The Mystery of Vibrationless-Vibration in Kashmir Shaivism

Vasugupta's Spanda Kārikā & Kṣhemarāja's Spanda Sandoha

Revealed by
Swami Lakshmanjoo

WITH ORIGINAL AUDIO

John Hughes, Editor

Lakshmanjoo Academy

Published by:

Lakshmanjoo Academy

First printing 2016

Printed in the United States of America

For information, address:
Lakshmanjoo Academy
http://www.lakshmanjooacademy.org

ISBN 978-0-9966365-7-5 (paperback)
ISBN 978-0-9966365-5-1 (hardcover)
ISBN 978-0-9966365-6-8 (ebook)

This sacred text is dedicated to Swami Lakshmanjoo, our teacher, our spiritual father, who has given us everything. Glory be to Thee!

Table of Contents

Guide to Pronunciation vi

Preface vii

Introduction ix

Acknowledgements xv

Author xix

Spanda Kārikā – (audios 1 to 3)

First Flow

Verses 1 – 25 1

Second Flow

Verses 1 – 7 44

Third Flow

Verses 1 – 19 52

Vasugupta's Conclusion

Verses 1 – 2 85

Spanda Sandoha – (audios 4 to 10) 87

Kṣhemarāja's concluding verses 259

Additional Questions 265

Appendix 271

Bibliography 299

Index 303

Published works 320

Instructions to download audio 322

Guide to Pronunciation

The following English words exemplify the pronunciation of selected Saṅskṛit vowels and consonants. The Romanized Saṅskṛit vowel or consonant is first listed and then an English word is given to aid you in its proper pronunciation.

a	as	a in ***A***merica.
ā	as	a in f***a***ther.
i	as	i in f***i***ll, l***i***ly.
ī	as	i in pol***i***ce.
u	as	u in f***u***ll.
ū	as	u in r***u***de.
ṛi	as	ri in mer***ri***ly.
ṛī	as	ri in ma***ri***ne.
e	as	e in pr***e***y.
ai	as	ai in ***ai***sle.
o	as	o in st***o***ne.
au	as	ou in h***ou***se
ś	as	s in ***s***ure.
ṣ	as	sh in ***sh***un, bu***sh***
s	as	s in ***s***aint, ***s***un

Preface

A central theme of the philosophy of Kashmir Shaivism is the highly esoteric principal known as *spanda*. Swami Lakshmanjoo tells us that the word '*spanda*' means established stable movement. That is, it is movementless-move-ment, vibrationless-vibration. It is this secret, mysterious and yet essential principle that Swami Lakshmanjoo clarifies and elucidates in his revelation of the two texts dealing specifically with this principle, the *Spanda Kārikā* and the *Spanda Sandoha*.

The theory of spanda is not new. It was hidden in the body of the Tantras and extracted by Vasugupta, founder of the Shiva Sutras, and initiator of monistic Shaivism in the valley of Kashmir. Vasugupta composed the *Spanda Kārikā*, a text filled with the fundmental precepts (*kārikās*) regarding *spanda* and the philosophy surrounding it.

Kṣhemarāja, the chief disciple of the very important and central figure in the tradition of Kashmir Shaivism, Abhinavagupta, is the author of the second pivotal text regarding spanda, the *Spanda Sandoha*. This text is an extensive exposition (*sandoha*) on the first verse of the *Spanda Kārikā*.

The text that Swami Lakshmanjoo chose to reveal also contains the enlightened commentary (*nirṇaya*)[1] of the Shaiva philosopher Kṣhemarāja, the chief disciple of the very important and central figure in the tradition of Kashmir Shaivism Abhinavagupta. Kṣhemarāja is also the author of the second pivotal text regarding spanda, the *Spanda Sandoha*. This text is an extensive exposition (*sandoha*) on the first verse of the *Spanda Kārikā*.

In 1917, a Sanskrit edition of The *Spanda Sandoha* was published in Srinagar by the Research Department of the

1 For the most part Swami Lakshmanjoo has translated only Vasugupta's original *kārikā* verses, yet in places he also quotes Kṣhemarāja's *nirṇaya*.

government of Jammu and Kashmir as volume 16 of the Kashmir Series of Texts and Studies. Seven years later (16th of January, 1925) the Research Department published the Sanskrit edition of Vasugupta's *Spanda Kārikā* with the *nirṇaya* (commentary) of Kṣhemarāja, as volume 42 in the Kashmir Series.

In his preface of the Kashmir Series of Texts and Studies edition of the *Spanda Kārikās* written in 1925, Pandit Madhusudan Kaul Shastri, expresses his thanks to Pandit Maheshvara Razdan, for his contribution to the preparation of this text. It may be of interest to note that in that same year (1925), at the age of 17, Swami Lakshmanjoo began his formal study of Sanskrit grammar under the private tutelage of Pandit Maheshvara Razdan. Over the next seven years he devoted himself to an in-depth study of the teachings of Kashmir Shaivism under the learned Pandit, who at the time was recognized throughout Kashmir as the foremost authority on Kashmir Shaivism.

For the sake of the reader, and those interested in the history of these Spanda texts, we have reproduced, in part, Pandit Madhusudan Kaul Shastri's preface to the original edition of the *Spanda Kārikā*, published in 1925. We have also added a few lines taken from Kṣhemarāja's introduction and concluding verses, which were published in that same volume of the Kashmir Series.

John Hughes
Lakshmanjoo Academy
Los Angeles, 2016

INTRODUCTION
from Kashmir Series of Texts and Studies (1925)

Ever since the beginning of the Christian era until, more or less definitely, the close of the seventh century, the Valley of Kashmir remained in close contact with the Buddhists. They carried on their proselytizing propaganda successfully and the whole of Kashmir came under their sway.

Teachers like Dignaga and Dharmakirti appealed most to the minds of the people and consequently the belief of the populace in the tenets of Shaivism received a great shock. The voice of the Shaivistic teachers of this period was feeble in comparison with that of the Buddhists. The former busied themselves with the work of giving the coloring of the dualist Shaivism to the extant Shaiva agamas. The present idealistic monism was unknown or less heard and spoken of. It was in the 8th century that Vasugupta was born and studied the Shaiva agamas from the standpoint of the idealistic monism. The power of argumenting was so strong in the Buddhist philosophers that even he felt in a fix to meet them and come out triumphant in creedal controversies.

Some of the Buddhist teachers, headed by Nagabodhi, engaged him in a wordy warfare of discussions. When all his intellectual resources failed him to gain victory over them, he tried to seek divine help and implored the favour of Shiva. Shiva appeared to him in a dream and instructed him to go to Mahādeva mountain, where he could find the Shiva Sutras engraved on a rock.[2] Thus, receiving this holy command, Vasugupta, filled with great joy, hurried to this spot where he found them. The Sutras were copied and published by him.

The Spanda system owes its origin to them and concerns itself with their elucidation and popularization. The Spanda Kārikās,

---

2 This rock, known as Shankapala (the rock of Shiva), still exists to this day and is located at the foot of Mahādeva mountain, nestled beside a small stream, in the valley of Harvan.

which have already been presented to the public in the recensions of Ramakantha and Utpala Bhatta, form a detailed commentary on the Shiva Sutras. On this point all Shaivistic writers are agreed. It is only the authorship of the Kārikās that remains in dispute.

Utpala Bhatta the author of the Spanda Pradipika, a commentary on the Spanda Kārikās, together with a host of other Spanda students endorses the view that they are the work and production of Kallaṭa, the chief disciple of Vasugupta.[3] The fifty-third stanza in the Spanda Pradipika reads as follows:

वसुगुप्तादवाप्येदं गुरोस्तत्त्वार्थदर्शिनः
रहस्यं श्लोकयामास सम्यक् श्रीभट्टकल्लटः

vasuguptādavāpyedaṁ gurostattvārthadarśinaḥ
rahasyaṁ ślokayāmāsa samyak śrībhaṭṭakallaṭaḥ

"Kallaṭa Bhaṭṭa rightly versified the secret doctrine after he received it from his teacher Vasugupta who had discerned the real state of Being."

It may be borne in mind in this connection that the stanza is not found in the recensions of Ramakantha and Kṣhemaraja.

Kṣhemarāja upholds the view that they were written by Vasugupta himself. What lends weight to his assumption is the presence of the following stanza in his recension of the Spanda Kārikās[4]:-

---

3 A number of contemporary scholars also attribute the authorship of the *Spanda Kārikā* to Bhatta Kallaṭa, but, on this point Swami Lakshmanjoo was adamant, as stated in his first English publication: "Some teachers think that the '*Spanda Kārikās*' were not composed by Vasuguptanātha, but rather by his disciple Kallaṭa. This theory, however, is absolutely incorrect." *Kashmir Shaivism, The Secret Supreme*, Swami Lakshmanjoo, ed. John Hughes (Lakshmanjoo Academy Book Series, Los Angeles, 2015), footnote 5, page 135.

4 This is the concluding verse of the 4th chapter of the *Spanda*

लब्ध्वाप्यलभ्यमेतज्ज्ञानधनं हृद् गुहान्तःकृतनिहितेः
वसुगुप्तवच्छिवाय हि भवति सदा सर्वलोकस्य ।।

labdhvāpyalabhyametajjñānadhanaṁ hṛdguhantakṛtanihiteḥ
vasuguptavacchivāya hi bhavati sadā sarvalokasya //*4.2*[5]

The occurrence of the word 'Vasuguptavat' in the above stanza is very important for the solution of the riddle. The probable objection that might be raised against this view is the absence of this stanza in other recensions. But it does not seem to vitiate the view of Kṣhemarāja as Maheśvarānanda, the reputed author of the Mahārthamañjari, quotes it in toto in the commentary on his own Mahārthamañjari. (See page 8 bottom Trivandrum edition.)

The name of the commentary written by Kṣhemarāja is Spanda Nirṇaya. It was undertaken at the request of his own pious pupil Sura. The material, that the author used in preparing it, is openly declared to have been obtained from Abhinavagupta, the illustrious exponent of the Shaivagama.

ARRANGEMENT OF THE KĀRIKĀS

Kṣhemarāja in his own recension of the Kārikās follows partially the same order and division as was adopted by

---

Kārikā, where Vasugupta say "I pray to God that, as Lord Śiva made this treasure fully living in the mind of Vasugupta, in the same way, let this treasure of knowledge remain living in the whole universe." See page 86 for Swami Lakshmanjoo's full translation of this verse.

5 Jaidev Singh, studied this text with Swami Lakshmanjoo (1980), and dedicated his translation with the following words:

> *With profound respects to Swami Lakshmanjoo,*
> *the doyen of Shaiva Agama'.*

Singh's translation of this verse is as follows:
"As on the attainment of this treasure of knowledge which is difficult of attainment, and on its being well preserved in the cave of the heart, it has been for the good of Vasugupta, so also on the attainment and on its being well preserved in the cave of the heart, it would always be for the good of all."

Ramakantha. The Kārikās, numbering in all fifty, are arranged into three chapters and each chapter is called Niḥsyanda[6], i.e., vibration. The first vibration goes by the name of the vitality in real nature, the second by the energy in the rise of intuition and the third by the energy in and of glory. The last chapter, though called Niḥsyanda, does not form part of the main body of the book and is a mere panegyric on the author's spiritual teacher and the author.

[The following are the introductory and concluding *ślokas* from Kṣhemarāja's *nirṇaya*:[7]]

Shankara's Spanda Energy, out of Her own nature, portrays on the background of Her pure self, the totality of categories, as a mirror does the city, from earth up to Shiva, which (totality) is one in substance with Her own self. She is the divinity representing the faculty of cognition. She forms the vitality of mantras and is ever abloom. Identical with the universe of sound and with the supreme egoity or infinite consciousness, She exults in glory all the wide world over.

My Spanda Sandoha has already thrown light in a measure on the principles of Spanda, and now an adequate effort is directed to giving a detailed and satisfactory exposition of the same principal.

This gloss on the Spanda system is calculated to explain the right interconnection of the sūtras of the Spanda Kārikās; to enable a student to acquire a close approach to the highest principle; to teach the method of pointed reasoning and the right application of the means (*upāya*); to help in the proper understanding of the self-evident truths and lastly to bring home the secret philosophy of Kashmir Shaivism. The intelligent should hence pin their attention to this gloss and thereby acquire the wealth of spanda.

---

6 Note: Swami Lakshmanjoo translates *niḥṣyandaḥ*, which forms part of the title of each of the first three chapters, not as vibration, but as 'flow'.

7 These verses were not translated by Swami Lakshmanjoo's in his rendering of the *Spanda Kārikā*.

[Kṣhemarāja's concluding ślokas:]

Although the counting is not possible of the commentaries on this Shastra and although the intelligent people are mostly indifferent by nature, yet those few critics are sure to know that special merit of my commentary, who, being, as it were, the swans of intelligence, are keen enough to detect the essence.

My teacher [Abhinavagupta] did not like to be bracketed with the common herd of other numerous commentators, and hence, did not comment on the Spanda Śāstra.

I have before given a summary statement of the chief differences in my Spanda Sandoha, and today, because of the fervent prayer of my own pupil, Sura, who feels glorified by the inspiration of Rudra Śakti and who has become one with Śiva, I, Kṣhemarāja, explain that Śāstra through the help of the great instruction of my own teacher.

Those are not qualified for the study of this Shastra, who have not acquired the intelligence purified by instruction from the right sort of teachers, whose doubts are not cleared up by the secret philosophy of the sacred teachings of Shaivism and who, being of tender intellect, have not previously tasted the nectar of the Shri Pratyabhijñā. This may be properly digested by the high-minded.

The supreme energy of consciousness exults in all glory as the abode of the unique and ever-manifest bliss. It represents the expansive emanation of paths from Shiva to earth and is diversified by the manifestation of various states of creation, maintenance and absorption. A drop of its current stands in the form of this universe.

Here ends the Shri Spanda Nirṇaya, the work of Shri Kṣhemaraja, pupil of Mahāmaheśvarācharya Shrimad Abhinavaguptanatha, a great grand pupil of the author of the Shri Pratyabhijñā[8].

HAPPINESS TO ALL!

8 Shri Utpaladeva was the author and founder of the Pratyabhijñā System, a philosophy unique to Kashmir Shaivism. His immediate disciple was Lakṣmanagupta who was Abhinavagupta's teacher in the Pratyabhijñā. Kṣhemarāja was Abhinavagutpa's chief disciple.

Acknowledgements

First of all I would like to thank our team of associate editors comprised of Viresh Hughes, George Barselaar, Denise Hughes and Stephen Benson. They took the raw unedited audio transcript and, at Swamiji's direction, transformed it into a polished document ready for publication. Being closely attuned to Swamiji's vision they were able to lightly edit the manuscript without tarnishing the flow of the narrative. Recognizing that these revelations were meant to be used as an aid to gaining understanding of the philosophy and practice of Kashmir Shaivism they added exhaustive footnotes and appendices to aid the student in this quest. To Michael Van Winkle, our audio engineer, who enhanced the original audio. To Claudia Dose, our creative director, who typed the Devanāgarī and was responsible for creating the overall design. To Shanna Hughes, who managed this project, so it would be completed in a timely manner.

Swami Lakshmanjoo

Swami Lakshmanjoo

The Author

Swami Lakshmanjoo was born in Srinagar, Kashmir, on May 9, 1907. He was the most recent and the greatest of the long line of saints and masters of the Kashmir Shaiva tradition. From his early childhood, Swamiji spent his life studying and practicing the teachings of this unique and sacred tradition. Having a complete intellectual and spiritual understanding of the philosophy and practice of Kashmir Shaivism, he was a true master in every respect.

Being born with a photographic memory, learning was always easy for him. In addition to possessing a complete knowledge of Kashmir Shaivism, he had a vast knowledge of the traditional religious and philosophical schools and texts of India. Swamiji would freely draw upon other texts to clarify, expand, and substantiate his lectures. He could recall an entire text by simply remembering the first few words of a verse.

In time, his reputation as a learned philosopher and spiritual adept spread. Spiritual leaders and scholars journeyed from all over the world to receive his blessings and to ask him questions about various aspects of Kashmir Shaiva philosophy. He gained renown as a humble devotee of Lord Shiva and as an accomplished master (*siddha*) of the non-dual tradition of Kashmir Shaivism.

Throughout his life, Swamiji taught his disciples and devotees the ways of devotion and awareness. He shunned fame and recognition and did not seek his own glory. He knew

Kashmir Shaivism was the most precious jewel and that, by God's grace, those who desired supreme knowledge would be attracted to its teachings. He taught freely, never asking anything in return, except that his students, young and old, should do their utmost to assimilate the teachings of his cherished tradition. His earnest wish was for Kashmir Shaivism to be preserved and made available to all humankind.

On the 27th of September, 1991, Swami Lakshmanjoo left his physical body and attained *mahasamādhi*, the great liberation.

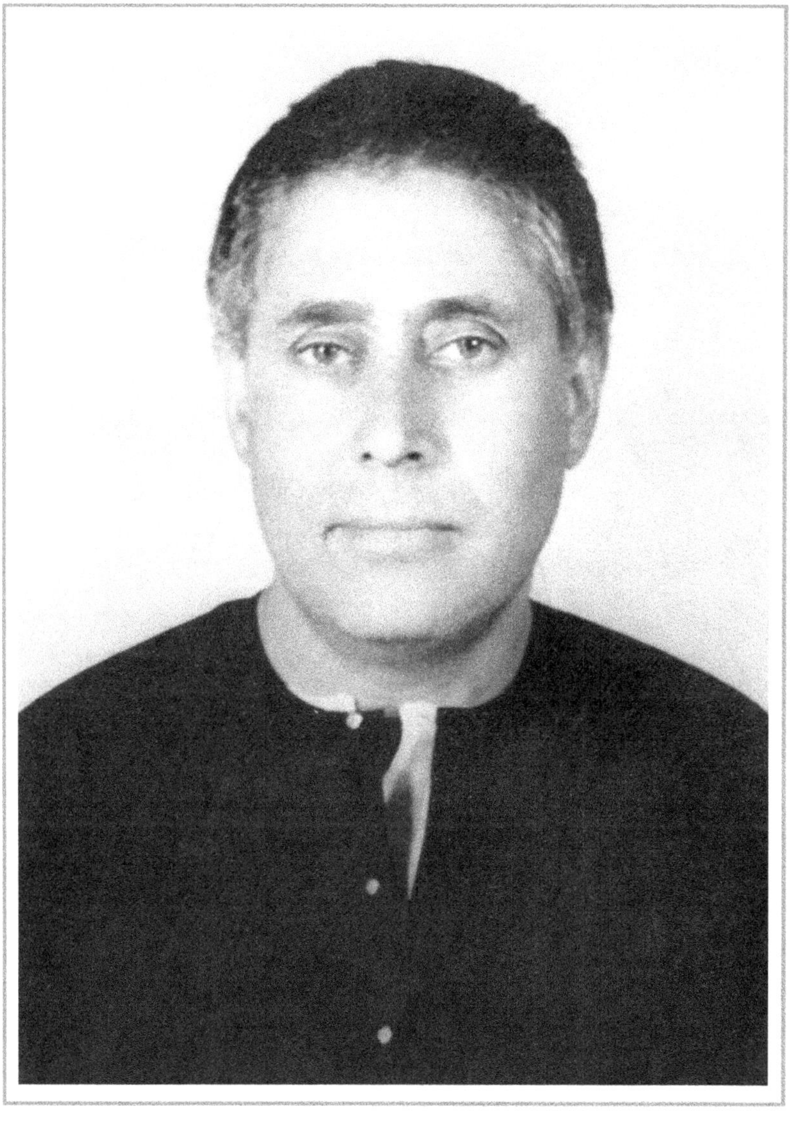

Swami Lakshmanjoo

The Spanda[1] Kārikā of Vasugupta[2]

First Flow
Svarūpa Spanda
(The Essential Nature of Spanda)

Audio 1 - 00:00

SWAMIJI: The first *kārikā*[3]:

यस्योन्मेषनिमेषाभ्यां जगतः प्रलयोदयौ ।
तं शक्तिचक्रविभवप्रभवं शङ्करं स्तुमः ॥ १ ॥

yasyonmeṣanimeṣābhyāṁ jagataḥ pralayodayau /
taṁ śakti-cakra-vibhava-prabhavaṁ śaṁkaraṁ stumaḥ //

We prostrate before Śaṁkara[4].

Prostration–what is meant by "prostration"?

Prostration means, we put [ourselves] at the feet of Śaṁkara, we surrender at the feet of Śaṁkara–our self.

What is the self?

The self is the gross body, the subtle body, and the subtlest

1 Swami Lakshmanjoo translates *spanda* as 'vibrationless-vibration'. See Appendix 1 for a detailed explanation of *spanda*.

2 Abhinavagupta's principal disciple, Kṣhemarāja, wrote a commentary on Vasugupta's *Spanda Kārikā* called the *Spanda Nirṇaya*. For the most part Swamiji has translated Vasugupta's original *kārikā* verses only, yet in places he also quotes Kṣhemarāja's *nirṇaya*.

3 *Kārikā*: a concise statement in verse form (esp. philosophy and grammar doctrines).

4 An appellation of Lord Śiva. Lit., causing prosperity, auspicious, beneficent. "Śaṁkara is He who gives *śaṁ* (peace, entire peace). He who produces, who bestows, peace, entire peace, that is Śaṁkara." Swami Lakshmanjoo, trans., *Spanda Sandoha* (Lakshmanjoo Academy archive).

body; the body of *jāgrat* (*sthūla śarīra*[5]), the subtle body (*sūkṣma śarīra*), which conducts in the dreaming state[6], and the subtlest body, which conducts in the dreamless [state] (*suṣupti*[7]). These bodies we offer at the feet of Lord Śiva. That is "*śaṁkaraṁ stumaḥ*".

Which Śaṁkara?

yasyonmeṣanimeṣābhyāṁ jagataḥ pralayodayau /

By whose *unmeṣa* and *nimeṣa*, by whose twinkling of the eyes (*unmeṣa* is "the opening of [His] eyes", *nimeṣa* is "closing His eyes"), you find *jagataḥ pralayodayau*, the rise[8] and the dissolution of one hundred and eighteen worlds.[9] One hundred and eighteen worlds rise when He opens His eyes, one hundred and eighteen worlds are destroyed when He closes His eyes. He is Śaṅkara.

And He is the *śakti cakra vibhava prabhavaṁ*, He is the master of all the gathering of all the cycle of His energies, all the cycle of His numberless energies (*śakticakra* is, the wheel of energies). The glory of the wheel of energies, He is holding, He is handling.

Audio 1 - 02:10

यत्र स्थितमिदं सर्वं कार्यं यस्माच्च निर्गतम् ।
तस्यानावृतरूपत्वान्न निरोधोऽस्ति कुत्रचित् ॥ २ ॥

yatra sthitamidaṁ sarvaṁ kāryaṁ yasmācca nirgatam /
tasyānāvṛtarūpatvānna nirodho'sti kutracit //2//

In which state (*yatra*, in which state), *sthitaṁ idaṁ sarvaṁ kāryam*, this whole cycle of *kārya*, . . .

This whole cycle of *kārya* is cause and effect. The cause is "*kāraṇa*" and the effect is "*kārya*". *Kārya varga* is that which

5 The waking state (*jāgrat*) is also known as the gross (*sthūla*) body (*śarīra*).

6 *Svapna*.

7 Deep sleep.

8 That is, the creation.

9 In general, Hinduism claims the existence of 108 worlds. Kashmir Shaivism, however, claims the existence of 118 worlds.

is brought into manifestation. That which is brought into manifestation, that is *kārya varga*. What is brought into manifestation? One hundred and eighteen worlds. The rise of one hundred and eighteen worlds is brought into manifestation. This is *kārya varga*.

. . . this *kārya varga*, in which this whole cycle of *kārya varga*, which is brought into manifestation, is existing (*yatra sthitaṁ idaṁ sarvam*), *yatra yasmin svarūpe*, in which *svarūpa*[10] all this cycle of *kārya varga*, all the cycle of one hundred and eighteen worlds, are existing, is existing, *yasmāt ca nirgatam*, and from whom this cycle of *kārya varga* comes out (where this is existing and from where it comes out in manifestation), for Him (*tasya*), *anāvṛtarūpatvāt*, He is never veiled.

DEVOTEE: Concealed.

SWAMIJI: Covered. He can never be covered by these movements, outer movements and inner movements. If, in His own nature, these one hundred and eighteen worlds are existing–[Vasugupta] has told that these one hundred and eighteen worlds are existing in His own nature–by the existence of one hundred and eighteen worlds, His nature of God consciousness is not subsided, does not become blocked.

ERNIE: Less.

SWAMIJI: Less. And by the offshoot of these one hundred and eighteen worlds from that God consciousness, It does not become affected, It does not become less. The state of God consciousness remains the same.

> Abhinavagupta has explained this through the example of a mirror. In a mirror you'll find the reflection of a mountain. If your mirror is two pounds in weight (it has got the weight of two pounds), after the reflection of a huge mountain in that mirror, it won't become more. The weight will remain the same in the mirror. The weight won't increase by the reflection of this mountain.[11]

---

10 Swamiji often translates *svarūpa* as "nature".

11 See *Kashmir Shaivism–The Secret Supreme*, ed. John Hughes, Lakshmanjoo Academy Book Series (Los Angeles 2015), "The Theory

JOACHIM: Where does Abhinavagupta tell this? In the *Tantrāloka*?

SWAMIJI: In the *Tantrāloka*, yes.

JOACHIM: Where? The first chapter or . . . ?

SWAMIJI: The third chapter, yes.

Tasya anāvṛtarūpatvāt, so, He is never being covered, His nature never becomes subsided. So, *kutracit na nirodhaḥ*, He has no *nirodha* (no obstacle) anywhere. He can remain in His nature, He can come out from His nature–everywhere He is divine.

Audio 1 - 06:03

जाग्रदादिविभेदेऽपि तदभिन्ने प्रसर्पति ।
निवर्तते निजान्नैव स्वभावादुपलब्धृतः ॥ ३ ॥

jāgradādivibhede'pi tadabhinne prasarpati /
nivartate nijānnaiva svabhāvādupalabdhṛtaḥ //3//

Tat, that *spanda tattva*, that element of *spanda*, that element of stable movement, . . .

Spanda means "stable movement". It is that kind of movement which is stable, which is not in movement. You don't find It in movement but It is in movement.

GANJOO: Motion-less movement.

SWAMIJI: Motion-less movement. That is *spanda*.

. . . and [from] that *spanda*, *jāgrat ādi vibhede'pi tat abhinne prasarpati* (*tat abhinne jāgrat ādi vibhede'pi prasarpati*), this *jāgrata* (the cycle of wakefulness), the cycle of the dreaming state, and the cycle of the dreamless state (*suṣupti*), come out in manifestation, but it does not come out in manifestation after becoming disconnected [from] that *spanda tattva*, it is [always] connected with that *spanda tattva*. While being connected with that *spanda tattva*, it comes out.

What?

---

of Reflection–*Pratibimbavāda*", 4.29. "This is the *nirmalatā*, this is the refinement of the mirror." Swami Lakshmanjoo, trans., Abhinavagupta's *Tantrāloka* (Lakshmanjoo Academy archive), Los Angeles, 1972-1981), 3.8.

The state of wakefulness, the state of the dreaming state, and the state of the dreamless state (*suṣupti*). It comes into manifestation, but it holds within, with this, the state of that *spanda*. It is still one with *spanda*. It cannot remain, it can't exist, in the outside cycle of the world without *spanda*. *Spanda* is [always] adjusted with it because *spanda* is the life for this world. You can't ignore *spanda*! [Even] in the absence of *spanda*, *spanda*s presence is a must. In the absence of *spanda*, when you ignore *spanda*, there is *spanda*.

DENISE: Like in a rock, you mean, there is *spanda*.

SWAMIJI: There is *spanda*.

DENISE: Although it seems solid and still, there is *spanda*.

SWAMIJI: But there is *spanda*.

jāgradādivibhede'pi tadabhinne prasarpati /
nivartate nijānnaiva svabhāvādupalabdhṛtaḥ //3//

When the state of wakefulness is over, [when] the state of dreaming is over, [and when] the state of the dreamless state is over (*nivartate*)–*nijāt naiva svabhāvāt upalabdhṛtaḥ*, it is over, it takes its end; *jāgrat*, etc., takes its end–but the state of *jāgrat*, etc., does not take the end of [their] attachment of *spanda*. *Spanda* is there in the ending also. In the ending state of *jāgrat*, *spanda* is not ending; in the ending state of *svapna*, *spanda* is not ending, *spanda* is there; and in [the ending state of] *suṣupti* also, *spanda* is there. No matter if they end, if they end their drama, if that drama is over, but the drama of *spanda*'s attachment is there in that also. This is what he says in the third *śloka*.

Audio 1 - 09:13

अहं सुखी च दुःखी च रक्तश्चेत्यादिसंविदः ।
सुखाद्यवस्थानुस्यूते वर्तन्तेऽन्यत्र ताः स्फुटम् ॥४॥

ahaṁ sukhī ca duḥkhī ca raktaścetyādicaṁvidaḥ /
sukhādyavasthānusyūte vartante'nyatra tāḥ sphutam //4//

"I am joyful" (*ahaṁ sukhī*, I am joyful), "*ahaṁ duḥkhī*" (I am filled with torture, I am filled with crises, I am sad), "*raktaśca*" (I am attached to such and such person), *ityādi saṁvitaḥ*, these kinds of perceptions rise in a human being [always], they go on rising and ending–these perceptions.

Which perceptions?

JOHN: "I am happy", "I am sad", . . .

SWAMIJI: "I am happy", "I am sad", "I am attached", "I have got this weakness. I have got such and such weakness. I have got weakness for my master. I want to remain with my master always"–this is weakness–"I have got this weakness".

All these perceptions *vartante* (exist), *vartante anyatra*, in some other Being, on another basis, and that basis is *sukhādi avastha anusyūte*, where *sukha*, *duḥkha*, and *raktabhāva* (*sukha* means "pleasure", *duḥkha* means "pain", and *rakta* means "attachment") are . . . "woven"?

ERNIE: Yes, sir.

SWAMIJI: What is "woven"?

ERNIE: Like cloth?

SWAMIJI: No.

DENISE: Interwoven.

SWAMIJI: Interwoven, yes.

DENISE: Woven together . . .

SWAMIJI: Yes, woven together.

ERNIE: Like the cloth.

SWAMIJI: Yes. *Sukha*, *duḥkha*, and *rāga* are woven in that *spanda* (that motion-less motion), and they are residing in That. This perception that, "I am happy", this perception that, "I am sad", "I am attached, I have got attachment for such and such person", these kinds of perceptions *vartante* (exist) in that state of God consciousness where all these perceptions are woven altogether–they are There.

This is the exposition of *spanda* here!

Audio 1 - 11:40

न दुःखं न सुखं यत्र न ग्राह्यं ग्राहकं न च ।
न चास्ति मूढभावोऽपि तदस्ति परमार्थतः ॥५॥

na duḥkhaṁ na sukhaṁ yatra
na grāhyaṁ grāhakaṁ na ca
na cāsti mūḍhabhāvo'pi
tadasti paramārthataḥ //5//

But what is–in brief words–what is *spanda*?

DEVOTEES: (laughter)

SWAMIJI: I[12] want to explain what *spanda* is. *Spanda*, that motion-less movement, what is that motion-less movement.

Where *na duḥkhaṁ*, where there is no pain, that is motion-less movement; *na sukhaṁ*, where there is no pleasure, that is that *spanda*; *yatra na grāhyam*, where there is no objective perception; *grāhakam na ca*, when there is no subjective perception. There is neither an object nor a subject, neither pain nor pleasure. *Na cāsti mūḍha bhāva api*, when there is nothing, there is neither pain nor pleasure, neither object nor subject.

[The objector:] Then it is a rock! Then your *spanda* is just like a rock, dead, a dead being!

[Vasugupta] says, it is not dead also (*na cāsti mūḍha bhāva api*, it is not dead also). *Tadasti*, that is, in reality, *spanda*, the essence of *spanda*.

ERNIE: Is that like Brahma in the *Veda*s?

JOHN: No, this is *svātantrya*.

SWAMIJI: This is *svātantrya*, yes, *svātantrya*.[13]

---

12 Vasugupta, the author. Vasugupta (860-925 CE) was the sage to whom Lord Shiva revealed the *Śiva Sūtras*, and although there has been some debate, Swami Lakshmanjoo was absolutely clear that Vasugupta was also the author of the *Spanda Kārikā*, which is considered to be a commentary on the *Śiva Sūtras*.

13 Absolute freedom/independence. Kashmir Shaivism is also known as *Svātantryavāda*, the Doctrine of Absolute Freedom. "The singularly unique aspect of Lord Śiva is complete independence, *svātantrya*. This complete independence is not found anywhere except in the state of Lord Śiva." Swami Lakshmanjoo, trans., *Śiva Sūtras–The Supreme Awakening*, ed. John Hughes (Lakshmanjoo Academy Book Series, Los Angeles, 2015), 1.12. See Appendix 2 for an explanation of *svātantrya*.

Audio 1 - 13:11

यतः करणवर्गोऽयं विमूढोऽमूढवत्स्वयम् ।
सहान्तरेण चक्रेण प्रवृत्तिस्थितिसंहृतीः ॥६॥
लभते तत्प्रयत्नेन परीक्ष्यं तत्त्वमादरात् ।
यतः स्वतन्त्रता तस्य सर्वत्रेयमकृत्रिमा ॥७॥

yataḥ karaṇavargo'yaṁ vimūḍho'mūḍhavatsvayam /
sahāntareṇa cakreṇa pravṛttisthitisaṁhṛtīḥ //6//
labhate tatprayatnena parīkṣyaṁ tattvamādarāt /
yataḥ svatantratā tasya sarvatreyamakṛtrimā //7//

Now he directs us how to find out that state of *spanda* in your own self.

Yataḥ karaṇa vargo'yam, just go to[14] the cycle of your organs. These cycles of the organs, they rise and they subside. You see [something] and you close your eyes: "Oh, this is such and such thing", [then] you close your eyes. You want to have sex, you have sex, finished, [then] you close that chapter. In the same way, *śabda*, *sparśa*, *rūpa*, *rasa*, and *gandha*[15], all these sensual objects, they rise and they end.

And this *karaṇavarga*, this cycle of *karaṇavarga*, this cycle of the organs, *yataḥ*, from where this rises? This cycle of the organs, from which it rises?

This *karaṇavarga* rises from that *spanda*. After rising from *spanda*, this, generally, by itself, this *karaṇavarga* is *vimūḍhaḥ*, is dead, is lifeless–the eyes are left lifeless, the ear is lifeless. If they were not lifeless, what has happened to these *karaṇavargas* in a dead body? All of his organs are okay but he can't see, he can't hear, he can't feel the sensation of touch, he can't smell. He can't do anything but his organs are okay. His organs are quite normal but there is no feeling, sensation. So, actually, this cycle of organs is *vimūḍhaḥ*, is just dead.

ERNIE: Even when you are alive.

14 That is, observe and examine.
15 Sound, touch, form, taste, and smell, respectively.

SWAMIJI: Of course. And *yataḥ*, from which power this dead cycle of organs *amūḍhavat*, becomes just like filled with life, as if [they] is filled with life. And he does so many things by only one organ, like this (Swamiji demonstrates).

DEVOTEES: (laughter)

SWAMIJI: It has got so much life in it, but otherwise it is lifeless. In itself, it is lifeless, but by the installment of *spanda*, when *spanda* is installed in it, and then it becomes life-full–*yataḥ karaṇavargo'yaṁ vīmūḍho*, and [this organ] becomes *amūḍhavat*, just as if it is filled with life (*amūḍhavat*).

Svayaṁ sahāntreṇa cakreṇa, pravṛtti sthiti saṁhṛtīḥ labhate, and, by itself, without the aid of, without the support of, any other agency, this cycle of the organs does everything independently–he sees, he touches, he smells, he hears, he has sex, he does everything, good and bad. *Sahāntareṇa cakreṇa*, along with the *antaḥkaraṇa*, along with the internal organs (the internal organs are the mind, intellect, and ego; the mind, intellect, and ego are also adjusted in this *karaṇavarga*), this whole cycle of *karaṇavarga* becomes filled with life.

From which?

JOHN: *Spanda*. The injection of *spanda*.

SWAMIJI: From which grace of *spanda*! And *pravṛtti sthiti saṁhṛtī labhate*, and he can do and undo; whatever he likes, he can do by this *karaṇavarga*, by this cycle of the organs.

So, *tat prayatnena parīkṣyam*, and now, what we have to do is to find out what that power is, which is installed in this dead cycle of organs. You have to find out that, that Being, which is installed in it and it becomes filled with life. *Prayatnena*, with great effort you have to find out that Being; *prayatnena parīkṣyam*, you have to find out again and again. If you can't succeed in finding out once, do it again, do it again, do it again, do it again, and that is meditation–*parīkṣyam*[16]. And this finding out should be done not with force and you should not get bored.

ERNIE: With effort?

SWAMIJI: Not only with effort, *ādarāt*, with great

---

16 Lit., careful examination, inspection, observation.

enthusiasm, with great . . .

DEVOTEES: Devotion.

SWAMIJI: . . . devotion. *Yataḥ svātantratatā tasya sarvatreyam*, then he will find, then the *sādhaka* will find, the *svatantratā*. When he gets entry in that God consciousness, he will find *svātantratā* (absolute independence).

It is why in the *Veda*s it is said, "He sees without the eyes, He smells without the nose." Who?

DENISE: Lord Śiva.

SWAMIJI: Lord Śiva. He hears without the ears, He touches without the skin–all that.

> *apāṇyapādojavanograhītā*
> *paśyatyacakṣu sa śṛoṇtyakaraṇaḥ*
> *sa vetti vedyaṁ na ca tasyāsti vettā*
> *tam āhur agryaṁ puruṣaṁ mahāntam* / /[17]
> [not recited in full]

> He hears without the ears; *apāṇyapāda*, He has no hands, He has no feet; *javano grahītā*, He holds without hands, He walks fast without feet, without legs (*javano grahītā*[18]); *paśyatyacakṣu*, He observes forms of each and every form without eyes; *sa śṛṇotyakaraṇaḥ*, He hears all sounds without ears; *sa vetti vedyaṁ*, He observes all the objective world [but] *na ca tasyāsti*, no one observes Him. *Tam āhur agryaṁ puruṣam*, He is the topmost Being in this world. He is to be sought.

[Now] this is a question: You have already said that, *tatastattvat cetanatāmivāsādyendriyāṇi svayaṁ pravṛtyādi labhanta iti*[19], that *spanda tattva* is that power which infuses Its

17 *Śvetāśvatara Upaniṣad*, 3.19.

18 With speed and velocity (*javana*), he seizes, takes, is occupied with or undertakes (*grahītā*).

19 Abhinavagupta's principal disciple, Kṣhemarāja, wrote a commentary on the *Spanda Karikā* called the *Spanda Nirṇaya*, the substance of which Swamiji occasionally discusses throughout this revelation. This question is from Kṣhemarāja's introduction to the

power in dead, lifeless, organs, [and they] function just as if they are filled with life–the organs of the senses. How can it be possible? How can lifeless organs become life-full by the mere touch of that *spanda*? *Yāvatā*, and this too is also life-full: *ayameva grāhaka icchayā dātrādīnīva karaṇāni prerayati*[20], this individual [soul] infuses, inserts, power in the organs, just like [when] you have to cut grass, you want something to cut it, but the cutter is the individual himself. The instrument does not cut it, the cutter cuts it. So these are just like [that cutting] instrument–these organs. These are just instruments. How can these instruments work without the [involvement] of the cutter, the individual?

And another point is doubtful: You have already explained in the previous *śloka* that *spanda*, that reality of *spanda*, must be observed with great effort and with great devotion. How can it be possible because, generally, our desire is always [extroverted], the movement [of our desire], it is extroverted? It always goes on *viṣayas*[21] (*śabda*, *sparśa*, *rūpa*, *rasa*, and *gandha*). It is never focused on one point of God consciousness. How can it be possible?

JOHN: What? To focus it.

SWAMIJI: To focus it.

JOHN: If it is never focused, ever.

SWAMIJI:

Audio 1 - 22:35

न हीच्छानोदनस्यायं प्रेरकत्वेन वर्तते ।
अपि त्वात्मबलस्पर्शात्पुरुषस्तत्समो भवेत् ॥८॥

na hīcchānodanasyāyaṁ prerakatvena vartate /
api tvātmabalasparśātpuruṣastatsamo bhavet //8//

This is not the case here as [where] there is one section of the cutter and one section of those instruments. This is not

---

eighth *śloka*.
20 Kṣhemarāja's commentary.
21 The external objects of the senses.

the case here in the organic field.[22] These organs get the power of God consciousness in their own nature and [then] they begin to work, they begin to function. [It is] not just that the cutter is also adjusted with that [instrument] and [then] they do that [cutting]–it is not like that. [The organs] become absolutely filled with [God] consciousness and they work. There is no need of the adjustment of the individual in it. They become powerful in functioning . . .

JOHN: In their own self.

SWAMIJI: . . . in their own way. This is how the infusion of power from God consciousness appears in the organs of the senses. You don't feel that the organs of senses are infused from another agency. You feel that they are themselves powerful, that they are themselves capable of seeing, capable of touching, capable of doing, tasting, everything.

Api tvātmabala sparśāt puruṣas tat samo bhavet, *puruṣa* becomes an organ there.[23] *Puruṣa* is not adjusted there [as the principal agent]. For instance, when you perceive a form, when you perceive some taste, when you perceive some touch, at that time, only that organ of touch (the skin) works. There is no other agency who is adjusted with that *Ātma*[24]. There is no *ātma*[25] there. [The individiual self and the organs] become one with that God consciousness [and then they work]. It is how it works in this field of the world.

But now, there is one point to be discussed. That point is, how can we know that they have become conscious through the grace of the adjustment of Lord Śiva (or God consciousness)?

ERNIE: The organs of perception.

SWAMIJI: The organs of perception. How can we know? Why don't we know that?

---

22 Swamiji uses the word "organic" throughout to refer to the organs of knowledge and action.

23 In any given sensation or activity, the individual self (*puruṣa*), like the organs, is also a mere instrument.

24 The universal soul, God consciousness.

25 The individual soul.

Audio 1 - 25:22

निजाशुद्ध्यासमर्थस्य कर्तव्येष्वभिलाषिणः ।
यदा क्षोभः प्रलीयेत तदा स्यात्परमं पदम् ॥९॥

nijāśuddhyāsamarthasya kartavyeṣvabhilāṣiṇaḥ /
yadā kṣobhaḥ pralīyeta tadā syātparamaṁ padam //9//

Only one point is to be observed here (this is the most important point): There is impurity found in the cycle of the organs. That impurity is *nija aśuddhi*, one's own impurity. It is the impurity of the organs. By the impurity, these organs think [about] right and wrong, good and bad, pleasure and pain. All of these things happen through the impurity. And that impurity rises from [their] extroverted tendency. If these organs are focused inside consciousness, then the impurity will vanish at once. It is due to the impurity that *kartavyeṣvabhilāṣiṇaḥ*, he craves for other things. He craves for lust, he craves for a badminton game, he craves for cinema–he craves for all these things–he craves for taste, he craves for sex, because these organs are impure.

By which they are impure? What is the cause of their impurity?

The cause of the impurity is that they are extroverted. They don't focus their nature [upon] where[from] they have got this force of the capacity of consciousness. You must find out the consciousness, wherefrom this consciousness has risen in this organic field.

Yadā kṣobhaḥ, and this is agitation. [The organs] are agitated by this, by being [focused towards an] extroverted position. The position [of awareness] must be diverted inside. *Yadā kṣobhaḥ pralīyeta*, when that position [of awareness] will be diverted inside and this agitation will be vanished, *tadā syāt paramaṁ*, then the supreme state of God consciousness will be there, in the organs also. The organs will be divine!

ERNIE: So, it's one organ, you take one organ and go inside of that . . . ?

SWAMIJI: Yes, take one organ and find out wherefrom this life has been inserted in this organ. When you find that, the source of that life, then you are inside, then you are in your own God consciousness, you have realized your Self. *Tadā syāt paramaṁ padam*, then the supreme state is shining already there.

Here, in the *Vijñāna Bhairava Tantra* also, [Kṣhemarāja] has quoted:

mānasaṁ cetanā śaktirātmā ceti catuṣṭayam /
yadā priye parikṣīṇaṁ tadā tadbhairavaṁ vapuḥ //[26]

[Bhairava:] O Pārvatī, there are four elements. One is the mind[27], and one is the intellect[28], one is force (organic force[29]), and one is the individual[30]. *Yadā priye parikṣīṇam*, these must be vanished. The mind must not function and the intellect must not function . . . at that stage where the mind does not function, the intellect does not function, and this force is introverted in God consciousness, and the self, the individual self, the limited self, has vanished, when these four vanish, *tadā tat bhairavaṁ vapuḥ*, that Bhairava state will take place. It is there. And, at that very moment, . . .

Another *śloka*, the tenth:

Audio 1 - 29:30

तदास्याकृत्रिमो धर्मो ज्ञत्वकर्तृत्वलक्षणः ।
यतस्तदेप्सितं सर्वं जानाति च करोति च ॥ १० ॥

tadāsyākṛtrimo dharmo jñatvakartṛtvalakṣaṇaḥ /
yatastadepsitaṁ sarvaṁ jānāti ca karoti ca //10//

At that point, *akṛtrimo dharma*, the un-artificial aspect will rise in [the *yogī*'s] nature. Un-artificial, because these organs, this cycle of the organs, have got consciousness but that is

---

26 See *Vijñāna Bhairava–The Manual for Self Realization*, ed. John Hughes, Lakshmanjoo Academy Book Series (Los Angeles, 2015), verse 138, *Dhāraṇa* 112.
27 The organ of differentiated thoughts.
28 The organ of differentiated perceptions.
29 *Śakti*, the energy of breath, inhale and exhale.
30 The limited ego.

artificial, that is loaned, borrowed, borrowed consciousness. The organs, the cycle of the organs, have got consciousness, [which is] not their own. It is borrowed from another department and that department is God consciousness.

And then, that cycle [of God consciousness] which is not borrowed, which is your own natural property, that is your own aspect (*akṛtrima dharma*, an un-artificial aspect), will rise, and that un-artificial aspect, which is *jñatva kartṛtva lakṣaṇa*, all-knowledge and all-action, not particular knowledge and particular [action]. As long as there is particular knowledge and particular action, it is . . .

ERNIE: Imperfect.

SWAMIJI: . . . it is imperfect. When it is all-knowledge and all[-action], it is perfect. And that perfect knowledge and perfect action will appear then, when you are introverted in your own nature.

Yatastat epsitaṁ sarvaṁ jānāti ca karoti ca, and, at that state, whatever you will, will come true, whatever you know, it will be absolutely correct. That knowledge will be correct and that will will be perfect.[31] As long it is not there[32], our will is always imperfect, our knowledge is always imperfect. Whatever we desire, it does not take place. We wish this and that but it does not occur, it does not happen like that, it goes the opposite. But here, at that stage [of un-artifical God consciousness], it won't go [unrealized]. Whatever you desire will be there, whatever you know will be there. It will be absolutely un-artificial knowledge and un-artificial action.

Audio 1 - 32:15

तमधिष्ठातृभावेन स्वभावमवलोकयन् ।
स्मयमान इवास्ते यस्तस्येयं कुसृतिः कुतः ॥ ११ ॥

---

31 "*Icchā śaktirūmā kumārī*, for such a *yogi*, his will is one with the energy of Lord Siva–unobstructable, completely independent, always given to play." *Śiva Sūtras–The Supreme Awakening*, 1.13.
"*Saktisandhana sarirotpattiḥ*, by infusing his energy of the will, the embodiment of that which is willed occurs at once." Ibid., 1.19.

32 That un-artificial aspect, which is *jñatu kartṛtva lakṣaṇa*, all-knowledge and all-action.

tamadhiṣṭhātṛbhāvena svabhāvamavalokayan /
smayamāna ivāste yastasyeyaṁ kusṛtiḥ kutaḥ //11//

When, at that stage, when *adhiṣṭhātṛ bhāvena svabhāvam*, that *svabhāva*, that nature of your own Self, when you perceive the nature of your own Self by *adhiṣṭhātṛ bhāva* [33], . . .*

By *adhiṣṭhātṛ bhāva* means, not by *adhiṣṭheya bhāva*[34]. These are two states of perception: One state is *adhiṣṭheya bhāva*, perception in the boundary, in the cycle, of *adhiṣṭheya bhāva*, and another perception is in the cycle of *adhiṣṭhātṛ bhāva*. When you perceive this pencil, "This is a pencil", this is the perceiving of this pencil in *adhiṣṭheya bhāva*, in the objective cycle. When you perceive, "This is my Self", this is perceiving this object in the subjective cycle, on the subjective cycle, and that is the real perception, that is the real perception of that object. That is *adhiṣṭhātṛ bhāvena*. You should perceive this whole world as your own Self. You should not perceive in this-ness, you should perceive everything in I-ness, full consciousness. That is *adhiṣṭhātṛ bhāvena*.

*. . . and then, when you perceive your nature, *adhiṣṭhātṛ bhāvena*, by the adjustment of subjective consciousness (not objective consciousness, not the adjustment of this-ness), . . .

By the adjustment of what?

DEVOTEES: I-ness.

SWAMIJI: I-ness.

. . . *smayamāna ivāste*, at that time, you will get wonderstruck (*smayamāna iva*, you will get wonderstruck), you will feel wonders in your nature![35] You will realize that state of God consciousness which you have not realized in the past so many centuries.[36] You will be wonderstruck in realizing that

---

33 That state which superintends or governs, i.e., subjectivity.
34 That state which is superintended or governed, i.e., objectivity.
35 "*Vismayo yogabhūmikāḥ*–The predominant sign of such a *yogi* is joy-filled amazement." *Śiva Sūtras–The Supreme Awakening*, 1.12.
36 "At the moment, He realizes His own nature and is filled with knowledge. He has the experience that the state of knowledge was already there. So there was never really any separation. Separation only *seemed* to exist." *Self Realization in Kashmir Shaivism–The*

God consciousness.

ERNIE: And that is the *spanda*.

SWAMIJI: That is the *spanda*. *Tasyeyam*, for that person, where is the place for *saṁsāra*[37]? *Saṁsāra* does not exist for him. This question does not arise. Pain and pleasure, this cycle of births and rebirths and deaths, it is finished!

JOHN: What is the word for "wonderstruck"?

SWAMIJI: Wonderstruck, when you realize your nature.

JOHN: What is the word for that here in the . . . ?

SWAMIJI: *Smayamāna. Smayamāna ivāste yaḥ tasyeyaṁ kusṛti kutaḥ. Kusṛtiḥ* means, that disgusting pathway, the journey/traveling on the disgusting pathway. What is the disgusting pathway?

ERNIE: Limitation.

SWAMIJI: Sexual pleasure, taste, *śabda* (sound), touch, cinema, etc. These are "disgusting" because you are never satisfied with it. As soon as you finish it, you try some other thing, then you try some other thing, then you try . . . and this goes on for centuries and centuries and no perfection. And when once you realize your nature, at that time you will be wonderstruck. Because it is not realizing your nature as routine-like. It is not a routine-like realization. It is just fresh, new, always new, and you will be wonderstruck!

ERNIE: Let's say, with hearing, or taste, or smell, you go with that one and you find That.

SWAMIJI: You will find that something else in that sex. You will find something else in that form.

ERNIE: In that pencil.

SWAMIJI: In that pencil [you will find] something else. That *śabda* (sound), that *sparśa* (touch), that *rūpa* (form), *rasa* (taste), and *gandha* (smell), will be divine! All actions are divine!

Oral Teachings of Swami Lakshmanjoo, ed. John Hughes (State University of New York Press, Albany, 1995), 1. *Bodhapañcadaśikā–15 verses on Wisdom*, verse 5, page 24.

37 The repeating cycle of birth, life, and death.

ERNIE: It doesn't matter which one. You can take any one.

SWAMIJI: Any, anything. Anything, it will be filled with God consciousness.

ERNIE: And all the other [sensations] will benefit from that.

SWAMIJI: Yes, yes.

ERNIE: And then, each one, e.g., the eye, is independent? It has its own *spanda*?

SWAMIJI: Yes, yes.

ERNIE: Its own *spanda*?

SWAMIJI: Yes.

ERNIE: And taste has its own *spanda*?

SWAMIJI: But it will be divine. That God consciousness will be inserted there, at that moment, after realization. After realization, everything will be [divine].

ERNIE: You said it wasn't like the cutters tool, . . .

SWAMIJI: No (affirmative).

ERNIE: . . . that they are independent, that they have their own life?

SWAMIJI: Yes.

ERNIE: Hearing has its own [life]?

SWAMIJI: Own life, because God consciousness is inserted there. It is one with God consciousness. But it will only take place when there is not the individual cycle of consciousness. That individual cycle of consciousness is dependent on breath, breathing. As long as you breathe, you are an individual. As long as breath has stopped, you become divine.[38]

JOHN: But there's a point in a later time when you breathe

38 "Automatic stoppage will take place through meditation, through the power of meditation. You will see, you will feel, that this is blocked, this ordinary two-way path [i.e., inhale and exhale] is blocked and my breath is entering from some other pathway. Only when there is the grace of God, the grace of your master, and the grace of your strength to maintain awareness, then this pathway will be cleared for you and you will rise." *Tantrāloka* (LJA audio archive), 15.102-103.

and you are also universal, isn't it?

SWAMIJI: Then you are universal. Then that breathing does not matter. That breathing is just like the breathless state. That is what [Bhairava] says:

na vrajenna viśecchaktirmarudrūpā vikāsite /
nirvikalpatyā madhye tayā bhairavarūpatā //[39]

This *prāṇa śakti* (the energy of breath), it does not function at all.[40] It functions in God consciousness afterwards because his mind is one-pointed. His mind becomes one-pointed and it does not function as it functioned previously.

Audio 1 - 38:21

नाभावो भाव्यतामेति न च तत्रास्त्यमूढता ।
यतोऽभियोगसंस्पर्शात्तदासीदिति निश्चयः ॥ १२ ॥
अतस्तत्कृत्रिमं ज्ञेयं सौषुप्तपदवत्सदा ।
न त्वेवं स्मर्यमाणत्वं तत्तत्त्वं प्रतिपद्यते ॥ १३ ॥

nābhāvo bhāvyātāmeti na ca tatrāstyamūḍhatā /
yato'bhiyogasaṁsparśāttadāsīditi niścayaḥ //12//
atastatkṛtrimaṁ jñeyaṁ sauṣuptapadavatsadā /
na tvevaṁ smaryamāṇatvaṁ tattattvaṁ pratipadyate //13//
[not recited]

Now, there is another point to be discussed. That point is of Vedānta, the schools of Vedānta, the thought derived from the school of Vedānta (that is *śrutyantavid*), Akṣapāda [which] is

39 *Vijñāna Bhairava*, verse 26.
40 "*Madhye nirvikalpatayā*, when you establish one-pointedness in the central path, the central vein (*suṣumnā*), then what happens? *Marut rūpā śakti*, this energy of breath neither goes out nor enters in, *na vrajet na viśet*, because *madhye vikāsite*, this central vein is *vikāsite,* it is already illuminated. And, by this process, *bhairava rūpatā bhavati*, one becomes one with Bhairava." Ibid., 26.

Gautama[41], and Madhyamaka[42] [which] is just like Buddhism, etc.

kṣobhapralaye viśvocchedarūpamabhāvātmakameva tattvam-avaśiṣyate[43]

They conclude that when this agitation of the world ends, *nābhāvo bhāvyātāmeti*, this *abhāva*–which they have concluded that It is *abhāva*, It is nothingness–when you melt in nothingness, that is the real state of God consciousness.

ERNIE: The void.

SWAMIJI: The void. That is the theory of Vedānta, Akṣapāda, and Buddhism. Nothingness, to get entry in nothingness, is the reality of God consciousness.

JOHN: Vedāntists believe [in] this nothingness?

SWAMIJI: Yes, that is *śūnya*, *śūnyātmatā*.

JOHN: I thought Brahman was full for them?

SWAMIJI: [For them, Brahman is] *śūnya* because they don't believe in *svātantrya*.[44] When there is not *svātantrya*, it is just like *śūnya*.

JOHN: But the Vedāntists themselves, they argue with the Buddhists, they argue that, "The Buddhists say It is *śūnya* and we don't say It is *śūnya*. They say, we say It's . . ."

SWAMIJI: But it is also *śūnya*.

ERNIE: (laughter)

JOHN: Because there is nothing there.

SWAMIJI: Yes. But that *śūnya*, how can you perceive *śūnya*?

---

41 Akṣapāda, also known as Gautama, was the compiler of the *Nyāya Sutra* and the founder of *Nyāya*, the first of the six classical systems of Indian Philosophy.

42 A school of Mahāyāna Buddhism founded by the sage Nāgārjuna.

43 Kṣhemarāja's introductory commentary for verses 12 and 13.

44 "The singularly unique aspect of Lord Śiva is complete independence, *svātantrya*. This complete independence is not found anywhere except in the state of Lord Śiva." *Śiva Sūtras–The Supreme Awakening*, 1.1, page 12. See Appendix 2 for an explanation of *svātantrya*.

This is the . . .

ERNIE: The question?

SWAMIJI: No, this is the argument from Shaivism. The Shaivite master [asks]: How can you perceive *śūnya*? When it is a void, how can you perceive it? If it is nothing, how can you perceive it?

Audio 1 - 40:24

Na bhāvo bhāvyatāmeti, if you once perceive that nothingness, it is something. *Na ca tatrāstyamūḍhatā*, because, when a Vedānta master enters in *samādhi*, [afterwards] he says, "I was residing in *samādhi*"[45], and when you ask him, "What was it like?" he says, "I can't explain. It was just going in nothingness, that *abhāva*" (*abhāva* means, that nothingness). They conclude that that state of nothingness is the reality of God consciousness. But how can it be perceived? Because, at the time of its perception, you don't perceive it. At the time of *abhiyoga*[46] you perceive it. When you come out from *samādhi*, you tell your friends that, "I was in *samādhi*". But, at that very moment [during *samādhi*], you can't perceive that it is *samādhi* because it is *śūnya*, it is the void. The void cannot be perceived in the cycle of voidness. Afterwards, when you get out from that voidness, you perceive that there was something.

ERNIE: Like deep sleep.

SWAMIJI: Deep sleep. *Yato abhiyoga saṁsparśāt tadāsīd*, [when the *yogi* says], "That was existing, that *samādhi* was existing", this kind of perception rises at the time of

45 *Samādhi*, which literally means "putting together, joining or combining with", is an intense spiritual absorption or trance. As Swamiji will explain in his commentary on verse 3.6, there are different kinds of *samādhi*. Swamiji defines *samādhi* as, "The thought-less state of consciousness, *samādhi*, *grāhya grāhakabhedā asaṁcetana rūpa*, when the state of *grāhya* (objectivity) and the state of *grāhaka* (subjectivity) both vanish in an instant. That is *samādhi*." Swami Lakshmanjoo, trans., *Śiva Sūtra Vimarśinī* (LJA archives). See Appendix 3 for an explanation of *samādhi*.

46 In this instance *abhiyoga* carries the sense of "a declaration".

vyutthāna[47], at the time when he comes out from *samādhi*.

Audio 1 - 42:10

Atastad, so it is artificial *samādhi*. This is the conclusion of the Shaivite master [that] this kind of *samādhi* is artificial *samādhi*, it is adjusted *samādhi*, not real *samādhi*. *Atastat kṛtrimam jñeyam*, it is *sauṣapta padvat*, it is just like *suṣupti*, it is just like deep sleep.[48] [The Vedāntins, etc.] have tried for that, they have served their masters for twelve years and gone in this deep sleep, . . .

ERNIE: (laughter)

SWAMIJI: . . . [but] we go in deep sleep every day. What is the sense in serving your master for twelve years [in order to] attain the state of deep sleep?

DEVOTEES: (laughter)

SWAMIJI: We attain it . . .

DENISE: Naturally.

SWAMIJI: . . . naturally. *Atastat kṛtrimam*, so this [supposed] state of God consciousness is *kṛtrimam* (artificial), it is just adjusted, it is just poetry, *sauṣupta padavat*, [it is] just like *suṣupti*.

Na tvevaṁ smaryamāṇatvam, that reality of God consciousness is not perceived this way that, "It was something!" just like [recalling] the sweetness of a sugar cube, that sugar candy.[49] [Further,] you say [that] It cannot be told, It cannot be

---

47 Waking up to the external world.

48 Deep sleep is the condition of the *pralayākala pramātṛin*. See Appendix 4 for an explanation of the seven perceivers.

49 "That moment when you realize God consciousness, it means the moment existing in the present tense, not in the future tense, not in the past tense. It is not a past moment, it is not a future moment. It is the present moment, the present situation, the present period of realizing God consciousness. But by telling you, "The present moment", you must not think that there are two other moments also, [that] in the past there is one moment and in the future there is another moment. So this *vartamānakṣaṇasya*, this present moment, is restricted. It is restricted–there is no past moment, there is no future moment. Past moment and future moment, both moments are

explained, [in the same way] that [one cannot explain] what taste is existing in sugar candy, [but] this kind of example does not adjust here. [According to Shaivism], It is that state of God consciousness which can be explained properly, how It is like. So, this kind of *samādhi* derived from Vedānta, Buddhism, and Gautama (Nyāya) is absolutely incorrect.

Audio 1 - 44:09

अवस्थायुगलं चात्र कार्यकर्तृत्वशब्दितम् ।
कार्यता क्षयिणी तत्र कर्तृत्वं पुनरक्षयम् ॥ १४ ॥

avasthāyugalaṁ cātra kāryakartṛtvaśabditam /
kāryatā kṣayiṇī tatra kartṛtvaṁ punarakṣayam //14//

There are two states in this world, two states which we experience in this world. There is *kāryatā*[50] and this *kartṛtā*[51].

Kāryatā is just what you do. For instance, you work, you go to the office, you marry, have children, have babies (get yourself married and then have children), and then . . .

ERNIE: Your activities in the world.

SWAMIJI: All things. You . . .

---

digested in this present moment. Whenever you realize God consciousness, at the time of realization, at the moment of realizing God consciousness, you feel that, "I was in the past also there [in the state of God consciousness]", and you feel at that present moment, "I'll be [in God consciousness] in the future also in the same way. Nothing has happened, nothing has been lost. Nothing has been lost, I was there in the past, I'll be there in the future also." This is the present situation of that moment. So there is not the past existing, there is not the future existing. So all of these three periods are finished. Because this period is *tattva paryavasāyyeva*, when you realize It, at the time of realization, you find that you had already realized It. You can't remain without this, you can't exist without this realization. You had already realized It, you had realized It, and you will be realizing It in the future also. There is no other way of Its realization." Swami Lakshmanjoo, trans., *Parātrīśikā Vivaraṇa* (Lakshmanjoo Academy archive, Los Angeles) 1982-1985.

50 The state of being an effect.

51 The state of being the agent of an action.

JOHN: Rear your children.

SWAMIJI: . . . you make money, you have got a big bank balance, . . .

ERNIE: You spend money.

SWAMIJI: . . . and you have got a big bungalow afterwards–motor cars, everything, society, friendship. This is *kāryatā*.

Kartṛtā is the one who is the hero, who has done all this–the hero. The time will come [when] this whole cycle of *kāryatā* will vanish altogether. There will be no son, there'll be no children, there will be no money, there will be nothing, no wife, no house, no . . . you'll be just like a pauper. But *kartṛtvaṁ punarakṣayam*, but the doer, the hero, is still there. The hero does not get vanished. Which hero?

JOHN: The doer, the real doer.

SWAMIJI: The real doer. *Kāryatā kṣayiṇī tatra kartṛtvaṁ punarakṣyaṁ*, *kartṛtva* (doership) is [always] there. The done, whatever is done by that doership, let it be vanished, let it vanish, let it go to hell, but the doership is still existing. *Kāryonmukhaḥ* . . . what happens to this cycle [of *kāryatā*] then? [Vasugupta] says:

Audio 1 - 46:06

कार्योन्मुखः प्रयत्नो यः केवलं सोऽत्र लुप्यते ।
तस्मिँल्लुप्ते विलुप्तोऽस्मीत्यबुधः प्रतिपद्यते ॥ १५॥

kāryonmukhaḥ prayatno yaḥ kevalaṁ so'tra lupyate
tasmiṁllupte vilupto'smītyabuddhaḥ pratipadyate //15//
[not recited in full]

The *prayatna*, the effort, the trouble, all this, that vanishes, that is finished. There is no son, there is no wife, there is no . . . nothing remains, only that . . .

ERNIE: Doer.

SWAMIJI: . . . doer is there. That *prayatna* is finished, that *pratyana* has vanished. *Tasmiṁllupte*, when the *prayatna* is vanished, [when] his effort, his fruit, along with his effort, along with his fruit, has vanished, he concludes, "I am vanished, I am no more, I am finished! [Swamiji beats his chest] I am finished", [but] he[52] [is not] finished, he is still there. *Tasmiṁllupte vilupto asmi iti abudhaḥ*, this is the perception of ignorance, this is the perception derived from ignorance that he says, "I am nothing. I am ruined. I am spoiled. I have no wife. I have no children. They all were crashed in an air crash. Finished. I am . . . *bas.*"

ERNIE: "I will kill myself."

SWAMIJI: "I am nothing. There is no fun in . . . there is no meaning in my life now." (laughter) He says that. *Tasmiṁllupte vilupto'smītyabudhaḥ*, but this is the perception perceived by that person who is ignorant, who is not fully elevated.

Audio 1 - 47:44

न तु योऽन्तर्मुखो भावः सर्वज्ञत्वगुणास्पदम् ।
तस्य लोपः कदाचित्स्यादन्यस्यानुपलम्भनात् ॥ १६ ॥

na tu yo'ntramukhobhāvaḥ sarvajñatvaguṇāspadam /
tasya lopaḥ kadācitsyādanyasyānupalambhanāt //16//
[not recited]

Na tu yo'ntramukhabhāvaḥ, that *antar mukha bhāva* . . .*
Antar mukha bhāva is that . . .

GANJOO: Introvertedness.

SWAMIJI: . . . introverted God consciousness.

*. . . the state of introverted God consciousness, which is *sarva jñatva guṇās padam*, which is the basis of all knowledge and all action, *tasya lopaḥ kadācitsyāt*, It cannot be vanished, It will never vanish if Its function, Its action, has vanished. [When] Its action has vanished, It cannot vanish along with Its action, along with Its force, Its creative force. That [Self] remains eternally one-pointed and just in one shape, one form.

---

52 The doer, the hero.

Audio 1 - 48:32

तस्योपलब्धिः सततं त्रिपदाव्यभिचारिणी ।
नित्यं स्यात्सुप्रबुद्धस्य तदाद्यन्ते परस्य तु ॥ १७॥

tasyopalabdhiḥ satataṁ tripadāvyabhicāriṇī /
nityaṁ syātsuprabuddhasya tadādyante parasya tu //17//

Tasyopalabdhiḥ satataṁ tripad vyabhicāriṇī, there are three states [of the limited individual]: wakefulness, dreaming, and the dreamless state. There are three states, and in these three states also, that elevated soul who has realized that which was to be realized, . . .*

What was to be realized?

JOHN: His own real nature.

SWAMIJI: No. [The state of] *kartṛtva* (doership), not the done! Whatever is done, it is done; it is outside, it is in the outside cycle. You are the doer, you are existing in your own nature–that will never vanish!

Tasyopalabdhiḥ, there are [three] sections of *yogi*s: *suprabuddha yogi*, *prabuddha yogi*, and [*apr*]*abuddha yogi*. *Suprabuddha yogi* is that kind of *yogi* who is always alert in his nature, who is naturally alert in his own way. That *suprabuddha yogi* perceives that nature of God consciousness of doership.

*. . . that state of doership he perceives in all the other three states–in wakefulness, in the dreaming state, and in the dreamless state. In wakefulness, in the dreaming state, and in the dreamless state, he perceives the state of that doership. As he used to perceive that [state] in *turya* and *turīyātitā*[53], in the same way, he perceives that state in these three states also–in

53 "The difference between *turya* and *turyātītā* is, in *turya* you find in *samādhi* that this whole universe is existing there in the seed form, a germ. The strength, the energy, of universal existence is existing there, but here he has [yet] to come out [into activity]. In *turyātītā*, he comes out in [the field of] action and feels universal consciousness. This is the difference between *turya* and *turyātītā*. So, *turyātītā* is just like *jagadānanda* and *turya* is *cidānanda*." *Tantrāloka* (LJA archives), 10.288. See Appendix 5 for an explanation of *turya* and *turyātītā*.

jāgrata, in *svapna*, in *suṣupti* also–always (*nityaṁ syāt suprabuddhasya*).

Tadādyante parasya tu, and that *para*, the next *yogi* of the next section (that is the *prabuddha yogi*), the *prabuddha yogi* perceives that state of God consciousness in-between these three states. He does not perceive [God consciousness] in the cycle of wakefulness, he perceives [God consciousness] in the beginning of the cycle of wakefulness and in the end of the cycle of wakefulness and in the beginning of the cycle of the dreaming state and in the end of the cycle of the dreaming state.

ERNIE: The junction, the gap.

SWAMIJI: The gap. The source and the end, the source point and the ending point. In these two points, he perceives the state of God consciousness. Who? The *prabuddha yogi*. The *suprabuddha yogi* perceives the state of God consciousness always–in the beginning, in the end, and in the center also. This is the greatness found in the *suprabuddha yogi*. And the *prabuddha yogi* only perceives that God consciousness . . .

ERNIE: In the gap.

SWAMIJI: . . . in the gap only. And the *aprabuddha yogi* does not find it at all. The *aprabuddha yogi* does not find it at all.

ERNIE: Because?

SWAMIJI: Because he is kept away from God consciousness altogether.

ERNIE: Then, but he is still a *yogi*.

SWAMIJI: He does practice just as we do, without knowing anything (laughter). But you must be a *prabuddha yogi*; at least you must be a *prabuddha yogi*. You must find out the reality of this *turya* in-between these two states: *jāgrat* (wakefulness) and *svapna* (dreaming), in the center of *jāgrat* and *svapna*, or in the center of *svapna* and *suṣupti* (deep-sleep), or in the center of *svapna* and *jāgrat*. You have to find out! If you don't find It out, then there is no hope. So you must strive for It! You must struggle for It! And this is done by the grace of the master. *Bas*.

Audio 1 - 55:39

[suprabuddhasya] triṣu padeṣu yādṛśī upalabdhistāṁ vibhāgena darśayati[54]

There are three classes of *yogis*. One class is of the *[apr]abuddha yogi*, and the next is the *prabuddha [yogi]*, and the third is the *suprabuddha yogi*.

The *suprabuddha yogi* is that *yogi* who is fully elevated, who is just like a *siddha yogi*.[55] For him, how he deals with these three states (waking, dreaming, and the dreamless state), how he treats them, how he deals [with] them, that he explains in this *śloka*:

Audio 1 - 56:30

ज्ञानज्ञेयस्वरूपिण्या शक्त्या परमया युतः ।
पदद्वये विभुर्भाति तदन्यत्र तु चिन्मयः ॥ १८॥

jñānajñeyasvarūpiṇyā śaktyā paramayā yutaḥ /
padadvaye vibhurbhāti tadanyatra tu cinmayaḥ //18//

Lord Śiva appears to him, to that *yogi*, the *suprabuddha yogi*, in wakefulness and in the dreaming state with *jñāna śakti* and *jñeya śakti* (the energy of knowledge and energy of the object; cognitive energy and objective energy).

JOACHIM: Is it *kriyā śakti*? The same . . . ?

SWAMIJI: *Kriyā śakti*[56] and *jñāna śakti*, not *icchā śakti*[57]–with *jñāna śakti* and with *jñeya śakti*. *Jñāna śakti* is the energy of knowledge, *jñeya śakti* is the energy of the object

---

54 Kṣhemarāja's introductory commentary for verse 1.18.
55 Lit., an accomplished (*siddha*) *yogi*. "He is a *jñāni*. He is called a *siddha yogi*. He can initiate people. The *siddha yogi* will give [the initiate] *bhoga*, *mokṣa*, and *vijñāna*. *Bhoga* means, worldly success, success in the world. *Mokṣa* means, liberation, final liberation. And [*vijñāna* means], knowledge of Shaivism. All these three are worth to have." *Tantrāloka* (LJA archives), 13.332-338.
56 Viz., *jñeya śakti* (objective energy).
57 Energy of the will.

(*jñeya*, *prameya bhāva*[58]).

[The *suprabuddha yogi*] feels the Lord's energy of *prameya bhāva* is functioning in wakefulness and Lord Śiva's cognitive energy is functioning in his dreaming state. So, his dreaming state and wakefulness are also divine. But this is an additional adjustment in that: he feels in wakefulness the objective energy [of Lord Śiva], and in the dreaming state, [he feels] the cognitive energy of Lord Śiva. *Padadvaye vibhurbhāti*, Lord Śiva appears to him like this.

Tadanyatra, in the other, the third state, . . .

JOHN: Deep sleep.

SWAMIJI: . . . deep sleep (*suṣupti*), *cinmayaḥ*[59] appears to him as absolutely one with God consciousness. So his *suṣupti* is just as *samādhi*. Whose?

JOHN: This *suprabuddha yogi*.

SWAMIJI: The *suprabuddha yogi*. Not [ordinary] sleep–the *suprabuddha yogi's suṣupti* (deep sleep) is just like *samādhi*. There is no difference between *samādhi* and *suṣupti* for him. For whom?

JOHN: For the *suprabuddha yogi*.

SWAMIJI: Yes.

Audio 1 - 55:36

> *yatheyaṁ jāgrādimadhyadaśāpi prabuddhaṁ na badhnāti tathā upapādayati*[60]

Now he explains in this next *śloka* that this elevated *yogi* does not get bondage, does not get bound, entangled, by these three states (*jāgrat*, *svapna*, and *suṣupti*).

---

58 *Prameya bhāva* (the objective state). See Appendix 6 for an explanation of *prameya, pramāṇa, pramātṛ* and *pramiti bhāva*.

59 The fulness of consciousness, Lord Śiva.

60 Kṣhemarāja's introduction to verse 1.19.

Audio 1 - 56:01

गुणादिस्पन्दनिष्यन्दाः सामान्यस्पन्दसंश्रयात् ।
लब्धात्मलाभाः सततं स्युर्ज्ञस्यापरिपन्थिनः ॥ १९ ॥

guṇādispandaniṣyandāḥ sāmānyaspandasaṁśrayāt /
labdhātmalābhāḥ satataṁ syurjñasyāparipanthinaḥ //19//

Jñasya means, that *yogi* who is absolutely elevated (*jñasya*). He who has known, in the real sense, the state of Lord Śiva, he is *jñasya* (*jñasya* means, a fully-elevated *yogi*).

For him, *guṇādispanda niṣyandāḥ*, all these cycles of the *guṇās*[61], all these cycles of organs, the activity of the organs, all organs (the organs of action and the organs of knowledge), . . .*

> The organs of action are five and the organs of knowledge are also five. *Śabda*, *sparśa*, *rūpa*, *rasa*, and *gandha* are the organs of knowledge, and *vāk*, *pāṇī*, *pāda*, *pāyu*, and *upastha* are the organs of action. *Vāk* means, [speech], speaking; *pāṇi* is handling, holding; *pāda* is walking; *pāyu* is excretion of *mala*[62]; and *upastha* is the sexual [organ]. [These are] the five acts of *kriyā*, action.

*. . . that elevated soul takes hold of *sāmānya spanda* in that.

There are two sections of *spanda*s explained in this *spanda śāstra*, movement. One *spanda* is *viśeṣa spanda* and another *spanda* is *sāmānya spanda*. *Viśeṣa spanda* is distinctive movement. Distinctive movement is found in the daily activity of life–distinctive movement. Going here and there, talking, eating, sleeping, joking, laughing, going to the movies, all these activities are distinctive, they are separated from each other ("distinctive" means, they are separated from each other).

JOHN: Beginning and end?

---

61 *Guṇas* here means, the organs. See *Spanda Sandoha*, page 237.
62 Lit., impurity, here referring to urine and feces, etc.

SWAMIJI: Not beginning and end. They are separated, e.g., one movement of talking is different from the movement of walking, the movement of walking is different from the movement of enjoying (the movement of playing)–all of this. They are different from each other. In this [differentiation], you find *spanda*. *Spanda* is existing there, but that *spanda* is existing in *viśeṣa bhāva* (*viśeṣa bhāva* is distinctive), in a distinctive manner.

And there is another *spanda*, that is *sāmānya spanda* (universal *spanda*). That is *sāmānya spanda*. *Sāmānya spanda* is found everywhere, just unchangeable and just in one formation. *Sāmānya spanda* is one [whereas] *viśeṣa spanda*s are many, hundreds, thousands.

But that elevated soul takes hold of that *sāmānya spanda*, not *viśeṣa spanda*. In the activity of *viśeṣa spanda*, he takes hold of *sāmānya spanda*. So he is fine, he does not go down, he is not trodden down from the kingdom of God consciousness. His kingdom of God consciousness is still prevailing there, in *viśeṣa spanda* also. So, [taking hold of *sāmānya spanda*] while acting, that is what is called *karma yoga* (*yoga* in action).

Yoga in inaction, that is *jñāna yoga*[63]. When you don't act, you remain in *samādhi*, meditating, all-round meditating, that is inactive *yoga*. In that inactive *yoga*, there is the possibility of coming down from that state, but in active *yoga* . . .

> when you rise along with thieves, who will steal your property? You are with thieves, you are rising along with your thieves, who would [otherwise] snatch all your good property from you–if you deal with, along with, thieves also. What are "thieves"? The temptations of the world, temptations of the world. There are so many temptations in the world. Those snatch away the treasure of God consciousness from you. You lose that treasure of God consciousness by those thieves. But you make friendship with the thieves. When you remain in the action of the world, [then] you are on friendly terms with the thieves also. What can they snatch from you? They will never snatch from you.

---

63 *Yoga* in knowledge (*jñāna*).

ERNIE: So, for a *jñāna yogi*, they are thieves, and for . . .

SWAMIJI: . . . the *karma yogi*, they are not thieves, they are friends–no problem.

JOHN: So *jñāna yoga* is inactive *yoga*.

SWAMIJI: Inactive, yes.

JOHN: So *karma* [*yoga*] is much higher than *jñana yoga*.

SWAMIJI: Of course. *Karma* is, *kriyā śakti* is, best!

JOACHIM: It's *kriyā śakti*?

SWAMIJI: *Kriyā śakti*, yes. *Jñāna śakti* is lower and *icchā śakti* is lowest. But in Vedānta, you will find *icchā śakti* the highest, *jñana śakti* a bit lower, and *kriyā śakti* as wretched. They call *kriyā śakti* "*bhrama*", illusion. But this is not an illusion for us. For Shaivites, *kriyā śakti* is just the real element to rise.

So, for those elevated souls, these *guṇādi spanda niṣyandāḥ*, these classes of the organs of the senses, they become *labdhātmalābhaḥ*, they just push him in the center of God consciousness.

Who?

The organs of action and the organs of knowledge. The organs of action and the organs of knowledge just push you inside God consciousness.

Whom?

Those elevated *yogis*. It is not found in those who are not elevated–they are kicked down by these senses.[64]

And this is the way [that] *jñasya āparipanthinaḥ*, for an elevated soul, they become friends, not enemies. For those who are not elevated, they are enemies for them. How are they enemies? That is clarified in the next *śloka*:

64 "At the time of enjoyment of those senses, *vidyudvat ābhāsanam*, that God consciousness is shining just like lightning for one second, in a flash. *Tena tattadavasareṣu*–but what you have to do there?–*tattadavasareṣu*, at those points, at those points of lightning, you have to be absolutely aware. If you are not aware, finished, you are as good as an individual being." Swami Lakshmanjoo, trans., *Śiva Sūtra Vimarśinī* (LJA archives).

Audio 1 - 01:03:30

अप्रबुद्धधियस्त्वेते स्वस्थितिस्थगनोद्यताः ।
पातयन्ति दुरुत्तारे घोरे संसारवर्त्मनि ॥२०॥

aprabuddhadhiyastvete svasthitisthaganodyatāḥ /
pātayanti duruttāre ghore saṁsāravartmani //20//

Aprabuddhadhiyaḥ, he whose intellect is not elevated, those *yogi*s whose intellect is not fully elevated in the cycle of God consciousness, for those *yogi*s, *ete*, these senses, these organs of the senses, . . .

Do you understand, sir?

JOACHIM: Yes.

SWAMIJI: . . . these organs of the senses are just bent upon *svasthitisthaganod*, just to conceal his real nature. They just do this business only.

What business?

DENISE: Just conceal his nature.

SWAMIJI: Just conceal his nature. If you see, your God consciousness is concealed. If you touch, your God consciousness is concealed. For whom? Those who are not elevated. [For] those who are fully elevated, by touch [they] will rise, by seeing [they] will rise. It will [provide] a strong push to go inside God consciousness by being in the activity of the world. So be in action and be elevated. This is what is taught by Shaivism. Good?

JOHN: Yes.

SWAMIJI: *Aprabuddhadhiyastvete*, so, these organs of the senses, for those who are not elevated, *svasthitisthagana-udyatāḥ*, are bent upon concealing the nature of God consciousness (for those un-elevated souls), and *pātayanti duruttāre ghore* [*saṁsāra*], and they kick him down in the ditch of *saṁsāra* of repeated births and deaths. He is entangled in that cycle forever, for centuries and centuries.

So what we have to do is explained in the next *śloka*:

Audio 1 - 01:05:33

अतः सततमुद्युक्तः स्पन्दतत्त्वविविक्तये ।
जाग्रदेव निजं भावमचिरेणाधिगच्छति ॥२१॥

ataḥ satatamudyaktaḥ spandatattvaviviktaye /
jāgradeva nijaṁ bhāvamacireṇādhigacchati //21//

So, what you have to do is, *satatam udyuktaḥ*, you must develop that kind of zeal of action, that kind of zeal of effort (*udyuktaḥ*, that zeal of effort)–for what?–*spanda tattva viviktaye*, to find out the reality of *spanda*. The one who is bent upon finding out the reality of *spanda* always (*satatam*), in the dreaming state also–not only in wakefulness, in the dreaming state also–who is bent upon finding out the reality of God consciousness, does not lose even one hundreth part of his breath. So, 21,600 breaths[65] he does not lose, not even one breath, day and night.

JOHN: "Lose" means? Goes out of his awareness?

SWAMIJI: [When your breath] goes out [or in] without awareness. You should be aware with each and every breath. You should watch your breath, day and night. So you have to do this kind of effort.

Then, what will happen to him?

Jāgrat eva, not [only] in the dreaming state, not in the center only, he will find out the truth of *turya*. He will find out the truth of *turya* in wakefulness also (*jāgrat eva*)! In wakefulness also, *nijaṁ bhāvam*, his real nature of *turya*, *acireṇādhigacchati*, he will, . . .

JOACHIM: In a short time . . .

SWAMIJI: . . . in a very short period, he will achieve. Now, there are some states of daily life where this kind of process is very easily done, easily conducted.

ERNIE: This watching of the breath?

---

65 "This automatic recitation of breath in twenty-four hours takes place twenty-one thousand and six hundred times–*ṣat ṣatāni*, six hundred, *divā rātrau*, in the day and night, *sahasrāṇi ekaviṁśati*, and twenty-one thousand." *Vijñāna Bhairava*, 156.

SWAMIJI: Not watching of the breath, [but] . . .

JOHN: Catching hold of the *sāmānya* [*spanda*].

SWAMIJI: Catching hold of that *spanda*, . . .

ERNIE: The gap.

SWAMIJI: . . . *spanda* in action.

JOHN: Which *spanda* are we talking about here? This *sāmānya spanda* or this . . . ?

SWAMIJI: *Sāmānya spanda*, not *viśeṣa spanda*. *Viśeṣa spanda* we are already . . .

ERNIE: There is no problem.

SWAMIJI: There is no problem for *viśeṣa spanda* for us. We are living in *viśeṣa spanda*. The problem is *sāmānya spanda*, you must realize *sāmānya spanda*, what *sāmānya spanda* is.

Audio 1 - 01:08:00

अतिक्रुद्धः प्रहृष्टो वा किं करोमीति वा मृशन् ।
धावन्वा यत्पदं गच्छेत्तत्र स्पन्दः प्रतिष्ठितः ॥२२॥

atikruddhaḥ prahṛṣṭo vā kiṁ karomīti vā mṛśan /
dhāvan vā yatpadaṁ gacchettatra spandaḥ pratiṣṭhitaḥ //

This *sāmānya spanda* you will find easily, existing in these, at these, points. Which points? *Atikruddhaḥ*, when you are extremely angry–wrath, filled with wrath (Swamiji demonstrates), *bas*, because your breathing also does not work there.[66]

When you did that.[67]

ERNIE: (laughs)

SWAMIJI: It is that period (laughter). At that time, you ought to have done this. You would have entered in that *sāmānya spanda*.

ERNIE: Shall I get angry again?

---

66 "You can't enter in God consciousness when there is breathing." *Tantrāloka* (LJA archives), 5.88.

67 Swamiji is referring to an incident in which Ernie had become extremely angry.

SWAMIJI: Of course!

JOHN: If he does this.

SWAMIJI: Yes.

ERNIE: But why does it happen then?

SWAMIJI: Because, at that time, *sāmānya spanda* is vivid, vividly found. Because, at that time, you have no other thought, only anger. Only the flood of anger is . . .

ERNIE & DENISE: One-pointed.

SWAMIJI: . . . one-pointed there–the flood of anger, the flood of wrath.

ERNIE: And your breath is . . .

SWAMIJI: The breath also stops at that time, the breath does not work, and all your organs do not work. Only, all the senses are diverted towards wrath (Swamiji demonstrates).

DEVOTEES: (laughter)

SWAMIJI: Like this, huh?

This is what happens. *Atikruddhaḥ*, this is the state of *atikruddhaḥ bhāva* (*atikruddha*, extreme wrath). When you get that extreme wrath, the state of extreme wrath, *tatra spandaḥ pratiṣṭhitaḥ*, there you will find [*sāmānya*] *spanda*, if you just get diversion in internal diversion at that period.

DENISE: You mean, just sit and meditate at that time?

SWAMIJI: Just meditate on "Why I am so angry" (*ati kruddhaḥ*).

Prahṛṣṭo vā, or when you are overjoyed (*prahṛṣṭaḥ*, supreme joy), at the time of supreme joy also, your breath does not work, your actions also . . .

GANJOO: Vanish.

SWAMIJI: . . . just stop, they don't function. At that period, *tatra spanda* [*pratiṣṭhitaḥ*], that *sāmānya spanda* is existing, and you must find it out if you are a *yogi*.

Kiṁ karomīti vā mṛśan, or at the time when this was falling, . . .

DENISE: Skylab?

SWAMIJI: . . . the Skylab[68] was falling, and the time was supposed [that] just after half an hours time, Kashmir will be nothing, finished–and you live in Kashmir.

ERNIE: (laughter)

SWAMIJI: At that moment, what will you do? Where will you go? That is *kiṁ karomi* ("What should I do now?").

ERNIE: That is fear.

SWAMIJI: That is fear. At that [rise of] fear, that *sāmānya spanda* is existing.

JOHN: The more fear, the better. The more . . .

ERNIE: Frightened.

JOHN: . . . the more frightened you are, the more that *sāmānya* [*spanda*] is present.

SWAMIJI: *Sāmānya spanda* is present. Because you have no choice [at that moment]. If a beautiful lady is with you, will you think of embracing her? "Just damn her head! I am dying just in another minute." (laughter) You won't do any action in this world. All of your organs are in a standstill position.

ERNIE: Suspended.

SWAMIJI: Suspended, all actions are suspended there. This is *kiṁ karomi*, this state. At that very moment, that *spanda* is existing; *sāmānya spanda* is there, very near.

Dhāvan vā, or, you are just walking in a forest and a lion comes and . . .

GANJOO: Chases you.

SWAMIJI: . . . chases after you, it runs after you, and you run, you run so fast, God alone knows how fast you run to save yourself, but you can't escape from his clutches, but still you run to save yourself. This is the position where *spanda* is existing, that *sāmānya spanda*. If you just go inside, *sāmānya spanda* will be there.

DENISE: But he may eat you.

SWAMIJI: No, then he won't eat you.

DENISE: He really won't?

---

68 Referring to the space station of that name launched by NASA, which orbited the earth between 1974 and 1979.

SWAMIJI: This is what happened to Sudāmā. In a forest he was going to see his friend, Lord Kṛṣṇa, and in the forest, that black bear came to chase him, to eat him, and he thought [the bear] was Lord Kṛṣṇa in a black coat. And that *sāmānya spanda* was existing there. And he embraced [the bear]. They embraced each other.

JOHN: So what's the difference between this one and *kiṁ karomi*?

SWAMIJI: This is *dhāvan.* It is *dhāvan* (running), when you are running fast! *Dhāvan* means "running".

ERNIE: So, if you are not afraid and you are just running, it's also possible?

SWAMIJI: Yes, by running, you run and just see which is the force that makes you so much run.

One of my sisters was absolutely crippled. She is still living–Tekker Ded[69], that [lady] with the *pheren*[70].

DENISE: Who is bent over?

SWAMIJI: Yes, bent over. And she was crippled in those days when she was young. She was crippled, she couldn't walk, she couldn't move. And a big earthquake came, an earthquake happened, and she went walking, running, and she came down and all her disease was over. With fear, she . . . (laughter)

ERNIE: (laughter) She cured herself.

SWAMIJI: Yes (laughter).

ERNIE: So that's really the most active *spanda*.

SWAMIJI: Active *spanda*.

ERNIE: When you try and grasp that.

SWAMIJI: Yes.

JOHN: So we have three so far. Three–fear, anger, and running.

SWAMIJI: *Bas*?

ERNIE: No, and overjoyed.

---

69 Tekker Ded was one of Swamiji's elder sisters

70 A traditional long Kashmiri robe.

JOHN: Where is overjoyed?

SWAMIJI: *Prahṛṣṭo, prahṛṣṭo.*

JOACHIM: Swamiji, can we take [this] in every *kriyā*[71]? *Sthāyī bhāva*, for example, if I am [in a] completely erotic mood, or if I am in an aesthetic scenery, or [any of] these nine or eight *sthāyī bhāvas*, it must be possible that in any *spanda*, *sāmānya spanda* can happen from there when the emotion is completely clear.

SWAMIJI: No, not the emotion. You have to find out wherefrom this intensity has come, wherefrom this intensity of anger or intensity of running or intensity of joy has come.

JOACHIM: In the end, I have to refer it to my subjective, to the center.

SWAMIJI: When you go inside, yes. [When you earnestly inquire] wherefrom this has come, you will find *spanda*, you will find that *sāmānya spanda* there, existing, shining, without any problem.

Audio 1 - 01:15:19

यामवस्थां समालम्ब्य यदयं मम वक्ष्यति ।
तदवश्यं करिष्येऽहमिति सङ्कल्प्य तिष्ठति ॥२३॥

yāmavasthāṁ samālambya yadayaṁ mama vakṣyati /
tadavaśyaṁ kariṣye'hamiti saṁkalpya tiṣṭhati //23//

Now, he explains here the way how to do it in those states. In which states?

JOHN: In these four states of joy, anger, fear, and running.

SWAMIJI: In these four states of extremity, intensity–these four states of intensity.

JOACHIM: When I feel very disgusted, can it happen also when I am so disgusted, that I am completely out of myself because of disgust?

SWAMIJI: Yes, yes, that too, yes. Yes, yes, all these.

JOACHIM: That is *jugupsa*, to feel disgusted.

71 Activity.

SWAMIJI:

yāmavasthāṁ samālambya yadayaṁ mama vakṣyati /
tadavaśyaṁ kariṣye'hamiti saṁkalpya tiṣṭhati //23//[72]
[repeated]

This *saṁkalpa*[73] must take place at that moment for this elevated soul, for this *yogi*, who wants to get entry in that God consciousness at that moment: he must say that, "*Yāmavasthāṁ samālambya yadayaṁ mama vakṣyati*, this extreme state of anger, this extreme state of joy, this extreme state of running, this extreme state of all these", what he has explained in the previous *śloka*, "*yadayaṁ mama vakṣyati*, I want to find out what it means, what is the meaning of this." Just find out the meaning of this, how it has risen, risen in [you]. Just find out the meaning of this. And "*tadavaśyaṁ kariṣye'ham*, I want to remain in that meaning, what is meant by this wrath" (Swamiji demonstrates wrath). And there is no breathing also. Everything[74] is finished in all these states. *Iti saṁkalpya tiṣthiti*, this *saṁkalpa* must be held at that moment–this thought. This thought must prevail there. When this thought prevails, then what happens next to him?

DENISE: Which thought?

SWAMIJI: This thought to find out wherefrom this intensity of wrath, anger, etc., has come out.

JOACHIM: But not reduce it to an object creating it. For example, when I get angry because, for example, you know, a cow is cutting my view or something, not reducing it to what is creating it.

SWAMIJI: No, no, no. Just seeing what has happened in my mind, how this has happened in that [mind], this position of thought. Then what happens if he does this?

72 See Appendix 3 for an alternate explanation of this verse in relation to the state of *turya* and *samādhi*.

73 Conception or idea or notion formed in the mind or heart.

74 That is, the activity of the organs.

Audio 1 - 01:18:06

तामाश्रित्योर्ध्वमार्गेण चन्द्रसूर्यावुभावपि ।
सौषुम्नेऽध्वन्यस्तमितो हित्वा ब्रह्माण्डगोचरम् ॥२४॥
तदा तस्मिन्महाव्योम्नि प्रलीनशशिभास्करे ।
सौषुप्तपदवन्मूढः प्रबुद्धः स्यादनावृतः ॥२५॥

tāmāśrityordhvamārgeṇa candrasūryāvubhāvapi /
sauṣumne'dhvanyastamito hitvā brahmāṇḍagocaram //24//
tadā tasminmahāvyomni pralīnaśaśibhāskare /
sauṣuptapadavanmūḍhaḥ prabuddhaḥ syādanāvṛtaḥ //25//
[not recited]

Then, his breath stops altogether. At once his breath stops and it rushes in *suṣumnā*, in the central vein – at once, at that moment. When he just thinks of that intensity of joy, anger, etc., his breath stops altogether and his breath enters in the central vein of *suṣumnā*. *Candra sūryāu ubhāvapi*, both these breaths, inhaling and exhaling, both these breaths, *sauṣumne adhvani astamitaḥ*, they vanish in the path of *suṣumnā nāḍī*. *Hitvā brahmāṇḍa gocaram*, and it, [the force of breath], rises from *mūlādharā*, then up to *sahaśrārdha cakra*[75]. What happens? This wrath has been transformed in that supreme God consciousness.

At that moment also, there is another problem, there is another problem there. Where? When your breath has stopped, it has rushed in *suṣumnā nāḍī*, and from *mūlādharā* it has risen to the state of *sahaśrārdha cakra*. At that very moment also, if you are not fully attentive in that God consciousness, [then] you are kicked down on the path of *suṣupti*. You will become just . . .

JOHN: Asleep.

SWAMIJI: . . . just asleep. If you don't have the character and strength of maintaining that [awareness] there, you will just fall on the ground unconscious, and doctors will be attending you when you wake up [and they will wonder],

75 The thousand petal lotus is located above the crown of the head.

"What has happened to this man?" But *prabuddhaḥ syād*, that [*yogi*] who is fully elevated, fully alert, [has the character and strength of maintaining awareness there]. Because, this point of God consciousness is so refined that you . . .

JOACHIM: It requires the *prabuddha* state [inaudible] . . .

SWAMIJI: It requires full attention. If you are [unaware] just for half a second, one hundredth part of a second, if you don't maintain attentiveness, you will fall down.

ERNIE: You go back to the anger or you . . . ?

SWAMIJI: No, not anger. *Bas*, you are just as . . . you remain in an unconscious state, and everybody will think, "He is dying, he is on [his] deathbed", and you will come out and you will see doctors around you.

ERNIE: But you remember that experience before you fainted?

SWAMIJI: Yes, after that. After that you remember what had happened.

ERNIE: How close.

SWAMIJI: Yes. "How close I had reached and how I was kicked out."

JOHN: Isn't this state, though, very [difficult to achieve]? It seems to me the key of this is that God's grace, that you think that thought at the moment of anger.

SWAMIJI: It is why in Vedānta also, in the *Veda*s, [it is said]:

utiṣṭhata jāgrata prāpya varān nibodhataḥ[76]

"O soul, be attentive! Be awake! Hear this message of Lord Śiva: *Kṣurasya dhārā*, this is treading on the path, on the edge of a sword. *Durgampatha*, this is a very difficult path to tread on."[77]

Just for one second's mistake you will be kicked down. It is

---

76 *Uttiṣṭhata jāgrata prāpya varān nibodhata*: *kṣurasya dhārā niśitā duratyayā; durgam pathas tat kavayo vadanti–Kaṭha Upaniṣad*, 1.3.14.

77 See also *Self Realization in Kashmir Shaivism*, 2.49.

so precious. So you must maintain It, you must have It, you must devotedly have It.

ERNIE: But, if you maintain It, then you have It forever?

SWAMIJI: Forever! Devotion and effort.

JOACHIM: How can it be maintained?

SWAMIJI: With devotion and effort, devotion and effort–devotional effort. It must not be routine-like effort. It must be devotional effort, with enthusiasm.

JOHN: So the key of this one, though, is that you have to be, when you have this anger, somehow the thought has to come to you–when you have this anger or these other states–first you have to get the thought that you should . . .

ERNIE: Look inside.

JOHN: . . . look inside.

SWAMIJI: Look inside, yes.

JOHN: Many times, the thought will come afterwards, "Oh, if I'd have looked inside during that time . . ."

SWAMIJI: Afterwards, it comes afterwards (laughter).

DEVOTEES: (laughter)

SWAMIJI: That is the mistake. It comes afterwards.

JOHN: But you don't have any choice on this, though.

SWAMIJI: Huh?

JOHN: This is all God's grace. You don't have . . . when you are just centered in wrath, you don't . . . somebody has to come and throw this idea in your mind to look inside. That's God's grace, isn't it?

SWAMIJI: It needs God's grace, it needs your own effort, it needs the grace of your master. All three are needed, *bas*.

Second Flow
Niḥṣyanda Sahaja Vidyodaya
(Rise of the Innate Knowledge of Consciousness)

SWAMIJI: It is *niḥṣyanda. Niḥṣyanda* does not mean "chapter", *niḥṣyanda* means "flow".

JOHN: Flow. This is the second flow?

SWAMIJI: The second flow of *spanda*, yes.

JOHN: Just like *unmeṣa* means "second awakening" or . . .

SWAMIJI: Yes.

Audio 2 - 10:50

तदाक्रम्य बलं मन्त्राः सर्वज्ञबलशालिनः ।
प्रवर्तन्तेऽधिकाराय करणानीव देहिनाम् ॥ १ ॥
तत्रैव सम्प्रलीयन्ते शान्तरूपा निरञ्जनाः ।
सहाराधकचित्तेन तेनैते शिवधर्मिणः ॥ २ ॥

tadākramya balaṁ mantrāḥ sarvajñabalaśālinaḥ /
pravartante'dhikārāya karaṇānīva dehinām //1//
tatraiva saṁpralīyante śāntarūpā nirañjanāḥ /
sahārādhakacittena tenaite śivadharmiṇaḥ //2//

All *mantras*, pure or impure (all *mantras*), . . .*

JOHN: What would be an impure *mantra*?

SWAMIJI: An impure *mantra* is just black magic, *mantras* for black magic, *mantras* for . . .

DENISE: Destroying.

SWAMIJI: . . . destroying some person. Those deadening *mantras*; you die at once by those *mantras* (black magic, all those *mantras*). And pure *mantras* also. Pure *mantras* are those *mantras* which, if you are weak, it will give you strength. If you have some problem, you will get its solution by that *japa*[78].

*. . . but all those *mantras*, *sarvajña bala śālinaḥ*, get that strength of functioning, functioning strength, only when they are located in that supreme *mantra* of God consciousness–[*sāmānya*] *spanda*. On the basis of [*sāmānya*] *spanda*, they work. If [*sāmānya*] *spanda* is not there[79], you can't [succeed]. It won't work, that black magic [or pure magic] won't work, it will fail.

DENISE: But isn't [*sāmānya*] *spanda* existing everywhere?

SWAMIJI: No, it[80] must be based on [*sāmānya*] *spanda*, then it will work, yes.

JOHN: What is the *spanda mantra*? [Is it the] "*ahaṁ*" *mantra*?

SWAMIJI: No, the *spanda mantra* is God consciousness, I-consciousness, universal consciousness. That is [*sāmānya*] *spanda*.

ANDY: How does a *mantra* acquire that *spanda*?

SWAMIJI: *Mantra*? No. *Mantras* actually reside in that [*sāmānya*] *spanda*, but you must know that, that it is in [*sāmānya*] *spanda*.

JOHN: So it's the *mantra*-user that has . . .

DENISE: So the *yogi* must have that power of awareness while reciting.

SWAMIJI: Yes, yes, yes, and that works, that will work. And so, this *mantra* of black magic won't work . . .

DENISE: Unless the *yogi* is powerful.

SWAMIJI: . . . unless the *yogi* is powerful. And a [realized] *yogi* won't produce this black magic because [he is] one with God, [so he] won't destroy anybody.

JOHN: So, who were those *yogis* in those days?

---

78 Recitation.

79 That is, if *sāmānya spanda* is not held in awareness while reciting a *mantra*.

80 The recitation of *mantra*.

SWAMIJI: Intense, when there is the intensity of . . . for instance, some person acts unlawfully. When you are fed up with that person, then you produce that black magic to destroy him. Otherwise never. Who?

DENISE: The *yogi*.

ERNIE: The rascal.

SWAMIJI: The *yogi*, the real *yogi*. The unreal *yogi*s, if they produce [*mantra*s], they won't work, so there is no worry.

ANDY: So, all *mantra*s have potential . . .

SWAMIJI: Power, yes, only when they reside in [*sāmānya*] *spanda*. When they are introduced in the cycle of [*sāmānya*] *spanda*, then they will become powerful, otherwise they will be useless. [When *mantra*s reside in *sāmānya spanda*], they become *sarvajña bala śālinaḥ*, the strength of all-action and all-doing comes in them. *Pravartante adhikārāya*, and they function properly, accordingly, just like *karaṇānīva dehinām*, the organs (the sensual organs–the organs of action and the organs of cognition) work because they reside in God consciousness. Otherwise, the eyes won't be able to see if [they are] not residing in God consciousness. The ear won't hear, the nose won't smell, the skin won't get the sensation of touch, unless it resides in God consciousness. In the same way, all those *mantra*s, they function only when they reside in God consciousness.[81]

DENISE: So what does that mean, like when someone is blind or they can't smell, some people can't smell, they can't taste, you know, they can't hear? What does that mean?

SWAMIJI: No, that is . . .

DENISE: That has nothing to do with that.

SWAMIJI: No, that is a defect in the body.

tatraiva saṁpralīyante śāntarūpā nirañjanāḥ /
sahārādhakacittena tenaite śivadharmiṇaḥ //2// [repeated]

---

81 Even though *mantra*s, like the organs, reside in God consciousness–everything resides in God consciousness–but *mantra*s, unlike the organs, do not function without maintaining awareness of God consciousness.

And those *mantras*, pure and impure (all *mantras*), *tatraiva saṁpralīyante*, they get dissolution in that supreme God consciousness. When they work, after their functioning, they rest in God consciousness. *Sahārādhaka-cittena*, and that *mantra*, the person who has produced that *mantra*, he also rests in that God consciousness after the functioning of this *mantra*.

Tenaite śiva dharmiṇaḥ, so, in brief words, all *mantras* have aspects of God consciousness. [When] they possess aspects of God consciousness and nothing else, then they work. Otherwise, [if the] aspects of God consciousness are not present in those *mantras*, that *mantra* is useless.

Audio 2 - 05:44

यस्मात्सर्वमयो जीवः सर्वभावसमुद्भवात्।
तत्संवेदनरूपेण तादात्म्यप्रतिपत्तितः ॥ ३ ॥
तस्माच्छब्दार्थचिन्तासु न सावस्था न या शिवः ।
भोक्तैव भोग्यभावेन सदा सर्वत्र संस्थितः ॥ ४ ॥

yasmātsarvamayo jīvaḥ sarvabhāvasamudbhavāt /
tatsaṁvedanarūpeṇa tādātmyapratipattitaḥ //3//
tasmācchabdārthacintāsu na sāvasthā na yā śivaḥ /
bhoktaiva bhogyabhāvena sadā sarvatra saṁsthitaḥ //4//

[Although] it is quite true that *sarvamayo jīvaḥ* (*jīvaḥ* means, the individual), the individual is universal, . . .

In reality, the individual is universal. Always the individual is universal. In the cycle of individuality, universality is not absent.

. . . because *sarvabhāva samud bhavāt*, all aspects, all things, are produced from that universal God consciousness (*sarvabhāva samud bhavāt*, all flow out from that God consciousness), *tat saṁvedana rūpeṇa tādātmya pratipattitaḥ*, [but] when they act, when they work, in the daily routine of life, those individuals, they work only when *tādātmya*, when they are attached to that God consciousness.[82] When they are detached from God consciousness, it won't work.

For instance, you desire for something. It won't come true because it is not attached to God consciousness. If it is attached to God consciousness, your desire will come true, your dream will come true; your everything, whatever you think, whatever you do, it will be fruitful. Otherwise, it is fruitless.

So, in conclusion, what is in the background of this God consciousness?

Tasmāt śabdārthacintāsu na sāvasthā na yā śivaḥ, all words, all activities of worldly things, they reside in Śiva *bhāva*, in the state of Śiva. *Bhoktaiva bhogyabhāvena*, all these, the cycle of the objective world (*bhogya bhāvena*, the objective world), also resides in the cycle of subjective consciousness. There is only one God consciousness, which pervades everywhere. This is the reality of [*sāmānya*] *spanda*. And It pervades everywhere, at the time of knowing [It] and at the time of not knowing [It]. If you know [It], still It pervades. If you don't know [It], still It pervades.

Somānanda[83] has produced this *śloka*, written this *śloka*, in the *Śivadṛṣṭi*:

> *atha sthite sarvadikke śivatattve'dhunocyate* /
> *tasmiñjñāte'thavājñāte śivatvamanivāritam* //[84]
> [not recited in full]

"I am explaining now the reality of Śiva, the element of Śiva. *Tasmin jñāte*, if you know It, *tasmin jñāte'thavājñāte*, or, if you don't know It, It is still there. If you know It or if you don't know It, It is still there–the state of Śiva *bhāva* is not gone."

---

82 When they perceive and feel (*saṁvedana*) the sameness or identity of nature or character (*tādātmya*) with God consciousness.

83 Somānanda (875–925 CE) wrote the first philosophical treaty on non-dual *Kashmir Shaivism* called the *Śivadṛṣṭi*. His illustrious disciple Utpaladeva, commented upon this text and in doing so, laid the framework for the Pratyabhijña System of Kashmir Shaivism.

84 *Śivadṛṣṭi*, 7.1.

ERNIE: Affected.

SWAMIJI: No, It has not gone anywhere. It is there.

JOHN: It doesn't depend on your knowing or not knowing.

SWAMIJI: And this kind of treatment will act only at the time of the realization of God consciousness in *samādhi*. When you enter in *samādhi*, then you feel that, "It was already there. I had nothing to achieve." When you realize the state of God consciousness in *samādhi*, at that time, this memory comes in your mind, in the background of your mind: "It was already with me. It is not new."

DENISE: "And I ignored It"?

SWAMIJI: "I ignored It. I didn't want It."

Audio 2 - 09:58

इति वा यस्य संवित्तिः क्रीडात्वेनाखिलं जगत् ।
स पश्यन्सततं युक्तो जीवन्मुक्तो न संशयः ॥५॥

iti vā yasya saṁvittiḥ krīḍātvenākhilaṁ jagat /
sa paśyansatataṁ yukto jīvanmukto na saṁśayaḥ //5//
[not recited]

Iti vā yasya saṁvittiḥ, if you know, if you know in this way, that God consciousness is there, if It is known, It is there; if It is not known, [still] It is there; [even] if It is ignored, It is there . . . God consciousness will never be separated from your consciousness, from your individual consciousness.

God consciousness is still there because God consciousness is the life of individuality. Individual consciousness will not live without the background of God consciousness.

And in this way, if you know, if you understand, this kind of philosophy (*iti vā yasya saṁvittiḥ*, anybody who knows this way), *krīḍātvenākhilaṁ jagat*, this whole universal activity is, for him, just a play; *krīḍātvenākhilaṁ jagat*, he feels everything–good, bad, whatever he feels in the daily routine of life–he feels that it is only the play of God consciousness, it is just a drama. *Sa paśyan satataṁ yukto*, he feels that because he is always alert, always alert and adjusted to God consciousness.

Jīvanmukto na, he is *jīvan mukta*[85], there is no doubt about it.

Audio 2 - 11:22

अयमेवोदयस्तस्य ध्येयस्य ध्यायिचेतसि ।
तदात्मतासमापत्तिरिच्छतः साधकस्य या ॥ ६ ॥

ayamevodayastasya dhyeyasya dhyāyicetasi /
tadātmatāsamāpattiricchataḥ sādhakasya yā //6//

When a *yogi* with this determination sits for meditation, that, "I will not leave this meditation until I realize the real truth. I won't come out of this meditative functioning. I won't leave this function. I won't leave this meditation until I realize God consciousness", . . .

ayamevodayastasya dhyeyasya dhyāyicetasi /
tadātmatāsamāpattiricchataḥ sādhakasya yā //6//
[repeated]

. . . when the *sādhaka-yogi* sits for meditation and becomes one with God consciousness, that means, the rise of God consciousness has taken place in his thought (*ayameva-udayas-tasya dhyeyasya*).

Dhyeya means, that which is to be meditated. What is to be meditated? The state of God consciousness. That is to be meditated upon. And the rise of the state of God consciousness is that [determination]. In other words, it is the rise of the state of God consciousness.

What?

Tad ātmatā samāpattir icchataḥ, when one person with this determination sits for meditation that, "I will have It", [then] he has got It, he has got It on the very first start of that meditation. But that [kind of] meditation must be done, not this distracted meditation.

85 Lit., liberated while living. "Whatever you do, you remain in that universal state. This is the state of *jīvan mukti*, liberated in life. This state is experienced, not by ordinary *yogis*, but only by great *yogis*." *Kashmir Shaivism–The Secret Supreme*, 17.120.

ERNIE: Ten minutes here, twenty minutes . . .

SWAMIJI: Keep your watch here and meditate and see . . .

DEVOTEES: What is the time (laughter).

SWAMIJI: (laughter) Yes, for how much time I have meditated on. This is not the thing. You should meditate with this determination [that], "I will never leave it until I realize the reality of God consciousness." [Your very determination] means, It has risen in the background of your consciousness– that reality of God consciousness.

Audio 2 - 13:55

इयमेवामृतप्राप्तिरयमेवात्मनो ग्रहः ।
इयं निर्वाणदीक्षा च शिवसद्भावदायिनी ॥७॥

iyamevāmṛtprāptirayamavātmano grahaḥ /
iyaṁ nirvāṇadīkṣā ca śivasadbhāvadāyinī //7//
[not recited]

Iyameva, this is the attainment of *amṛta* (nectar, supreme nectar). The supreme nectar he has attained. *Ayam eva ātmano*, this is the controlling of your mind, this is one-pointedness of your mind. *Iyaṁ nirvāṇa dīkṣā ca*, and this is the real initiation, which sentences you to liberation, ultimate liberation, *śiva sadbhāvadāyinī*, which will give you *śiva sat bhāva*, the state of Śiva *bhāva*.

Third Flow
Vibhūti Spanda
(The Glory of *Spanda*)

Audio 3 - 00:00

Tṛtīyo niḥṣyandaḥ, the third flow of *spanda*.

In the third flow of *spanda* is [the explanation of] the *yogic* power which [the *yogi*] derives in wakefulness and the *yogic* power which he derives in, attains in, the dreaming state. [Vasugupta] explains this.

यथेच्छाभ्यर्थितो धाता जाग्रतोऽर्थान् हृदि स्थितान् ।
सोमसूर्योदयं कृत्वा सम्पादयति देहिनः ॥ १ ॥

yathecchābhyarthito dhātā jāgrato'rthān hṛdi sthitān /
somasūryodayaṁ kṛtvā saṁpādayati dehinaḥ //1//

Dehinaḥ, but that *yogic* power is [attained by] that person, that *yogi*, who has not yet been liberated from the attachment of bodily attachment; bodily attachment, who has bodily attachment, who has still . . .

JOHN: That means, he wants *bhokta*? That means, he wants also enjoyments or . . . ?

SWAMIJI: No, there is some gap in the state of his God consciousness [because of the fact] that he wants to get power.

ERNIE: In this *yogi*?

SWAMIJI: The *yogi*, yes.

ERNIE: He has this desire for . . .

SWAMIJI: For showing people the *yogic* powers. It means, he wants some money, or he wants some fame, or he wants some . . .

DENISE: Recognition.

ERNIE: Praise.

SWAMIJI: Praise and . . .

So, he has put that *yogi* as "*dehinaḥ*" (*dehinaḥ* means, he who is attached to his body). As long as he's attached to the body, this desire is there. Which desire?

ERNIE: Fame, recognition.

SWAMIJI: Fame and showing *yogic* powers, flying and everything, whatever it is.

Yathecchābhyarthito dhātā (*dhātā* means, Parameśvara, Lord Śiva), when [the *yogi*] sits for meditation with this determination that, "I want such and such thing to come true, such and such thing must happen in reality", and with this desire, he sits and meditates on God consciousness, . . .

> *yathecchābhyarthito dhātā jāgrato'rthān hṛdi sthitān* /
> [repeated]

. . . *jāgrato'rthān hṛdi sthitān*, those objects that he wants to achieve in wakefulness, with this determination that he will achieve them in wakefulness, he goes on meditating on God, Lord Śiva, and at that time of *samādhi*, when he achieves the reality of God consciousness–he enters in that state of *samādhi*–and afterwards, when he comes out from *samādhi*, as the thought for attainment of power was there in the beginning, but not in the course of meditation, . . .*

[Not] in the course of meditation because meditation won't work if there is any other thought. Only you have to put that thought in the beginning of meditation, that such and such thing must happen.

ERNIE: I want to accomplish this.

SWAMIJI: Yes, and then you meditate.

*. . . when you come out from *samādhi*, this thought comes to you, [and] when this thought comes to you–then what you have to do?–*soma sūryodayaṁ kṛtvā*, then you have to breathe in and out several times (for instance, ten times breathe in and out with giving it length) with this thought that, "This must happen"–just after coming out from *samādhi*; *soma-*

sūryodayaṁ kṛtvā–saṁpādayati dehinaḥ, [then] that will come true.[86]

JOHN: The thought that one carries while he maintains this breathing in and out with length is that he wants some power, or he wants this or that, what[ever] he wants.

SWAMIJI: Yes, and this is the way how he achieves that power. He has to breathe in and out very slowly with giving it force, just as we do in *cakrodaya*[87], like that. *Saṁpādayati dehinaḥ*, that power comes to that *yogi* who is attached to his body.

DENISE: Power or desire?

SWAMIJI: Any desire, any desire. For instance, Viresh is not well, Viresh is always weak. You want him to get strong, and with this desire you meditate, go in *samādhi* and then come out, breathe in and out several times and he will get his health as he ought to [have].

This is the power that is achieved in the state of wakefulness. And now he explains the power that is achieved in the state of dreaming.

Audio 3 - 5:06

तथा स्वप्नेऽप्यभीष्टार्थान्प्रणयस्यानतिक्रमात् ।
नित्यं स्फुटतरं मध्ये स्थितोऽवश्यं प्रकाशयेत् ॥ २ ॥

tathā svapne'pyabhīṣṭārthān praṇayasyānatikramāt /
nityaṁ sphuṭataraṁ madhye sthito'vaśyaṁ prakāśayet //2//

86 "A 'day' is when you breathe out. *Antarniśā*, when you breathe in, that is a 'night'. *Enendu*, so this is functioned by the sun and the moon. The functioning of the moon (*soma*) will be the night and the functioning of the sun (*sūrya*) will be the day." *Tantrāloka* (LJA archives), 6.64-65.

87 For a description of the practice of *cakrodaya*, please refer to *Self Realization in Kashmir Shaivism*, 2.42-43. See also *Vijñāna Bhairava*, 156, and the seventh *āhnika* (chapter) of *Tantrāloka* (LJA archives), which is entirely devoted to the description of the practice of *cakrodaya*.

Now, the *ādeśa*[88] of our masters. *Adeśa* means, the masters have . . .

DEVOTEE: Ordered.

SWAMIJI: Not ordered. The masters have taught us that in *svapna*, when this kind of *yogi* enters in the dreaming state and he begins to dream, at the time of beginning the dream, he feels that he is dreaming. [He knows that] he is not in wakefulness. This is the power he gets by the strength of his meditation.

JOHN: That he knows he is in the dreaming state.

SWAMIJI: He knows that. He knows in the dreaming state that he is dreaming. [He knows that] he is not in wakefulness. He dreams and talks to you in the dreaming state and [knows] that it is a dream. He does ignore this kind of . . .

JOHN: So he has awareness in the dreaming state.

SWAMIJI: He has awareness in the dreaming state. Awareness must be. It is a must. It is the first . . .

ERNIE: Criterion.

SWAMIJI: . . . the first point.

Svapne'pi, in that *svapna*, *abhīṣṭhārthān praṇayasyānatikramāt*, he goes on meditating in *svapna* also; in the dreaming state also, he meditates. He meditates [while dreaming] because of the intensity of his meditation during wakefulness. He meditates in the dreaming state also and perceives all experiences of this, the world of dream–he goes to see Denise, he goes to see Kamala and Bruce and Marion.

ERNIE: In dreaming?

SWAMIJI: In the dreaming state. And, at the same time, he thinks that he is dreaming.

But what has he to do for getting power in the dreaming state?

Tathā svapne'pyabhīṣṭhārthān, whatever he wants to dream, *praṇayasyānatikramāt–praṇayasya* means, the power of meditation is *anatikramāt*, has not gone anywhere there in the dreaming state also, to him–*praṇayasya anati kramāt*, as he does not [lose] that power of meditation in that dreaming

---

88 Advice, instruction.

state also, *nityaṁ spuṭataraṁ madhye*, and in that state of meditation, he meditates and *sphuṭataraṁ* (vividly), *sthito'-vaśyaṁ prakāśayet*, he dreams those kind of dreams.[89]

If he wants to go into *samādhi*, that is well and good. In the dreaming state, it is very easy to go into *samādhi*–most easy. When you are alert in the dreaming state and you feel that you are dreaming, if you just breathe in and out with great awareness, just after ten or twenty . . .

ERNIE: Breaths.

SWAMIJI: . . . breaths, you will enter in *samādhi*. In the dreaming state, it is very easy to go in *samādhi* because *kārmamala* is not there; there is only *āṇavamala* and *māyīyamala*.[90] In which state?

DEVOTEE: In the dreaming state.

SWAMIJI: In wakefulness, there are all the three *mala*s existing; in wakefulness, there is *kārmamala*, there is *māyīya-mala*, there is *āṇavamala*. In the dreaming state, there is only *māyīyamala* and *āṇavamala*. *Kārmamala* is finished, though the traces of *kārmamala* are there as long as he has not entered fully in the state of God consciousness. So, it is very easy to go inside [while in the dreaming state]. And, for instance, there is *sadyojātabālaka*. *Sadyojātabālaka* is [one who is] just born. He has only one *mala*–*āṇavamala*. Who?

GANJOO: A newborn child.

SWAMIJI: The newborn child. There is no *kārmamala*, there is no *māyīyamala*, in a child. So it is very easy for him to go in *samādhi*, enter in *samādhi*. It is why I entered in *samādhi* when I was three years old, four years old. It is very easy there because there are not the two *mala*s; only one *mala* is there–*āṇavamala*.

BRUCE H: When does that disappear? When do those *mala*s become stronger?

SWAMIJI: As you grow, as you grow, they become stronger, they grow also.

ERNIE: The impressions.

---

89 That is, whatever he wants to dream.

90 See Appendix 7 for an explanation of the three *malas*.

SWAMIJI: Yes, the impressions, thoughts, distinction, e.g., "This is good", "This is bad", "This is best", "This is . . . "

ERNIE: "This is a tree", "This is a car".

GANJOO: "This is mine, this is yours."

DENISE: "I am pretty", "I am ugly".

SWAMIJI: Yes.

DENISE: A small child never thinks these kind of things.

SWAMIJI: No, no (affirmative). If you give [a child] one piece of gold–this is the absence of *māyīyamala*–you give him one piece of gold and, at the same time, you give him one cookie, he will throw that piece of gold and get the cookie. He will like the cookie because he has not [the sense of] distinction that comes in the surface of *māyīyamala*.

Svapna api abhīṣṭārthān praṇayasya anati kramāt. I told this to my master that, "I have achieved this power in the dreaming state by this practice". He said, "I will only believe that you have achieved this power when you go in the dreaming state and you wish that, 'I want to see Lord Śiva in His . . .'"

ERNIE: Full glory?

SWAMIJI: "'. . . in His full glory in [His] body (in *sākāra*[91]), with the *triśūla*[92], with the *candrika*[93]', and you try that. If it comes true, then it is perfect *svapna svātantrya*." It is called *svapna svātantrya*[94]. That is *svapna svātantrya*, that is *svapna svātantrya*. I tried many times to see Lord Śiva in His body, but I couldn't. [My master] said, "No, this is not perfect *svapna svātantrya*. Perfect *svapna svātantrya* is when you see Lord Śiva existing before you."

ERNIE: That is very rare though, isn't it?

SWAMIJI: That is very . . . Lord Śiva does not appear to everybody. It is very . . .

ERNIE: Rare.

SWAMIJI: And dear also. What is "dear"?

---

91. Having form, having any shape or definite figure.
92. Lord Śiva's trident.
93. The crescent moon in Lord Śiva's hair.
94. Complete independence (*svātantrya*) while dreaming (*svapna*).

ERNIE: To see [Him] physically.

SWAMIJI: What is "dear"?

ERNIE: Lord Śiva.

JOHN: Dear means "precious".

SWAMIJI: Precious, precious, dear, costly, costly.

Audio 3 - 12:00

अन्यथा तु स्वतन्त्रा स्यात्सृष्टिस्तद्धर्मकत्वतः ।
सततं लौकिकस्येव जाग्रत्स्वप्नपदद्वये ॥ ३ ॥

anyathā tu svatantrā syātsṛṣṭistaddharmakatvataḥ /
satataṁ laukikasyeva jāgratsvapnapadadvaye //3//
[not recited]

Anyathā tu, if your meditation, the power of meditation, becomes loose, becomes lessened, . . .

JOHN: When? In daily activity?

SWAMIJI: In daily activities, when the power of meditation is less, then *svatantrā syāt sṛṣṭis tat dharmakatva*, the natural creation overpowers him, overpowers that *sādhaka*.

What do you mean by "overpowering by natural creation"?

JOHN: Takes his mind away from his . . .

SWAMIJI: That nature[95] does not allow him to go in the dreaming state with consciousness. Nature does not allow him to go in wakefulness with awareness. That, he, snatches the state of awareness from him. When you are meditating, not with that zeal, not with that continuity–when you don't meditate in wakefulness in that continuity which you ought to have done–then *svatantrā syāt*, then the kingdom of nature will rule on you. So, there is no hope of getting [*svapna*] *svātantrya*, the power of that, "I will dream like this, I will dream

95 The kingdom of *aparā prakṛti*. "*Prakṛti* is explained in the *śāstras* (scriptures) in two ways. *Aparā prakṛti*, which is said to be eightfold, is the combination of the five great elements, along with mind, intellect, and ego. *Parā prakṛti* is that energy of being which governs and contains all the activities and conceptions of this universe." *Kashmir Shaivism–The Secret Supreme*, 95.

this, I will. . . .” That won’t come true.

Satataṁ lakikasyeva, you are just . . . you are not a *yogi*! Vasugupta says, “He is not a *yogi. Satataṁ laukikasyeva*, he is just like an ordinary man. I won’t call him a *yogi*, who has not that capacity, who has not attained that capacity and that power of going in a dream with . . .”

ERNIE: Full awareness.

SWAMIJI: “. . . awareness, with full awareness.” *Jāgrat svapna pada dvaye*, so he is tossed here and there in these two states by nature, according to the will of nature, not according to his will. He will go into the dreaming state and won’t understand if he is dreaming or if he is in wakefulness. He feels that he is in wakefulness [and he] goes on [dreaming]. This is his state.

Audio 3 - 14:20

यथा ह्यर्थोऽस्फुटो दृष्टः सावधानोऽपि चेतसि ।
भूयः स्फुटतरो भाति स्वबलोद्योगभावितः ॥४॥
तथा यत्परमार्थेन येन यत्र यथा स्थितम् ।
तत्तथा बलमाक्रम्य न चिरात्सम्प्रवर्तते ॥५॥

yathā hyartho’sphuṭo dṛṣṭaḥ sāvadhāne’pi cetasi /
bhūyaḥ sphuṭataro madhye bhāti svabalodyogabhāvitaḥ //4
tathā yatparmārthena yena yatra yathā sthitam /
tattathā balamākramya na cirātsaṁpravartate //5//

No matter, there is no worry still, if you are governed by nature (universal nature), if you don’t govern universal nature and you are governed by universal nature, if this *prakṛti* governs you, rules on you, if the kingdom of *prakṛti* prevails, [and if] the kingdom of your consciousness does not prevail, it does not work, it does not act.

Do you understand?

DENISE: Yes, I understand.

SWAMIJI: I think you all understood this, no?

STEPHANIE: A bit.

SWAMIJI: A bit? (laughter)

Yathā hyartho, there is no worry; you should not worry if you go in the dreaming state and don't know that you are dreaming, if you know that [dreaming state] as if you are in wakefulness, as . . .

ERNIE: No difference.

SWAMIJI: . . . as before. *Yathā hyartho'sphuṭo dṛṣṭaḥ.* He gives an example. For instance, there is a thing which I cannot perceive properly [as to] what it is. There is something in front of me, and from a distance, I can't perceive what kind of thing it is. Is it a pot? Is it . . . what? What is that?

ERNIE: This is in the dream state?

SWAMIJI: No, in wakefulness. In wakefulness, you don't perceive properly what it is.

JOHN: [It's] something.

SWAMIJI: *Yathā hyartho asphuṭo dṛṣṭaḥ*, it is not vividly seen; any object which is not vividly seen. *Sāvadhāne*, when you put all the force of your attention towards it, then you come to see it [and realize] that, "Oh, this is this thing". *Sāvadhāne'pi cetasi bhūyaḥ sphuṭataro bhāti*, it is your own power of will that you make it vividly perceived. This is the example.

In the same way, no matter if you are caught in the dreaming state, or if you are caught in wakefulness by the government, by the kingdom, of *prakṛti*–the kingdom of *prakṛti* rules on you, so you have nothing, you have no power; all power is gone from you–don't worry.

> *tathā yatparmārthena yena yatra yathā sthitam /*
> *tattathā balamākramya na cirātsaṁpravartate //5//*
> [repeated]

So, what you have to do in this position?

You have to do *tat-* . . .

Whatever [happens], this reality of your God consciousness, the reality of God consciousness, is still there. The reality of God consciousness has not gone away from your cycle, only you don't attend to It. And you are caught by, you are overpowered by, the kingdom of *prakṛti*, the kingdom of nature.

. . . *tattathā balam*–what you have to do there?–*tattathā balam*, get fully strengthened, strengthen yourself with willpower, and go on meditating in continuity, *na cirāt saṁpravartate*, it will come again, that power will come again in you. It has not gone anywhere.

Audio 3 - 17:50

Durbalo'pi tadā . . . it is not only in this way.

दुर्बलोऽपि तदाक्रम्य यतः कार्ये प्रवर्तते ।
आच्छादयेद्बुभुक्षां च तथा योऽतिबुभुक्षितः ॥ ६ ॥

durbalo'pi tadākramya yataḥ kārye pravartate /
ācchādayedbubhukṣāṁ ca tathā yo'tibubhukṣitaḥ //6//

Durbalo'pi, for instance, there is a feeble person, a feeble *yogi*. If a feeble *yogi* is there and you want him to ascend a mountain, . . .

For instance, tomorrow, on Saturday, there is Janmāṣṭamī.[96] On Janmāṣṭamī, people go to that peak of this mountain.

DENISE: Here?

SWAMIJI: Yes, here. That is called Sarveśvara, Sarveśvara mountain.[97] This is Sarveśvara mountain, and people go there. At least, each year, twenty or thirty people go there on this day, on Janmāṣṭamī.

. . . for instance, a *yogi* is there, a *yogi* wants to go there, and he is weak, he is feeble, there is some physical trouble in his body, he can't walk, *durbalo'pi*, because he is very weak–he can't walk, so there is no hope for him to ascend that peak–

96 Lord Kṛṣṇa's birthday.

97 Sarveśvara mountain is directly to the east of Swamiji's ashram at Ishber, Gupta Ganga, Srinagar. Ancient history has it that Lord Shiva once performed the Tandava dance on a stone platform near the peak of that mountain. Kalhan's Rājataraṅgani also mentions this as a sacred shrine to goddess Durga Sureśvarī.

durbalo'pi, although he is so weak, *tadākramya*, if he holds that power of God consciousness, if he just breathes in and out as we already explained–how you should breath in and out after getting out from *samādhi*; breathe in and out, in and out, in and out, for several [breaths]–*tadā kārye pravartate*, [then] he gets that strength that he can climb the hill.

Ācchādayedbubhukṣāṁ ca, [or if] he has too much appetite and there is nothing to give him, if he has poverty and he can't afford food and he has an appetite (*ācchādya-bubhukṣām ca*), [he should] just go in meditation. If he is a *yogi*, he will go in meditation, enter in *samādhi*, and come out from *samādhi*, breathe ten times in and out, in and out with great awareness, [then] he will be full; he will feel that he is full, he has no appetite.

DENISE: And full of strength.

SWAMIJI: And with strength. *Tathā*, [in the same manner], *yo'tibubhukṣitaḥ*. For instance, *yo ati bubhukṣitaḥ*, then if some of his disciples get a big dish, a rich dish for him, [but] he has no appetite, . . .

The first was [the *yogi*] who had an appetite and there was nothing for him to eat, so he has subsided that appetite by the power of God consciousness. Now, [the *yogi*] who has . . .

ERNIE: No appetite.

SWAMIJI: . . . who has no appetite and some of his disciples come with a very rich dish and place that dish before him to eat–and he has no appetite. What he has to do? He has to meditate on that [desire for an appetite] and enter in *samādhi*, give rise to his breathing for ten times with awareness, [then] he will be fully . . .

ERNIE: Hungry.

SWAMIJI: . . . he'll be so hungry that he would like to get more dishes to eat (*tathā yo'tibubhukṣitaḥ*). But this is only meant for those *yogi*s who have attachment for this body, not those *yogi*s who have gone above the cycle of bodily attachment.

ERNIE: So, there are different kinds of *samādhi*.

SWAMIJI: No, *samādhi* is the same. *Samādhi* is the same, [but] the way how to produce it is different.

DENISE: Not everybody can just go into *samādhi*.

SWAMIJI: No, it is for *yogis*, but [for those] with bodily attachment. Those *yogis* who have no bodily attachment won't do these things! They will never think of doing these things.

ERNIE: But is it possible to go into *samādhi* with bodily attachment?

SWAMIJI: There is some bodily attachment for *yogis*.

ERNIE: It's possible.

SWAMIJI: Yes, it is possible. [But] when you have got complete *samādhi*, then these things won't happen.

ERNIE: So then there are different *samādhis*?

SWAMIJI: Then there is different [*samādhis*], yes. That is complete *samādhi* when you are detached from bodily love, bodily [attachment].[98]

ERNIE: So this really a very low *samādhi*.

SWAMIJI: Yes, a lower *samādhi*.

JOHN: But not as low as Vedānta's–higher than [Vedānta].

SWAMIJI: No, it is higher than [Vedānta].

JOHN: It is Shaivite *samādhi*.

SWAMIJI: Yes.

ANDY: If a *yogi* is above bodily attachment, will he not be in a position of hunger?

SWAMIJI: No, for him, Lord Śiva will [provide] his dish! There is no worry for him. If he has not attachment for his body, Lord Śiva will serve him all-round. He will look after him. Just a pretty girl will look after him, lipsticks and everything (laughter). He is the prettiest man in this world. Who?

DENISE: Lord Śiva.

SWAMIJI: No, that *yogi* who has not attachment for his body. [Lord Śiva] has to do it [i.e., provide for him]. It is said in

---

98 "This is the real *samādhi* when you get entry in *jagadānanda*." *Tantrāloka* (LJA archives), 5.62 commentary. See Appendix 3 for an explanation of *samādhi*, and Appendix 8 for an explanation of the Seven States of *ānanda* (bliss).

the *Bhagavad Gītā* also: "*Ananyaścinta*[99] . . .", those who are attached to Me only in this world, not anything else, *teṣāṁ nityabhiyuktānāṁ yogakṣemaṁ vahāmyaham*, I protect his, I take care of his, position of his household things."

ERNIE: Daily life.

SWAMIJI: No, for instance, "I take care that a thief doesn't come in his premises. I do that job for him." Who says that? Lord Kṛṣṇa. "I do that job for him because he is meditating on Me. And I arrange for his . . ."

ERNIE: Daily food.

SWAMIJI: ". . . daily food and everything. I have to arrange that. I will do that. He has nothing to worry."

Audio 3 - 24:41

अनेनाधिष्ठिते देहे यथा सर्वज्ञतादयः ।
तथा स्वात्मन्यधिष्ठानात्सर्वत्रैवं भविष्यति ॥७॥

anenādhiṣṭhite dehe yathā sarvajñatādayaḥ /
tathā svātmanyadhiṣṭhānātsarvatraivaṁ bhaviṣyati //7//

There are two beings: one is the individual being and one is the universal Being. *Anenādhiṣṭhite dehe*, when in individuality, in your body, the pervasion of God consciousness takes place in the body–*anena adhiṣṭhite dehe*, in the body, when the pervasion of God consciousness exists and It is induced in the body–*sarvajñatādayaḥ*, then in all the organs you feel all-pervadingness. You become capable of seeing, touching, tasting, smelling, everything. Your consciousness pervades in the whole body. This is the strength of [*sāmānya*] *spanda*. That strength of [*sāmānya*] *spanda* pervades the whole body in the cycle of individuality. In the same way, *tathā svātmanyadhiṣṭhanāt*, when you insert this God consciousness in the universe, then you can handle everything in this universe [just] as you handle each and every part of your body by your

99 *ananyaścinta yanto māṁ ye janāḥ paryupāsate, teṣāṁ nityabhiyuktānāṁ yogakṣemaṁ vahāmyaham*, *Bhagavad Gītā*, 9.23.

sweet will.[100]

For instance, if you want to move your finger, you can move your finger without any others help. *Bas*, you can move it like this just [by your] will, just will. In the same way, if you pervade, if the pervasion of God consciousness takes place in the whole universe (you see that through meditation), then you can move everything by [your] will. You become one with God. This is what he says in this *śloka*.

Anenādhiṣṭhite dehe yathā sarvajñatādayaḥ (this is an example for individuality), as in the individual body, you feel the pervasion [of consciousness] throughout the whole body without any other additional effort (e.g., you can move your eyes just by will, or you can move your nose)–the pervasion of God consciousness is fully existing in the body–in the same way, if you pervade this God consciousness everywhere in the universe, you can move the whole universe. You can take this mountain and dash it down by will. You can [do this] just as you do in your body.

Audio 3 - 27:43

ग्लानिर्विलुण्ठिका देहे तस्याश्चाज्ञानतः सृतिः ।
तदुन्मेषविलुप्तं चेत्कुतः सा स्याद्हेतुका ॥८॥

glānirviluṇṭhikā dehe tasyāścājñānataḥ sṛtiḥ /
tadunmeṣaviluptaṁ cetkutaḥ sā syādahetukā //8//

The only obstacle is *glāniḥ*[101]. *Glāniḥ* is the absence of God consciousness. When the absence of God consciousness is there, that is *viluṇṭhikā dehe*; that loots, that absence of God consciousness loots, everything, all the good treasury in your body. All treasure is lost by the absence of God consciousness. And that absence of God consciousness takes place *ājñānataḥ*, by ignoring the state of God consciousness. *Tat unmeṣa*

---

100 "*Svaśaktipracayo'sya viśvam*, for him, this universe is the embodiment of his collective energies." *Śiva Sūtras–The Supreme Awakening*, 3.30, 3.37.

101 *Glāni* literally means, exhaustion, fatigue of the body, lassitude, languor, depression of mind, debility.

viluptaṁ cet, and that ignoring of God consciousness must be *viluptam*, must be dashed down, must be killed, must be crushed, must be just . . .

ERNIE: Eliminated.

SWAMIJI: . . . eliminated, *tad unmeṣa*, by *unmeṣa*[102], by the rise of [*sāmānya*] *spanda*. When the rise of [*sāmānya*] *spanda* takes place in your nature, then this absence of God consciousness is kept away. So, *kutaḥ sā syādahetukā*, that absence of God consciousness will never take place after that. You will become one with Lord Śiva.

Audio 3 - 29:11

Now, how to give rise to [*sāmānya*] *spanda* is explained in the next *śloka*:

एकचिन्ताप्रसक्तस्य यतः स्यादपरोदयः ।
उन्मेषः स तु विज्ञेयः स्वयं तमुपलक्षयेत् ॥९॥

ekacintāprasaktasya yataḥ syādaparodayaḥ /
unmeṣa sa tu vijñeyaḥ svayaṁ tamupalakṣayet //9//

You just watch your movement of your mind. You just be attentive to the movement of the mind. When, in the mind, one *vikalpa* (one thought) rises, remain in that thought! Don't let that thought go away from your mind. Be attentive to that thought only, that one thought only. And, if you remain attentive in continuity to that one thought, *yataḥ syāt aparā-udayaḥ*, then after some time another thing will take place, another thing will rise, and that is [*sāmānya*] *spanda*.

JOHN: What is that other thing?

ERNIE: Thought? Another thought?

SWAMIJI: No, another thing. Another thing will take place, that is [*sāmānya*] *spanda*. *Spanda*, that is [*sāmānya*] *spanda*, [which arises] when you remain attentive to one thought only.

102 "*Unmeṣa*" here means the "rise", "blossoming", or "appearance" of *spanda*. It does not here refer to its first meaning of "opening the eyes".

Don't let your mind be scattered to various thoughts, variegated thoughts, e.g., "This is a [microphone]", "This is a book", "This is that", "This is that"–not this way. "This is a mike", "This is a mike!", "This is a mike!", "This is a mike!", "This is a mike!", don't let it go from [the thought of a] mike. If there is one thought of a mike, remain in that one thought.

ERNIE: Concentrate.

SWAMIJI: Concentrate on that one point!

JOHN: It can come again and again–the thought.

SWAMIJI: Again, again, put your mind towards one thought only. And, after a few minutes or seconds or half an hour, if you remain like that on one thought only, what will happen? This thought will give rise to [*sāmānya*] *spanda*. *Yataḥ syāt aparodayaḥ*, something else will take place, and *unmeṣa sa tu vijñeyaḥ*, that is *unmeṣa*, that is the rise of [*sāmānya*] *spanda*. *Svayaṁ tam*, you have to observe it yourself; *svayaṁ tam upalakṣayet*, you have to observe it yourself, and that will be [*sāmānya*] *spanda*, and you will be one with God.

This is the way how to give rise to [*sāmānya*] *spanda*.

And when you give rise to [*sāmānya*] *spanda* with less effort, when you put one-pointedness on one thought, not in full attentiveness, then what will happen after this thought gets its end?

Audio 3 - 32:05

अतो विन्दुरतो नादो रूपमस्मादतो रसः ।
प्रवर्तन्तेऽचिरेणैव क्षोभकत्वेन देहिनः ॥ १० ॥

ato vindurato nādo rūpamasmādato rasaḥ /
pravartante'cireṇaiva kṣobhakatvena dehinaḥ //10//

Ato bindurato nādo rūpamasmādato rasaḥ, you will enter in God consciousness, but in God consciousness you will find the internal world of powers. *Ato bindur*, you will find, you will feel, the rise of light in your mind[103], you will feel the rise

---

103 Swamiji recited "*bindu*" in place of "*vindu*". Both words convey the same meaning–a "drop" or a "point of light".

of *nāda* (*nāda* is sound, divine sound), divine *rūpa* (divine forms), divine taste on your tongue, and this you will find just after being attentive to that one thought.

JOHN: Now, are there two things we are talking about here? One thing is when you are really attentive to it, that's one *unmeṣa*, and if you are not so attentive to it, then at the end of that thought, you slip into God consciousness, but it's a lower God consciousness.

SWAMIJI: This is lower God consciousness.

JOHN: He's talking about two kinds here.

SWAMIJI: Yes.

JOHN: One where you enter through the thought itself, one where you . . .

SWAMIJI: Wholeheartedly, with great effort, then you just rush in God consciousness directly.

JOHN: And the second one . . .

SWAMIJI: If you don't keep that attentiveness firmly established there, then, after it is over, [after] that one thought is over, you will enter in *turya*, that inferior state of *turya*, and in the inferior state of *turya*, you will experience . . .

JOHN: Divine *tanmātra*s[104].

SWAMIJI: . . . divine light, divine sound, divine form, and divine taste. These are obstacles.

JOHN: These are the obstacles you talk about[105] in your lectures, these divine *tanmātra*s here.

SWAMIJI: Yes.

JOHN: So this is *śāktopāya*[106] here, entering in the gap between two thoughts? This second one, your thought ends . . .

SWAMIJI: No, the first one is *śāktopāya*. The first one is *śāktopāya*, and if that *śāktopāya* is not adopted with full effort,

104 The five rudimentary or subtle elements from which the *mahābhūta*s are produced.

105 *Self Realization in Kashmir Shaivism,* 2.49

106 See Appendix 9 for an explanation of the three *upāyas*: *āṇavopāya*, *śāktopāya*, and *śāmbhavopāya*.

full attentiveness, then you slip in that inferior state of God consciousness. There, it has nothing to do with *śāktopāya*. It is just when your effort is lessened, when your effort of *śākto-pāya* like this is lessened–it is less, it is not so strong, it is not so filled with will power–then you slip in the cycle of God consciousness, which is inferior. And yet that inferior God consciousness will give rise to divine things, divine sounds, divine forms, divine tastes. And there is an apprehension of being stuck in that world.

DENISE: Because it is so tasty.

SWAMIJI: It is very tasty! You can't imagine how tasty [it is]. So you will get stuck and you will lose that divine element of God consciousness. And these take place very rapidly (*pravartante acireṇaiva*, rapidly), *kṣobhaka* . . .*

JOHN: Rapidly, what takes place? These . . . ?

ERNIE: These four *tanmātra*s.

SWAMIJI: These divine ways.

JOHN: Divine taste and so forth.

SWAMIJI: Yes.

*. . . *kṣobhakavena*, just to kick this *yogi* from God consciousness. It is just . . .

JOHN: . . . to irritate him, to cause agitation so he falls from That.

SWAMIJI: Yes, he falls from That reality.

ERNIE: Swamiji, if you have [the thought], "The mike", and then you have the thought, "Oh no, I have to keep my attention on the mike . . . "

SWAMIJI: But there is the interruption of another thought: "No, no".

ERNIE: "No, no."

SWAMIJI: "No, no" also must not take place.

JOHN: No thought!

ERNIE: Not possible.

SWAMIJI: It is not possible? It is possible. It is possible when you have got strength, courage. It requires courage! If you have the courage to play badminton wholeheartedly, why not this?

ERNIE: (laughter) So then there can be not even the thought, you can't even have another thought of, "Oh, I am off, I have to go back".

SWAMIJI: No, no.

ERNIE: Not even that?

SWAMIJI: Then, if there are such leakages, then you slip in this other world of God consciousness.

ERNIE: No, but then it has to be . . . there is really nothing that you can do.

SWAMIJI: No, just be attentive to only this awareness on that one point.

ERNIE: And then when you slip? Then when there is a leakage?

SWAMIJI: Why? Leakage is only possible when you are not attentive fully.

ERNIE: No, but what if you are not strong? [It's] not just attentive, you have to have the strength. If the strength is not there?

SWAMIJI: I think you should fully nourish your system with *ghee*, with butter, and everything, so you have got good strength.

DEVOTEES: (laughter)

DENISE: That helps?

SWAMIJI: It may help. It means, strength of mind. You need strength of mind, thought power.

ERNIE: Which comes from meditation.

SWAMIJI: Yes.

JOHN: Well, *āṇavopāya* is supposed to prepare us for this.

SWAMIJI: It is not *āṇavopāya*. It is only *śāktopāya*.[107]

JOHN: No, this is *śāktopāya*, but *āṇavopāya* strengthens your awareness.

SWAMIJI: Yes, *āṇavopāya*, yes, *āṇavopāya* makes you strong.

---

107 See Appendix 9 for an explanation of the *upāyas*.

Audio 3 - 37:35

दिदृक्षयेव सर्वार्थान्यदा व्याप्यावतिष्ठते ।
तदा किं बहुनोक्तेन स्वयमेवावभोत्स्यते ॥ ११ ॥

didṛkṣayeva sarvārthānyadā vyāpyāvatiṣṭhate /
tadā kiṁ bahunoktena svayamevāvabhotsyate //11//

Didṛkṣayeva sarvārthān, when, on the other side, if I have slipped from that one-pointedness, if you have slipped [from] one-pointedness, and that [point of having] slipped, where you have slipped down, . . .

ERNIE: Slipped to.

SWAMIJI: . . . if you feel that that point is also one with that God consciousness–*sarvārthān*, wherever you go, wherever your mind travels, think that it is filled with God consciousness–that way too is also helpful in this process.

Yadā vyāpyāvatiṣṭhate, when you pervade everything, it is said there, *yatra yatra mano yāti*[108], let you keep your mind loose, let it go anywhere, but be attentive . . .

JOHN: Where it goes.

SWAMIJI: . . . where it goes, be attentive, and feel that, "This is also God consciousness", "This also is God", "This is also God consciousness". *Bas*, divert it to God consciousness, then there is no worry. That way too is also helpful. *Svayameva avabhotsyate*, this you can feel by your own self. You will feel that yourself, how it works. That too works.

ERNIE: This is inferior though.

SWAMIJI: No, this is not inferior. That too is not inferior. If

108 *"yatra yatra mano yāti bāhye vābhyantare'pi vā / tatra tatra śivāvasthā vyāpakatvātkva yāsyati //* Keep your mind absolutely loose; don't put any effort to control it. Keep your mind loose [in the] outside objective world and [in the] inside objective world. . . . and see that this is only the expansion of God, the expansion of your own consciousness, and that your consciousness is pervading outside, in the outside objective world and the inside objective world, [then], where [will] that state of *śiva bhāva* will go? It is there!" *Vijñāna Bhairava*, *dhāraṇa* 90, verse 116.

you feel God consciousness, the existence of, the presence of, God consciousness everywhere, then let it be loose, let your mind take place according to its own nature. That too works.

ERNIE: And just having the idea that this is God consciousness is enough?

SWAMIJI: *Bas*, yes. Only remain in God consciousness [and feel that], "This is divine, divine, everything divine".

ERNIE: Yes, but doesn't that have to be . . . I mean, it can't be a fantasy, it can't be imagination.

SWAMIJI: No, you can't remain away from God consciousness. If you don't remain away from God consciousness anywhere, in any step, then no worry. That too also works.

JOHN: This is imagination? I mean, infusing all your thoughts with God consciousness. First you have to imagine that, "This is God consciousness", "This is God consciousness", in the beginning. It's not a . . .

SWAMIJI: Yes, yes. God consciousness is, just remain attentive between two breaths, in the center of two breaths. If you don't move your consciousness from the center of two breaths in any case, no worry. That works.[109]

So, what you have to do? Next *śloka*:

Audio 3 - 40:24

प्रबुद्धः सर्वदा तिष्ठेज्ज्ञानेनालोक्य गोचरम् ।
एकत्रारोपयेत्सर्वं ततोऽन्येन न पीड्यते ॥ १२ ॥

prabuddhaḥ sarvadā tiṣṭhetjñānenālokya gocaram /
ekatrāropayetsarvaṁ tato'nyena na pīḍyate //12//

109 "Only by maintaining an unbroken chain of awareness will he be able to discover the reality between any two thoughts or actions. The practice of centering is meant to function between any two actions or any two thoughts. He can center between any two thoughts or any two movements, between one thought and another thought, between waking and dreaming, between one step and the next step, between one breath and the next breath. All actions and all thoughts are the proper framework for the practice of *śaktopāya*. The *śaktopāya yogi* must simply insert continuous awareness in the center of any two actions or thoughts." *Kashmir Shaivism, The Secret Supreme*, 36.

Prabuddaḥ sarvadā tiṣṭhet, always remain *prabuddhaḥ* (alert), alert in your own nature. *Jñānenālokya gocaram*: *gocaram* means, the whole cycle of the objective world, you should perceive with *jñāna*[110]. For instance, [when] you play with Viresh, think that you are playing with God. If you think that you are playing with Viresh . . .

DENISE: And you are not playing with God.

SWAMIJI: . . . [and lament that], "He teases me, he does everything naughty", then you are down. If you see that he is also divine, then there is no worry.

DENISE: [Viresh] said, "No" (laughter).

SWAMIJI: *Ekatrāro* . . . (laughter) you have not to ask him. You have to feel in your own self.

ERNIE: But that's very . . . what I am trying to say is that people who walk around the world thinking, "I am God, I am God, everything I see is God", but they are nothing, they are . . . you understand what I mean?

SWAMIJI: That imagination is transformed into reality afterwards, if you do it, if you practice it like that.

DENISE: You don't go around telling everybody, do you?

SWAMIJI: If you feel One couple, one couple you feel that, "This is Gaurī and Śaṅkara, [they are] Śiva and Pārvatī, Śiva and Pārvatī, Śiva and Pārvatī", [then] there is no worry–you are with Śiva and Pārvatī. This is the diversion of your thought, sir. You have to divert your thought from individuality to universality.

ERNIE: Right, but it's a secret and it's a private thing. You don't . . .

SWAMIJI: No, you have not to show. It is to be done inside.

ERNIE: Secretly.

DEVOTEE: Within yourself.

SWAMIJI: Within yourself.

JOHN: But with imagination.

SWAMIJI: Yes, imagination! Imagination works! Imagination is transformed into reality afterwards, after some time

110 Knowledge (*jñāna*) of God consciousness.

of this practice.

Prabuddhaḥ sarvadā tiṣṭhet, always remain attentive, alert! *Jñānenālokya gocaram*, feel everything as one with divine consciousness. *Ekatrāropayet sarvam*, just focus each and every activity of your world towards God consciousness. *Tato 'nyena na*, so there is no worry afterwards [because] you are one with God consciousness, you are living in God consciousness.

[Kṣhemarāja] gives a reference of the *Utpalastotrāvalī*[111] here:

> *yo'vikalpamidamarthamaṇḍalaṁ*
> *paśyatīśa nikhilaṁ bhavadvapuḥ /*
> *svātmapakṣaparipūrite jagat-*
> *yasya nityasukhinaḥ kuto bhayam //*[112]

That person who perceives this whole universe, the whole cycle of the universe, as just one with God consciousness–*svātmapakṣaparipūrite jagati*, in this world, he sees that everything resides in God consciousness–*tasya nitya sukhinaḥ*, he is always filled with that supreme blissful state. *Kuto bhayam*, there is no fear for him from anything, any other substance in this world.

Now, on the other side, if you don't do like this, what will happen?

Audio 3 - 44:17

शब्दराशिसमुत्थस्य शक्तिवर्गस्य भोग्यताम् ।
कलाविलुप्तविभवो गतः सन्स पशुः स्मृतः ॥ १३ ॥

śabdarāśisamutthasya śaktivargasya bhogyatām /
kalāviluptavibhavo gataḥ sansaḥ paśuḥ smṛtaḥ //13//

---

111 *Utpalastotrāvalī* is another name for the *Śivastotrāvalī*, a collection of devotional hymns composed by Utpaladeva. See Swami Lakshmanjoo, trans., *Hymns to Shiva–Shivastotrāvalī* by Utpaladeva, ed. John Hughes (Lakshmanjoo Academy Book Series, Los Angeles, 2015).

112 *Śivastotrāvalī*, 13.16.

Sabdarāśi samutthasya, there are the biggest cycle of energies of God consciousness; God consciousness has produced the biggest cycle of Its energies–that is *śabdarāśi*. *Śabdarāśi* is, the cycle of sounds, the cycle of words, the cycle of sentences. It has got great power.

For instance, somebody will tell you, "Some kith and kin of yours is dead." "Some-kith-and-kin-of-yours-is-dead", these words, this is the combination of words, and it will carry you to torture. These words, the hearing of these words, will carry you to torture and kick you in that pit of sadness if you think that such and such kith and kin of yours is dead. "Such-and-such- . . . ", you will concentrate on [the meaning of] these words. If you concentrate on these words, not on the meaning of these words, just concentrate on these words themselves, then there is no worry, it is all divine. "Such and such a person is dead." "Such and such a person is dead." D-e-a-d, what is that?

DENISE: Nothing, without meaning.

SWAMIJI: It is without meaning. That is the power of *śabdarāśi*. *Śabdarāśi* means, these sounds, letters, and sentences. They produce such power that they will kick you in the pit of sadness. But if you remain attentive to those words themselves, not go to the background of those words. . . . The "background" is in the inserted meaning, it is the inserted meaning. "D-e-a-d", it is "d-e-a-d", it is not "dead". "Dead", it is dead, but it does not mean that it is lifeless. It is only "d-e-a-d." Remain in "d-e-a-d", not in that "death". *Śabdarāśi samutthasya*, so this is the *śakti varga*, this is the power that is produced from these sounds, letters, and words.

Śakti vargasya bhogyatām, one who has become the object of these *śabdarāśi* (an object is [like a] football, when you become a football of these *śabdarāśi*), they will kick you from one side to another side, and you will be nowhere existing. You will be sometimes blissful, sometimes happy, sometimes sad, sometimes tortured, sometimes crying, sometimes screaming– all this will happen. *Kalā vilupta vibhava*, and by these energies[113], your glamour of God consciousness will be

113 Here, Swamiji is refering to the class of energies (*śakti vargas*),

destroyed altogether. When it is destroyed, you are just like a *paśu*, just like a beast then, and you have to undergo this, the repeated cycle of repeated births and deaths. So you should not do that.

Audio 3 - 48:00

परामृतरसापायस्तस्य यः प्रत्ययोद्भवः ।
तेनास्वतन्त्रतामेति स च तन्मात्रगोचरः ॥१४॥

parāmṛtarasāpāyastasya yaḥ pratyayodbhavaḥ /
tenāsvatantratāmeti sa ca tanmātragocaraḥ //14//

The *apāya*, you should see that there is not *apāya*, there is not the supreme nectar of God consciousness is not destroyed (*apāya* is "destruction").[114] The destruction of the supreme [divinity] of God consciousness should not take place at anytime. *Parāmṛta*, the supreme nectar, the supreme nectar of God consciousness, when It is *apāya*, when It is destroyed, *tasya yaḥ pratyayodbhavaḥ*, after Its destruction, *tena asvatantratām eti*, he[115] becomes absolutely dependent in this world, dependent to everything. He becomes the slave of those who are already slaves in this world. *Sa ca tanmātragocaraḥ*, and that will make you travel only on the pathway of the *tanmātras* (*śabda*, *sparśa*, *rūpa*, *rasa*, and *gandha*[116]). You are only traveling on that [path], and That path is absolutely neglected, that supreme path of God consciousness.

---

which function the various classes of letters. "*Kavargādiṣu māheśvaryādyāḥ paśumātaraḥ*, in the world of letters, words and sentences, the eight energies of the Lord, who are the mothers of beasts [*paśu*, limited individuals] (take control and hold him)." *Śiva Sūtras–The Supreme Awakening*, 3.19, page 175.

114 "Destroyed" in the sense of appearing to be absent on account of being neglected.

115 The one who "neglects" the supreme nectar of God consciousness.

116 Sound, touch, form, taste and smell, respectively.

Audio 3 - 49:20

स्वरूपावरणे चास्य शक्तयः सततोत्थिताः ।
यतः शब्दानुवेधेन न विना प्रत्ययोद्भवः ॥ १५ ॥

svarūpāvaraṇe cāsya śaktayaḥ satatotthitāḥ /
yataḥ śabdānuvedhena na binā pratyayodbhavaḥ //15//

Now, you must find, you must observe, that there are energies of God consciousness, numberless energies of God consciousness, who are bent upon destroying your field of the rise of God consciousness. They just destroy that, destroy that cycle of God consciousness. *Satatotthitāḥ*, they are always attentive to destroy that.

It is His will, it is the will of God that His energies, [His] numberless energies, are bent upon destroying, taking you away from, God consciousness.

Vighnāyuto sahasraṁ . . . Abhinavagupta has said in his *Pratyabhijñā Vivṛtti Vimarśinī*, *Bṛhat Pratyabhijñā*, a big book he has composed (it is called *Vivṛtti Vimarśinī* of the *Pratyabhijñā*):[117]

vighnāyuto sahasraṁ tu parotsāha samanvitam
praharatyaniśaṁ jantoḥ sadvastvabhimukhasya ca /
viśeṣato bhavāmbodhi samuttaraṇakāriṇaḥ //
[not recited in full]

Vighna ayuta sahasram. *Vighna* means–what is *vighna*?–obstacles. Not one obstacle, not two, not three, not a hundred, not one thousand, *ayuta sahasram*, 10,000 into 10,000, so many obstacles will take place. So many obstacles . . .

GANJOO: Exist.

SWAMIJI: No, take place. Work, they work (*vighnāyuto sahasraṁ tu*), *parotsāha*, with great . . .

ERNIE: Vigor.

SWAMIJI: . . . with great vigor, they work like this. *Praharati*, and they attack, *aniśam*, day and night. *Jantoḥ*,

117 *Iśvarapratyabhijñā Vivṛtti Vimarśinī*, Vol.1, page 18. See also *Special Verses on Practice,* (LJA archive), 38, 39.

they work on that person, *sat vastvabhimukhasya*, who wants to do something good. He who wants to do something good, they don't, they won't, let him to do that good.

DENISE: Why?

SWAMIJI: This is His will. This is the world. If you want to do something good in this world, for that, those . . .

ERNIE: 10,000 times 10,000.

SWAMIJI: . . . 10,000 times 10,000 obstacles will take place. They will prepare themselves . . .

ERNIE: Distract.

SWAMIJI: . . . to distract you from that intention. *Viśeṣato*, and [the obstacles work] in greater effort to that person, *viśeṣato bhavām bodhi samuttaraṇa*, who wants to rise from individuality to God consciousness.

JOHN: They try harder.

SWAMIJI: [For one] who wants to rise, they try hard, they push him down, they try to push him down and down and down so that this thought does not exist in his mind.

DENISE: Well then, how does he have a chance with so many obstacles?

SWAMIJI: No, there is courage, you must develop courage, strength [when] *viśeṣato bhavāmbhodi samuttaraṇakāriṇaḥ*. It is why he says, *svarūpāvaraṇe cāsya śatkyaḥ satatotthitāḥ*, always they are attentive, they are bent upon destroying your God consciousness as soon as you begin to meditate. When you don't begin to meditate, [when] you don't meditate, [when] you work, you are fine, your mind is one-pointed. When you make your mind one-pointed [in meditation], all distractions take place, e.g., "Oh, that thing I have to do, that thing I have to do, that thing I have to do"–they will take place.

ERNIE: Somebody knocks at the door.

SWAMIJI: Yes, everything will . . . everything, every blunder will take place during that period of meditation. So, this meditation is not a joke. If you meditate, you must [just] meditate. As soon as you get a moment, meditate, meditate! Don't waste your time. Go on meditating, because something absurd will happen–it will, it has to, it is sure!

ERNIE: Guaranteed.

SWAMIJI: Guaranteed. So, *svarūpāvaraṇe cāsya śaktayaḥ satatothitāḥ*, [Lord Śiva's energies] are attentive to destroy your one-pointedness, *yataḥ śabdānu vedhena na vinā pratyayodbhavaḥ*, because this *pratyaya*[118] [will distract you]. For instance, if you meditate wholeheartedly, "*oṁ namaḥ śivāya, oṁ namaḥ śivāya, oṁ namaḥ śivāya, oṁ namaḥ śivāya*", wholeheartedly, if you are doing this with great strength, those energies of God consciousness, which are bent upon destroying this state of your . . .

ERNIE: Disturbing you.

SWAMIJI: Disturbing you, they will disturb you in your own way. For instance, you will say, "*oṁ namaḥ śivāya, oṁ namaḥ śivāya*, I must do always '*oṁ namaḥ śivāya*'." Another thought has come: "I must always do '*oṁ namaḥ śivāya*'. Oh, it is very fine to do '*oṁ namaḥ śivāya*'." So, it is a distraction, a distraction takes place. Don't attend to that thought also. Be only, "*oṁ namaḥ śivāya, oṁ namaḥ śivāya*", *bas*, not this, "*oṁ namaḥ śivāya* is fine", because he will destroy you in a friendly state. He will become your friend and destroy you. This happens. So, this is a very difficult way you are treading on.

ERNIE: So, you could do, "*oṁ namaḥ śivāya, oṁ namaḥ śivāya* . . . gosh, I am a good boy for doing this."

SWAMIJI: No, not this.

ERNIE: No, no, but this is the "friend"–"Oh, I am such a good boy."

SWAMIJI: Yes, yes (laughter), this is what happens.

DEVOTEES: (laughter)

SWAMIJI:

Audio 3 - 55:15

सेयं क्रियात्मिका शक्तिः शिवस्य पशुवर्तिनी ।
बन्धयित्री स्वमार्गस्था ज्ञाता सिद्ध्युपपादिका ॥ १६ ॥

---

118 A notion or idea, which is produced by Lord Śiva's energies.

*seyaṁ kriyātmikā śaktiḥ śivasya paśuvartinī /
bandhayitrī svamārgasthā jñātā siddhyupapādikā //16//*

This is the active energy of God consciousness. This is the active energy of God consciousness that plays, that functions, in this world, in this cycle of the worldly cycle and the spiritual cycle, both. In the worldly cycle, it works, and in the spiritual cycle also, it works. And, in the spiritual cycle, it works just to make Śiva transform into the individual *paśu bhāva*, just into the state of a beast, becoming a beast. He wants that Śiva should become a beast.

DENISE: Who wants?

SWAMIJI: The energies. The energies of God try to make Śiva as a beast by their own power. This is *śakti*, this is the powerful active energy of Lord Śiva. *Bandhayitrī*, so it gives bondage to that person, to that Śiva, [but] *svamārgasthā*, when you are fully attentive [to one point], when you are fully attentive and you don't listen to those energies, [when] you turn a deaf ear to those energies [that manifest in the form of thoughts such as], "No, do this meditation this way, this way it will work, this way it will work", . . .*

This is a friendly . . .

ERNIE: Deception.

GANJOO: Distraction.

SWAMIJI: . . . distraction. This also you should not allow. Go on with your own point.

*. . . and when you are *svamārgasthā*, you are attentive to one point only–don't listen, keep a deaf ear, to all those outside activities of the energies–*jñātā siddhyupapādikā*, then you will rise in God consciousness, there is no fear.

ERNIE: So, in the worldly everyday life, if a person tries to do good, these energies work against him.

SWAMIJI: Yes.

ERNIE: And if a person does it on the spiritual [path], they try to work . . .

SWAMIJI: They try him more, mostly.

ERNIE: That's even more strong.

SWAMIJI: More strong, yes.

Audio 3 - 57:39

तन्मात्रोदयरूपेण मनोऽहम्बुद्धिवर्तिना ।
पुर्यष्टकेन संरुद्धस्तदुत्थं प्रत्ययोद्भवम् ॥ १७॥
भुङ्क्ते परवशो भोगं तद्भावात्संसरेदतः ।
संसृतिप्रलयस्यास्य कारणं सम्प्रचक्ष्महे ॥ १८॥

tanmātrodayarūpeṇa mano'haṁ buddhivartinā /
puryaṣṭakena saṁrūddhastadutthaṁ pratyayodbhavam //17
bhuṅkte paravaśo bhogaṁ tadbhāvātsaṁsaredataḥ /
saṁsṛtipralayasyāsya kāraṇaṁ saṁpracakṣmahe //18//

The thing is, *tanmātrodaya rūpeṇa*, the rise of the *tanmātras* is the point, is the distraction–the rise of the *tanmātras* (*śabda*, *sparśa*, *rūpa*, *rasa*, and *gandha*). Don't be attentive to these: any sound (*śabda*), any *sparśa* (touch), *rūpa* (form), *rasa* (taste), and *gandha* (smell)–these *tanmātras*–and the mind, and the ego, and *buddhi* (intellect). So they are eight: *śabda*, *sparśa*, *rūpa*, *rasa*, *gandha* (the five *tanmātras*), the mind, the intellect, and the ego. And this is *puryaṣṭaka*[119], this is the body of the subtle body. This is the subtle body, this is the substance of the subtle body.[120]

Which is the substance?

Eight-fold.

JOHN: The five *tanmātras* and the three inner organs.[121]

---

119 Lit., the city of eight.

120 The limited subject is comprised of and limited to four states or "bodies" of objective experience: *deha*, *puryaṣṭaka*, *prāṇa*, and *śūnya*. "*Deha* means, the body existing in wakefulness, [*puryaṣṭaka* is the] body existing in dreaming state, [*prāṇa* is the] body existing in the dreamless state, and the body existing in the *śūnya* state, nothingness. In these four bodies, you think that, "I am this". Although this is not *ātma*, but, he perceives, "This is *ātma*". *Paramārthasāra–Essence of the Supreme Reality,* (Lakshmanjoo Academy Book Series, Los Angeles, 2015), verse 31.

121 "When the five *tanmātras* give rise to the three intellectual organs (intellect, mind, and ego), then collectively there are eight

SWAMIJI: Five *tanmātras* and the three internal organs. *Saṁruddhaḥ*, *bas*, you are stuck by this. This is the only cycle which makes you travel in unlimited repeated births and deaths of this world.[122] [But] if you hold these *tanmātras* [and the inner organs] in your own nature, if you fix them, focus them, in your own God consciousness, then there is no fear. Otherwise, there is fear from all sides.

Taduttharṁ pratyayodbhavam bhuṅkte, so [the individual] has to face and he has to enjoy the cycle of this universe. He enjoys the cycle of universe through these eight cycles, eight cycles of *puryaṣṭaka*.[123]

Tadbhāvāt, by this *puryaṣṭaka*, by the functioning of this eight[-fold] cycle of *puryaṣṭaka*, *saṁsare*, he goes in *saṁsāra*–he comes, goes, he dies, he gets birth. So this happens without any stoppage.

Saṁsṛti pralayasyāsya, how it will be stopped? I will tell you how to stop it, how to stop the cycle of travelling in the cycle of repeated births and deaths.

---

organs. These eight organs are said to be *puryaṣṭaka* and they function in our dreaming state. This *puryaṣṭaka* prevents you from getting through to the reality of your Self. When the reality of your nature is ignored, then you are dependent on enjoyment which cannot be refused. Because of this you are played and entangled by the wheel of repeated birth and deaths." This is Swamiji's translation of verses 17 and 18, which appear in his *Śiva Sūtra–The Supreme Awakening*, 3.2.

122 "*Puryaṣṭaka* carries the impressions again and again, [stores] impressions. Otherwise, if *puryaṣṭaka* is not existing, at the time of death you'll be united with God automatically, without doing anything. *Puryaṣṭaka* is the trouble maker." *Parātrīśikā Vivaraṇa* (LJA archive).

123 *Niyatyaiva yadā caiṣa*, whenever *eṣa*, Lord Śiva, *svarūpācchādan kramāt*, hides His nature [by] taking hold of your past actions, taking hold of the past actions of individuals, and that individual, *bhuḥkte duḥkha vimohādi*, then he enjoys pleasure, pain, and negligence, and all these things. And then you should know that *tadā karma phala kramaḥ*, this is the action due to your own *karmas*." Swami Lakshmanjoo, trans., *Tantrāloka* (LJA archives), 14.5.

Audio 3 - 01:00:17

यदा त्वेकत्र संरूढस्तदा तस्य लयोदयौ ।
नियच्छन्भोक्तृतामेति ततश्चक्रेश्वरो भवेत् ॥ १९ ॥

yadā tvekatra saṁrūḍhastadā tasya layodayau /
niyacchanbhoktṛtāmeti tataścakreśvaro bhavet //19//

Just be attentive to one-pointedness, that is all (*yada ekatra saṁrūḍha*). *Tadā tasya pralayodayau niyacchan*, *bas*, see that it is not destroyed–don't give rise to it, don't let it fall.

JOHN: In other words, don't pay attention to it at all, don't care for it to come up or . . .

SWAMIJI: No, no. For instance, there is one-pointedness, develop one-pointedness. You have not to develop it again and again. Just see that it does not fall [and that] it does not rise.

ERNIE: Not rise?

SWAMIJI: It must remain in one level, one level without any flickering state. *Bhoktṛtām eti*, then he becomes *bhoktā*, then he becomes . . .

JOHN: Real enjoyer.

SWAMIJI: . . . the enjoyer. *Tataḥ cakreśvaraḥ*, he becomes, he governs, the cycle of the numberless energies of Lord Śiva. So the numberless energies, those [very energies] who had done so much mischief before, they become [his] slaves.

ERNIE: Not rise?

SWAMIJI: Don't give it to rise. Rise will also make you disturbed, make your one-pointedness disturbed. Don't give it rise. Be attentive, *bas*!

JOHN: So "attentive" means?

SWAMIJI: *Hastam hastena saṁrūddhya*, just squeeze your hands, squeeze your fingers, squeeze your body, and . . .

JOHN: . . . clench your teeth.

SWAMIJI: Yes, that I have told you.[124]

---

124 *hastaṁ hastena saṁpīḍya dantairdantāṁśca pīḍayan / aṅgāny-*

JOHN: But get that at all costs.

SWAMIJI: *Bas*, put your mind in one-pointedness.

JOHN: So, this verse refers to that other earlier verse where it gave those two kinds of meditation–one where you hold the thought and you don't lose it, and one where you lose it and you go to those divine *tanmātras*. So, he is talking about here [that] "holding this without rise and fall" means, just having it in one point.

SWAMIJI: One point. This is the first . . . this is the first . . . this is the first.

---

aṅgairsamākramya jayedādau svakaṁ manaḥ // Yogavāsiṣṭhasāra. "Ball your fists, clench your teeth, and tense all the muscles of your body, but conquer your mind. This is the advice of Vasiṣṭha to Rāma. He tells him that he must first conquer his mind." *Self Realization in Kashmir Shaivism*, 2.44. See Appendix 10 for Swamiji's complete exposition of this verse from the *Yoga Vasiṣṭha*.

Vasugupta's Conclusion

Audio 3 - 01:02:47

This fourth chapter is not the philosophy. This fourth chapter is an homage to the master.

अगाधसंशयाम्भोधिसमुत्तरणतारिणीम् ।
वन्दे विचित्रार्थपदां चित्रां तां गुरुभारतीम् ॥ १ ॥

agādhasaṁśayāmbhodhi-samuttaraṇatāriṇīm /
vande vicitrārthapadāṁ citrāṁ tāṁ gurubhāratīm //1//
[not recited]

Agādhasaṁśayāmbhodi, I, for this attainment, *vande vicitrārthapadāṁ citrāṁ tāṁ*, I bow, I prostrate, before the *bhāratī* of the master (*bhāratī* means, the word, that supreme word of the master). I prostrate before the supreme word of the master, which is *vicitrārthapadām*, which gives rise to various meanings and various states–this *bhāratī*, this word of the master. I bow before that word of the master, which is *agādha saṁśayāmbhodhi samuttaraṇatāriṇīm*; *saṁśaya-ambhodhi*, [Vasugupta] has put that this whole world is filled with doubts and that the cycle of doubts, which is existing in the world, is a great ocean, a big ocean, and this word of the master will take you from one individual shore to that Universal shore [by carrying you over] that doubt. I bow to that word.

Audio 3 - 01:04:24

लब्ध्वाप्यलभ्यमेतज्ज्ञानधनं हृद्गुहान्तकृतनिहितेः ।
वसुगुप्तवच्छिवाय हि भवति सदा सर्वलोकस्य ॥२॥

labdhvāpyalabhyametaj-
jñānadhanaṁ hṛdguhāntakṛtanihiteḥ /
vasuguptavacchivāya hi
bhavati sadā sarvalokasya //2// [not recited]

Labdhvāpyalabhyametat, if you once achieve this state of God consciousness, you will not achieve It–*labdhvā api alabhyam etat*.

This [achievement], what is that?

Jñānadhanaṁ, this is the treasure of knowledge. This is the treasure of knowledge, which if you once achieve, still there is the apprehension of losing it at once, altogether. So, I pray to God that *vasuguptavat*, as Lord Śiva made this treasure fully living in the mind of Vasugupta, in the same way, let this treasure of knowledge remain, living in the whole universe.

This is the prayer of the author.

Spanda Sandoha
Kṣhemarāja's commentary on the first verse of the Spanda Kārikā

Audio 4 - 00:00

SWAMIJI: This *Spanda Sandoha* is the exposition of the *spanda* principle based on the first *śloka*[125] of Vasugupta, "*yasyonmeṣanimeṣābhyāṁ* . . . ", of the *Spanda Kārikā*. [Kṣhemarāja] has put that base to expose this, the theory of *spanda*.

akalitamahimā yaḥ kṣmādisādāśivāntaṁ
kalayati hṛdi viśvaṁ citrasaṁyojanābhiḥ /
prathayati ca vicitrāḥ sṛṣṭisaṁhāralīlāḥ
sa jayati śiva ekaḥ spandavānsvapratiṣṭhaḥ //1//

Glory be to that one being, Śiva, who is filled with *spanda* and [who is] established in His own nature. Glory be to Him.

Now [Kṣhemarāja] gives the qualification of that Śiva.

Akalita-mahimā, whose greatness, glamour, is not counted. You can't count, you . . .

JOHN: It can't be calculated.

SWAMIJI: It can't be calculated, yes. And who creates this whole universe of thirty-six elements, right from *pṛthvī*[126] to *sadāśiva tattva*[127], in His own heart, in His own nature. And at the same time, who *citrasaṁyoja-nābhiḥ prathayati ca vicitrāḥ sṛṣṭi-saṁhāra-līlā*, in this universe of thirty-six elements, who creates the *līlā* (the *līlā* is "play"), the play of creation and destruction of this universe in varieties. The

125 Verse.
126 Earth.
127 See appendix 11 for a chart of the 36 elements.

various creations and destructions of this universe, who creates in this cycle of thirty-six elements, let that Śiva, Lord Śiva only, unique Lord Śiva, be glorified, who is always established in His own nature and filled with *spanda*.

The second *śloka*:

Audio 4 - 02:31

caitanyābdheḥ prasaradamṛtaṁ troṭitāyāsatantraṁ
sarvasyāntaḥ sphuradapi mahāmudrayā mudritaṁ yat /
pūrṇānandapradamatitarāmetadunmudrya yuktyā
yo'ntarvaktraṁ rasayati jayatyeṣa vīraḥ kulendraḥ //2//

As in the milky ocean, when the milky ocean was churned by the gods and those demons, they had to do all the effort they could to churn it and get out of it that supreme nectar by which they became immortal–they had to put all of the struggle and all of the effort to do that–in the same way, *caitanyābdheḥ prasarad-amṛtam*, from the ocean of *caitanya*[128], from the ocean of God consciousness (the ocean of God consciousness he has [described] just like the milky ocean), from the ocean of God consciousness, the supreme nectar has risen. The supreme nectar has appeared from the ocean of God consciousness, but without churning It. [The gods had] churned it with great effort and then they got that nectar out of that milky ocean. But from this ocean, from this ocean of God consciousness, the supreme nectar appears, it comes out, without any effort (*troṭitāyāsa-tantram*, there is no *āyāsa*; *āyāsa* means "effort"). Effortlessly it comes out.

What? This nectar.

And that nectar, *sarvasyānta-sphuradapi*, although that nectar is residing in each and every being in this world, everybody has got that, has possessed that nectar, but at the same time, *mahāmudryā mudritaṁ yat*, it is concealed with the great stamp of *svātantrya śakti*.[129] It is not exposed. You have that nectar, but you can't see it, you can't feel the glory

128 "*Caitanya* means 'complete freedom of universal consciousness.'" *Śiva Sūtra–The Supreme Awakening*, 1.2, page 20.

129 "The singularly unique aspect of Lord Śiva is complete independence, *svātantrya*. This complete independence is not found anywhere except in the state of Lord Śiva." Ibid., 1.1, page 12.

and glamour of that nectar within you. It is within you, that nectar, but it is stamped and locked . . .

GANJOO: Sealed.

SWAMIJI: . . . sealed by *mahāmudrā*, the supreme *mudrā*[130] of *svātantrya śakti*.

Audio 4 - 05:26

Pūrṇānandapradam, and this nectar is *pūrṇānanda*, it bestows you the supreme, first-class, bliss (*pūrṇa-ānanda-pradam*; *pradam*, it bestows *pūrṇānanda*, supreme *ānanda*).

JOHN: Full and complete, huh?

SWAMIJI: Yes.

GANJOO: Complete bliss.

SWAMIJI: But it is concealed by this *svātantrya śakti*. Nobody can experience the glamour of that nectar, supreme nectar.[131]

JOHN: So, *svātantrya śakti* is *māyā śakti* here? I mean, *svātantrya* . . .

SWAMIJI: Yes, *māyā śakti*.[132]

JOHN: *Māyā śakti*.

SWAMIJI: Yes. And that *vīra kulendra–vīra kulendra* is that *vīra* (hero); *kulendra* is he who has got authority to expose that, to expose that nectar, to open that seal of that nectar–

---

130 A stamp.

131 "This kind of action cannot be accomplished by any power in this universe other than Lord Śiva. Only Lord Śiva can do this. Only Lord Śiva, by His own *svātantrya,* can totally ignore and mask His own nature. Lord Śiva wants, in His creation, to disconnect His God Consciousness completely and then to discover that it was never disconnected. Although it is disconnected, it is not disconnected. In the real sense, it is not disconnected. This is the supreme action." *Self Realization in Kashmir Shaivism*, 1.7, page 25.

132 "*Svātantrya śakti* and *māyā* are one. *Svātantrya śakti* is that state of energy which can produce the power of going down and coming up again. And *māyā* is not like that. *Māyā* will give you the strength of coming down and then no ability of going up–then you cannot go up again. This is the state of *māyā*." *Kashmir Shaivism–The Secret Supreme*, 47.

and he can open that seal by *antar vaktra*.

There are two cycles of openings. One is *antar vaktra* and another is *bahir vaktra*. *Bahir vaktra* is when you are turned outside.

GANJOO: Introspection and outer-spection?

SWAMIJI: And when you are introverted, inside your own consciousness, that is *antar vaktra*. And you can open it, you can expose it, through *antar vaktra*. It is not *bahir vaktra*'s job. External substance is not needed to open this seal. This is the internal substance of the alertness of God consciousness that can open it. And that hero who can open it, he is to be nominated as "*kulendra*". *Kulendra* is the chief of the cycle of all beings–a supreme being. That is a *yogi*, *yogīndra*. *Kulendra* means, *yogīndra*, *yogīrāja*.

JOHN: The ruler of *yogi*s.

SWAMIJI: Yes.

JOHN: Why do they call it "*kula*"? *Kula* means, referring to the Kula system[133] here?

SWAMIJI: No, *kula* is "the class".

JOHN: The class.

SWAMIJI: The *yogic* class. *Indra* means, the ruler, the chief of *yogi*s.

Let he be glorified, that chief of *yogi*s, who can open the seal of this supreme nectar of God consciousness. He opens it, *yuktyā*, by the technique of his master. *Yuktyā* means, *guru yuktyā*.

JOHN: [It] means, by word of mouth of his master? *Yuktyā* means, by telling or saying of his master?

SWAMIJI: No, by the technique, by the production of the technique of the master.[134] The master reveals to him the

---

133 "The Trika System is comprised of four sub-systems: the Pratyabhijñā system, the Kula system, the Krama system, and the Spanda system. These four systems, which form the one thought of the Trika system, all accept, and are based on, the same scriptures." Ibid., 129.

134 For attaining these two powers (the powers of creative energy [*mantra vīrya*] and the powers of establishment in that creative

technique of how to open it, how to open this seal (*mudrā*). Otherwise, this seal cannot be opened.

ERNIE: In the internal way.

SWAMIJI: Internal way.

The third [*śloka*]:

Audio 4 - 08:51

unmīlitaṁ spandatattvaṁ mahadbhirgurubhiryataḥ /
tata eva tadābhoge kiṁcitkautukamasti naḥ //3//

[Kṣhemarāja]: What was the need for me to expose, to give, the exposition of the *spanda* principle here? It is because *mahat bhirgurubhir*, because *mahadbhirgurubhir*, Vasuguptanātha, the great master, he has *unmīlitaṁ*, he has hinted upon this *spanda* principle in his *Spanda Kārikā*. He has given the indication of the *spanda* principle in his *Spanda Kārikā*.

Who?

DEVOTEES: Vasugupta.

SWAMIJI: Vasugupta.[135]

It is why I have got a curiosity to open it. I have developed a curiosity to open the principle of this *spanda*.

tatra ādyameva sutraṁ vimṛśyate, paramādvaya-
prakāśāndamayamaheśvarasvarūpapratyabhijñāpanāya
samastaśāstrārthgarbhāṁ samucitāṁ
stutimimāmupadideśa śrīmān vasuguptaguruḥ

Ādyameva sūtraṁ vimṛśyate, the first *sūtra* is being exposed. This first *sūtra* of the *Spanda Kārikā* is being exposed here. The first *sūtra*, you know? It is:

---

energy [*mudrā vīrya*]), for attainment of these two powers–*gururupāyaḥ*–the master is the means. It can be attained through the master only, no one else. *Shiva Sutras–The Supreme Awakening*, 1.6.

135 Vasugupta is credited with the authorship of the *Spanda Kārikā*, which is an exposition of his own *Shiva Sutras*, the seminal text of Kashmir Shaivism that was revealed directly to him by Lord Śiva.

Audio 4 - 10:22

यस्योन्मेषनिमेषाभ्यां जगतः प्रलयोदयौ ।
तं शक्तिचक्रविभवप्रभवं शङ्करं स्तुमः ॥ १ ॥

yasyonmeṣanimeṣābhyāṁ jagataḥ pralayodayau /
taṁ śakti-cakra-vibhava-prabhavaṁ śaṁkaraṁ stumaḥ //

This is the first *sūtra* of the *Spanda Kārikā*. You have already read it.

And this *sūtra* is here exposed, will be exposed exhaustively by me.

Who is ["me"]?

JOHN: Kṣhemarāja.

SWAMIJI: Kṣhemarāja.

Audio 4 - 10:47

paramādvaya prakāśānandamaya maheśvarasvarūpaprat-yabhijñāpanāya samastaśāstrārtha garbhāṁ samucitāṁ stutimimāmupadeśa śrīmān vasuguptaguruḥ [repeated]

Paramādvaya prakāśa ānanda maya maheśvara svarūpa pratyabhijñā, just to recognize (*pratyabhijñāna*, just to recognize) the nature of Maheśvara[136], the nature of Maheśvara's *svarūpa*[137], which is filled with supreme *prakāśa* and *vimarśa* of nectar, . . .

Supreme *prakāśa* means "light" and *vimarśa* means "the feeling of supreme nectar". Where there is *prakāśa* and *ānanda* (light and nectar), that is Maheśvara *svarūpa*, that is the reality of Maheśvara.

. . . just to recognize that reality of Maheśvara, Vasugupta *guru* (master), the previous master, the ancient master, Vasugupta, has *samasta śāstrārtha garbhāṁ samucitāṁ stutim imām upādeśa*, this first *śloka* of the *Spanda* [*Kārikā*] he has put forth, this first *śloka* in which you find *samasta-*

136 An appellation of Lord Śiva. Lit., a great lord, sovereign, chief.
137 Own condition, peculiarity, character, nature.

śāstrārtha, you find the treasure of all *śāstras*[138]. You find that the treasure of all *śāstras* is existing in this first *śloka* of the *Spanda Kārikā*. And so, this *samucitām stutim*, this [hymn that is] *samucitām*, which is just to the point, just an appropriate *stuti*, he has put here in this first *śloka*, and this first *śloka* is:

Audio 4 - 12:53

yasyonmeṣanimeṣābhyāṁ jagataḥ pralayodayau /
taṁ śakti-cakra-vibhava-prabhavaṁ śaṁkaraṁ stumaḥ //

Do you understand it?

ERNIE: Um-mmm (disagreement).

SWAMIJI: It is very easy to understand it. You just put your attention.

By whose *unmeṣa* and by whose *nimeṣa* (*unmeṣa* is "opening your eyes" and *nimeṣa* is "closing your eyes"), with the opening of your eyes and with the closing of the eyes, you find–by whose opening and closing of the eyes–you find the destruction and creation of this whole universe. You find that the universe is destroyed and it is created. By *unmeṣa*, this universe is destroyed, and by whose *nimeṣa* (closing His eyes), the universe gets rise.

JOHN: Withdrawn or . . .

SWAMIJI: No, it is not withdrawn. It rises. The universe is created by closing His eyes. By opening His eyes (*unmeṣa*), the universe is destroyed. When He opens His eyes, the universe is destroyed. When He closes His eyes, the universe rises.

JOHN: Why that way?

ERNIE: Whose eyes?

JOHN: God's.

SWAMIJI: God's eyes.

JOHN: Why when He closes His eyes is it . . . ?

SWAMIJI: When He opens His eyes, this means, when He opens, when His eyes are open, He is in His own nature.

ERNIE: Really open.

138 Scriptures.

SWAMIJI: Yes.

ERNIE: Not like we think of . . .

SWAMIJI: No, no. He has not these [physical] eyes. When He opens His eyes, it seems He is residing in His own nature, so you won't find this universe, you will find . . .

ERNIE: He sees the real world.

SWAMIJI: When He opens His eyes, it means He opens His nature. When He opens His nature, that is, in other words, the destruction of the universe, the destruction of the differentiated universe. When He closes His eyes, that means, when He ignores His nature, the universe appears into its being.

Audio 4 - 15:27

Taṁ stumaḥ, I bow to that Lord Śaṁkara who is *śakti cakra vibhava prabhavaṁ*, who is the creator and producer of the wheel of His numberless energies, who is the creator of the wheel of His numberless energies.

And who is Śaṁkara? Śaṁkara is, He who gives *śaṁ* (peace, entire peace). [He] who produces, who bestows, peace, entire peace, that is Śaṁkara. I bow to that Śaṁkara.

Śaṁ- . . . what is "*śaṁkara*"? First, he gives the exposition of the word "*śaṁkara*" in this *śloka*. He has not yet started the exposition of *spanda*. [Here] it is just the foundation stone for the exposition of the *spanda* principle.

ERNIE: But it is still on the first . . . ?

SWAMIJI: The first *śloka*.

The first *śloka* says, "*śaṁkaraṁ*"–"*śaṁkara*" is one word there–"I bow to that Śaṁkara." What is "*śaṁkara*"? *Śaṁ karotīti śaṁkara*, He who gives peace, that who gives entire peace, is Śaṁkara. What is "peace"? *Śaṁ* . . . you should put a dash after "*śaṁ*".

Audio 4 - 17:03

śaṁ-aśeṣa-upadrava-rahita-paramānandādvaya-caitanya prakāśa-pratyabhijñā-panātmakam anugrahaṁ

Śaṁ means, *anugrahaṁ*. *Anugrahaṁ* means, supreme grace. What is that grace? *Aśeṣa upadrava rahita*, when all *upadravas* (all of those confusions), all of those confusions get their end, when all confusions end.

JOHN: What confusions is he talking about here? "*Upadrava*" means?

SWAMIJI: "This is mine", "This is not mine", "This is a pot", "This is a bath", "This is good", "This is bad", "This is money", "I have to earn money", this is all confusion. This is *upadrava*. *Upadrava* is torture.[139] When that . . . which[ever] confusion, this is just torture.

When all of that torture ends, gets its permanent end, and *param ānandam caitanya prakāśa pratyabhijñā*, and you recognize the supreme *caitanya*[140], who is filled with light and bliss, and that is *anugraha*. This kind of *anugraha*, this kind of grace, is produced by whom? That is Śaṁkara. *Śaṁ* is grace. The [bestower] of grace is Śaṁkara.

JOHN: He's giving different interpretations of "Śaṁkara" depending on the verse.

SWAMIJI: Yes.

Taṁ svātmaparamārthaṁ, and that is the reality of your nature; this Śaṁkara is the reality [of your nature]. Śaṁkara is not residing in the seventh cycle of the world.

JOHN: Seventh heaven or . . . ?

SWAMIJI: Seventh heaven. He is your own nature. *Svātmaparamārthaṁ*, It is the nature of your own Self. And that Śaṁkara, I, we, *stumaḥ*, we prostrate before that Śaṁkara.

JOHN: So he's differentiating this Śaṁkara from that Rūdra, who is with [Brahma] and Viṣṇu, and that seventh heaven, all of those gods and . . . ?

SWAMIJI: No, not that Śaṁkara.

JOHN: Yes, he is saying, not that one–this.

SWAMIJI: I bow to that Śaṁkara who is residing in each and every being.

---

139 Lit., that which attacks or occurs suddenly, any grievous accident, misfortune, calamity, mischief.

140 "*Caitanya* means 'complete freedom of universal consciousness.'" *Śiva Sūtra–The Supreme Awakening*, 1.2, page 20.

What is "prostration"? "I prostrate before that Saṁkara." What is "prostration"? Prostration is not just [to] say, "*Jai Guru Dev*!" "*Jai Guru Deva*" won't do only!

DEVOTEES: (laughter)

Audio 4 - 19:42

samastadehaprāṇādi-parimitapramātṛpadam adhaspadīkṛtya

When you destroy, when you subside, your ego on wakefulness[141], ego on dreaming state[142], ego on dreamless state[143], and ego on *turya* state[144], . . .*

What is ego on wakefulness, [etc.]?

Ego on wakefulness is, "I am awake" , [ego on the dreaming state is], "I am dreaming", [ego on deep sleep is], "I am in sound sleep", [and ego on *turya* is], "I am resting in *samādhi*". This is only ego. I subside all of these ego's! That is *samasta-deha-prāṇadi-parimita-pramātṛ*, this is the state where *parimita pramātṛ bhāva* is residing, ruling, governing.

JOHN: *Pramiti*?

SWAMIJI: No, *parimita*. *Parimita* is the inferior state of the ego. The inferior state of the ego is divided in four classes. One class is the inferior state of the ego that resides in wakefulness, the second class that resides [is the] ego in the dreaming state, the third is that resides in deep sleep, and the fourth is that resides in *samādhi*. In *samādhi*, it is the same. When you feel that, "I am in *samādhi*", it is just *māyā*, it is just illusion. *Samastadeha-prāṇādi-parimita-pramātṛ-padam*, so this is *parimitaṁ*, this is, all of these four [states] are, the states of the inferior way of *pramātṛ bhāva*[145].

* . . . *adhaspadīkṛtya*, when you subside it, *vikalpa-avikalpa-ādi-rūpāsu sarvāsu daśāsu*, subside it in all of these states, in all of these four states where you find *vikalpa* in some states and in some states [where] you find the absence of

141 *Jāgrat*.
142 *Svapna*.
143 *Suṣupti*.
144 Lit., the fourth state. See Appendix 5 for an explanation of *turya*.
145 The state (*bhāva*) of subjectivity (*pramātṛ*).

*vikalpa, . . .**

Vikalpa is present only in the first two states–thoughts. The cycle of thoughts is present in the first two states of being.

ERNIE: Wakefulness and . . .

SWAMIJI: And the dreaming state. And *vikalpa* is absent in the other two states.

ERNIE: Deep sleep and *turya*.

SWAMIJI: Deep sleep and *turya*. That is what he says.

*. . . *vikalpa-avikalpa-ādi-rūpāsu sarvāsu daśāsu*, in all of these four states, *sarvotkṛṣṭatayā parāmṛśāmaḥ*, when I feel that I am above these four states, that is "*Jai Guru Dev*", that is the meaning of "*Jai Guru Dev*"[146]. It is not *Jai Guru Dev* only by saying, "*Jai Guru Dev*", when you have done *praṇām*[147] [while saying], "*Jai Guru Dev*". It is not that. It is to do it practically: When you subside the ego existing in all of these four states, in the first two states in *vikalpa daśā*[148] and in the other two states in *nirvikalpa bhāva*[149].

STEPHANIE: Isn't that also your ego when you say, "I am above the four states"?

SWAMIJI: I am . . . ?

STEPHANIE: "Above the four states." What is that? That's not your ego?

SWAMIJI: No, when [you are] above the four states. But that [state] is not nominated. If it is nominated, then it is ego. Then it is ego.

STEPHANIE: Because you said, "I am above the four states".

SWAMIJI: Above, above. Above what? I[150] have not spoken that. I say, "I am above", [but] I don't know what that is. When

---

146 That is the real meaning of prostration (*stumaḥ*).
147 Bowing.
148 The state or condition (*daśā*) of thought (*vikalpa*)–*jāgrat* (wakefulness) and *svapna* (dreaming).
149 The state (*bhāva*) of thought-lessness (*nirvikalpa*)–*suṣupti* (deep-sleep) and *turya* ("the fourth state").
150 One who is actually above these four states.

you are above and you don't know what that "above" is, that is not ego. When you know what is "above", then it will be connected with the ego. The ego is [existing] when it is nominated. It is above the nomination–above.

ERNIE: It is.

SWAMIJI: It is, it is above.

ERNIE: And you experience that.

SWAMIJI: Yes.

JOHN: So, what's the difference here then? The difference is that the affirmation of 'I' doesn't have to come into that . . . ?

SWAMIJI: 'I' does not come.

JOHN: Like you said before, "I am Denise, I am Denise, I am John, I am John", . . .

SWAMIJI: Yes.

JOHN: . . . that is the same thing. These four states are, "I am this, I am this".

SWAMIJI: Yes.

JOHN: But you don't have that situation . . .

SWAMIJI: No (affirmative), in above.

JOHN: Because there is nothing to identify.

SWAMIJI: Yes.

ERNIE: So you don't . . . do you know?

GANJOO: "This" is dissolved; *idantā* is dissolved.

SWAMIJI: "This" and "I-ness", both [are dissolved].

ERNIE: Yes, but do you know?

SWAMIJI: How can we know? We can't know the knower. The knower cannot be known, only the known can be known. What is known, that is known. The object is known, the subject is not known.

JOHN: But in that state–*pramiti bhāva*.

SWAMIJI: *Pramiti bhāva*.

JOHN: Is this *pramiti bhāva*?

SWAMIJI: Yes, it is *pramiti bhāva*.[151]

STEPHANIE: So, above those four states, nothing is known?

SWAMIJI: Nothing is known, yes.

JOHN: But it's not nothing.

SWAMIJI: No, it is that thing which is . . .

ERNIE: Everything.

STEPHANIE: Motionless-motion or something.

SWAMIJI: Yes, it is just like next to *spanda*.

Audio 4 - 24:33

JOHN: So, the knower and the known become one at this state . . .

SWAMIJI: Yes.

JOHN: . . . so there is nothing to . . .

SWAMIJI: Nothing to realize, yes.

ERNIE: Does a person who has that, does he know that he has that?

SWAMIJI: He experiences that in I-consciousness, not with "this-ness".

JOHN: In other words, he becomes that thing.

SWAMIJI: He does not become his object. He knows in such a way.

ERNIE: "I am dreaming", "I am eating", not that way.

SWAMIJI: No (affirmative).

JOHN: That makes it an object, doesn't it?

SWAMIJI: Yes.

JOHN: So, he knows this state more than he knows anything in his life. When he has this state, this will be a more firm knowledge than any other knowledge he ever had.

SWAMIJI: Firm knowledge and he will . . . no, it will not be objective knowledge. It is subjective consciousness. He resides

151 "*Pramiti* is that state where subjective consciousness prevails without the agitation of objectivity. Where the agitation of objectivity is also found in subjective consciousness, that is the state of *pramātṛ.*" *Kashmir Shaivism–The Secret Supreme*, 11.81.

in subjective consciousness where he does not know anything.

ERNIE: No, but would it be possible for someone to have this state of . . .

SWAMIJI: He knows that unknown state.

ERNIE: But could you have this state and not know that you were elevated?

SWAMIJI: Elevated, what . . . ? "Elevation" and "non-elevation" do not rise there.

ERNIE: But if you have this experience, . . .

SWAMIJI: Yes.

ERNIE: . . . is it possible that you don't know that you are in that place?

SWAMIJI: Who are "you"? Are you not one with That? You are not separate from That.

ERNIE: No. Now I am [separated from That] because I have this "I", but . . .

SWAMIJI: *Bas*, this separated soul will never enter in That state.

ERNIE: No, but for a person who has . . .

SWAMIJI: Whenever you enter, you enter only when you melt away.

ERNIE: Yes, but then is it possible that you don't know that you have melted away?

SWAMIJI: You don't know. He knows. That remains. Afterwards, That remains.

JOHN: But after that state, let's say . . .

SWAMIJI: When you come out from that, you know it as, "It was something above".

ERNIE: Something.

SWAMIJI: Yes.

JOHN: But it's something great, it's a flashy . . .

SWAMIJI: Yes.

JOHN: Isn't it like this *vedha*, this piercing? I mean, it's like a shock, it's not a . . .

SWAMIJI: Yes.

JOHN: It's not a nothing.

BRUCE H: Is it a state you hold in the external world, I mean in wakefulness?

SWAMIJI: No, not external. It is an internal state first.

JOHN: First.

Audio 4 - 26:41

SWAMIJI: *Sarvāsu daśāsu sarva-utkṛṣṭatayā parāmṛś-āmaḥ*, I see that after that, after getting contact with that supreme God consciousness, I experience that God consciousness as above everything and residing in each and every blade of grass, afterwards. It is one God consciousness everywhere, found everywhere then. There is no objective . . . the objective cycle just melts away. Only the subjective cycle remains. Subjective consciousness cannot be perceived [because] it is the perceiver; it is the state of the perceiver, not the [state of the] perceived. But [It is] not the perceiver also. As long as you say, "perceiver", it means that there is something to be perceived. It is above that. It is not known, It is unknown. That person who resides in That, he resides, he just resides. That person who feels that, "I have known It", he has not known It.

ERNIE: (laughter)

JOHN: So, "knowing" means here?

SWAMIJI: "Knowing" means, This cannot be an object, This can never remain in the cycle of objectivity. You can't know It.

JOHN: So this is that . . .

SWAMIJI: You feel that state as one with God consciousness.

ERNIE: So either you live It or you don't have It.

SWAMIJI: No (affirmative), that is right.

JOHN: This is *anākhyā*, this unspeakable.

SWAMIJI: *Anākhyā*, yes. *Anākhyā*, yes.[152]

Bahuvacanam, now he has put this in the plural–"*stumaḥ*". *Stumaḥ* means, "we prostrate before that *spanda*". "We prostrate before that *spanda*." He does not say, "I prostrate

152 Transcendence beyond the description of words.

before that *spanda*, I bow."

JOHN: He says, "we", in the plural.

SWAMIJI: "We". What does the plural mean? Why has Vasugupta kept ["*stumaḥ*" in the] plural, this that, "We bow before That?" By "we" we must understand–*bahuvacanam* is that plural, putting it in a plural way–*ātmikṛta-aśeṣa-anugrāhya-jana-abheda-prathanāya*, he wants that, "Let this whole cycle of one hundred and eighteen worlds, the individuals of the whole cycle of one hundred and eighteen worlds, let them melt in that God consciousness, not only myself." He wants that everybody should just melt in that supreme God consciousness. It is why he has put the plural. He does not want to enter in that God consciousness alone. He wants to enter with all of [the universe], whatever is created in this universe. It is why he has put *bahuvacanam*, the plural.

Have you understood?

JOHN: Yes, sir.

SWAMIJI: And "*taṁ*". *Taṁ* is, "I bow to *that* Śaṁkara". "That", what "that" means?

Audio 4 - 29:58

Taṁ iti ca asādhāraṇa-svarūpa-pratyabhijñāpanāya, "that" means, I bow to *that* Śaṁkara, I bow to *that* supreme God consciousness.

What is "that"? By "that", what do you mean?

By "that" you mean, *asādhāraṇa svarūpa pratyabhijñāpanāya*, "that" means that God consciousness which is not perceived by anybody. "That" [means] "unique".

So, he has put "that", not "this". If he would have put "this", then it would be something else. He has put "that" God consciousness. "That" is that unknown, unknown to anybody. It is known to His nature only.

Ko'sau śaṁkaraḥ, who is that Śaṁkara? For that he says, "*yasyonmeṣanimeṣābhyāṁ jagataḥ pralayodayau*", by whose *unmeṣa* and by whose *nimeṣa*[153] you find the rise and dissolution of this whole universe, the rise and the destruction

153 Opening of the eyes and closing of the eyes, respectively.

of this whole universe. By *unmeṣa* you find the destruction of the universe, by whose *nimeṣa* you find . . .

JOHN: Rise of the whole universe.

SWAMIJI: . . . the rise of His universe. When He closes His God consciousness [i.e., *nimeṣa*], the rise of the universe takes place. When He opens the door of God consciousness [i.e., *unmeṣa*], the destruction of the universe takes place.

Now for "this". "*Atra*", from "*atra*", this is the conclusion of various masters, various . . .

JOHN: Various schools or teachers of various schools?

SWAMIJI: . . . various schools, teachers.

Audio 4 - 31:45

atra eke svarūpa prakāśana tadgopanābhyāṁ yatkartṛkābhyāṁ unmeṣanimeṣābhyāṁ jagato viśvasya pralayodayau vināśasargau iti vyākhyātavantaḥ tadeke na sehire

Some masters (*eke*, some masters) on this point of *unmeṣa* [and *nimeṣa*], what is *unmeṣa* and what is *nimeṣa*, [say that] *unmeṣa* and *nimeṣa* is *svarūpa-prakāśana tadgopanābhyāṁ*, *unmeṣa* is *svarūpa prakāśana*, to reveal His nature is *unmeṣa*, to conceal His nature is *nimeṣa*. Some masters say that the exposition of *unmeṣa* and *nimeṣa* means, *svarūpa prakāśana* and *svarūpa nimeṣana*. *Svarūpa prakāśana* takes place by His *unmeṣa*, i.e., the nature of God consciousness rises when He opens His eyes, and the nature of God consciousness is subsided . . .

JOHN: When He closes His eyes.

SWAMIJI: . . . when He closes His eyes. And, in the same way, *unmeṣanimeṣābhyāṁ jagato viśvasya pralayodayau*, in the same way, they say that this universe, by His *svarūpa prakāśana*, takes its end–this universe ends when He reveals His nature. When He conceals His nature, this universe gets its rise, as we [explained] it previously. *Iti vyākhyātavantaḥ*, this way they believe the exposition of *unmeṣa* and *nimeṣa*.

Tadeke na sehire, but for this point, this point they do not tolerate; this point of exposition, some schools of thought do not tolerate. They can't tolerate . . .

JOHN: This idea, this way of understanding.

SWAMIJI: . . . this way of exposition of *unmeṣa* and *nimeṣa*, that *unmeṣa* is *svarūpa prakāśana* and *nimeṣa* is *svarūpa nimeṣa*. *Svarūpa prakāśana*, when you reveal your nature, that is *unmeṣa*, [and] when you conceal your nature, that is *nimeṣa*. And when you reveal your nature, this world is destroyed, [and] when you conceal your nature, . . .

GANJOO: This world comes into being.

SWAMIJI: . . . this world comes into being.

ERNIE: Why can't they accept that?

SWAMIJI: They don't tolerate this kind of exposition. *Tathāhi*, that will be explained.

Audio 4 - 34:35

Unmeṣanimeṣau kādācitkau, opening His eyes and closing His eyes, it is *kādācitkau*[154]. Some philosophers say that, by *unmeṣa* and *nimeṣa*, it means [*unmeṣa*] is [occurring at] one time and the next time is *nimeṣa*. The first time, in the first second at 8:38, *unmeṣa* [occurs, and at] 8:39, *nimesa* [occurs]. So it is *kādācitkau*. *Kādācitkau* is "sometimes", sometimes *unmeṣa* and sometimes *nimeṣa*. *Kādācitkau* is *kādācit bhāvau kādācitkau*, when *unmeṣa* takes place, *nimeṣa* is not there, [and] when *nimeṣa* takes place, *unmeṣa* is not there. So, they are *kādācitkau*, they are in separate times, they take place at separate moments. That is *kādācitkau*.

JOHN: They are exclusive, mutually exclusive. When one takes place, the other is not taking place.

SWAMIJI: Yes. At one point [in time] . . .

JOHN: Only one can exist.

SWAMIJI: . . . only one can exist, not both.

ERNIE: Never simultaneous.

SWAMIJI: Never simultaneously.

JOHN: This is the second . . .

SWAMIJI: That is *kādācitkau*.

---

154 Appearing now and then, produced sometimes, occasional, incidental.

Audio 4 - 36:00

Kādācit-kajagat-nāśodaya-hetu kathaṁ nitye bhagavati syātām, but That is eternal, God consciousness is eternal. There is no question of *kādācitaka bhāva*. If He is *unmeṣa*, if He is [ever] opening His eyes, He must remain always like that. He is eternal, He has not breaks of His nature.

Do you understand?

The breaking of His nature means that it is *unmeṣa*, sometimes *unmeṣa*, and sometimes *nimeṣa*; sometimes opening His eyes and sometimes closing His eyes. It means He is not eternal. If He is not eternal, He will die, He will disappear some day. When there are two kinds of behavior . . .

ERNIE: Two states.

SWAMIJI: . . . behaviors of states, then it means it will end sometime. When there is only one behavior, one continuous behavior of God consciousness, that is tolerable, that can be tolerated. This cannot be tolerated that sometimes He is in the *unmeṣa* state and sometimes He is in the *nimeṣa* state. At the time of the *unmeṣa* state of His being, the world is destroyed, and at the time of His *nimeṣa*, the world is created–it cannot be tolerated in [consideration of] that eternal God consciousness. This is the logic of those other schools of thought [concerning] this point.

It will be explained later on, i.e., our school, what is our school's [position] regarding this *unmeṣa* [and *nimeṣa*]. What is opening the eyes, and what is the meaning of opening His eyes, and what is the meaning of closing His eyes? If the opening of His eyes [really] means the opening of His eyes and the closing of His eyes really means closing His eyes, then it means that He is not eternal [because] He is sometimes closing His eyes, sometimes opening His eyes. When there are two aspects of His being, it means it will end sometime. Eternity won't remain in His being.

ERNIE: Not monistic.

SWAMIJI: It won't be monistic.

JOHN: What about that first objection we heard? That wasn't an objection. Was that an objection also?

SWAMIJI: What?

JOHN: That when God opens His eyes, He's revealing His nature, and when He closes His eyes, He's concealing His nature.

SWAMIJI: But, he is objecting [to] that point now, here.

JOHN: This man.

SWAMIJI: Yes.

JOHN: But our view is more that first view that when He opens His eyes, He is revealing His nature. Because you said what it means when He closes His eyes is that He conceals His nature and the world comes into being.

SWAMIJI: But that is not our Shaivism.

JOHN: That is not?

SWAMIJI: No.

DEVOTEES: (laughter)

SWAMIJI: It will be . . .

GANJOO: You must wait for the further explanation of it.

SWAMIJI: The reality of Shaivism will be explained later on. It is just building up to the meaning of this *śloka*.

By *unmeṣa* and *nimeṣa* . . . really, *unmeṣa* and *nimeṣa* does not mean the opening and the closing of His eyes. The real meaning of *unmeṣa* and *nimeṣa* he will explain it later on from his viewpoint of Shaivism.

ERNIE: What Vasugupta was trying to say.

SWAMIJI: Yes. So this cannot exist, this *unmeṣa* and *nimeṣa*, these two activities of movement, cannot exist in an eternal Being, who is always one, the same.

Audio 4 - 39:35

ata unmeṣa-nimeṣa-dharmaka-jagat kāraṇatvāt ekaiva bhagavacchaktiḥ unmeṣanimeṣa-śabdābhyām vyavahriyate

So, they say that *unmeṣa-nimeṣa-dharmaka-jagat-kāraṇa-tvāt*, when *unmeṣa* and *nimeṣa*, these two aspects of the rise and dissolution of the universe, [when you say that] the rise of the universe takes place by His *nimeṣa* and the destruction of the universe takes place by His *unmeṣa* (*unmeṣa nimeṣa dharmaka jagat kāraṇatvāt*), so, *ekaiva bhagavat śaktiḥ unmeṣa nimeṣa śabdābhyāṁ vyavahriyate*, so you must say that *unmeṣa* and *nimeṣa* does not mean "opening His eyes" and "closing His eyes". You must say, you must translate the word "*unmeṣa*" and the word "*nimeṣa*" as, "by the supreme energy of God". It is [by the] supreme energy of God [that] it has become *unmeṣa* and *nimeṣa*. The supreme energy of God gives rise to *unmeṣa* and gives rise to *nimeṣa*. It is energy that works, it is not *unmeṣa* and *nimeṣa* that works. It is energy, eternal energy. God is eternal, God is always the same, and He gives rise to *unmeṣa* and *nimeṣa*. This way you should expose this, these two words of *unmeṣa* and *nimeṣa*.

Do you understand?

This is only one energy that puts, that manifests, these *unmeṣa* and *nimeṣa*.

ERNIE: This is *śakti*? That energy is His *śakti*?

SWAMIJI: *Śakti*, yes, *svātantrya śakti*.[155]

JOHN: This is another school.

SWAMIJI: This is another school of thought. That also won't be accepted later on.

ERNIE: (laughs)

SWAMIJI: Why [do you laugh]?

ERNIE: I thought that was the Shaivism!

SWAMIJI: (laughs) No, no, no.

DENISE: I did, too.

ERNIE: So, this other school says that it's the energy . . .

SWAMIJI: The energy that puts, gives . . .

ERNIE: . . . that is eternal.

SWAMIJI: Energy is eternal and it gives rise to *unmeṣa* and *nimeṣa* by which you find the destruction and the rise of the universe.

ERNIE: That explains it.

SWAMIJI: It is the explanation of that other school of thought.

BRUCE H: What other school is that?

---

155 Lord Śiva's energy of absolute independence. See Appendix 2 for an explanation of *svātantrya śakti*.

SWAMIJI: Damn its head! We have to see our school, what is our school.

ERNIE: (laughs)

JOHN: These are all local schools.

SWAMIJI: These are all, yes, adjustments of Shaivism.

ERNIE: These.

SWAMIJI: These, yes.

JOHN: Masters in the valley arguing amongst themselves on what is what–these guys.

SWAMIJI: Yes.

Audio 4 - 42:25

tathā ca yathāsaṁkhyaṁ tyaktvā yathāsaṁbhavaṁ yasya unmeṣāt jagadudayo, yannimeṣāt ca pralayaḥ iti vyācacakṣire /

So, they translate these two words, "*unmeṣa*" and "*nimeṣa*", not *yathā saṁkhyaṁ*, [but rather], *yathā saṁbhavaṁ*. [Not] *yathā saṁkhyam*, not one and two, not in one and two. They . . .

GANJOO: Not in corresponding . . .

ERNIE: Like a lightbulb, on and off.

SWAMIJI: On and off, not like on and off, but *yathā saṁbhavam*, but just by an adjustment: the energy adjusts *unmeṣa*, the energy adjusts *nimeṣa*.

ERNIE: Doesn't matter which, the energy is there.

SWAMIJI: Doesn't matter which, the energy is there.

JOHN: Energy is one.

SWAMIJI: Energy is one, and it is the energy's adjustment in *unmeṣa* and *nimeṣa* that gives the rise and the dissolution of this universe. [They say that] this way you should explain these two words of *unmeṣa* and *nimeṣa*.

Audio 4 - 43:32

atrāpi ca śāstrārthopadeśadṛśā śaṁkarasvarūpābhinnasya jagato'pi kathaṁ kādācitkau vināśodayau bhavetām? iti tulye prasaṅge, . . .

Atrāpi ca, in this point also, if you go in the depth of this exposition, this second exposition . . .

JOHN: About *śakti*.

SWAMIJI: About *unmeṣa* and *nimeṣa* through *śakti*, through one energy, *śāstra ārtha upadeśadṛśā*, *śāstra ārtha*, the essence which is residing in the background of our Shaivism, by that we conclude [that] *śaṁkara-svarūpa ābhinnasya*, Śaṁkara is one always, the reality of God consciousness is always one. *Jagato'pi*, so, when He has produced this universe, this universe also must be one, because foreign matter cannot come from one matter, e.g., a pencil will produce only a pencil, a pencil won't produce water. So, Lord Śiva can produce only the substance of Lord Śiva in the universe, not a separated universe.

ERNIE: Only unity.

SWAMIJI: Only unity of God consciousness. He can produce only that. Whatever is in [your] pocket, you can produce that, that thing, not [some] foreign matter. When this "foreign matter" has been created, i.e., this universe of repeated births and deaths, where are repeated births and deaths [existing]? Are these repeated births and deaths existing in God consciousness?

Why are these produced from God consciousness?

What is it? This is . . .

ERNIE: Not possible.

SWAMIJI: . . . this is not real, this is not possible. It cannot be! How will darkness come out from light? How can mortality come out from an immortal being? Otherwise, you have to accept that mortality also exists There. If mortality and immortality exist There, that way it is not possible because It is only one being. There [can't] be two there existing in God consciousness. So, *kādācitkau vināśodayau bhavetām*, so if there is only one energy existing, one energy is accepted, . . .*
Whose energy?

JOHN: Lord Śiva's.

SWAMIJI: Lord Śiva's energy, which produces that *unmeṣa* and *nimeṣa*. [His energies] produce by their power, *unmeṣa* and *nimeṣa*.

*. . . [then] why *unmeṣa* and *nimeṣa*? Why not only one, one thing? Because the energy is one, [so] it must produce only one [thing]. [One] energy cannot produce two [things]. If there is oneness, from oneness you will find only oneness. The production of oneness must be one with that which produces [it]. *Iti tulye prasaṅge*, it is one and the same thing in both ways of thinking, both ways of school.

Audio 4 - 47:00

yadi ābhāsaparamārthānusāreṇa tathābhāsaparam-ārthasya śaṁkarasvabhāvābhinnasya jagataḥ thatābhāsana-mayāveva vināśodayau iṣyete, unmeṣa-nimeṣāvapi tathābhāsa-paramārthau bhagavati kiṁ na iṣyete / kālo'pi ābhāsanasāro, na tu tadvyatiriktaḥ kaścit, iti kathamasau varākaḥ ābhāsāyitari bhagavati bhedaśaṁkāspadam /

Now, if we put [forth] *ābhāsa paramārtha*, . . .*

Ābhāsa paramārtha is the reality of our thought. *Ābhāsa paramārtha*, whatever shines, it exists in God consciousness–whatever shines, it exists in God consciousness. That is *ābhāsa paramārtha*, the reality of *ābhasā*.

JOHN: So, "*ābhāsa*", how will you translate into English?

SWAMIJI: *Ābhāsa* is whatever is existing, whatever is felt. Anything existing, anything felt, is *ābhāsa*. Whatever is shining is one with God. This is *ābhāsa paramārtha*. [Kashmir Shaivism] is called *ābhāsavāda* also, the theory of *ābhāsa*[156]. Whatever is shining, e.g., if a baby from . . . you

156 Lit., splendor, light, color, appearance, i.e., perception. The Doctrine of Kashmir Shaivism is known by a number of names: *Ābhāsavāda*, the Doctrine of Appearances; *Advaita Darśana*, the Monistic Teaching; *Svātantryavāda*, the Doctrine of Freedom/Independence; *Pratyabhijñāvāda*, the Doctrine of Spontaneous Recognition; and *Rahasya sampradāya*, the Secret Tradition (sometimes referred to as the *Tryambaka sampradāya*). Abhinavagupta uses the terms *Trika Śāsana* (Trika Teaching) or *Trika Śāstra* (Trika Scripture) in his *Tantrāloka*, and the term *Anuttara Trika* (The Excellent Trika) in his commentary on the *Paratrīśikā*

know a barren woman?

ERNIE: The milk of a bird.

SWAMIJI: The milk of a bird. As long as the milk of a bird comes in our mind, it is existing. This is *ābhāsa paramārtha*. Whatever has come in thought, in your thought only, [although] it may not exist in the external world, it is existing. This is *ābhāsa paramārtha*, this is the reality of *ābhāsa*. Whatever is found in the inside and the outside of the world, if it is found, if it is felt, it is existing. This is *ābhāsa paramārtha*.

*. . . according to that theory, *tatha ābhāsa paramārthasya śaṁkara svabhāva ābhinnasya jagataḥ*, this universe, if we say that this universe is one with God in that way, in that way in which it exists, it is one with God consciousness[157], *tatha ābhāsana-mayāveva vināsodayau iṣyet*, so *unmeṣa* and *nimeṣa* is just like that. There is no difference between *unmeṣa* and *nimeṣa*. As long as you will accept that *unmeṣa* is the same and *nimeṣa* is the same, it may be the rise of God consciousness, what then? It may be the dissolution of God consciousness, what then? God consciousness is still there!

Audio 4 - 49:54

atha sthite sarvadikke śivatattve'dhunocyate /
tasmiñjñāte'thavājñāte śivatvamanivāritam //[158]

If you say that Śiva *tattva*[159] is known, [that] here Śiva *tattva* is known [and] here Śiva *tattva* is not known [or] here Śiva *tattva* is present [and] here Śiva *tattva* is not present, what then? Śiva *tattva* is present in Its presence, Śiva *tattva* is present in Its absence also. Because He has given rise to the absence of Śiva *tattva*, and that is Śiva *tattva*. When you say, "no", that is "yes". When you say, "yes", that is also "yes". If

---

Vivaraṇa.

157 Because the *savikalpa* state (differentiated perception/thought/appearance) is just an offshoot of the *nirvikalpa* state (the undifferentiated, thought-less state of Lord Śiva). Paraphrase taken from *Parātrīśikā Vivaraṇa* (LJA audio archives).

158 Somānanda's *Śivadṛṣṭi*, *āhnika* 7, *śloka* 1.

159 The element (*tattva*) of Śiva.

you know Siva *tattva*, well and good, you know. If you don't know, well and good, you know still. It does not mean that in not-knowing, in the state of not-knowing, It is not known. It is known there also. That is *abhāsavāda*. If you take that *abhāsavāda* in view and explain these two words of *unmeṣa* and *nimeṣa*, then it is well and good.

JOHN: Who is saying that? Kṣhemarāja is agreeing that that's a valid argument?

SWAMIJI: Yes, yes.

Vināśodayau iṣyati, then *unmeṣa nimeṣāvapi*, *tathābhāsa parmārthau bhagavati kiṁ na iṣyete*, then why can't you tolerate *unmeṣa* and *nimeṣa* also in that supreme Being? If everything is okay, it is not to be discarded, . . .*

What is not to be discarded? The absence of God consciousness. The presence of God consciousness is not to be discarded because God consciousness is still there. The absence of God consciousness is not to be discarded because in the absence of God consciousness, It exists–It exists, It is not discarded.

*. . . so why should you not tolerate *unmeṣa* and *nimeṣa* also? Why the opening of [His] eyes is good and the closing of His eyes is bad?

JOHN: So this closing and opening of the eyes here, . . .

SWAMIJI: It is one and the same.

JOHN: . . . which is good and bad, . . .

SWAMIJI: If you achieve God consciousness, you have achieved [It]. If you don't achieve [It], you have still achieved [It]. This is the reality of Shaivism.

JOHN: But this earlier viewpoint where when you open the eyes that is good and when you close the eyes that is bad, this is the Vedāntic point of view where *māyā* is something other than God and . . .

SWAMIJI: No. As long as *unmeṣa* and *nimeṣa* are separately explained, that is bad. [When] *unmeṣa* and *nimeṣa* are explained . . .

GANJOO: As one.

SWAMIJI: . . . as one with God consciousness, then it is fine. The reality of eternity . . .

ERNIE: It doesn't matter if His eyes are closed.

SWAMIJI: It doesn't matter if your eyes are closed or open. If you achieve Him, you are existing in Him. If you don't achieve Him, you are still existing in Him. What is there?

DENISE: Then what's the point in trying?

SWAMIJI: So don't do anything, don't meditate, don't do . . . *bas*, just remain as [you are]. This is the reality of Shaivism[160]. *Bas*!

DEVOTEE: Same in nothingness.

GANJOO: Same in nothingness!

SWAMIJI: *Kālo'pi abhāsanasāro, na tu tad vyatiriktaḥ*. And if you say, "No, I am twenty years old", "I am thirty years old", "I am seventy years old", "I am going to die", what then? It is only one cycle of God consciousness. *Kālo'pi*, this time, this cycle of time, is also *ābhāsanasāra*[161], it is just *ābhāsanasāra*, it is just residing in the state of God consciousness.

ERNIE: Like the milk of a bird.

SWAMIJI: *Na tu tadvyatiriktaḥ*, it is not separated from God consciousness. *Kathamasau varākaḥ ābhāsayitari bhagavati bhedaśaṁkāspadam*, how can it differentiate the state of God consciousness?

---

160 Abhinvagupta says, "This *saṁsāra* (the cycle of repeated births and deaths), this drama is not existing at all. It is only the glory of Śiva. When you are born, it is the glory of Lord Śiva. When you die, it is the glory of Lord Śiva. When you live, it is the glory of Lord Śiva. Everywhere there is the glory of Lord Śiva. So, where is the question of bondage? When there is no question of bondage, why meditate? It is useless to strive for liberation when you are already liberated. So, liberation and bondage is just a misconception. Don't abandon anything and don't accept anything, remain just as you are. There is nothing to be done!" Paraphrase of Swamiji's translation of the second verse of Abhinavagupta's hymn on the highest reality (*anupāya*), the *Anuttarāṣṭaka*. See *Parātrīśika Vivaraṇa* and also the *Tantrāloka* 4.92 commentary (Lakshmanjoo Academy archive).

161 The essence (*sāra*) of appearances (*ābhāsana*).

Audio 4 - 53:49

ekacintāprasaktasya yataḥ syādaparodayaḥ . . . .[162]

iti ca unmeṣa lakṣaṇamatraiva asti / tadanusāreṇa ca nimeṣa-lakṣaṇam-api svarūpa-gopanā-rūpam-ūhyam iti yathā-saṁkhye'pi na kṣatiḥ iti apare / tad-alamākhyāyikā varṇanena / prakṛtamucyate - yasyonmeṣa iti /
[not recited]

We have explained this in the *Spanda Kārikā* also, in this *kārikā* of *spanda*, [that] when you give rise to one thought, give rise to another thought, just be attentive and you will reside in God consciousness. Go on thinking various thoughts but be attentive. Attentively think, that is all.[163] *Iti ca unmeṣa lakṣaṇamatraiva asti*, this is the reality of *unmeṣa*, what is *unmeṣa*.

Tadanusāreṇa ca nimeṣa-lakṣaṇam-api svarūpa-gopanā-rūpam-ūhyam. Now *nimeṣa*, which subsides the nature of God consciousness. When you close your eyes, that is when you subside the nature of God consciousness, that also should be explained in this way: When you subside the nature of God consciousness, in that way also, God consciousness is still existing–in a subsided [way] also.

Audio 4 - 55:00

Iti yathāsaṁkhye'pi na kṣatiḥ iti apare, and some Śaivites, some good scholars [among] Śaivites, say that, "*yathā-*

162 *Spanda Kārikā* 3.9, page 66.

163 Kṣhemarāja will later refer to the *Svacchanda Tantra* to further expand upon this point. This appears to be Kṣhemarāja's interepretation of the original *Spanda Kārikā* verse which states: "You just be attentive to the movement of mind. When in the mind one *vikalpa* (one thought) rises, remain in that thought, don't let that thought go away from your mind. Be attentive to that thought only, that one thought only. And if you remain attentive in continuity to that one thought, *yataḥ syādaparodayaḥ*, then after some time, another thing will take place, another thing will rise, and that is [*sāmānya*] *spanda*." Swami Lakshmanjoo, trans., *Spanda Kārikā* 3.9. page 66.

saṁkhye'pi na . . .", you can believe in numbers also[164] – "It is *unmeṣa*", "It is *nimeṣa*", "It is good", "It is bad", "It is this", "It is that", "It is. . . ." – this can also be tolerated, no harm.

ERNIE: (laughter)

SWAMIJI: *Tadalamākhyāyikāvarṇanena*, these are the theories of Shaivism. These are the three kinds of theories of Shaivism. Now, I will give you the real thinking of Shaivism, what Shaivism means . . .

ERNIE: The understanding.

SWAMIJI: The real understanding of Shaivism.

JOHN: So these three theories are just to . . . theory one is, to open your eyes is to reveal God consciousness, and wanting to close [your eyes], that is to conceal it.

SWAMIJI: Yes.

JOHN: And then another man says that this God consciousness is like moments in succession–opening and closing the eyes, opening and closing the eyes.

SWAMIJI: Yes.

ERNIE: That it's the energy that . . .

JOHN: The third guy says, "No, it's the energy that . . ."

SWAMIJI: Energy that . . .

JOHN: ". . . opens and closes these eyes so that's the oneness, so that one . . ."

SWAMIJI: Yes.

JOHN: And then the final one, which wasn't a theory, was he is saying that we can accept that one of . . .

SWAMIJI: But there is also some adjustment to be done in that fourth understanding. That adjustment he will do now.

ERNIE: And that fourth understanding was that, whether It's there or not there, it does not matter, It is still there.

SWAMIJI: It does not matter, It is still there, It is still there. *Bas*.

164 *Saṁkhyā* literally means, to reckon or count up, sum up, enumerate, calculate.

Audio 4 - 56:48 / Audio 5 - 00:00

Prakṛtamucyate, now we will go to our subject, to our point. *Yasyonmeṣa iti*, *unmeṣa* and *nimeṣa*, rise and dissolution, what is that?

> *iha parameśvarasya mahāprakāśātmano vimalasyāpi ekaiva parāmarśaśaktiḥ kiñciccalattābhāsarūpatayā spandaḥ iti, sphurattā iti, ūrmiḥ iti, balam iti, udyogaḥ iti, hṛdayam iti, sāram iti, mālinī iti, parā ityādyananta-saṁjñābhiḥ āgameṣu udghoṣyate* /

Iha, in this field of the Trika system, Parameśvara, the supreme Lord, is *mahā prakāśa*, filled with supreme light.[165] *Vimalasyāpi*, and He is pure. And His *ekaiva parāmarśa*, He has only one energy which is called *parāmarśa śakti*, the energy of consciousness. That energy of consciousness, It is just the embodiment of *spanda*, It is just the embodiment of movement, stable movement. Because It is *kiñcit calatta ābhāsa rūpatayā*, movement, you feel that It is moving, otherwise It is not moving, but It is in movement. It is that kind of movement [that] is just a vibrating movement.

You know "vibrating movement"?

But not vibrating to that extent. For instance, just as the heart vibrates, but it expands also in girth–it expands–but It does not expand, because there is no other room, no other place, for It to expand. So It vibrates in His own nature. That is *spanda*.

And this *spanda* is nominated as *sphurattā* (*sphurattā* is just "flow"), *ūrmiḥ* (tide), *balam* (strength), *udyoga* . . .

Udyoga is not "effort".

ERNIE: Concentration?

SWAMIJI: No. *Udyoga* is just "force".

. . . *hṛdayam* (heart), *sāram* (essence), and *mālinī* (supreme energy). These are the nominations which are attributed to this *spanda* in the *śāstra*s.[166]

---

165 See Appendix 12 for an explanation of *prakāśa*.
166 Scripture.

sā ca ekāpi yugapadeva unmeṣa-nimeṣamayī /
[not recited in full]

Although that energy of *spanda*, the energy of vibrating energy, is only one, *yugapadeva unmeṣa-nimeṣamayī*, you feel that vibrating energy rising and [dissolving] simultaneously. It rises and It dissolves simultaneously. From one point [of view] you feel It is rising and [from] another point [of view] you feel at the same time It is . . .

JOHN: Dissolving.

SWAMIJI: . . . It is dissolving. It will be clarified now.

Audio 5 - 03:20

[tathāhi] sadāśivādikṣitiparyantasya tattvagrāmasya prāksṛṣṭasya yā saṁhārāpekṣayā nimeṣabhūḥ saiva srakṣyamāṇabhedāpekṣayā unmeṣadaśā /

When, right from *sadāśiva* to *pṛthvī* (earth), all of these elements, all of these cycles of elements[167], *prāksṛṣṭasya*, are created, although it is created, when, after its creation, it is to be destroyed, *saṁhārāpekṣayā*, when it is destroyed, *nimeṣa-bhūḥ*, that is the dissolution of this cycle of the elementary world–it dissolves–but at the same time, that dissolution, *saiva srakṣyamāṇabhedāpekṣayā unmeṣadaśā*, that is the rise of Śiva. When it dissolves, . . .

What? The cycle of the universe right from *sadaśiva* to *pṛthvī*, it gets dissolution, it dissolves, it is destroyed.

. . . but the destruction of this elementary world is the creation of the state of Śiva. So it is a rise also, the rise also of Śiva. Śiva's rise is the destruction of the universe.

Audio 5 - 04:47

prāksṛṣṭabhedasaṁhārarūpā ca yā nimeṣadaṣā saiva cidabhedaprathāyā unmeṣabhūḥ /

On the other hand, just to clear it, *prāk-sṛṣṭa bheda saṁhāra rūpā*, when you destroy *bheda*, when you destroy the differentiated cycle of the world, destroying this differentiated

167 See Appendix 11 for a list of the thirty-six elements (*tattvas*).

cycle of the world is to [cause] the rise of the undifferentiated cycle–the undifferentiated cycle rises and that is God consciousness.

So, the *nimeṣa*, the state of *nimeṣa* of the differentiated cycle, is the state of *unmeṣa* for the undifferentiated movement. So, both ways this is the movement. You can't say what is right and what is wrong there. That is also in its own way right and the other [one] is also in its own way right.

bhedāsūtraṇarūpā ca yā unmeṣadaśā saiva cidabheda prathāyānimeṣabhūḥ / māyāpade'pi ca [not recited in full]

When you *āsūtraṇa-rūpā*, when you put the foundation stone for *bheda*, the differentiated world (*unmeṣa daśā* means, when you give rise to *bheda*, the differentiated cycle), and that rise of the differentiated cycle is *cit abheda prathāyā nimeṣa-bhūḥ*; when the differentiated cycle rises, *cit abheda prathāyā*[168] is *nimeṣa*, that is dissolved, that gets dissolution.

What? God consciousness. God consciousness is subsided.

So both are working, both are working simultaneously.

JOHN: So, from the point of view of differentiation, un-differentiation doesn't exist.

SWAMIJI: It doesn't exist.

JOHN: From the point of view of un-differentiation, differentiation doesn't exist.

SWAMIJI: It exists, but [only] in the cycle of *svātantrya*. In the cycle of *svātantrya*, these both exist simultaneously.[169]

---

168 The spreading out (*pratha*) of non-dual (*abheda*) consciousness (*cit*).

169 "That essence of *svātantrya* is *anavacchinna*, beyond limitation, all-round beyond limitation. There is no such limit found in that state. *Vicchinna camatkāra maya viśrāntyā*, and this limited state of being is also found there. [Lord Śiva] is unlimited, but the limited cycle of God consciousness is also found There. So It is both limited and unlimited. That being who is limited only, he is not true. That being who is unlimited only, he is not true. Why? Because he is limited. The being who is unlimited is not true because he is unlimited only [and] not limited. That fullness of God consciousness

Māyāpade'pi ca, now, leave that cycle of *svātantrya* aside. Go to the daily activity of the world, *māyā pade*, in the state of *māyā*, in the state of illusion.

Audio 5 - 07:17

nīladidṛkṣātmaprāgbhūmirūpā unmeṣāvasthaiva sphurita nīla-pūrva-pitāvabhāsana-viśrāntyātmakanimeṣarūpā sarvasya svasaṁvitsiddhā /

In the daily routine of life also, you'll see that *spanda* works both ways. It has got both . . .

ERNIE: Characters, characteristics.

SWAMIJI: . . . both factors. *Nīla-didṛkṣya-ātma-prāg-bhūmi-rūpā*, when you want to see something blue, you want to see [some] blue object, some object which is blue, blue colored–*nīladṛkṣātmaprāg bhūmirūpā*; *nīladidṛkṣyā*, just to see a bluish object[170]–when you want to see a bluish object, that is the rise of a bluish object, that is the *unmeṣa* of a blue object. *Sphurita-nīla-pūrva-pīta-āvabhāsana-viśrānti-ātmakanimeṣa-rūpā sarvasya svasaṁvitsiddhā*, and that very state is the *nimeṣa* of what you had seen before, e.g., that *pīta*, that yellow, that yellowish object. First you had seen a yellowish object, now you want to see . . .

JOHN: A blue object.

SWAMIJI: . . . a blue object. You give rise to a blue object (*unmeṣa*), and that rise of a blue object is the *nimeṣa* of the yellowish object, which you have already seen. So, in the daily routine of life, these two factors work simultaneously. And everybody knows that (*sarvasya svasaṁvit siddhā*, everybody knows this).

api ca . . .

---

is found [in one] who is limited and at the same time unlimited also. That is the fullness of God consciousness, the fullness of God consciousness where nothing is excluded. Whatever is excluded, it is also one with That. That is the fullness of God consciousness." *Parātrīśikā Vivaraṇa* (LJA archives).

170 The color blue (*nīla*) is often used in Shaivite philosophy as an example of an object of perception.

There is one more point to be discussed.

Audio 5 - 09:16

... iyaṁ didṛkṣābhūmiḥ nīlasya idantāvabhāsanāsūtraṇa-svabhāvonmeṣarūpāpi, tadaiva tasyaiva parameśvarābhinnasvabhāvanimeṣa-paramārthāpi,...

There is another point in this cycle of the daily routine of life to be noted. That is, when you see that *nīla* (bluish object), when you want to see a bluish object, that is the rise of a bluish object. You give rise to a bluish object and simultaneously you give the previous [object], which you have perceived previously (that yellowish object), that is dissolved, you destroy it.

Not only this.

At the same time, *tadaiva tasyaiva parameśvara-ābhinna svabhāva nimeṣa paramārthāpi*, at the same time, another third cycle also is vividly seen subsided in dissolution, and that third object is Parameśvara, Parameśvara *bhāva*, the state of God consciousness. The state of God consciousness is subsided also. It is not only [that the] state of the yellowish object is subsided, it is the dissolution of the yellowish object, . . .

What is the dissolution of the [yellowish object]?

JOHN: Seeing the blue object.

SWAMIJI: When you see a bluish object.

. . . not only the dissolution of the yellowish object, it is the dissolution of God consciousness also at the same time. Because, when you are engrossed in the outward cycle of the world, God consciousness is subsided always. It does not mean that God consciousness is subsided and [therefore] God consciousness is not existing. It is existing in a subsided form.

DENISE: In an undifferentiated way, isn't it?

ERNIE: Where?

SWAMIJI: Everywhere! Everywhere[171] It is in a subsided state.

JOHN: So, It is not seen just like the yellow is not seen.

---

171 In the field of differentiation.

SWAMIJI: No (affirmative). It is *sūkṣma* (*sūkṣma*, subtle), in the background. God consciousness is in the background, rising and dissolving.

JOHN: He said, "God consciousness is seen here". Is he trying to show this proof also that God consciousness weaves these states altogether, or he is not saying that?

SWAMIJI: That will be seen further, later on.

ERNIE: Was It there when the yellow object was there? You said that when you see the blue, then that third is also, that God consciousness is also, destroyed.

SWAMIJI: Yes.

ERNIE: Was It there when it was only yellow?

SWAMIJI: No, It was not there also.

ERNIE: It wasn't there also.

SWAMIJI: No.

ERNIE: So then how can It be destroyed . . . ?

SWAMIJI: In the daily routine of life, It is subsided.

ERNIE: No, but then he makes the point of when you make it blue, then that is destroyed.

SWAMIJI: When you [perceive] blue, God consciousness is subsided. When you [perceive] yellow, God consciousness is subsided. God consciousness is also existing there in a subsided form.

GANJOO: In the background.

SWAMIJI: In the background, but in a subsided state. You understand?

DENISE: Yes.

SWAMIJI: It is there.

Vastutastu māyāpade'pi . . . in fact, if we go to the depth of this theory, *vastutastu māyāpade'pi*, in the daily routine of life, in the worldly routine of life, . . .

Audio 5 - 12:41

. . . māyāpade'pi nimeṣonmeṣapalakṣitasarvaśakti vilolatārūpā iyaṁ parā vimarśabhūmireva sarvadā sarvasya sphurantyapi māyādaśāyāṁ na nirūḍhiṁ lambhayati saṁvidaṁ svātmani, . . .

Bas, this point is to be noted here. In reality, *māyāpade'pi*, in the daily routine of life, *nimeṣa unmeṣa upalakṣita sarva śakti vilola rūpā*, one [perception] is *nimeṣa*, one is in a subsided form, one is in dissolution . . .

JOHN: Dissolved state.

SWAMIJI: . . . dissolved state, and one has risen[172], . . .

ERNIE: Yellow and blue.

SWAMIJI: Yellow and blue.

. . . but that *iyaṁ parā vimarśa bhūmireva*, this supreme state of God consciousness, *sarvadā sarvasya sphuranti*, although It is in the background alive, although the supreme state of God consciousness is in the background alive in both these states of rise and dissolution, but *māyādaśāyāṁ na nirūḍhiṁ lambhyati saṁvidaṁ svātmani*, but, in the daily routine in the activity of the world, this [God consciousness] is not held, This is not known. Although It is existing, It is not known, It is dissolved.

Audio 5 - 14:06

tatrāpi madhye madhye prakaṭībhavati / yatsvarūpa ābhijñānāya sphuṭayiṣyati [not recited]

Tatrāpi, in the daily routine of life also–another important point is in the daily routine of life also–sometime, sometime, at some points, you will see the rise of God consciousness alive there.

Yatsvarūpa ābhijñānāya sphuṭayiṣyati, this *svarūpa*[173] [of God consciousness] is clarified in this *śloka* of the *Spanda Kārikā*:

atikruddhaḥ . . . . / [174]

When you are extremely angry, filled with anger, [or] when you are extremely filled with excitement of sexual desire, [or] when you are extremely filled with fear–as you have already been explained that–in those states, God consciousness is alive. It is in Its . . .

---

172 *Unmeṣa*.

173 The self-form or nature.

174 *Spanda Kārikā* 1.22, page 35.

ERNIE: Seed form?

SWAMIJI: No. It is *unmeṣa*.

JOHN: Expanded form or . . .

SWAMIJI: No, *unmeṣa*. It has risen there, It is not subsided. Although It is subsided always [in the field of differentiated perception], but sometimes . . .

GANJOO: It rises.

SWAMIJI: . . . It rises at times, in the daily routine of life also. When you sleep, and sleep has not yet come–this wakefulness, the state of wakefulness is ending [but] sleep has not yet come–in that gap, It rises. So, that God consciousness is not [absent, It] is alive everywhere.

JOHN: But That also is hidden, isn't it? Like in that gap, . . .

SWAMIJI: Yes.

JOHN: . . . isn't that hidden by *tirodhāna śakti*[175]?

SWAMIJI: Yes, that is quite true, but . . .

Audio 5 - 15:41

. . . . *prabuddhaḥ syādanāvṛtaḥ* / /[176]

One who is alert, he can experience that state in the daily routine of life also.

JOHN: So it is only hidden for that person who is not alert. *Tirodhāna śakti* works for . . .

SWAMIJI: Who is not alert, yes.

ityantaṁ śloka catuṣṭayam /

These four *ślokas* explain the same point there in the *Spanda* [*Kārikā*].[177]

---

175 Lord Śiva's concealing energy as opposed to His *anugraha śakti* (revealing energy).

176 *Spanda Kārikā* 1.25, page 41.

177 The four *ślokas* are *Spanda Kārikā* 1.22 to 1.25, pages 35-41.

Audio 5 - 16:01

paraśaktipātaprakāśadhvastamāyāvaraṇasya tu śivapadāvāptau karālambanaṁ dadatyeva paraṁ pūrṇatayā sarvadā na parisphurati /

Paraśakti-prakāśa-dhvasta māyāvarṇasya, that blessed soul whose veil of *māyā*, the veil of illusion, has been removed by supreme *śaktipāta*[178], for that person, *śivapadāvāptau*, to hold the state of *śivapada*[179] in these states, at these points, . . . Which points?

ERNIE: Joy, anger.

SWAMIJI: Joy, anger, . . .

JOHN: Great fear.

SWAMIJI: . . . threat, fear . . .

ERNIE: Sleep, the gap.

SWAMIJI: Everything.

. . . so, *karālambhanaṁ dadhatyeva*; *karālambhanaṁ*, that energy shakes hands with that person who is blessed with *śaktipāta*.

ERNIE: Who has the veil of . . .

SWAMIJI: Who has removed the . . . whose veil of ignorance is removed by *śaktipāta*. At that time, that state shakes hands with that person. So, She appears [at] that [time]. That state of God consciousness appears to him.

yadvakṣyati . . .

[Vasugupta] will explain this later on in the *Spanda* [*Kārikā*], . . .

yadā kṣobhaḥ pralīyeta [*tadā syātparamaṁ padam*] //[180]
[not recited in full]

. . . *yadā kṣobhaḥ pralīyeta*, when agitation is over, there is

178 Grace.

179 The abode (*pada*) of Śiva. *Śivapadāvāptau*, *śivapada*, the state of Śiva, is *avāpta*, held or achieved.

180 *Spanda Kārikā* 1.9, page 13.

paramaṁ pada[181], the supreme God consciousness is still there. It is just a veil that makes you keep away from that God consciousness. Otherwise, It is there.

. . . . *jānāti ca karoti ca* / /[182]

He knows everything, he does everything.[183]

tathā[184] *"jāgradādi"* . . . [1.3] *ityārabhya "tadasti parmārthataḥ"* / [1.5]

In wakefulness, in the dreaming state, [and] in the dreamless state, that God consciousness exists. It is explained in these *ślokas* of the *Spanda* [*Kārikā*].[185]

tathāhi – . . .
It will be clarified again more:

Audio 5 - 18:12

. . . *yadā prathamāyāḥ śivātmanaḥ sāmarasyabhūmeḥ pūrṇāhantātma-sāmarasyāvasthitaṁ viśvaṁ yadi na bhavati avidyamānaṁ kathaṁ sṛjyeta*, . . .

Sāmarasya bhūmeḥ is that state of God consciousness where the whole cycle of one hundred and eighteen worlds exists. The whole cycle of one hundred and eighteen worlds exists in that God consciousness, but in *sāmarasya*[186], [just] as the peacock's feathers, the various colors of feathers, exists in the water of an egg of a peacock. It exists, but in *sāmarasya*, in oneness.

JOHN: Sameness.

SWAMIJI: In sameness. It is *sāmarasya*, it is not vividly

---

181 The supreme abode.
182 *Spanda Kārikā* 1.10, page 14.
183 "And that perfect knowledge and perfect action will appear then, when you are introverted in your own nature." *Spanda Kārikā* 1.10.
184 So, in this way . . .
185 *Spanda Kārikā* 1.3 and 1.5, pages 4 to 7.
186 Lit., having equal feelings.

seen there. But when it comes out, it is seen. In the same way, . . .

JOHN: "*Sāmarasya*" means?

SWAMIJI: *Sāmarasya* means, . . .

JOHN: Same flavor?

SWAMIJI: No. *Sāmarasya* means, one with oneness. For instance, you put water in water–it is *sāmarasya*. You can't find out that cup of water in the ocean then.

GANJOO: (Inaudible)

SWAMIJI: Oneness. That is *sāmarasya*. So in that *sāmarasya* state [of God consciousness], the whole cycle of one hundred and eighteen worlds exists.

Prathamāyāḥ śivātmanaḥ sāmarasyabhūmeḥ pūrṇāhanta-ātma-sāmarasyāvasthitam, and it is, the one hundred and eighteen worlds are, one with God consciousness there, existing, in that supreme state of . . .

ERNIE: *Sāmarasa*.

SWAMIJI: . . . *sāmarasa*.

If It would not have been existing there, [then] how this whole cycle of one hundred and eighteen worlds would have come into manifestation afterwards? It has come into manifestation only [because] it was there. It has come out from that God consciousness in the cycle of manifestation. So, you must know that it is existing in That un-manifested state. What?

ERNIE: The world.

SWAMIJI: This cycle of . . .

ERNIE: One hundred and eighteen worlds.

JOHN: Everything.

SWAMIJI: Everything is There.

Audio 5 - 20:19

nīlādidṛkṣārūpā tuṭipātāparaparyāyā daśā uditā, . . .

Now, *nīlādidṛkṣārūpā*, when you want to see a blue object, [when] you are just going to see a blue object, that is *didṛkṣā*, the state of . . . just, it is the tendency . . .

JOHN: Just about to see.

SWAMIJI: Just about to see. You have not seen it yet, but you want to see it. You are going to see it in the next moment. At that first moment, at that first moment, what exists? That is what he explains here.

JOHN: The first moment, just before you . . .

SWAMIJI: Just before you want to see this blue object, that is *tuṭipāta*, that is a *tuṭi*, that is one *tuṭi* of God consciousness. There you find the state of God consciousness visible.

JOHN: Why does he call it a "*tuṭi*"? Two and a quarter finger spaces. Why does he say it's a "*tuṭi*"? Just to show it's a small bit or a . . . ?

SWAMIJI: Just a . . .

JOHN: Poetic?

SWAMIJI: . . . fraction, . . .

JOHN: Just a little bit.

SWAMIJI: . . . a fraction of a whole, a fraction of one big body.[187]

Tuṭipātāparaparyāyā daśā uditā, It is rising there, It has risen there.

Audio 5 - 21:42

tadā nīlamātrāpekṣayā ahantācchāditedantāsūtraṇarūpā tāvatī sadāśiveśvaratā ucyate /

And *nīlamātrāpekṣayā*, *nīlamātrā*, [the blue object], which you have to see now in the next moment, taking that in view, taking that seeing in your view, *ahantācchādita idantā sūtraṇarūpā*, that *nīlatā*[188] is subsided, *nīlatā* is dissolved in that state, [in] that previous state of a *tuṭi*, and that [*tuṭi*] is

---

187 In his *Tantrāloka*, Abhinavagupta uses the word "*tuṭi*" to describe the fractional movements of breath: "*Tuṭi* means, time, time which is taken by the movement of breath in two fingers spaces and one fourth of a finger space. That much time is called a *tuṭi*." (*Tantrāloka*, 6.64) In this instance, however, *tuṭi* refers to the initial fraction of time in the span of a perception.

188 The blue object or any given object of perception.

sadāśiva-īśvara daśā, that is *ahaṁ-idaṁ* and *idaṁ-ahaṁ*.[189] You will find the rise of *ahaṁ-idaṁ* or *idaṁ-ahaṁ*. It is the rise of *sadāśiva* or the rise of *īśvara* in the first moment. The next moment you will feel . . .

ERNIE: Blue.

SWAMIJI: . . . blue, the blue object. The first moment you will feel the blue object as one with Lord Śiva. That is *idaṁ-ahaṁ*, that is *īśvara*. Or you will feel that blue object, in the first moment, in 'I-ness in this-ness'.

JOHN: *Ahaṁ-idaṁ*.

SWAMIJI: *Ahaṁ-idaṁ* (*sadāśiva*). These two states are found. So, these two states, the rise of these two states, is the stoppage of going to [the perception of] *nīla*. And when you go to [the perception of] *nīla*, this is the dissolution of these two states, *sadāśiva* and *īśvara*. When it is in the *unmeṣa* state, [when] *sadāśiva* and *īśvara* is the *unmeṣa* state, then seeing *nīla* (the blue object) is in the *nimeṣa* state. When the blue object is in the *unmeṣa* state, the state of *sadāśiva* and *īśvara* is in . . .

JOHN: *Nimeṣa*.

SWAMIJI: . . . *nimeṣa*.

ERNIE: So, that happens then with every new experience, every new perception?

SWAMIJI: Every new experience, it is going on. This cycle is going on in each and every human being although he does not know, he is not aware of it.

JOHN: So, everytime . . .

SWAMIJI: Everytime.

---

189 The words *ahaṁ idam*, "I am this universe", express the experience in *sadāśiva* [*tattva*]. The words *idam aham* signify, "this universe is not separate from myself." This is the perception in the state of *īśvara* [*tattva*]. The words *aham aham idam idam* mean, "though this universe seems separate actually this universe is not separated from me." This is the experience in the state of *śuddhavidyā* [*tattva*]." *Self Realization in Kashmir Shaivism, Entrance Into the Supreme Reality*, Kṣhemarāja's *Parāprāveśikā*, 3.61

JOHN: If I look at this microphone and then I look at [something else], that happened.

SWAMIJI: Yes.

JOHN: Between each thought also.

SWAMIJI: Between each thought also, *aham̐-idam̐* and *idam̐-aham̐* . . .

JOHN: So this is that gap that we must catch?

SWAMIJI: . . . will be the gap, yes. That gap is to be . . .

ERNIE: It's the glue of this universe, then.

SWAMIJI: Yes.

ANDY: Are *īśvara* and *sadāśiva* the same?

SWAMIJI: *Īśvara* and *sadāśiva* is just . . . 'this-ness' first[190] is *īśvara*, 'this-ness' afterwards is *sadāśiva*.[191]

Audio 5 - 24:27

tadaiva saiva ca pūrṇāhantātmasāmarasyāvasthita-viśvāpekṣayā śivatāpi, . . .

And in that state of *sadāśiva* and *īśvara*, in that, when *pūrṇāhantā*[192] comes, [he experiences] *ahameva*[193]. When *sadāśiva*, at the state of *sadāśiva*, you go inside and see the cycle of *unmeṣa* and *nimeṣa* also, . . .

When you go [inside] from this outside cycle (*nīla*–when you find *nīla*, this is the utmost outside cycle), the inner cycle is the state of *sadāśiva* and *īśvara* (*aham̐-idam̐* and *idam̐-aham̐* is the inner cycle), the the innermost cycle is *aham̐*[194] (that is the state of Śiva).

---

190 Before 'I-ness'.

191 See Appendix 11 for a list of the thirty six elements (*tattvas*).

192 "When the supreme Creative Energy is directed towards Her internal nature (*svarūpā*), where all movement ends, She there relishes Her true state – the fullness of I-Consciousness (*pūrṇahantā*) completely filled with God Consciousness. Then that I-Consciousness is diluted in consciousness-of-this, and consciousness-of-this is diluted in I-Consciousness." Self Realization in Kashmir Shaivism – *Kuṇḍalinī Vijñāna Rahasyam*, 5.113.

193 That is the state of "I" (*aham̐*) alone (*eva*).

194 I-ness.

. . . and when *ahaṁ-idaṁ* is rising, the rise of *ahaṁ-idaṁ* is the dissolution of *ahaṁ*, [and] the rise of *idaṁ-ahaṁ* is the dissolution of *ahaṁ*. When *ahaṁ*, the supreme *ahaṁ*, only *ahaṁ*, the embodiment of *ahaṁ*, rises, that is the destruction of *sadāśiva* and *īśvara–sadāśiva* and *īśvara* exist no more. So [the instruction] is, you have to go deep in the inner cycle also and find the *unmeṣa* and *nimeṣa* working ahead also in . . .

JOHN: It works on all levels.

SWAMIJI: In all levels. In the external flow also and the internal flow also, the *unmeṣa* and *nimeṣa* are working.

ERNIE: So, but what was the middle one?

SWAMIJI: What is middle?

ERNIE: The one in-between.

SWAMIJI: *Sadāśiva* and *īśvara*.

JOHN: You mean, the gap?

ERNIE: No, no, I thought there are three. There was the . . .

SWAMIJI: There was blue.

ERNIE: Blue, and there is the *ahaṁ*.

SWAMIJI: *Ahaṁ* is the supreme. The gap is *sadāśiva* and *īśvara* (*ahaṁ-idaṁ*, *idaṁ-ahaṁ*)–that is the center.

Audio 5 - 26:22

yadi tu[195] *anyā sadāśivaprakāśātmatayā nāvasthitā syāt kathaṁ uttarakālaṁ sṛjyeta cidrūpavyatirekeṇa anyasya sraṣṭṭatvānupapatteḥ* /

Yadi tu anyā sadāśiva prakāśa ātmatayā na āvasthitā syāt. This *sadāśiva* and *īśvara*, if *sadāśiva* and *īśvara* would not have come out from that supreme *ahaṁ* (only I-consciousness), [then] how would it have existed in the center? The central state [i.e., the fullness] of God consciousness is also existing when It is pushed from that supreme state of oneness (I-consciousness, *ahaṁ*). *Kathaṁ uttarakālaṁ sṛjyeta*, how could it be created if it were not existing in that I-ness, I-consciousness? Because *cidrūpa vyatirekeṇa anyasya sraṣṭṭatvānupapatteḥ*, nothing can be "created", only the creation is

195 Swamiji says "*tu*" but the text reads "*hi*". Both convey the same meaning.

attributed to *cidrūpa*, only consciousness, God consciousness. God consciousness has become coagulated.[196] It is half-coagulated in *sadāśiva* and *īśvara*, and fully coagulated in the blue object (it is fully coagulated), and it is un-coagulated in the state of . . .

JOHN: *Ahaṁ*.

SWAMIJI: . . . *ahaṁ*, Śiva.[197]

Audio 5 - 27:52

pramāpitaṁ ca etat pratyabhijñāyām [not recited]
cidātmaiva hi devo'ntaḥ sthitamicchāvaśādbahiḥ /
yogīva nirūpādānamarthajātaṁ prakāśayet[198] / /[199]

Just like a *yogi*, the acting of a *yogi* is just like the acting of Śiva. Śiva acts just as a *yogi* acts. *Cidātmaiva*, *cidātma* (Śiva, God consciousness, filled with consciousness) is *antaḥ sthitaṁ icchāvaśādbahiḥ arthajātam*, this whole cycle of one hundred and eighteen worlds is existing in Lord Śiva, in *cidātmā*, in God consciousness, and by His sweet will of the energy of *svātantrya śakti*, He pushes it out, outside His consciousness, in one hundred and eighteen worlds just like a *yogi* does (*yogīva*, just like a *yogi* does), without any outside gathering of substances.

[If] you have to construct this house, you want an outside gathering of substances, e.g., you want stones, you want

---

196 "God consciousness has been coagulated in these varieties of forms and shapes and time." Swami Lakshmajoo, *Special Verses on Practice* (LJA archive), verse 8.

"[God consciousness] takes the coagulated formation of one [thing] and the negation of all other things." *Parātrīṁśikā Laghvṛtti* (LJA archive).

197 "What do you mean by "coagulation"? When you understand that, "I am the universe", your understanding is not coagulated. When you understand, e.g., "I am somebody's wife and I have got two children", your understanding is coagulated, [it is] frozen in some limited cycle. When you experience that, "I am everything. All ladies are my wives, all ladies are my daughters, all ladies are my sisters"–finished! Where lies the difference? So your *bodha*, your understanding, is unlimited, divine." *Parātrīśikā Vivaraṇa* (LJA archive).

198 Swamiji says "*prakāśate*" where the text reads "*prakāśayet*".

199 Utpaladeva's *Īśvarapratyabhijñā Kārikā*, 1.5.7.

cement, you want workers. But this is not the case with Lord Śiva. [When] Lord Śiva creates this universe, He pushes this universe of one hundred and eighteen worlds outside His consciousness without the gathering of these . . .

ERNIE: Not dependent.

SWAMIJI: . . . substances. [He is] not dependent.[200]

JOHN: So how is that like a *yogi*?

SWAMIJI: Just like a *yogi*. A *yogi* also creates this universe [according to] his choice, with his choice, without any gathering [of external substances]. A *yogi* is just like Śiva.

ERNIE: So then it is possible that [the *yogi*'s] house would not be dependent on the rocks coming in the truck or the cement. He would just . . . and it would be there.

SWAMIJI: *Bas*, it will appear, it will appear at once.

iti ihāpi vakṣyati

In this *Spanda śāstra* also it will be said:

Audio 5 - 29:55

yatra sthitamidaṁ sarvaṁ[201] *kāryaṁ yasmācca*

---

200 "All of the thirty-six elements, from Śiva to earth, are created by that natural I-Consciousness. And not only are they created by that Consciousness, they also shine in that Consciousness. His creation is not outside of His nature, it exists in His own Self. He has created this whole universe in the cycle of His Consciousness. So, everything that exists resides in that Consciousness.

This must be your understanding. The creative energy which is attributed to Lord Śiva is not that energy of Lord Śiva that creates the universe outside of His Consciousness as we create outside of our consciousness. His creation is not insentient (*jaḍa*) as our creations are. This universe, which is created in His Consciousness, is dependent on that Consciousness. It is always dependent on that Consciousness. It cannot move outside of that Consciousness. It exists only when it is residing in His Consciousness. This is the way the creation of His universe takes place. *Self Realization in Kashmir Shaivism*, *Parāprāveśikā* (Entrance into the Supreme Reality) of Kṣhemarāja, 3.57.

201 Swamiji says "*viśvam*" but text has "*sarvam*".

nirgatam /[202]

"In which this whole universe exists and from which this whole universe comes out in manifestation . . ."[203]

DENISE: Swamiji, is it like, you know, we can imagine what the house is going to be like when it is finished, that's . . .

ERNIE: In a way, . . .

DENISE: . . . in one way, it's producing . . .

SWAMIJI: Yes.

ERNIE: . . . the idea of . . .

DENISE: . . . by mind.

SWAMIJI: It is in your idea, yes.

DENISE: But outwardly I can't do it (laughter).

SWAMIJI: Yes. *Bas*, we will do only this much.

Audio 5 - 30:27 / Audio 6 - 00:00

[*iti / te ca ete śivatā*] *sadāśiveśvarate parasparavyāptyā avasthite ekarūpe eva /*

So, this way, *śiva*, *sadāśiva*, and *īśvara*, these three elements, . . .*

Śiva indicates the *parāmarśa*[204] of *ahaṁ* (pure I-consciousness), *sadāśiva* [is the *parāmarśa* of] I-consciousness in this-consciousness, and *īśvara* [is the *parāmarśa* of] this-consciousness in I-consciousness.

You understand?

Pure I-consciousness is attributed to Śiva, and I-consciousness in this-consciousness is attributed to *sadāśiva*, and this-consciousness in I-consciousness is attributed to *īśvara*.

*. . . so these three elements, *paraspara vyāptyā*, they are one with each other, they are not separate from each other–these three elements. *Avasthite*, although they exist in three ways, *ekarūpe eva*, they are one.

---

202 *Spanda Kārikā* 1.2, page 2.

203 See the *Spanda Kārikā* 1.1 for a complete translation.

204 Reflection or awareness.

Audio 6 - 01:01

yadā tadā iti hi upadeśyāpekṣyā vāci kramo'yaṁ, na vastuni /

Sometimes you find these three-fold elements as three, three aspects of being, but it is just to make your disciple understand what really *śivatā* is, what *sadāśivatā* is, and what *īśvaratā* is. In fact, these are one.[205] It is just to make your disciples understand. For that understanding purpose, for the purpose of understanding, you . . .

JOHN: Differentiate these.

SWAMIJI: . . . differentiate these into three. They are one. *Na vastuni*, [they are] not [differentiated] in the background; in the background, they are one.

ata eva yugapadeva īyaṁ saṁvit sraṣṭrī ca saṁhartrī ca iti sakramābhāsā, . . .

So simultaneously, this God consciousness is in Its creative field (is established in the creative field) and the destructive field. In the creative field It is just like *unmeṣa*. In the destructive field It is *nimeṣa*. And *unmeṣa* and *nimeṣa* (creation and destruction) is *sakramābhāsā*, is [appearing] successively.

DEVOTEE: They look successive.

---

205 "Śiva has taken five formations of His pure nature, the pure nature of God consciousness. The first formation and supreme one is *śiva*, and the second is *śakti*, the third is *sadāśiva*, the fourth is *īśvara*, and the fifth is *śuddhavidyā*. *Śiva ādi śuddhavidyāntaṁ*, just right from *śiva* up to *śuddhavidya*, *yat śivasya svakaṁ vapuḥ*, these are the formations of Śiva Himself without any distinction. There is no distinction of *bheda* (duality) there. *Śiva* is filled with God consciousness, *śakti* is filled with God consciousness, *sadāśiva* is filled with God consciousness, *īśvara* is filled with God consciousness, and *śuddhavidya* is filled with God consciousness. God consciousness is already full in these five states. So hence, these five states are Śiva's own states, [His] own pure states." *Tantrāloka* 6.41 (LJA archive). For a further explanation of the *śuddha tattva*s (pure elements), see *Kashmir Shaivism–Secret Supreme*, 1.1-9.

Audio 6 - 02:33

SWAMIJI:

asraṣṭṭasaṁhartṛrūpā śudhāhantāprakāśamayī akramāpi [*ityalam*] /

Asraṣṭṭarūpā, when they remain in their own aspects, in their own state, then *śuddhāhantā prakāśamayī*, there you find pure *prakāśa* in these three elements. So, in that purity, it is *akrama*, it is without [succession], it is a simultaneous understanding for these three elements.

Let [us] stop this topic because . . .

upadeśadhanā evaṁ enāṁ bhūmiṁ cinvate [*iti*] /

. . . those who have the treasure of *upadeśa*[206], the treasure of *guru krama* (*guru krama* are those who have understood the reality of this secret from their master), only they can understand this.

In this *Spanda* [*Kārikā*] also (*ihāpi ca*, in this *Spanda* [*Kārikā*] also), in this *sūtra* and in these other *sūtra*s, the same point is discussed. *Didṛkṣayeva sarvārthān* . . . this *sūtra* is first:

Audio 6 - 03:41

didṛkṣayeva sarvārthānyadā vyāpyāvatiṣṭhate /
tadā kiṁ bahunoktena svayamevāvabhotsyate //*SpK 3.11*//

When a *sādhaka*[207] wants to learn what the collectiveness of the thirty-six elements are, what is the background of these thirty-six elements, and he pervades all of these thirty-six elements and finds that these thirty-six elements, the pervasion of these thirty-six elements, is pervaded by one Being only.

And another *sūtra* is:

---

206 Instruction, teaching, initiation.

207 Aspirant.

tamadhiṣṭhātṛbhāvena svabhāvamavalokayan /
smayamāna ivāste yastasyeyaṁ kusṛtiḥ kutaḥ //SpK 1.11//

That person, that *sādhaka*, who understands the nature of that supreme Being as the beholder (or as not that [state which] is held)–one [state] is held, one [state] is the beholder who holds–when you remain in the state of holding, not [in the state of] being held, [when you remain] in the state of subjective consciousness, not in the state of objective consciousness, then you will find your own nature (*svabhāvam avalokayan*) and you are just *smayamāna ivāste yaḥ*, you become wonderstruck in your own nature. *Tasyeyam*, for that person, there is no question of *saṁsāra*, there is no question of bondage or entanglement in the wheel of repeated births and deaths.

ityatra ca yameva upadeśārthaḥ /

This is what is taught by the *Spanda sūtras*. And in these *ślokas* also you will find *guruṇāmayameva āśyaḥ*, masters have this very object to be explained:

Audio 6 - 05:59

sadā sṛṣṭivinodanāya . . . . /[208]

He is always in a creative mood, *sadā sthiti*, He is always in a protective state, and He is always in a destructive state. You can't say that when He creates the world [that] He is not destroying this universe–He is destroying the universe. [You can't say that] when He is destroying the universe [that] He is not protecting the universe–He is protecting also at the same time. At the same time He creates, at the same time, at the moment of creation, He protects, [and] at the moment of protection, He destroys. What He destroys, what He creates, and what He protects, it will be explained later on. But He has not to create anything other than His own nature. He has not to destroy and He has not to protect [anything] other than His own nature. He destroys Himself, He protects Himself, He

208 *sadā sṛṣṭivinodanāya sadā sthitisukhāsine / sadā tribhuvanāhāratṛptāya svāmine namaḥ* / / Utpaladeva's *Śivastotrāvalī*, 20.9.

creates Himself.

pratikṣaṇam-aviśrāntaḥ . . . . /[209]

Every moment He is *aviśrāntaḥ*, He is not exhausted in creating, protecting, and destroying this universe of His own nature.

prākāmyamātmani yadā . . . . /[210]

When the freedom of the will[211] you perceive in your own nature, then you find everything, all of these three aspects, solved. The three aspects of creation, protection, and destruction are solved totally. This is the understanding of our masters.

Asti ca āgamaḥ, for this, *Tantra* also says:

Audio 6 - 07:33

lelihānā sadā devī sadā pūrṇā ca bhāsate /
ūrmireṣā vibodhābdheḥ śaktiricchātmikā prabhoḥ //[212]

"O Pārvatī,"–this is *Tantra*; Śiva addresses [His] better half, Pārvatī–"*lelihānā sadā devī*, this God consciousness is always in the state of tasting."

ERNIE: Of being enjoyed.

SWAMIJI: No. *Lelihānā*, She is destroying this whole universe.[213] She dissolves this whole universe in Her own nature, and when She dissolves [this universe in Her own nature], *sadā pūrṇā ca bhāsate*, She is always full. This whole cycle of the universe is existing in Her own nature, always,

---

209 *pratikṣaṇamaviśrāntastrailokyaṃ kalpanāśataiḥ* / Abhinavagupta quotes this verse in his *Īśvarapratyabhijñāvivṛtivimarśinī*, as being from Śri Bhaṭṭanārāyaṇa's *Stava Cintāmaṇi*, verse 112.

210 This verse is also quoted by Abhinavagupta in his *Īśvarapratyabhijñāvimarśinī*.

211 *Svātantrya śakti*. See Appendix 2 for an explanation of *svātantrya śakti*.

212 Abhinavagupta's quotes a similar verse in his *Īśvarapratyabhijñā Vivṛtti Vimarśinī*. The source is not known.

213 *Leilihānā* literally means, frequently licking or darting out the tongue.

because She dissolves that whole universe in Her own nature.

Ūrmireṣa vibhodhābdhe, and then whenever it comes out, it comes [out] just like a tide from the ocean. When a tide comes, [then] one hundred and eighteen worlds are created. This is one tide of that supreme ocean of God consciousness. In one tide you feel the existence of one hundred and eighteen worlds. In the next, when this tide is over, you find that fullness of [Her] nature–all of those one hundred and eighteen worlds are residing in Her own nature.

So, it is the energy of His free will–that is nothing. It is only the drama of the energy of His free will.[214]

What?

Creation, destruction, and protection.

JOHN: This first line of this *Tantra* was that, "She is always tasting"?

SWAMIJI: "Tasting" is dissolving this whole universe in Her own nature.

JOHN: Eating this world.

SWAMIJI: Yes . . . not "eating". Eating is when there is something much to eat. Before Her it is nothing, it is just a drop of water to take it inside. What "drop of water"? One hundred and eighteen worlds.

JOHN: And, at the same time She is taking it, She is always full also.

SWAMIJI: Yes.

JOHN: Or She gets filled with that. Does it mean that She is always full? She gets filled or She is always full?

SWAMIJI: No, She is full by this, by tasting.

JOHN: By tasting this world, She becomes full of that.

SWAMIJI: Yes.

JOHN: Then that's universal consciousness . . .

SWAMIJI: [When the universe] sprouts out, She becomes a bit weaker.

JOHN: "Weaker" means?

SWAMIJI: Huh?

---

214 *Svātantrya śakti*.

JOHN: "Weaker" means what?

SWAMIJI: The universe is outside now. But it [only] seems so. Actually, that outside universe also exists in Her own nature.

JOHN: This is speaking about existing in Śakti's nature here.

SWAMIJI: Yes.

JOHN: Why does he not say "Śiva's nature"?

SWAMIJI: No, Śiva is residing in Śakti. From Śakti, from that supreme energy, Śiva sprouts out, and then His Śakti sprouts out. The supreme *śakti* of *svātantrya śakti*–first.

JOHN: First.

SWAMIJI: First is the existence of *svātantrya śakti*, then is the existence of Śiva, then His Śakti. But the *svātantrya śakti* is the chief point from which these both sprout–Śiva and Śakti.

ERNIE: But this is just like I-ness and this-ness. There is no difference really. It's only for . . .

SWAMIJI: No, there is no difference. It is only one element.

JOHN: This is the thirty-sixth, the thirty-seventh *tattva* we are talking about.

SWAMIJI: No, the thirty-seventh and the thirty-eighth.

JOHN: Both, because when you go to one, you go to the other.

SWAMIJI: Yes. When the thirty-seventh [*tattva*] is perceived, that is Śakti, then Śiva will be the thirty-eighth. When the thirty-eighth is perceived, then the thirty-eighth will be Śakti and the thirty-seventh will be Śiva.[215] Śiva and Śakti are . . .

---

215 "As you find in the *Tantrāloka* also, when the thirty-sixth element is perceived, the reality of that thirty-sixth element will move to the thirty-seventh. And when the thirty-seventh also is perceived, the reality of the thirty-seventh element will move to the thirty-eighth element. When that thirty-eighth element is also perceived, that reality of thirty-eighth element will move down to thirty-seventh. It won't come in your clutches of perceiving." *Tantrāloka* 3.141 (LJA archive).

ERNIE: Inseparable.

SWAMIJI: . . . in fact, these are one.

JOHN: So, this Śiva and Śakti that we have in these thirty-six *tattva*s is really . . .

SWAMIJI: Involved.

JOHN: . . . it is only for explanation.

SWAMIJI: Yes.

JOHN: This is evolved Śiva and Śakti. So, this Pārvatī and Lord Śiva here are those lower Śiva and Śakti.

SWAMIJI: Yes.

JOHN: And he is talking about supreme . . .

SWAMIJI: Supreme, yes.

JOHN: . . . Paramaśiva.

SWAMIJI: Yes.

Audio 6 - 11:57

iti / evamiyam ekaiva avibhāgā vimarśabhū[miḥ] unmeṣanimeṣmayī unmeṣanimeṣaśabdābhyām-abhidhīyate /

So this way, this is only one *avibhāgā*[216], undifferentiated *vimarśa bhūmiḥ*, the state of *vimarśa.*[217] The state of supreme I-consciousness, this undifferentiated state, *unmeṣa nimeṣa mayī*, it is the state of rising and, at the same time, it is the state of dissolution.

JOHN: Simultaneously.

SWAMIJI: Simultaneously (*yugapat*). *Unmeṣa nimeṣa śabdābhyāmabhidhīyate*, so, from one point of view you can call it *unmeṣa* (rise), from another point of view you can call it dissolution (*nimeṣa*).

JOHN: So, when creation is happening, destruction is happening at the same time.

SWAMIJI: At the same time, yes. It is not after creation

---

216 No separation, no distinction.

217 Self-awareness. "*Spanda* is *vimarśa*". Swami Lakshmanjoo, trans., *Dehasthadevatacakrastotram* (LJA archive).

[that] destruction will take place–it is not like that. In creation, destruction is existing; in destruction, creation is existing. In rise, dissolution is existing; in dissolution, rise is existing.

JOHN: So, when a bud of a flower becomes a flower, that bud is really destroyed. That is the destroying we are talking about here.

SWAMIJI: Yes.

JOHN: Whatever state there was before is destroyed for causing that other . . .

SWAMIJI:

Audio 6 - 13:16

tataśca unmeṣau ca nimeṣau ca iti vigṛhya unmeṣasya nimeṣamayasya, nimeṣasya ca unmeṣamayasya, prādhānya -itaratāvibhaktasya dharaṇyādi-sadāśivāntaṁ jagat prati pralayodayahetutvaṁ vyākhyātavyam /

So, this way you should explain this *unmeṣa* and *nimeṣa*, [in] which way [that] I will tell you.

Unmeṣau ca nimeṣau ca, these are two, nominate these *unmeṣa* and *nimeṣa* in two, in the dual, not in the singular form.

JOHN: Dual form.

SWAMIJI: *Unmeṣau*. "*Unmeṣau*" means, *unmeṣa* and *nimeṣa*. "*Nimeṣau*" means two, *nimeṣa* and *unmeṣa* both. When you utter the word "*unmeṣa*" [in the dual form], *nimeṣa* is there. When you utter the word ["*nimeṣa*" in the dual form, *unmeṣa* is there].

JOHN: You see, in English, we only have singular and plural. But in Sanskrit, there is a dual form also . . .

SWAMIJI: Yes.

JOHN: . . . which is two. Singular, dual, and plural.

SWAMIJI: Singular, dual, and plural.

ERNIE: And that plural for *nimeṣa* is?

SWAMIJI: No, not plural. It is dual.

ERNIE: Dual.

SWAMIJI: Siva and Sakti.

ERNIE: Dual for *nimeṣa* is? "*Nimeṣo*".[218]

SWAMIJI: *Nimeṣa* and *unmeṣa*. When you utter "*unmeṣa*", the word "*unmeṣa*" [in the dual form], it means, *unmeṣa* and *nimeṣa*. When you utter the word "*nimeṣa*" (dissolution) [in the dual form], it means, dissolution and rise both.

ERNIE: But you said it a different way.

JOHN: Yes, you said [it in] Sanskrit, "*unmeṣo*" or something, in the dual form. What is the dual form of *unmeṣa*?

Audio 6 - 14:46

SWAMIJI: *Unmeṣau. John ca Ernie ca = Johnernieyau.* John and Ernie means, *John-and-Ernieyau* in Sanskrit. [The grammatical ending] '*au*' is the formation of duality, two. *Rāmaśca Kṛṣṇaśca = Rāmakṛṣṇau. Devadattaśca Dhanañjayaśca = Devadattadhanañjayau.* This is the grammatical rule for two.

JOHN: So, they speak of Śiva that way also?

SWAMIJI: *Unmeṣau* and *nimeṣau. Śivaśca śaktiśca = śivaśaktī. Śaktiśca Śivaśca = śaktiśivau.*

ERNIE: So, when you say "*nimeṣo*"[219], you mean both.

SWAMIJI: You mean both, *nimeṣa* and *unmeṣa*.

JOHN: Does that same thing go with, apply with, Śakti and Śiva? When you mean Śakti, you always mean Śiva at the same time?

SWAMIJI: Yes.

Unmeṣau ca nimeṣau ca vigṛhya, so, you should explain this *unmeṣa* and *nimeṣa* in the dual form. When you have to say "*unmeṣa*", don't say one *unmeṣa*, say it in the dual form: *unmeṣaśca nimeṣaca = unmeṣanimeṣau*. And "*unmeṣau*" will touch this.

JOHN: Carry the philosophical meaning.

SWAMIJI: Those both, these both (*unmeṣau ca nimeṣau ca*). So, in [saying] "*unmeṣa*", you must say "*unmeṣau*", in the dual form; "*nimeṣa*" you must say in the dual form: "*nimeṣau ca*".

218 That is, "*nimeṣau*".
219 That is, "*nimeṣau*".

So, *unmeṣasya nimeṣamayasya*, it means, whenever there is *unmeṣa*, there is *nimeṣa* there; whenever there is *nimeṣa* (dissolution), there is *unmeṣa* there. Both are existing there.

JOHN: Can we translate these words, almost literally, as "being" and "becoming"?

Audio 6 - 16:41

SWAMIJI: No, no.

JOHN: Not *unmeṣa* and *nimeṣa*?

SWAMIJI: No, no, no. "Being" and "becoming", they'll remain in two aspects. [*Unmeṣa* and *nimeṣa*] are not two aspects.

JOHN: But you also taught that Paṇḍitjī from Aurobindo's ashram that there is being and becoming.

SWAMIJI: But that was another subject. This is another subject. This is the theory of oneness in universality.

JOHN: Because you had taught him that being and becoming are that one . . .

SWAMIJI: Yes.

ERNIE: But this *nimeṣa* is rising and *unmeṣa* is . . .

SWAMIJI: Being is Śiva, becoming is Śakti. Yes?[220]

ERNIE: This is rising and falling, *unmeṣa* and *nimeṣa*.

SWAMIJI: "Rising and falling" not. Rising and dissolving.

ERNIE: Dissolution.

JOHN: But this is also universality in individuality, is it?

SWAMIJI: Huh?

JOHN: *Nimeṣa* and *unmeṣa* are universality and . . .

SWAMIJI: . . . individuality existing in both, in both. So, . . . Is it raining?

DENISE: No.

SWAMIJI: . . . *unmeṣasya nimeṣamayasya*, *unmeṣa* is always with *nimeṣa*; *nimeṣasya ca unmeṣamayasya*, *nimeṣa* is always with *unmeṣa*. So, *prādhānya itara avibhaktasya*, so the difference is only when you say "*unmeṣa*" [in the singular

---

220 Swamiji is responding to Ernie's question.

form], you must understand [that] *unmeṣa* is in predominance there and *nimeṣa* is in a subsided state. And when you say "*nimeṣa*" [in the singular form], by saying "*nimeṣa*" you must understand that *nimeṣa* is in predominance and *unmeṣa* is in a subsided state. So, that is *prādhānya* and *itara*; *prādhanya* is "in predominance", *itara* is "in subsided form".

So, in this way, *dharaṇyādi sadāśivāntaṁ jagat*, this whole universe existing in thirty-six elements, right from *pṛthvī* to *sadāśiva*, *pralayodaya hetutvam*, *unmeṣa* and *nimeṣa* is *pralayodaya hetutvam*, it is attributed to *pralaya* and *udaya*–*unmeṣa* and *nimeṣa*. *Pralaya* means [*nimeṣa*], "dissolution, destruction"; *unmeṣa* means [*udaya*], "rise, creation".

Audio 6 - 18:47

evaṁ ca pralayau ca, udayau ca iti vigṛhya pralayodayau iti vyākhyeyam /

So, *pralayau ca*, "*yasyonmeṣanimeṣābhyām jagataḥ pralaya-udayau*", by whose *unmeṣa* and *nimeṣa*, the universe finds its rise and dissolution (*pralaya* and *udaya*, destruction and [rise]), it is being created and destroyed.

So, in *pralaya* (*pralaya* means *nimeṣa*), when you say "*nimeṣa*", it is the *nimeṣa* of one thing (from one viewpoint of Śiva, it is *pralaya*), and from another point of view of Śiva, it is *unmeṣa*. When this [unmanifested] state of Śiva is destroyed–that is the destruction of, dissolution of, Śiva *bhāva*, the state of Śiva–the [unmanifested] state of Śiva is destroyed and the state of Śiva, universal Śiva, is created at the same time. So, It gets Its rise, Śiva gets Its rise in Its manifested form. When you say "unmanifested Śiva is destroyed", it means, manifested Śiva is created. When you say "manifested Śiva is destroyed", it means, unmanifested Śiva is created. So this way you should [understand *unmeṣa* and *nimeṣa*].

JOHN: So, which one of these is transcendental Śiva and [which] one is immanent?

SWAMIJI: Both, both are transcendental. They are one with each other.

tathāhi – . . .

I'll[221] clear it again more.

ERNIE: (laughter)

SWAMIJI:

Audio 6 - 20:54

. . . nīlādeḥ yo bahirūpatāyā udayaḥ sa eva ahantārūpatāyāḥ pralayaḥ, . . .

Suppose you perceive some object. This pot is here or this blue pot is here. You perceive this blue pot. For instance, you perceive this blue [pot] in front of you. So, *nīlādeḥ yaḥ bahirūpatāyāḥ udayaḥ*, so it rises, this perception of the blue pot rises. When the perception of the blue pot takes place [or] when the perception of this white handkerchief takes place, . . .

JOHN: In your mind.

SWAMIJI: No, when you see it, you see [that] it is a handkerchief.

. . . *nīlādeḥ yo bahirūpatāyāḥ udayaḥ*, it rises from outside. *Sa eva ahantārūpatāyāḥ pralayaḥ*–how did you know that this is a handkerchief?–the root of the perception of the handkerchief was lying in your super-consciousness, in your mind. When you feel this outside, [that] this is a handkerchief, it means the internal handkerchief, which was in your super-consciousness, it is destroyed, it is subsided, it is gone.

ERNIE: Which is destroyed?

SWAMIJI: The internal handkerchief.

ERNIE: The inside handkerchief.

SWAMIJI: Yes, inside . . .

GANJOO: Actually, one's conception.

DENISE: That is the universal manifestation inside of a handkerchief?

SWAMIJI: For instance, you know me. Do you know me? You go home and you won't see me there. Where is that? Where is Swamiji in your consciousness? It is inside your consciousness. That is the internal world. I have gone in the internal world of your consciousness there.

---

221 Kṣhemarāja.

ERNIE: You are here. I am there.

SWAMIJI: Yes. But you know me. I am existing in your brain.

ERNIE: If I talk with you with John . . .

SWAMIJI: I am existing in your brain. So, I am existing there in your internal consciousness. Whenever you see me here, you come and see me here, where is that [internal] Swamiji then? It is in the outside consciousness of yours. That is *bahirūpa*. So, when *bahirūpa*, when you find me outside, the internal [form] is dissolved. When the external [form] is dissolved, the internal [form] gets rise. This is what he says.

So, *unmeṣa* and *nimeṣa* is working on both sides. One *unmeṣa* for this [handkerchief], *nimeṣa* for another handkerchief; *unmeṣa* for this handkerchief, *nimeṣa* for this [other handkerchief], then it is nowhere existing, it is subsided. In the same way, *unmeṣa* and *nimeṣa* is explained in this *Spanda Sandoha*.

Audio 6 - 23:51

BRUCE H: What if you have never seen a handkerchief before?

SWAMIJI: Huh?

BRUCE H: What if this is the first handkerchief you ever saw?

SWAMIJI: But, a handkerchief you have seen.

BRUCE H: No, for a small child, he's never seen.

SWAMIJI: No, it is in super-consciousness.

BRUCE H: So, it is not "handkerchief"?

SWAMIJI: No, it is in super-consciousness. It is also existing there.

BRUCE H: For example, when Ernie . . .

SWAMIJI: For instance, when you teach him [that] this is a handkerchief, then he knows it is a handkerchief.

ERNIE: Like Viresh. This is the first time he is . . .

SWAMIJI: How can he know that this is a handkerchief [if] this handkerchief does not come out from his inner consciousness? It is all there, but in a subsided state in children.

BRUCE H: So, before Ernie met you, did you exist in his internal consciousness?

SWAMIJI: Yes, internal consciousness, yes.

BRUCE H: Still? Before?

SWAMIJI: Yes.

DENISE: Before hearing about you, you existed?

SWAMIJI: No, not even hearing also.

ERNIE: Even someone in Africa who has never met you or does not know where Kashmir is.

SWAMIJI: But you know that. You know that in your . . .

ERNIE: He knows a handkerchief. He knows . . .

SWAMIJI: He knows everything.

JOHN: Everything is contained in that universal state.

SWAMIJI: Yes, everything is there.

DENISE: So, nothing's new.

SWAMIJI: Nothing is new.

ERNIE: So really, I know everything then.

SWAMIJI: You are *sarvajña*[222]. It is why we call the individual as universal. This is the background of this *unmeṣa* and *nimeṣa spanda*.

ERNIE: God, I wish I could remember all of it.

DEVOTEES: (laughter)

SWAMIJI: *Nīlādeḥ yo bahirūpatāyāḥ udayaḥ*, so, when blue objects, blue or yellow objects, exist in the external state, *yo bahirūpatāyāḥ udayaḥ sa eva ahantārūpatāyāḥ pralayaḥ*, that means [that the object] is destroyed in your internal consciousness.

> *evaṁ yo bahirūpatāyāḥ pralayaḥ sa eva ahantārūpatāyā udayaḥ*

When an external object existing in the external side, the external world, is destroyed, *sa eva ahantārūpatāyā udayaḥ*, this means it has risen in internal consciousness. But it won't be [completely] destroyed at all. If you destroy it here, it will

222 All-knowing.

go in your consciousness. If you destroy it in your consciousness, this [object], it will come out here. It will never be destroyed. So, *udayaḥ* and *pralaya* are working simultaneously–rise and dissolution.

iti pralayo'pi udayarūpaḥ; udayo'pi pralayarūpaḥ.

So, when you say "dissolution", it means "rise"; when you say "rise", it means "dissolution"–both.

Audio 6 - 26:33

bhedābhedaprādhānyetaratākṛtastu atra vivekaḥ /

But differentiation rises only when you find something in predominance [and] something in a subsided form. In predominance, if it is the rise [of a form], an external rise, [then] it is [its] external rise and . . .

ERNIE: Subsided is internal?

SWAMIJI: . . . [its] subsided internal dissolution. When predominant is the internal rise, it is subsided . . .

ERNIE: . . . externally.

SWAMIJI: [It is its external] dissolution. It happens like this.

ERNIE: So they both exist at the same time.

SWAMIJI:

> *vastutaḥ cidātmaiva tathā bhāti [iti] akramataiva atra ityuktam* /

In fact, this is the drama of one's own consciousness, that consciousness of God consciousness, which is playing inside and outside.

Samāsaśca ithameva upapannaḥ, so, this *samāsa*[223] (*samāsa* is the combination of *unmeṣa* and *nimeṣa*), you must explain the combination of *unmeṣa* and *nimeṣa* like this: When you say "*unmeṣa*", you must say "*unmeṣa* and *nimeṣa*"; when you say "*nimeṣa*", you must say "*nimeṣa* and *unmeṣa*"–both. Both are existing in one.

---

223 A grammatical compound.

Audio 6 - 28:03

tathā ca dvanda samāse bhāṣyam

This is the *bhāṣya*[224] of Patañjali, in grammar also, while explaining the theory of *dvanda samāsa. Dvanda samāsa* [is used] when you have to explain two [nouns].[225] When you have to explain Rāma and Kṛṣṇa [together], e.g., "Rāma and Kṛṣṇa are going", [then] *rāmaśca kṛṣṇaśca* [becomes] *rāmakṛṣṇau*, [and you say], *"Rāmakṛṣṇau gacchataḥ"*. This is how we explain "Rāma and Kṛṣṇa are going": *Rāmakṛṣṇau gacchataḥ*. You put it in the dual form.

JOHN: Dual form.

SWAMIJI: *Gacchataḥ* is also [the conjugated] verb for two, not the verb for one, not the verb for three–*gacchataḥ*. *Gacchati, gacchataḥ, gacchanti.*[226] I think you should hold a class for a short period–a Sanskrit class.

DENISE: For us?

SWAMIJI: Yes, you will learn.

ERNIE: (laughter)

SWAMIJI: *Tathā ca dvanda samāse bhāṣyam*. This is the *bhāṣya*. *Bhāṣya* means, [a commentary]. Patañjali has commentated upon Pāṇini's grammar. Patañjali, you know Patañjali? Patañjali is the producer of the *yoga darśana*, the producer of grammar, and the producer of herbs, medicines.

Audio 6 - 29:29

yogena cittasya padena vācā /
malaṁ śarīrasya tu vaidikena
yo'pākarottaṁ pravaraṁ munīnām
patañjalirprāñjalirānato'smīm //[227] [not recited in full]

---

224 An explanatory work, exposition, explanation, commentary.

225 A *dvandva* compound (*samāsa*) is only comprised of nouns and each noun is equally important.

226 Singular, dual, and plural, respectively.

227 This verse does not appear in the original text of the *Spanda Sandoha*. This verse, which Swamiji recites from memory, is the invocation, which appears in the 11th century *Bhojavṛtti* (*Rāja-mārtaṇḍavṛtti*), King Bhojadeva's commentary on Patañjali's *Yoga*

He has produced in this world, he has produced three aspects of important factors. *Yoga–yoga* is the first aspect which he has produced. Who?

JOHN: Patañjali.

SWAMIJI: Patañjali. *Yogena cittasya*, by this producing of *yoga*, he wants to destroy the dirt in your mind. The dirt in your mind is destroyed by that *yoga*[228], by his production of *yoga*.

ERNIE: This is not the *āsanas*[229]. This is not . . . you are talking [about] philosophy.

SWAMIJI: No. It is meditation, meditation–*yoga*.

JOHN: *Yoga darśana*.

SWAMIJI: By *yoga darśana* he wants to destroy the impurity of the mind (*yogena cittasya*). *Padena vācā*, by grammar[230], when he produces grammar, when he has produced grammar, by grammar he wants to destroy the impurity of your speech, [by which] your speech becomes pure, you talk correctly. *Yogena cittasya, padena vācā, malam śarīrasya*, and he wants to destroy the impurity of your system of the body by *vaidikena*, by herbs[231]. So he has produced these three aspects in this universe–Patañjali. He was a great *yogi* and also a philosopher and a grammarian.

ERNIE: And doctor.

SWAMIJI: Doctor also.

DEVOTEES: (laughter)

SWAMIJI:

Audio 6 - 31:06

yadi nirdarśayituṁ buddhiḥ evaṁ /
nirdarśayitavyaṁ dhavau ca khadirau ca // [not recited]

Sūtras.

228 The last of the six traditional Hindu *darśanas*, or philosophical systems, the *yoga darśana* is codified in Patañjali's *Yoga Sūtras*.

229 Yoga postures.

230 Patañjali's *Mahābhāṣya* a commentary on Pāṇini's *Aṣṭādhyāyi* on Sanskrit grammar.

231 Patañjali has also been accredited with a treatise on the science of Ayurveda (*Carakapratisaṁskṛtaḥ*). This text is now lost.

Yadi nirdarśayituṁ buddhiḥ, if you want to make your clearance in your intellect . . .*

These are his words in . . .

ERNIE: Patañjali.

SWAMIJI: Patañjali's words in the *bhāṣya*, in [his] commentary of [Pāṇini's] grammar. These are his words.

*. . . if you want to clear your intellect in fullness, then *nidarśayitavyaṁ dhavau ca khadirau ca*, then you must feel it [like] *dhavau ca khadirau ca.*

Dhavau. "Dhavau" is in the dual form. *Dhavaḥ, dhavau, dhavāḥ; khadiraḥ, khadirau, khadirāḥ.*[232] Khadira is [an edible] plant which is very sour. Dhavau is . . . it is also [an edible plant, but] not sour, it is hot. *Dhavau ca khadirau ca.* When you say "*dhavau*", in the dual, it means, *dhavaśca khadiraśca = dhavau.* [Or], *khadiraśca dhavaśca = khadirau.*

JOHN: One includes the other.

Audio 6 - 32:23

SWAMIJI: So, if you say only "*dhavau*". . . . Dhava is the name of one plant, not two plants. Dhava and khadira, these are two plants. *Dhava* and *khadira* are two plants existing in this universe. *Dhava* is one plant and *khadira* is another plant. And if you want to indicate both, you can just make "*dhava*" in the dual–"*dhavau*". What is the meaning of *dhavau? Dhava* and *khadira.* And if you want [to include *dhava*] in *khadira* also (khadira is another plant), [say] "*khadirau*". If you put *khadirau* (in the dual form), it means *dhavaśca khadiraśca*[233]; *khadiraśca dhavaśca = khadirau.*

JOHN: But you have to indicate this earlier in the sentence, which are which.

SWAMIJI: And, at the same time, in our Shaivism also, if we want to say, "Śiva and Śakti", there is no need to say, "*śiva śakti*" [or] "*śakti śivau*"–there is no need. [Just say], "*śivau*", *bas.* "*Śivau*" means Śiva and Śakti. "*Śivau*", if you put "*śiva*", this word, in the dual form, it means Śiva and Śakti. It will consume Śakti also.

---

232 Singular, dual, and plural, respectively.

233 *Dhava* and *khadira.*

ERNIE: Can you say "*śaktyau*"?

SWAMIJI: No.

ERNIE: You can't say that.

JOHN: No dual form for "*śakti*"?

SWAMIJI: *Śaktī*, *śaktī*[234]. If you say "*śaktī*" . . .

ERNIE: *Śaktī*.

SWAMIJI: "*Śaktī*" is the dual form [of "*śakti*"]. Because "*śakti*" [ends in] '*i*', so for '*i*', the dual form will be '*ī*'–"*śaktī*". And '*a*', when it ends in '*a*' ("*śiva*" ends in '*a*'), for this '*a*', the dual form is '*au*'–"*śivau*". For "*śakti*", the dual form is "*śaktī*". When you say "*śaktī*", it means Śakti and Śiva. When you say "*śivau*", it means Śiva and Śakti.

This way you must say "*unmeṣa* and *nimeṣa*". When you say "rise", it means "dissolution" also. Two rises when you say "rise" in the dual–"*unmeṣau*".

Audio 6 - 34:37

What is "*unmeṣau*"?

JOHN: *Unmeṣa* and *nimeṣa.*

SWAMIJI: *Unmeṣaśca nimeṣaśca = unmeṣau.*

It is not only this kind of grammar that is existing in Pāṇini's system. "*Unmeṣanimeṣau*", this is also one way of explaining *unmeṣa* and *nimeṣa*. You [can combine] both words in the dual–"*unmeṣanimeṣau*". "*Unmeṣanimeṣau*" means, *unmeṣa* and *nimeṣa*.

Not only this!

"*Unmeṣau*" will do! "*Unmeṣau*", put only one word in the dual form [and] it will collect both–"*unmeṣau*". *Śaktiśivau*; "*śaktiśivau*" means, Śakti and Śiva. *Śivau*; "*śivau*" also means, Śiva and Śakti. This is the ruling and regulation of grammar also in both ways. So, in this second way, you must produce, you must explain, this *unmeṣa-nimeṣa*. Not *unmeṣa* separately and *nimeṣa* separately, [but rather] *unmeṣa* in *nimeṣa*, *nimeṣa* in *unmeṣa*. For instance, you say, "*unmeṣau*". What do you understand from "*unmeṣau*"?

DENISE: *Nimeṣa* and *unmeṣa*.

---

234 That is, with a long '*ī*'.

SWAMIJI: *Unmeṣa*. No, *unmeṣa* and *nimeṣa*.

DENISE: *Unmeṣa and nimeṣa*.

DEVOTEE: *Unmeṣa* in predominance.

SWAMIJI: When I say "*nimeṣau*"?

DENISE: *Nimeṣa* and *unmeṣa*.

SWAMIJI: . . . and *unmeṣa*. So, this way. When you say, "*śivaśaktī*", [it means], Śakti and Śiva. "*Śivaśaktī*" [means], Śiva and Śakti.

DENISE: "*Śivau*"?

SWAMIJI: "*Śivau*" [means], Śiva and Śakti, both. In both ways, they explain the same thing.

So, *unmeṣa* and *nimeṣa*, if you say separatedly "*unmeṣa*" and "*nimeṣa*", it will be *unmeṣa* and *nimeṣa* [separatedly]. If you say collectively only one word in the dual form, "*unmeṣau*", it means, *unmeṣa* and *nimeṣa*. "*Nimeṣau*" [means], *nimeṣa* and *unmeṣa*. This way.

ityādi / ihaiva ca svatantra-śivādvaya-darśane ekaikasya arthasya anekatvaṁ saṁgacchate /

In this philosophy, our philosophy, of *svātantryavāda*[235] (that is, Shaivism), *advaita darśana* (this monistic thought), *ekaikasya api arthasya*, even one object will collect, will [include], *anekatvam*, all objects. If you say only one object, it will contact this whole universal object.[236]

Audio 6 - 37:18

anyatra hi pratiniyatarūpā bhāvāḥ ityeko'pi dvyarthaḥ, aparo'pi dvyarthaḥ, iti kā saṁgatiḥ ityalaṁ aprakṛtena /

Anyatra hi, in other schools of thought, *pratiniyatarūpā bhāvāḥ*, they conclude that it is only one [object], e.g., when you say "handkerchief", it is only a handkerchief, it won't [include] other things. [According to Shaivism], when you say

---

235 The Doctrine (*vāda*) of Freedom (*svātantrya*).

236 *Sarvasarvātmakā bhāva*: "Everything resides in everything; in the cycle of God consciousness, everything is in everything." *Parātrīśikā Vivaraṇa* (LJA archive).

"handkerchief", the rise of a handkerchief is the dissolution of this [other object], the dissolution of this, the dissolution of this, the dissolution of this; the dissolution of one hundred and eighteen worlds and the rise of a handkerchief. So, the whole lot of one hundred and eighteen worlds is attached to [a single object] in a subsided [form].

ERNIE: In the dissolution aspect.

SWAMIJI: So, in one object, one main object, you will find the attached adjustment of all the universal objects.

ERNIE: But other schools hold . . .

SWAMIJI: Other schools hold that, when you say "this", "this" is only this [particular object].

ERNIE: No dissolution.

SWAMIJI: No dissolution. Now, this dissolution, they do not recognize dissolution as attached to this [created object].

ERNIE: They see only creation. It is only being created.

SWAMIJI: Yes. [They say:] when [an object] is only being created, it is [only] created, and it is not attached, it is not adjusted, to its dissolution. They think like that. But it is not the real . . .

JOHN: So they think that when you create something, . . .

SWAMIJI: . . . real understanding.

JOHN: . . . they don't realize you destroy everything else.

SWAMIJI: They don't realize [that the] destruction of everything else is there existing. Destruction is existing. When destruction is existing, creation is existing. The creation of this [particular object] is existing with this: the destruction of all the one hundred and eighteen worlds is existing. This is the theory of *unmeṣa* and *nimeṣa* here in [the theory of] *spanda*.

Audio 6 - 39:35 / Audio 7 - 00:00

[evaṁ ca] vyākhyāte satī yat pañca-vidha-kṛtya-kāritvaṁ-śrīsvacchandādi-śāstreṣu parameśvarasya ucyate tadapi svīkṛtam /

In this way as we have commentated [upon] the reality of

spanda, *yat pañcavidha-kṛtyakāritvam*, in the *Svacchanda Tantra*, the *pañcavidhakṛtyakāritvaṁ*, the fivefold activities of Lord Śiva[237], which is explained in the *Svacchanda śāstra*, is also admitted, is also agreed [upon] here, in this exposition of *Spanda*.

tathā ca – . . .

That will be cleared now.

Audio 7 - 00:53

. . . *bhedā-sūtraṇa-tadullāsena-rūpeṇa unmeṣeṇa kiṁcitsvarūpa-nimeṣamayena śuddhāśuddharūpā dvividhā ṣadadhvanaḥ sṛṣṭiḥ* /

The creation of these *ṣaḍ* (six) *adhvans*[238] takes place by this *unmeṣa* and *nimeṣa*. *Bhedāsūtreṇa tad-ullāsana-rūpeṇa unmeṣeṇa*; *bhedāsūtraṇa*, when *bheda* (differentiatedness) is created and [when] differentiatedness is expanded (*ullāsana rūpeṇa*), that is *unmeṣa*. And *kiṁcit-svarūpa-nimeṣamayena*, and when, at the same time, when differentiatedness is created, the undifferentiated state of being of God consciousness is closed, gets in the state of *nimeṣa*. The exposition of the differentiated state is, in other words, the *nimeṣa* of God consciousness.

JOACHIM: If I perceive it, you know, if I say, "I see this creation", when I say "I", this is already *nimeṣa* and the creation is *unmeṣa*. It is like this, isn't it?

SWAMIJI: This also. But, when it is created, when differentiatedness is created, [when] *dvaita*[239] is created,

---

237 The fivefold acts of Lord Śiva are creation (*sṛṣṭi*), protection (*sthiti*), destruction (*saṁhāra*), concealing (*pidhāna* or *tirodhāna*), and revealing (*anugraha*).

238 The six pathways (*adhvans*) of the world are the three objective paths (circles, elements, and worlds) and the three subjective paths (letters, words, and sentences). For a complete explanation of the *adhvans*, see *Kashmir Shaivism–The Secret Supreme*, The Sixfold Path of the Universe, *Ṣaḍadhvan*, 2.11.

239 Duality, i.e., differentiatedness.

advaita[240] is lost.

Śuddhāśuddharūpā dvividhā ṣad adhvanaḥ sṛṣti. So, at the same time, simultaneously, the creation of the six *adhvans* takes place in a pure way and in an impure way. The pure way is the undifferentiated way and the impure way is the differentiated way. These two take place simultaneously. So, *unmeṣa* and *nimeṣa* exist at the same time, at the same period.

Audio 7 - 02:59

evaṁ dvividha-bhedanimeṣeṇa kiñcid-abheda-spṛgūrdhvomeṣaṇa rūpeṇa saṁhāraḥ /

Dvividha-bheda-nimeṣeṇa, when this two-way differentiatedness is locked, takes the state of *nimeṣa*, the two differentiated states, . . .

What are the differentiated states? The creation of differentiatedness and the expansion of differentiatedness.

. . . when these two are locked inside, when these two get [their] end (that is *dvidhabheda nimeṣeṇa*), at that very time, *kiñcit-abheda-spṛk-ūrdha-unmeṣaṇa-rūpeṇa*; *kiñcit abheda spṛk*, there is the tendency of going inside *abheda* (undifferentiated-ness). When differentiatedness is locked, undifferentiatedness sprouts out.

JOHN: Sprouts out.

SWAMIJI: That is *saṁhāra*[241]. *Saṁhāra* of what? *Saṁhāra* of differentiatedness. And, at the same time, it is the creation of undifferentiatedness.

Audio 7 - 04:18

tathā unmeṣanimiṣābhyāṁ lolībhūtābhyām

So, this way, *unmeṣa* and *nimeṣa* is *lolībhūtām*. It is just like in this . . .

JOACHIM: Bathing. Floating or bathing.

SWAMIJI: What is that?

---

240 Non-duality, i.e., un-differentiatedness.

241 Destruction.

JOACHIM: Like a wave.

DENISE: Swinging.

SWAMIJI: Swinging, swinging. It is swinging *unmeṣa* and *nimeṣa*, *unmeṣa* and *nimeṣa*–both are functioning at the same time. *Unmeṣa nimeṣabhyāṁ lolībhūtābhyāṁ*, so it is *lolībhūtābhyāṁ*, it is just like swinging with each other. Here is *unmeṣa* and again there is *nimeṣa*.

Audio 7 - 04:58

ābhāsanānābhāsana-prasara-paramārthā sthitiḥ /

So this is *sthiti*[242]: *ābhāsana* and *anābhāsana*, the appearance of differentiatedness [and the] disappearance of undifferentiatedness, in-between it is *sthiti*.

JOHN: "*Sthiti*" means here? "In-between" means when neither have risen?

SWAMIJI: No, in the junction, in the center.

JOHN: In the junction, when the swing is in the middle.

SWAMIJI: Yes. That is *sthiti*, that is *sthiti*. *Ābhāsana anābhāsana prasara paramārthā sthitiḥ*. So, the reality of *sthiti* is, it gives a push and a pull to both. It gives a push to what?

JOHN: To both sides.

SWAMIJI: No. To one side a push and another side a pull–*sthiti*.

JOHN: Each way, though. Each way.

SWAMIJI: Each way.

JOACHIM: Yes, but it remains stable by this, you know, *sthiti*.

DENISE: It pushes it up and pulls it back.

SWAMIJI: Yes.

DENISE: And pulls it back and . . .

SWAMIJI: And pushes it up, yes.

JOHN: So where does this *sthiti* exist in the swing? In the middle of the swing or in the . . . ?

---

242 Lit., maintenance, preservation, or establishment.

SWAMIJI: In the middle of the swing.

JOACHIM: It's stable.

BRUCE H: What does that mean, Swamiji?

SWAMIJI: Huh?

BRUCE H: *Sthiti*.

SWAMIJI: There is *sthiti*, this is *sthiti*, this is the stableness.

JOACHIM: Stability.

SWAMIJI: *Lolībhūtā* . . . this is said in this verse:

'. . . . . *lolībhūtā parā sthitiḥ*' /[243]

The supreme state of consciousness is *lolībhūtā*, is just fond of creation and destruction.

iti siddhapādaiḥ / [not recited]

This is said by Siddhapāda. Siddhapāda is some ancient master. He was before Abhinavagupta.

Audio 7 - 06:51

tathā utpannsvarūponmeṣābhāsarūpo vastuto nirayādibhogamayo yaḥ pūrṇo nimeṣaḥ svasvarūpasya sa vilayaḥ /

Utpanna svasvarūpa unmeṣa ābhāsa rūpaḥ vastuto nirayādi bhogamayo yaḥ pūrṇo nimeṣaḥ. When God consciousness has risen, *utpanna svarūpa unmeṣa ābhāsa rūpaḥ*, risen and It is shining–when God consciousness has risen and It is shining in Its fullness–that is, in other words, *vastutaḥ*, in reality, *nirayādi bhogamayaḥ pūrṇo nimeṣaḥ*, [the *nimeṣa* of] going in hell. Going in hell, the state in which we go in hell, downwards, in darkness, absolute darkness, it is the *nimeṣa* of that. *Nimeṣa*, it is just . . .

243 The verse '*cakradvaye'ntaḥ kacati lolībhūtā parā sthitiḥ*' appears in Jayaratha's commentary on the first verse of abhinavagupta's *Tantrāloka*. As Swamiji points out, little is known about its author, Siddhapāda.

ERNIE: Reverse.

SWAMIJI: . . . closed. It is closed! It is closed totally!

DENISE: To anything dark or hellish.

SWAMIJI: Yes.

JOHN: Is closed to what?

SWAMIJI: *Niraya*, *naraka* (*naraka* means, this hell). Going to hell is finished. It is the *saṁhāra* of going to hell. The creation of God consciousness is the *saṁhāra* (destruction) of going to hell. So, the *unmeṣa* of God consciousness is the *nimeṣa* of hell.

Audio 7 - 08:29

sarvātmanā punaḥ yaḥ pūrṇaḥ unmeṣaḥ sa cāśeṣabheda-upaśamanāt-nirūpita-pūrvardhito nimeṣamayaḥ, so'nugrahaḥ . . .

Sarvātmanā punaḥ yaḥ pūrṇaḥ unmeṣaḥ, when totally you get the full exposition of God consciousness all-round, there is no question of the impression of going to hell [and] no question of [the impression of] the absence of going to hell. When the absence of going to hell is there, there is some impression of hell.

DENISE: If there is an apprehension that you may go to hell. Do you mean it like that?

SWAMIJI: No.

JOACHIM: No, no, the idea of hell is completely swept out somehow.

SWAMIJI: Yes, when the idea too is finished, that is *anugraha*, that is the grace of God (*so'anugrahaḥ*).

. . . iti parameśvarasya pañcavidhakṛtyakāritvaṁ anenaiva spṛṣṭam /

So, in this way, by *unmeṣa* and *nimeṣa*, the fivefold activities of God consciousness, the fivefold activities of the Lord, is proved.

ithaṁ pralayodayāvapi saṁgamanīyau /

In this way, *pralayaḥ* and *udayaḥ* (destruction and creation) also should be adjusted in the same way. When you destroy, you ignore creation. When you create, you ignore destruction.

pralayādikaṁ ca ābhāsyaniṣṭhaṁ ābhāsasārameva,. . .

It may be destruction, it is existing in God consciousness. It may be creation, it is existing in God consciousness. So it is *ābhāsa-paramārtha*, the basis of destruction and creation is based on *prakāśa*.[244]

na tu prakāśātmano asya parameśvarasya tat kiñcit /

In fact, the state of God, which is all-round *prakāśa*, It will never be *aprakāśa*, It can never be *aprakāśa*, It can never be concealed. In the state of concealment, in the state of *tirodhāna* also, It is existing there.

Yadvakṣyati[245]:

Audio 7 - 11:08

avasthāyugalaṁ cātra kārya-kartṛtvaśabditam /
kāryatā kṣayiṇī tatra kartṛtvaṁ punarakṣayam //SpK 1.14//

There are two states existing in this world: [*kāryatā*] and *kartṛtā*. *Kāryatā* means "action" and [*kartṛtā* means] "actor".

JOACHIM: Actor, yes.

SWAMIJI: The state of the actor and the state of the action. In these two sections, *kāryatā* (the action) is lost but the actor is still there. You know the actor, [the one] who acts, who does this action. The action is lost, [but] when the action is lost, you cannot say that the actor is also lost. For instance, I have created this universe. If the universe is finished, [if] the universe is destroyed, you can't say that the creator of the universe is also destroyed. He cannot be destroyed. *Kartṛtā* is always *akṣayam*[246] (*kartṛtvaḥ punar akṣayam*).

JOACHIM: That is, it starts with Śakti, the *kartṛtā* some-

244 The light of God consciousness.
245 This is explained (*yadvakṣyati*) in the *Spanda Kārikā*.
246 The actor (*kartṛtā*) is always imperishable (*akṣayam*).

how, because . . .

SWAMIJI: No, *kartṛtā*[247] is attributed to Śiva, *kāryatā*[248] is attributed to Śakti.

JOACHIM: Lord Śiva's *kartṛtā* is not due [to the fact] that He is *śaktimān*, that He has the *śakti*s that He (inaudible) . . .

SWAMIJI: Yes, He is indulging in *kāryatā. Kāryatā* is *śaktitā*, *kartṛtā* is *śivatā*. *Kartṛtā* remains always the same. Now, keep this state of Lord Śiva on one side. Take the state of the individual person.

ityantam / māyāpramātṛbhūmāvapi

That is the state of *māyā pramātṛ bhūmi. Māya pramātṛ bhūmi* is the state of individual God consciousness–individuality. *Māyā pra*[*mātṛ bhūmi*], in that state also, . . .

Audio 7 - 13:17

parameśvarasya prakāśātmanaḥ idaṁ pañca-vidha-kṛtya-kāritvaṁ sthitameva, . . .

. . . Parameśvara[249] indulges in the fivefold activities there also, in the individual state also, not only in the universal state. Parameśvara indulges in the fivefold activities in the universal state. Not only in the universal state, in the individual state also He indulges in the fivefold activities: *sṛṣṭi* (creation), protection (*sthiti*), destruction (*saṁhāra*), concealing (*tirodhāna*), and revealing (*anugraha*)–*idaṁ pañca-vidha-kṛtya-kāritvaṁ sthitameva*.

pūrṇaṁ tu tatsaṁbandhasāvadhānavijñānaśālisaṁcetyam /

But this kind of state of God, which is existing in both ways (in individuality and in universal ways), this activity of God is felt only by those who are *tat saṁbandha sāvadhāna vijñāna-*

---

247 Agency.

248 Action.

249 Lord Śiva.

śāli saṁcetyam, who are aware of that *saṁbandha*[250] of that activity, always–those *yogi*s. Those *yogi*s can feel the position of God in this way, that He is always indulging in the fivefold activities in the universal way and in the individual way also. This can be felt only by *yogi*s, not everybody.

JOACHIM: What is understood by "*yogi*s"? I always wanted to ask. Are those *sādhus* you see, for example, going to Amarnāth included in those *yogi*s? Because, with them, I do not believe that there is any activity in their mind.

DEVOTEES: (laughter)

SWAMIJI: (laughter) No, no, those are not *yogi*s, those are *bhogi*s[251].

JOACHIM: *Bhogi*s (laughter).

DEVOTEES: (laughter)

ERNIE: But [*yogi*s] can see both the universal and the individual.

SWAMIJI: . . . individual, yes.

ERNIE: But, do people who are not *yogi*s, can they see that also?

SWAMIJI: They can't feel [this kind of state of God].

ERNIE: Sometimes?

SWAMIJI: No, they can never feel [That]. They can feel [It] only at the time of the junction only.[252] Only for just a flash, a flash of one moment, when [they] go from wakefulness to dreaming state–there. But that point is not stable, that point does not exist for him.

ERNIE: So, that is the same point that stabilizes . . .

SWAMIJI: Yes.

Audio 7 - 15:52

evaṁ bhūtasya hi bhagavato nīlaprakāśādikāle nīlābhāse deśa-kālasaṁbhinne sraṣṭṭatā, deśakālākārāntara-saṁbhinna śaṁkāyāṁ saṁhāraḥ, prāksṛṣṭe nīlādyābhāsa-

250 Inherence, contact, association or connection.
251 Those who are attached to worldly enjoyments (*bhoga*).
252 Viz., the *prabuddha* (inferior) *yogi*.

sāmānye sthitihetutā, tatraiva abhedāṁśasarge vilayahetutā ityādi pītābhāsādāvapi yojyam /

For instance, take one object, say it is some blue object. *Evaṁ bhūtasya bhagavataḥ*, so when in the individual state and in the universal state, only God is existing, God is functioning, God is indulging in both ways–He indulges in the universal way and in the individual way–so, *nīla-prakāśa-ādikāle*, take the state of individuality, when this *nīla* (this blue object) is felt (*nīla-prakāśa-ādikāle*), *nīlābhāse deśa-kāla-saṁbhinne sraṣṭṭatā*, when this blue object is felt along with space, time, and form (along with its space, its time, and its form, this is felt), this means He creates this, He creates this blue object.

ERNIE: The individual.

SWAMIJI: This is the . . . huh?

ERNIE: The individual.

SWAMIJI: God.

ERNIE: God does.

Audio 7 - 17:35

SWAMIJI: God is the actor in both ways. It is admitted that God does this. In the individual way and in the universal way, in both ways, God is active.

So, this is the state of creation, the first act, when he experiences this blue object along with this space, time, and form. *Deśakāla ākārāntara saṁbhinna śaṁkāyāṁ saṁhāraḥ*, when your eyes move from this [blue object] to another object, [when] your eyes move from this blue object to another object, say another object, a pot, . . .

JOHN: A yellow pencil.

SWAMIJI: Yellow or anything.

JOACHIM: Anything (laughs).

SWAMIJI: . . . *deśakāla ākārāntara*, and that space, time, and form is something else; this is another space, time, and form of that object, for another object. *Saṁbhinna śaṁkāyāṁ saṁhāraḥ*, you feel that this [blue object] is destroyed. There, when you move your eyes from this [blue] object to another object, at that functioning of your consciousness towards another object, you destroy this [blue object]. So, the creation of this [other object] and the destruction of this [blue object] is proved.

JOACHIM: On a smaller level also taking place in the individual.

SWAMIJI: Yes, in the individual level. It is the individual level.

Prāksṛṣṭe nīlādi ābhāsa sāmānye sthitihetutā. Now, what is the *sthiti* of this? He has proved only the creation of this [other] object and the destruction of this [blue] object. What is the . . .

ERNIE: So there are fivefold acts.

SWAMIJI: No, where is the *sthiti* now?

GANJOO: Where is the central one.

SWAMIJI: The central one. Creation, protection (*sthiti*) . . . what is the protection? What is the protection of that? The protective act.

Audio 7 - 19:56

ERNIE: His memory?

SWAMIJI: No. That is what he says:

Prāksṛṣṭe nīlādi ābhāsa sāmānye sthiti-hetutā. Prāksṛṣṭe, [that] which is already created before, . . .*

Before what? Before this other object. When this other object is created, you destroy this [previous object]. When this [other object] is perceived, you create [it]. When another object is perceived, you destroy this [previous object] and you create this [other object]–you create this. This is the creation of this [other object], and that creation of this [other object] is the destruction for this previous object. And what is *sthiti*?

*. . . [its] *sthiti* is *prāksṛṣṭasya nīlādi ābhāsa sāmānye sthiti hetūtā*, the period in which way you were perceiving this [created object]. The period . . .

GANJOO: The intervening period.

SWAMIJI: . . . the intervening period in which you were perceiving this object, it is *sthiti*.

ERNIE: That's the protection.

SWAMIJI: That is the protection. And this is the creation; the creation of another object has . . .

JOHN: Destroyed this one.

SWAMIJI: No.

. . . has created the threefold acts of this previous object. The creation of another object has created the threefold acts of this [previous] object.

JOHN: How did it create threefold acts?

SWAMIJI: Creation, protection, and destruction.

JOHN: Yes, but they were always there before you saw that other object.

SWAMIJI: No, how can you destroy it if you don't move your eyes from [it]?

JOHN: But creation and preservation were there.

SWAMIJI: Creation was there, but creation was there [only] when [the previous] thing was destroyed.

ERNIE: So when . . .

SWAMIJI: No, it is in a chain, it is just like a chain . . .

ERNIE: When the transition is taking place . . .

Audio 7 - 21:51

SWAMIJI: No, you have not created it afresh. When you go to *nīla* (a blue object), prior to that, you were occupied with something else. So, the destruction of that [previous object] is the creation of this [blue object].

ERNIE: But then the preserving . . .

SWAMIJI: And creation of this . . . no, that period, that period . . .

ERNIE: That, your attention is on that . . .

SWAMIJI: Yes, as long as attention is towards only one object, that is its protection/ preservation.[253]

Tatraiva abhedāṁśasarge vilaya-hetūtā, when curiosity

253 In *sūtra* 11 of his *Pratyabhijñāhṛdayaṁ*, Kṣhemarāja equates *sthiti* with *rakti* (pleasingness or loveliness).

finishes, curiosity is lost, curiosity of perceiving this object, . . .*

DENISE: The next object.

SWAMIJI: Huh?

ERNIE: No, the one that you are watching?

SWAMIJI: No, when you have moved to another object, at that time, this is the destruction of this [previous object]. When you move to another object and, for some time, [after] some time, the curiosity is finished of going here and there.

*. . . when curiosity is finished, it is concealing, concealing this object. It is *vilaya*.[254] This is the fourth act of Lord Śiva. Creation, preservation, and destruction, and concealing.

JOACHIM: It is *tirodhāna*, concealing.

SWAMIJI: *Tirodhāna*. That is *tirodhāna* when curiosity is finished.

JOHN: Why is that?

SWAMIJI: Curiosity . . . e.g., this is specks[255]. "What is this? What is this? Oh, this is specks!" *Bas*, curiosity is finished. When curiosity is gone, it is *tirodhāna*, it is concealed. It is taken in that state where it does not exist.

Audio 7 - 23:53

ERNIE: But isn't the mind always jumping from one thing to the next?

SWAMIJI: Yes, it is fivefold. In fivefold ways, in fivefold ways it is moving. It is always moving. It is why it is *spanda*.

ERNIE: Yes, but then, isn't that jumping, curiosity? Where is it that . . . where do you have that rest from curiosity if the mind is always jumping?

---

254 Lit., dissolution, liquefaction, disappearance, death, destruction (esp. destruction of the world). When an object is destroyed and its differentiated impression remains in the *puryaṣṭaka* (mind, ego, intellect, and the *tanmātras*) of the perceiver, this leads to the fourth act of concealment. In his *Pratyabhijñāhṛdayam*, Kṣhemarāja describes this act of concealment as *vilaya* or "the setting of the seed" (*bījā-vasthāpana*).

255 Spectacles (eye-glasses).

SWAMIJI: No, when curiosity is finished, that is *vilaya*, . . .

ERNIE: No, but when does that happen?

SWAMIJI: . . . but the impression is there.

ERNIE: When does curiosity stop?

SWAMIJI: When you embrace your beloved, there is curiosity. At the first time, there is curiosity. When it is finished, curiosity is gone, then you are in *vilaya*, you reside in the state of *vilaya*.

ERNIE: Then I'm concealed.

SWAMIJI: When you eat delicious food and then no taste [for it] remains afterwards, you can't take [anymore and you say], "I am full, I am full". That is . . .

ERNIE: You are bored.

SWAMIJI: No, not bored. You can't take [any more]. You can't take even one drop afterwards. Can you take?

ERNIE: No.

SWAMIJI: You are full. That is *vilaya*, that is that state of *vilaya*. In the same way, *vilaya* takes place.

And then *anugraha*, the fifth-fold act of Lord Śiva, is to be [explained].

DENISE: Revealing.

SWAMIJI: Revealing. That is what he will say.

Tatraiva abhedāṁśasarge vilayahetutā, when *abhedāṁśasarge* (*abhedāṁśasarge* is "curiosity"), when curiosity is finished, *vilayahetutā*, then you go to its *vilaya*, to its *tirodhāna*[256]. *Ityādi pītābhāsādāvapi yojyam*, in this way, you must attribute this kind of fourfold activity in [the differentiated perception of] other objects also.

GANJOO: All actions.

SWAMIJI: All objects also. When you go to other objects, these four-fold activities take place.

Audio 7 - 25:57

tathā prathamābhāsitanīlatadgrāhakabhāvāpekṣayā saṁhartṛtvam, avabhāsamānapītatadgrāhakabhāv-

256 Concealment.

āpekṣayā sraṣṭṭatvam, vicchinnatābhāsādyapekṣayā sthitihetutā, antaḥ saṁskārarūpātāpāditābhāsāpekṣayā vilayakāritvam, śuddhasaṁvidaikyāpannapravilāpita-smṛtyādibījabhāvābhāsāpekṣayā anugrahītṛtvam . . .

Now, he adjusts this fivefold act, the fifth-fold activity also, in these fourfold [acts]. These fourfold activities take place in each and every individual. In each and every activity of the world, these fourfold activities [take place], [but] not the fifth. *Anugraha* does not take place always, only curiosity is there. [When] curiosity is finished, that is *vilaya*, it is finished. [For example, when] you have to construct a temple, the curiosity is there. When the temple is finished, it goes to *vilaya*, that activity goes in the state of *vilaya*.

But where is *anugraha*, the fifth-fold [act]?

That is what he says in other words. This is in the language of spirituality. He explains these fivefold activities in the language of spirituality. This is spiritual language, yes, again.

GANJOO: Once again.

SWAMIJI: Yes.

JOHN: Because he hasn't explained the fifth yet.

SWAMIJI: Hmm?

JOHN: The fifth doesn't exist.

SWAMIJI: No. No, he will explain now the fivefold activities. He has explained only four activities, which are existing in worldly activities.

JOHN: From the point of view of ordinary knowledge.

SWAMIJI: Ordinary knowledge.

Prathama ābhāsita nīla tat grāhaka abhāva apekṣayā saṁhartṛtvam. For instance, you perceive this [pencil]. When you perceive this pencil, what do you perceive before perceiving that pencil? Before that [perception], you perceive something red, redness only. First you feel something [with] redness, then you perceive that this is a pencil. First, a red shade comes in your view.

Just [listen], it is very important.

First a red shade comes in your view, then the pencil appears to you.

Audio 7 - 28:43

ERNIE: Like focusing.

SWAMIJI: No. When you first see it, when first your sight falls on it, the first journey, the first traveling of this sight goes to this [object], you feel first [that there is] something [with] color, [but] you cannot distinguish what it is. [You wonder], "Is it a pencil or is it a rod or what is it?" It is *nirvikalpa.*[257] And before that [perception of its color], what [do] you perceive? You perceive just a shade, something [of a] shade, before that. And before that you perceive something [that is] only *spanda*, the first *spanda*. That is *prathama ābhāsitam*. That is *prathama ābhāsita nīla tad grāhaka-bhāvāpekṣayā*, neither there is *nīla*[258], neither there is this redness, nor there is the perceiver of this redness before that.[259] This is the first state of your flow.

Do you understand?

JOHN: Yes, the first state.

SWAMIJI: When you first see this [object], before that, what

---

257 The state of thought-lessness. "The first flow of [perception], it is *nirvikalpa* (without impression). That is *prathama anusaṁ-dhāna*, the first movement of realization. That is *nirvikalpa*, that is the reality of God. It is just *ahaṁ* (I-ness), it is not *idaṁ* (this-ness). First there is some sensation. After that sensation you come to this [realization] that, "This is a pot", [or] "This is a jug", [or] "This is tape recorder". This is the next step from that point of God consciousness, the state of God consciousness. Otherwise, there is only sensation, vibration, some vibration of coming out. You don't come out first. It is only the vibrating force that makes you go outside." *Parātrīśikā Vivaraṇa* (LJA archive). See Appendix 13 for an explanation of *nirvikalpa*.

258 Though the literal meaning of *nīla* is "blue", it also refers to any object.

259 By "perceiver", Swamiji is referring to *pramātṛ bhāva*, not *pramiti bhāva*. "*Pramiti* is that state where subjective consciousness prevails without the agitation of objectivity. Where the agitation of objectivity is also found in subjective consciousness, that is the state of *pramātṛ*. . . . In other words, when he is residing in his own nature, that subjective consciousness is the state of *pramiti*." *Kashmir Shaivism–The Secret Supreme*, 11.81.

do you see? Before that, what do you see? Go inside and inside and inside and see what you see first. First you see nothing. First you see just only a flash of *spanda*, and that *spanda* is of that object and the object holder (*grāhaka*). *Grāhaka* is the perceiver. The perceiver and the perceived are gone.

Audio 7 - 30:27

JOHN: Are "gone" means?

SWAMIJI: They have not risen yet! They have not risen yet! They have not risen yet! They will rise after two or three seconds.

JOHN: Or microseconds.

GANJOO: Or just a moment, a flash of a moment.

JULIAN W: Is the very first thing to arise the perceiver?

SWAMIJI: That is the perceiver. No, before the perceiver, that is . . .

JOACHIM: Of course the perceiver, otherwise there would be . . .

SWAMIJI: . . . *prathamābhāsita nīla tadgrāhaka abhāva apekṣayā. Abhāva* means, when the perceiver and that perceived [object] has not risen yet, but you are going to perceive it in the next moment. That is its *saṁhāra*, that is its destruction. That is the destruction of this object–it is *saṁhāra*.

JOHN: How can we call it "destruction" when we haven't created it yet?

SWAMIJI: Huh?

JOHN: How can we say it's the destruction of the object when we haven't created it yet?

SWAMIJI: No, if you are there, that is the state of destruction. If you remain aware in that point[260], that is the state of destruction, from the spiritual viewpoint.

ERNIE: And what is being destroyed?

SWAMIJI: The thing which will be created in the next moment, that is destroyed there. The thing which will be created is destroyed first. This is the spiritual way of the

260 *Prathama ābhāsa.*

fivefold activities.

Audio 7 - 31:57

ERNIE: Right, so first is the spiritual world, and then you destroy this, . . .

SWAMIJI: Yes.

ERNIE: . . . then you create it . . .

SWAMIJI: Then, we will see what he . . .

JOACHIM: Isn't it a sort of destruction of the fullness, for example, of consciousness, when I perceive something. For example, when I tell this is a pencil and it is red, for example, and before that there is nothing. And for destroying that, you know, the fullness is negated, is that [what is] meant here? Because, for any perception, for any definite perception, you know, the fullness of consciousness . . .

SWAMIJI: It was destroyed first.

JOACHIM: It was destroyed first.

SWAMIJI: First.

JOACHIM: It means, first it gets destroyed.

SWAMIJI: Yes.

ERNIE: That is what you are talking about?

SWAMIJI: Yes.

JOHN: Fullness of consciousness is destroyed.

SWAMIJI: Consciousness is not destroyed.

JULIAN W: Call it "differentiation".

SWAMIJI: Differentiated perception is destroyed.

GANJOO: The slate was clear.

SWAMIJI: This is *saṁhartṛtvam*, this is the act of destruction [by] God consciousness. The act of destruction [by] God consciousness is [operating] there.

Avabhāsamāna-pīta-tad-grāhaka-bhāvāpekṣayā sraṣṭṭatvam. When *avabhāsamāna*, when in another next moment, this blue object and the perceiver of the blue object, [when] the blue object and the perceiver of the blue object takes place, this is the act of creation. This is the act of creation–this.

Do you understand?

Audio 7 - 33:27

Avabhāsamāna-pīta-tad grāhaka-bhāva apekṣayā sraṣṭṭatvam. This is the act of creation. *Vicchinnata ābhāsādy-apekṣayā sthiti-hetutā*; *vicchinnatā*, when you perceive this [creation] in a differentiated way, when you perceive this, "This is a pencil", . . .

GANJOO: It is different from your consciousness?

SWAMIJI: No, no.

. . . when you perceive this, "This is a pencil", and I am the perceiver of this pencil, this is creation, this is the creation of this pencil. What is the destruction of this pencil?

ERNIE: When you go before.

SWAMIJI: Before that, it took place before that.

JULIAN W: But it also takes place afterwards when you move to another object.

SWAMIJI: Yes, it will do that.

JOHN: No, but we are talking about spiritual, right?

SWAMIJI: This is spiritual.

JOHN: So why is this creation of this object the same here as in . . . ?

SWAMIJI: Creation is the same.

JOACHIM: Because something gets aware. It is very important, you know, when an object gets aware.

SWAMIJI: You see, you see . . .

JOACHIM: It's the destruction of the fullness of consciousness.

JOHN: No, but what [have] we created? We created fullness of consciousness . . .

SWAMIJI: No, when you perceive this [pencil], this is creation–this is creation when you perceive this. The moment of perceiving this object is creation. And, when you perceive this [pencil as] other than this cloth at the same time, . . .

JOHN: At the same time?

SWAMIJI: . . . at the same time, when you perceive, when you are perceiving it, only this, "This is a pencil", that is its creation. When you perceive this [pencil] as different from this other object, this is [the pencil's] preservation. That is *sthiti.* That is what he says. *Vicchinnata ābhāsādy-apekṣayā* (*vicchinnata* is the other object), [when] the other object is separated[261] from this [pencil], this is [the pencil's] . . .

JOACHIM: Its limited-ness.

SWAMIJI: . . . its limited-ness, it is its *sthiti.*

Antaḥ saṁskāra-rūpatā-āpādita-ābhāsāpekṣayā vilayakāritvaṁ. When [its] impression remains in your consciousness–in your mind, its impression, the impression of this pencil and the perceiver of this pencil, for some time, this impression remains in your mind–it is its *vilaya*, it is its *tirodhāna*[262].

And now you have to move upwards. Now you have to move upwards from the spiritual viewpoint.

Śuddha saṁvidaikyāpanna pravilāpita smṛtyādi bīja bhāva ābhāsa āpekṣayā anugrahītṛtvam. Śuddha (pure), when pure God consciousness remains in the end, pure God consciousness, and no [differentiated] impression of this pencil . . .

ERNIE: Exists.

SWAMIJI: . . . exists, that is its *anugraha*[263], that is its oneness with God consciousness.

ERNIE: But what if it is in your memory?

SWAMIJI: No, no, no, that is *vilaya.*

ERNIE: That is something else.

SWAMIJI: That is *vilaya*, that is *vilaya*. That is *tirodhāna.*

ERNIE: That does not matter.

SWAMIJI: No, when memory[264] is also gone, the memory is gone and you find nothing except God consciousness in the end, that is its *anugraha.*

JOACHIM: You find only 'I' without the object.

---

261 That is, differentiated.

262 Concealment.

263 The fifth act of revealing.

264 The memory or impression (*saṁskāra*) of the differentiated object.

Audio 7 - 37:09

SWAMIJI:

ityevaṁ sarvadā sarvāsu daśāsu pañca-vidha-kṛtya kāritvaṁ māheśvarameva ekarūpaṁ sarvatra jṛmbhamāṇavasthitam iti /

In this way, *sarvadā* (always), *sarvāsu daśāsu*, in each and every . . .

GANJOO: Condition.

SWAMIJI: . . . condition (*sarvāsu daśāsu*), *pañca-vidha-kṛtya-kāritvam*, these fivefold activities of the Lord is, in one way, *sarvatra jṛmbhamāṇam avasthitam*, all-round it is existing–these fivefold activities.

tatraiva cit-cakraiśvaryātmani svasvabhāve śaṁkararūpe svaprakāśe keṣāṁcideva anuttarasamādhi dhanānāṁ dhiṣaṇā adhirohati, na tu anyeṣām dehādyahaṁ-bhāvabhavinām / [last line not recited]

Tatraiva, and in this state of God consciousness, in this state of the state of *anugraha* (revealing), . . .

Do you understand? Be attentive to it.

. . . in this state, *cit-cakraiśvaryātmani*, [that] which is the *aiśvarya* (glory) of the wheel of [the energies of] God consciousness (*cit cakraiśvaryātmani*), *svasvabhāve*, which is your own nature and which is one with Lord Śiva, and which is *svaprakāśa*, always shining . . .

JOACHIM: By itself.

SWAMIJI: . . . by Itself, *keṣāṁcideva*, in this state of God consciousness, *keṣāṁ cideva anuttara samādhi dhanānām*, there are very few *yogi*s who have possessed the wealth of the awareness of supreme God consciousness, and their intellect touches this state (*adhirohati*[265]).

Na tu anyeṣām, other people who are *dehādyahaṁ-bhāvabhavinām*, who are focused in their own fourfold bodies

---

265 Ascend, mount, or ride.

(*deha*, *prāṇa*, *puryaṣṭaka*, and *śūnya*[266]), the intellect of those souls cannot reach That state.

yaduktaṁ bhargaśikhāyām

It is quoted in the *Bhargaśikhā śāstra*:

Audio 7 - 39:30

vīra bhairavadevo'pi paramānandavigrahaḥ /
udeti mohāpaṅkāṅke paśuhṛtkuhare katham //

The embodiment of the supreme bliss of God consciousness (*paramānanda vigraha*, the embodiment of the supreme bliss of God consciousness), which is *vīrabhairava deva*, the *devatā* of *vīrabhairava–vīrabhairava deva* means, the Lord who is a *vīra* (hero), who is the embodiment of the supreme bliss of God consciousness–and this state of Bhairava, how can this rise in the *kuhara*, in the cave of the heart of *paśu* (beasts, ignorant souls)? "Beasts" means, in other words, . . .

ERNIE: The rise of . . . ?

JOACHIM: How can this consciousness rise in the hearts of those?

SWAMIJI: No, how can this lotus of *vīrabhairava* . . .

ERNIE: This consciousness?

SWAMIJI: . . . *vīrabhairava* rise in the emptiness of the heart of beasts (*paśus*, ignorant souls)? And [whose heart], which is filled with *mohapaṅkāṅke*, which is filled with the . . .

JOACHIM: Mud of . . .

SWAMIJI: . . . mud of *moha* (ignorance), how can this rise,

---

266 The experience of individuality is comprised of, and limited to, these fourfold bodies. "*Deha* means the body existing in wakefulness, and [*puryaṣṭaka* means] the body existing in the dreaming state, and [*prāṇa* means] the body existing in the dreamless state, and [*śūnya* means] the body existing in the *śūnya* (void) state where [you experience] nothingness. In these [fourfold] bodies, you think that, "I am this". Although this is not *ātma*, but he perceives this is *ātma*." *Paramārthasāra*, verse 31.

[how can] this lotus rise, in those hearts?

iti / evaṁ ca vyakhyātopadeśaprakāraḥ ihaiva agre sphuṭibhaviṣyati

This kind of *upadeśa* . . .

JOACHIM: Instruction.

SWAMIJI: . . . instructions, the way of instructions, will be clarified in these *śloka*s in the *Spanda śāstra*:

'jāgradādi vibhede'pi[267] *. . .' –in this śloka.*

In wakefulness, in dreaming, and in the dreamless state, [although] that God consciousness has created these three states, but this God consciousness does not get subsided in these three states.

Audio 7 - 41:55

'tadasti paramārthataḥ . . . .'[268]

That is the reality of God consciousness, [which] is the essence found in these three states: wakefulness, dreaming, and the dreamless [state].

'tasyopalabdhiḥ satataṁ tripadāvyabhicāriṇī /'[269]

And the state of God consciousness is felt by those elevated souls in all of the three states–in wakefulness, dreaming, and in the dreamless state. But those who are not fully elevated, they find the state of God consciousness only in the end and in the beginning of these three states.

'ataḥ satatamudyaktaḥ spandatattvaviviktaye /'[270]

So, you must be fully alert and bent upon finding out the reality of God consciousness, always. And this way . . .

---

267 *Spanda Kārikā* 1.3, page 5.
268 *Spanda Kārikā* 1.5, page 7.
269 *Spanda Kārikā* 1.17, page 26.
270 *Spanda Kārikā* 1.21, page 43.

'iti vā yasya saṁvittiḥ . . . .' [271]

. . . whoever perceives in this way, for him, this whole universe is just a play.

'prabuddhaḥ sarvadā tiṣṭhet . . . .' [272]

So, you must be always attentive. You must be always alert to find out the reality of God consciousness.

ityādi sthāneṣu /

In all of these states, it is cleared.

granthānte ca idameva saṁhariṣyati /

In the end also, [Vasugupta] will clear this very point.

Audio 7 - 43:16

yadā tvekatra saṁrūḍhastadā tasya layodbhavau /
niyacchanbhoktṛtāmeti tataścakreśvaro bhavet //[273]

When a *yogi* is bent upon [developing] one-pointedness of God consciousness, then *tasya layodayau niyacchan*, he creates and destroys all the three states in his own nature. He creates wakefulness, he destroys wakefulness; he creates the dreaming state, he destroys the dreaming state; he creates the dreamless state, he destroys the dreamless state. Where? In his own state of *turya.*[274] *Bhoktṛtameti*, he becomes the enjoyer then. He really enjoys wakefulness, dreaming, and the dreamless state. *Tataḥ cakreśvaro*, he becomes the king of *cakra*, the whole wheel of energies.

JOACHIM: Is he referring to the Krama system, the *cakras* here? Because the *Spanda sūtra*, or the *Spanda Kārikā*s, are

---

271 *Spanda Kārikā* 1.25, page 41.
272 *Spanda Kārikā* 3.12, page 72.
273 *Spanda Kārikā* 3.19, page 83.
274 See appendix 5 for an explanation of *turya*.

quite close to Krama sometimes, isn't it?

SWAMIJI: *Kāma*?

JOACHIM: To the Krama system.

SWAMIJI: Krama system, yes, it is the Krama system. Yes, it is Krama.[275]

iti / layodayau hi atra vyākhyātaparamārthāveva /

But the reality, the essence here of *spanda*, is just *laya* and *udaya* (destruction and creation). When one thing is destroyed, another is created–at the same time, another is created. [When] another thing is created, the previous thing is destroyed, but on the basis of *spanda*, that reality of God consciousness.

Audio 7 - 44:54

idameva ca cakraiśvairyam – . . .

The glory of *cakra*, the glory of this wheel, is . . . when one is glorified in this wheel, what is that?

. . . yat sarvadā pañcavidhakṛtyakāricinmaya-svarūpāvasthānam

When one person, a *yogi*, is always established in that state of God consciousness, which is always indulging in the fivefold activities.

iti alaṁ katipaya-jana-hṛdaya-āśvāsadāyinībhiḥ kathābhiḥ /

So, we must close this chapter because this kind of state is not perceived by everybody. It is perceived only by those few persons (*katipayajana*; *katipaya*, just a few persons) who are filled with alertness and fully elevated in God consciousness.

Bas.

---

275 "In the Krama System, you must rise in succession, step by step. This system teaches that step-by-step realization makes your realization firm." *Kashmir Shaivism–The Secret Supreme*, "The Schools of Kashmir Shaivism", 133.

Audio 7 - 44:55 / Audio 8 - 00:00

SWAMIJI: There is another way to explain this "*yasyonmeṣa-nimeṣābhyām*".[276]

> [*api ca*] *yasya cidāndaghanasya ātmanaḥ unmeṣa nimeṣābhyāṁ svarūpa-unmīlana-nimīlanābhyām 'yadantaḥ tat bahiḥ' iti kṛtvā jagataḥ śarīrarūpasya,* [not rectied in full]

Unmeṣa and *nimeṣa* (rise and closing) of *cid-ānanda-ghanaḥ* (*cidānandaghanaḥ* means, the intensity of God consciousness[277]), when It gives Its rise (*unmeṣa*) and when It is subsided (that is *nimeṣa*), in other words, it is *svarūpa-unmīlana-nimīlanābhyām*, it is *svarūpa unmīlina*, the sprouting out of your own nature is *unmeṣa*, and the subsiding of your nature (*nimīlanābhyām*), when your nature is subsided, it is *nimeṣa*. But, *iti kṛtvā*, in fact, '*yadantaḥ tat bahiḥ*', whatever exists inside God consciousness, that exists outside also, not [any] other element. Only that element exists whatever exists inside God consciousness, that is outside. [There] is not a foreign element in this world.

So, *jagataḥ*, the world ("world" means *śarīrarūpasya*, your own body), your own body rises when the state of God consciousness subsides. This subsiding state of God consciousness is the rising state of your body.

Audio 8 - 01:49

> *tadanuṣaṅgeṇa ca bāhyasyāpi viśvasya, pralayodau nimajjanonmajjane iti samāveśavyuthānāpekṣayā yathāsaṁkhyenāpi yojyam* / [not recited]

Tadanuṣaṅgeṇa ca bāhyasyāpi viśvasya, and also, this is the rise [of], along with the body, the world of your body. Each and everybody has its own world. As many bodies [there are],

276 The first line of the first verse of the *Spanda Kārikā*: "By whose *unmeṣa* and by whose *nimeṣa* (*unmeṣa* is "opening your eyes" and *nimeṣa* is "closing your eyes"), you find the destruction and creation of this whole universe."

277 Lit., a heap (*ghana*) of consciousness (*cit*) and bliss (*ānanda*).

so many worlds are existing in this universe. Along with your body, there is your own world. Viresh has his own world. Everybody has his own world along with his body. And that is, this body along with its world gets its rise when God consciousness is subsided. That is *nimajjana unmajjane* (*nimajjana* means "diving down" and *unmajjane* is "sprouting out in existence"). So when *cid-ānanda-ghana* subsides, the [individual's] body and its world rises.

In the same way, *samāveśa vyutthāna*[278] *apekṣayā*, it means *samāveśa*, when there is *samāveśa*, when there is the trance of God consciousness, when you enter in God consciousness, then *vyutthāna* gets subsided. When God consciousness is subsided, *vyutthāna* rises. This is the state of *unmeṣa* and *nimeṣa*.

Now a question. He puts now a question here:

Audio 8 - 03:20

nanu ca śrīmatsvacchandādyāgamoktaprakāreṇa yathā brahmādīnāṁ svāpaprabohāvasthayoḥ tadadharavartilokānām vyatiriktānāmeva pralayodayau bhavataḥ, tathā parameśvara-apekṣayāpi viśvasya vyatiriktasyaiva pralayodau iti tāvat uktam /

So, in this way, in this explanation of yours, it seems that just as in *Svacchanda Tantra* and other *Tantra*s also it is said that, just like *brahmādīnām*, as *brahmādīnām* (Brahma, Viṣṇu, Rūdra, and Īśvara, all of those gods which are existing in the universe of the upper worlds), *brahmādīnāṁ svāpa-prabohāvasthayoḥ*, it is said there in *Svacchanda Tantra* and other *Tantra*s also [that] when they go to sleep (*svāpa*), *prabodhaḥ*, when they . . .

JOACHIM: Wake up.

SWAMIJI: . . . wake up, in these two states, *tad-adharavarti-lokānām vyatiriktānāmeva*, the worlds and the individuals existing in those worlds, which are existing below their surface, below their cycle, . . .*

For instance, Brahma. When he sleeps, at that time, the worlds which are existing below his cycle, . . .

---

278 Swamiji translates *vyutthāna* as "the world of action" or "the external state". *Śiva Sūtras–The Supreme Awakening*, 1.6, 3.14.

ERNIE: Not as elevated.

SWAMIJI: Yes. When he sleeps, they get destroyed. When he wakes up, they get created, they are created.

*. . . so, creation and destruction takes place of the lower worlds at the time of their sleeping and the waking up of the upper gods.

Audio 8 - 05:13

JOACHIM: Is this referring to Brahma's worlds or to Brahma as a tutelary deity of *pṛthvyaṇḍa*[279]?

SWAMIJI: Huh?

JOACHIM: Is this referring to Brahma as tutelary deity of *pṛthvyaṇḍa*?

SWAMIJI: What is *pṛthvyaṇḍa*?

JOACHIM: The world belonging to *pṛthvī tattva.*

SWAMIJI: Oh, *pṛthvī tattva*, *pṛthvī aṇḍa.*

JOACHIM: The *aṇḍa*s.

SWAMIJI: No, all the *aṇḍa*s.

JOACHIM: All the *aṇḍa*s.

SWAMIJI: All the *aṇḍa*s. All the *aṇḍa*s which are existing . . . those *aṇḍa*s which are existing below his cycle.

JOHN: Which is that? Only *prakṛti*?

JOACHIM: Does this mean, the hells or . . . ?

SWAMIJI: Brahma. For instance, Brahma, Brahma is the creator of *pṛthvī aṇḍa.*

ERNIE: So, everything . . .

SWAMIJI: So, all of the worlds which are existing in *pṛthvī aṇḍa*. How many worlds are existing in *pṛthvī aṇḍa*?

JOACHIM: One hundred and eighteen?

SWAMIJI: Sixteen. No, sixteen worlds.

---

279 The *aṇḍa*s (egg shaped circles) are the containers of the 36 *tattva*s and the 118 worlds. These are *pṛthvyaṇḍa*, *prakṛtyaṇḍa*, *māyāṇḍa*, *śaktyaṇḍa*, and they are analogous with the five *kalā*s: *nivṛtti kalā*, *pratiṣṭa kalā*, *vidyā kalā*, and *śanta kalā*, respectively. See *Kashmir Shaivism– The Secret Supreme* 2.12.

JOACHIM: Sixteen?

SWAMIJI: Only sixteen. From *kālāgnirūdra* to *vīra bhadra bhuvana*, only sixteen worlds are existing in the element of *pṛthvī*. So, those worlds get . . .

JOACHIM: Destroyed.

SWAMIJI: . . . they are destroyed at the time of his sleeping. At the time of his waking up, those are again created.

JOACHIM: In the higher worlds, not what . . . ?

SWAMIJI: The higher worlds are the same.

JOACHIM: Are the same, they stay the same.

SWAMIJI: Yes. And Viṣṇu and those worlds, which are existing below [Brahma's] cycle, they get destroyed and they get their creation.[280] And, in the same way, other gods also, [who] are existing in the upper worlds, [affect the creation and destruction of the worlds below their territory].

Audio 8 - 06:47

JOACHIM: Rūdra, Īśvara, and Śakti.

SWAMIJI: Huh?

JOACHIM: Rūdra.

SWAMIJI: Yes. There is Brahma, there is Viṣṇu, there is Rūdra, Īśvara, Sadāśiva, over *pṛthvī tattva*. These five gods exist to command the element of *pṛthvī*. There are other five gods existing in *jala tattva*[281]. There are other five gods existing in *agni tattva*[282]. [These worlds are] numberless. You can't imagine how much and how big and how vast this [universe] is. So there are thousands of [groups of] five gods existing in these worlds.

In the same way, and from his viewpoint, from Brahma's viewpoint, the worlds existing below his territory are separate from his territory, are separate from his territory, are not one with that territory. One with what?

JOHN: With the territory in which he lives.

---

280 In relation to Brahma's sleeping and waking, respectively.

281 The element of water.

282 The element of fire.

SWAMIJI: The territory of Brahma, yes. In the same way, why should we not admit in the same way that *parameśvara āpekṣayāpi viśvasya vyatiriktasyaiva pralayodau iti tāvat uktam*? Parameśvara, in consideration of Parameśvara, in consideration with Parameśvara, the other worlds are separated from Parameśvara, and they get rise and dissolution at the time of *unmeṣa* and *nimeṣa* of Parameśvara.[283] Why not admit that?

Audio 8 - 08:20

dṛṣṭaṁ hi kumbhakārādīnāṁ vyatiriktakāryakāritvam iti pramāṇasiddhameva kiṁ abhyupagamyate
[not recited in full]

I will give you an example for this. There is an example also. *Kumbhakārādīnāṁ*, just see a potter. When there is a potter, *vyatirikta kārya kāritvam*, he creates pots which are existing separate from him[self], separatedly from him[self]. From whom? The potter. In the same way, the great Potter creates that universe which is separated from Him[self]. Why not admit that?

JOHN: Somebody says.

SWAMIJI: Yes, this is a question.

āhosvita anyathā?

Or there is some other answer to this?

iti saṁśayaṁ śamayituṁ

To clear this doubt of the *pūrva pakṣa* . . .

JOHN: "*Pūrva pakṣa*" means?

SWAMIJI: *Pūrva pakṣa* means "the questioner".

viśeṣaṇadvāreṇa hetumāha /

283 The sense here is that by the *unmeṣa* and *nimeṣa* of Parameśvara, all the circles which contain the 36 elements and the 118 worlds get rise and dissolution.

The answer to all of these problems is:

'śakticakravibhava-prabhavaṁ' iti /

He is the creator of all of the cycle of His energies. This [universe] is the cycle of His energies, [which are] inseparable from Him, not separated from Him.

ERNIE: Not like the potter and the pot?

SWAMIJI: No (affirmative).

Audio 8 - 09:40

'śaktayo'sya jagatkṛtasnaṁ śaktimaṁstu maheśvara' /

It is said also in the *Maṅgala tantra*, the *Maṅgala śāstra*, that this whole universe is His energy, it is the collection of His energies. *Śaktimāṁstu maheśvara*, and the energy holder is Lord Śiva and nothing else. So, it is not separated; this universe, which is created and destroyed, is not separated from the creator and destroyer.

ityāgamasthityā yāvat kiṁcit ābhāsate, tat sarvaṁ prakāśamayameva aprakāśasya prakāśanānupapatteḥ iti yuktivaśena svapna-saṁkalpādau svapna saṁkalpādau [not recited in full]

Iti āgama sthityā yāvat kiṁcit ābhāsate, whatever exists and whatever is seen, perceived, in this universe, *tat sarvaṁ prakāśa mayameva*–that is absolutely one with God consciousness, it is not at all separated from Lord Śiva. Because *aprakāśasya prakāśanānupapatteḥ* whatever is separated from Lord Śiva cannot exist. You can't perceive that. It is beyond your perception. It is just like the milk of a bird, which is not existing.

Iti yukti vaśena svapna-saṁkalpādau, and there is one trick also how to understand this. *Svapna saṁkalpādau*, in the state of the dreaming state (or in the state of your psychic state, in the cycle of your psychic world), you can create and destroy this whole universe of your own, which is one with you. Because, when you dream, you dream that you are residing in your own house. Where is that house existing?

JOACHIM: In myself.

SWAMIJI: It is one with your self. And you call for a driver and he comes [and asks], "Master, what is your order?" "Get a car." And he gets a car. Where does that exist? It is only in you. In the same way, this universe is created and destroyed by God. This is what he says. So,

saṁvida eva ābhāsollāsanāhetutvaṁ dṛṣṭaṁ [*iti*] /

It is *anubhava siddha*, it is known to all that [the universe] is created by the creator [and that] it is one with that creator.

Audio 8 - 12:02

anubhavānusāreṇa ca prakāśasyaiva bhagavataḥ prakāśamānaṁ viśvaṁ asya śaktayaḥ, . . .

And *anubhava* also says, your own experience also admits, that *prakāśasyaiva bhagavataḥ*, Lord Śiva, who is filled with God consciousness, the light of God consciousness, *prakāśamānaṁ viśvam*, and from that light of God consciousness sprouts out the existence of this universe, which is one with His energy.[284]

tāsāṁ yat cakram

And the wheel of those energies, what is that wheel of energies?

saṁyojanādi vaicitryavyavasthitaḥ samudāyaḥ, . . .

---

284 "This One Being of infinite light is called Lord Śiva and the external collection which makes up the objective world is His Energy (Śakti). The external world is nothing more than the expansion of His Energy. It is not separate from His Energy. This Energy is filled with the radiance of the glory of God Consciousness. And so we see that Lord Śiva is the Energy holder, and the universal state of the objective field is His Energy, His Śakti." *Self-Realization in Kashmir Shaivism*, Abhinavagupta's *Bodhapañcadāśika*, verse 2.

The gathering of *saṁyojana* and *viyojana*, adjustment and separation.[285]

JOACHIM: Detachment.

SWAMIJI: Detachment?

JOACHIM: Detachment.

SWAMIJI: Detachment.

sa eva vibhavaḥ sphītatā, . . .

That is the glory of God. He detaches and He separates. He separates and He adjusts [objective phenomena] with His own nature. And . . .

tasya prabhavaḥ prabhavati [*asmāt*]

. . . and the creator of that is God.

Audio 8 - 13:13

iti kṛtvā tathātathāvabhāsana paramārthaḥ svasvabhāva eva yaḥ, [*tam*] /

So, God is appearing in all of these objects, whatever, which are existing in the outside universe.

ERNIE: But He is also detached from them also? He can do that, too.

SWAMIJI: Detachment and attachment, . . .

ERNIE: He is both.

SWAMIJI: . . . but they remain one with Him.

ERNIE: So simultaneously He does both.

SWAMIJI: Yes.

yasmātsarvamayo jīvaḥ sarva . . . yadvakṣyati

This will be explained in the same book, the *Spanda śāstra*.

yasmātsarvamayo jīvaḥ sarvabhāvasamudbhavāt /

---

285 *Saṁyojana*: the act of joining or uniting with. *Viyojana*: the act of separating.

"*Samudbhāva*" is [printed] there [but] you must correct it as, "*samudbhāvāt*", [with the stem of] '*ā*' and '*t*'.[286]

Audio 8 - 14:03

yasmātsarvamayo jīvaḥ sarvabhāvasamudbhavāt /
tat saṁvedanarupeṇa tādātmyapratipattitaḥ //[287]

As it is true that *sarvamayo jīvaḥ*, *jīva* is that being who gives life to everybody, who gives life to all objects, . . .

JOACHIM: It's *puruṣa*.[288]

SWAMIJI: *Puruṣa*, yes.

. . . and that *jīva*–it is *puruṣa*–[is] one with God, *sarvabhāva samudbhavāt*, because all cycles of objects rise from him, because *tat saṁ vedana rūpeṇa*, those objects are perceived by him. *Tādātmya-pratipattitaḥ*, and those objects are existing [as] one with him, they are not separated from him.

iti / *tādātmyāt tat saṁvedanaṁ*, *tasmāt hetoḥ* [*ityādi*] /

Because *tādātmyāt*, whatever you perceive, it is one with you. If you perceive these specks, at the time of its perception, it means that it is diluted in your consciousness–then you can perceive it. If it is not diluted in your consciousness, [then] you can't perceive it, you can't understand it, what it is.[289]

Yadvā . . . there is another way to explain this *unmeṣa* and *nimeṣa*.

---

286 Thus placing the word in the ablative case.

287 *Spanda Kārikā* 2.3, page 47.

288 That is, the individual soul.

289 Viz., *ābhāsa paramārtha* as explained above: "Whatever shines, it exists in God consciousness." In his translation of the *Bhagavad Gītā*, Swamiji explains: "The knower has become the known. The known is not separate from the knower. This is the manifestation of the knower that the known is known. The known is known in the manifestation of the knower. Otherwise, if the manifestation of the knower would not be there, then the known could not be known, it would remain unknown." Swami Lakshmanjoo, trans., *Bhagavad Gītā, In the Light of Kashmir Shaivism* (Lakshmanjoo Academy Book series), Los Angeles 2015.

yadvā śakti cakrasya . . .

Śakti cakra–this is the second explanation–*śakti cakra*, the wheel of energies of God, what is the wheel of energies?

indriyavargasya

All of the organs, the cycle of the organs. And the glory of the cycle [of the organs], . . .

yo vibhavaḥ

. . . what is the glory of that cycle of organs? That is . . .

Audio 8 - 15:53

nija-nija-viṣaya-pravṛtyādikaḥ

. . . to see, to feel, to touch, to . . . everything; *śabda*, *sparśa*, *rūpa*, *rasa*, and *gandha*, all of these [sensations].

tasya prabhavam [*prāgvat*] /

He gives rise to that. He gives rise to *śabda*, *sparśa*, *rūpa*, and *rasa*, and *gandha*. That is [the meaning of] "*śakti cakra vibhava prabhavaṁ*".

yato vakṣyati

In this connection, he will explain in this very book, in this very book of the *Spanda śāstra*:

yataḥ karaṇavargo'yaṁ . . . . /[290]

From which this cycle of organs has come out and by whom . . .

. . . . *pravṛtti-sthiti-saṁhṛtīḥ* //[291]

290 *Spanda Kārikā* 1.6, line 1, page 8.
291 *Spanda Kārikā* 1.6, line 2, page 8.

. . . this *karaṇa varga* (the cycle of the organs) possess the power of creating, protecting, and destroying. These organs, because it is *vimūḍha*, the cycle of these organs is just . . .

JOHN: A dead thing.

SWAMIJI: . . . just dead, without any life, but that God consciousness gives life in those organs and they act as if they are alive. For instance, if you want to say something and you don't want that any other person should understand it (Swamiji whispers), you'll say like this, and I will understand it, [but] nobody else will understand it. This is the trick of the organs, which are [inherently] dead, which are lifeless, and this life comes from what? From that God consciousness. So, *pravṛttiḥ*, *sthitiḥ*, and *saṁhṛtiḥ*, they get the power, they possess the power, of *pravṛttiḥ*, *sthitiḥ*, *saṁhṛtiḥ* (*pravṛtti* is creation, *sthitiḥ* is protection, *saṁhṛti* is destruction). [The organs] can destroy, they can create, and they can protect. And *labhate*, and they get this power from That *spanda*.

labhate tatprayatnena parīkṣyaṁ tattvamādarāt /[292]

That *spanda* should be sought with great effort and with great devotion.

atha ca

The third explanation of this [*unmeṣa* and *nimeṣa*]:

śakticakrasya

Śakti cakra. *Śakti cakra* does not only mean the cycle of the organs. *Śakti cakra* means:

karaṇeśvarīcakrasya

Karaṇeśvarī cakrasya means, organs which are introverted organs. There are extroverted organs, there is a cycle of organs which are extroverted, [and] those are [called] the *indriya vṛttīyan* cycle of organs. And there are *karaṇeśvarī*

292 *Spanda Kārikā* 1.7, page 8.

organs, when these organs are introverted, when you see [but] you do not see, [when] you perceive only the objective world [as] one with God consciousness, as one with that supreme awareness of God consciousness. That is the way how *yogi*s perceive this whole world. *Yogi*s do not perceive this world as we perceive this. We perceive separately, they perceive . . .

ERNIE: Unified.

SWAMIJI: . . . unified with That nature.

ERNIE: That *spanda*.

SWAMIJI: Yes. That is *karaṇeśvarī cakra*. That is *śakti cakra*. And the glory of *karaṇeśvarī cakra* is . . .

vicitra-sṛṣṭi-saṁhārādi-kāritvam

. . . the variety of creation, protection, and destruction.

tasya prabhavam

The creator of that *karaṇeśvarī cakra* is also This *spanda*.

Audio 8 - 19:51

prabhavaṁ kramārthāvabhāsanakāritva kṛtam
akramamahāprakāśamayam /

In the successive field, [the *yogi*] becomes without succession, he surpasses this succession. In the field of darkness, he surpasses this cycle of darkness and becomes light, enters in light. That is the state of *karaṇeśvarī*.[293] Whenever you perceive, whenever you eat, you get that taste also but you remain above that level. When your organs of senses are transformed in *karaṇeśvarī cakra*, you become divine. Everything becomes divine!

yadvakṣyati

It will be explained in *Spanda* in this *śāstra*:

293 "Those goddesses of all of the senses." *Parātrīśikā Vivaraṇa* (LJA archive).

sahāntareṇa cakreṇa pravṛttisthitisaṁhṛtīḥ //
labhate . . . . /[294]

iti antara cakra

Āntara cakra is the internal cycle of God consciousness. Along with the internal cycle of God consciousness, [the *yogi*] creates, he protects, and he destroys this whole objective world.

atra etadeva vyākhyeyam, . . .

This way you should explain this third way of explanation.

Audio 8 - 21:18

na tu antaḥkaraṇatrayam–

You should not translate "*āntaram cakram*" as *antar-karaṇaḥ* (mind, intellect, and ego) because . . .

tasya karaṇavargeṇaiva svīkṛtatvāt . . .

. . . that mind, intellect, and ego is also [included] in the cycle of the organs.

karaṇavargasya svātmanaḥ pravṛtyādi mātratvam, . . .

These organs are just meant to create, to protect, and to destroy. But the elevated form of creation, the elevated form of protection, and the elevated form of [destruction] is done by *karaṇeśvarī cakra*, not [by the] organs of senses.[295]

---

294 *Spanda Kārikā* 1.6-7, page 8.

295 "*Karaṇeśvarī cakra* is when you perceive [but] you perceive within. When you perceive this book, you perceive it not [externally], you perceive it in your own nature. When you hear some sound, you hear some sound not from an outside element, you hear it in your own nature. That is *karaṇeśvarī cakra*'s functioning. It is higher, higher than the outside cycle [of the organs]." Swami Lakshmanjoo, trans., *Spanda Saṅdoha*, additional audio (LJA archive).

karaṇeśvarī cakrasya tu sṛṣṭyādikāritvameva pravṛtyādi lābhaḥ, iti vyākhyeyam [*ityalam*] /

Karaṇeśvarī cakra, the cycle of *karaṇeśvarī cakra*, creates, protects, and destroys by the power of God consciousness. *Iti vyākhyeyam*, in this way you must explain the state of *karaṇeśvarī cakra*. *Iti alam*, let us stop here.

Now, *śakti cakraṁ*, the fourth way of explanation of *śakti cakra*:

Audio 8 - 22:43

mantragaṇa mudrāsamuhaśca, tasya yo vibhavaḥ tri-vidha-siddhi-sādhana-samarthatvaṁ, tasya prabhavaṁ iti prabhavo-palakṣitotpatti-viśrānti-sthānam / [not recited]

Śakti cakra is *mantragaṇa mudrā samuhaśca*, all *mantra*s and all *mudrā*s, postures and *mantra*s. Those are *śakti cakra* also. This is a cycle of energies.

What is a cycle of energies?

JOHN: *Mudrā*s and *mantra*s.

SWAMIJI: All *mantra*s and all *mudrā*s. *Mudrā*s are postures. And . . .

DENISE: Which postures?

SWAMIJI: Body postures for *yoga*, for meditation. And there is another posture (*mudrā*) that is the supreme *mudrā*, that is *khecarī mudrā*. *Khecarī mudrā*, that is beyond the cycle of the body. That is another . . . that is a divine *mudrā*.[296]

And *mantra–mantra*s are all "*so'haṁ*", "*ahaṁ*", "*sauḥ*", all of these are *mantra*s. But there is another *mantra*, supreme, above the cycle of these words. That is pure I-God consciousness, which is felt only in *samādhi*. That is the supreme *mantra*, divine *mantra*, and those *mantra*s which are existing in the outside cycle are these *mantra*s: "*sauḥ*",

296 "What is the real *khecarī mudrā*? When you are treading the way of totality (*kulamārgeṇa*), you must see the totality in a piece of the totality. Take one part of the universe and see the whole universe existing there. That is the way of totality. So, just as it is said in the *Tantrasadbhāva* [*Tantra*], this *khecarī mudrā* is becoming one with supreme consciousness." *Shiva Sutras–The Supreme Awakening*, 90.

"*ahaṁ*"–all of these–"*om namaḥ śivāya*", "*rām*", whatever it is.

JOHN: All of these *mantra*s.

SWAMIJI: Yes. And *mudrā*s are also postures outside, and another *mudrā* is:

Audio 8 - 24:11

mudhaṁ svarūpalābhākṣyaṁ ārāti, arpayati /[297]

Mudaṁ is "taste". Taste is not that taste of the senses, the five senses. The taste of the five senses is not actually *mudaṁ* (taste). That is only [momentary] taste, it is not permanent taste. When you perceive *śabda*, *sparśa*, *rūpa*, *rasa*, and *gandha*, this will give you some taste, but it does not remain permanently in you. And there is another taste. That is *svarūpa lābhaḥ*, when you enter in God consciousness.

ERNIE: That is a *mudrā*?

SWAMIJI: That is the real *mudrā*. When you are There, that is *mudrā*. So, that is *śakti cakra*, all of these. First is the objective world; *śakti cakra* is the objective world, first. The second is *indriya vargasya*, the organs, organs of senses. The third is . . .

JOHN: The internal organs.

SWAMIJI: . . . the internal organs of the senses. The fourth is *mantra* and *mudrā*.

Mantragaṇa and *mudrāgaṇa* are also explained (*yadvakṣyati*). He will explain this *mantragaṇa* and *mudrāgaṇa* also in these *ślokas*:

Audio 8 - 25:36

---

297. This appears to be a paraphrase of a verse from Abhinavagupta's *Tantrāloka*: *mudaṁ svarūpalabhākhyaṁ dehadvāreṇa cātmanām* | *rātyarpayati yattena mudrā śāstreṣu varṇitā* || *Tantrāloka* 32.3 || In his explanation of the *Parātriśīka Vivaraṇa* (LJA archive), Swamiji translates this same verse as: "*Mudham*, there in the universal state (*mudham* means *ānanda*), that blissful state of His nature, when it is produced in its own way, then that is *mudrā*, that is called *mudrā*."

tadākramya balaṁ mantrāḥ . . . . / [298]

And *tad balaṁ ākramya*, all *mantra*s exist when they hold the state of God consciousness. All *mantra*s exist . . . what is the "existence" of *mantra*s? Just [that] they work out.

DENISE: They work.

SWAMIJI: They work out.

DENISE: You mean, they work?

SWAMIJI: They work. *Mantra*s, . . .

DENISE: They have power then.

SWAMIJI: . . . they get power. For instance, "*oṁ namaḥ śivaya*, *oṁ namaḥ śivāya*", if you recite this "*oṁ namaḥ sivāya*" for 400, 4,000 centuries, nothing will happen [without holding the power of God consciousness]. If you recite "*oṁ namaḥ śivāya*, *oṁ namaḥ śivāya*" with that . . .

GANJOO: Consciousness.

SWAMIJI: . . . with that God consciousness, after five minutes time you will get entry in God consciousness. This is the power of that *mantra*. And that power of *mantra* is held from within.

JOHN: So, it means all of these *mudrā*s and *mantra*s have to be held with . . .

SWAMIJI: Yes.

JOHN: . . . with awareness.

SWAMIJI: *Tadākramya*, with that awareness of That *spanda*, adjustment of *spanda*. *Spanda* must be there.

JOHN: What is "*nirañjanāḥ*"?

SWAMIJI:

Audio 8 - 26:42

. . . . *nirañjanāḥ* / [299]

Nirañjanāḥ[300] [means that] they don't spoil you in the

298 *Spanda Kārikā* 2.1, page 44.

299 *Spanda Kārikā* 2.2, page 44.

300 Lit., unpainted, spotless, pure, simple.

outside world, i.e., those *mantra*s, then.

JOHN: "Spoil you" means?

DENISE: What do you mean?

SWAMIJI: For instance, I have given you a *mantra*. [If] you recite this *mantra* without that power of God consciousness–"*oṁ namaḥ śivāya, oṁ namaḥ śivāya, oṁ namaḥ śivāya*"–[when] you fall asleep, you don't . . .

ERNIE: (laughter)

SWAMIJI: . . . you [will] perceive dreams as you perceived before that also.[301] [But] when you fall asleep with awareness of that *mantra*, whatever you dream, you dream that divinely. You have got that power in dreaming state also.[302] That is what he explains here.

Now, the fifth explanation [of *śakti cakra*]:

Audio 8 - 27:37

> *ityantam / vyakhyātena ca śakticakravibhavena mantrādi-sāmarthyātmanā prabhā diptiḥ yasya sādhaka-cittasya, . . .*

By the glory of *śakti cakra*, the glory of *śakti cakra* which is already explained (*vyākhyatena ca śakti cakra vibhavena*, the glory of *śakti cakra* which is already explained), by that glory, *mantrādi sāmarthyātmana prabhā dīptiḥ yasya sādhaka cittasya*–now take *śakti cakrasya–prabhā* (*prabhā* means "light"), the glory of *śakti cakra* gives light in the mind of the *sādhaka*, in the mind of the *yogi*. The mind of the *yogi* possesses the light of God consciousness by this *śakti cakra*.

---

301 "The one who is not aware of that God consciousness, he is unaware everywhere, in each and every corner of movement. Whenever you sleep [and] you go to the dreaming state, you don't know from which point you had entered in the dreaming state. When you come out from the dreaming state, you don't know when you came out from the dreaming state to wakefulness." *Śiva Sūtra Vimarśinī*, 1.19.

302 Viz., *svapna svātantrya*. "So also in the dreaming state, he can dream whatever he wishes to dream. This is called the independent world of the dreaming state (*svapna-svātantrya*)." *Shiva Sutras–The Supreme Awakening*, 90.

Tat–prabhā, prabhavam, śakti cakra vibhava prabha-vam – "*vaṁ*" is:

vāti gacchati prāpnoti adhitiṣṭhati gandhayati ca vināśayati svātmani viśrāmayati yaḥ [*tam*] /

That is *va*, this is *prabha-vaṁ*. *Prabhā* is translated as *prabhā* (*prabhā* is light, internal light of God consciousness), which exists, which appears, in the mind of the *sādhaka-yogi*. And by that internal light, which is existing in the mind of the *sādhaka-yogi*, by that light, *vāti gacchati prāpnoti adhitiṣṭhati gandhayati ca vināśayati svātmani viśrāmayati yaḥ* (*vāti* means *gacchati*), it gives you a push in that journey. It gives you a push in that journey; you get a push on that path of journey.

JOACHIM: It blows somehow. *Vāti* means "blows", huh?

SWAMIJI: Yes, blows, blows on that journey. And *gacchati*, when you travel on that path, the pathway of God consciousness, then you *adhitiṣṭhati*, then you are established and you get the smell, perfume, of that God consciousness (*gandhayati*), *vināśayati svātmani viśrāmayati*, and the whole outside world is destroyed, and *svatmani viśrāmayati*, you are established in your own nature. That is *prabha-vaṁ*.

yat sphuṭībhaviṣyati

This will be cleared in this very *Spanda śāstra*:

Audio 8 - 30:26

sahārādhakacittena tena te [*śivadharmiṇaḥ*] /
tatraiva saṁpralīyante śāntarūpāniranjanāḥ //*SpK* 2.2//

Sahārādhakacittena tena te śivadharmiṇaḥ, it is the *śloka* of the *Spanda* [*Kārikā*]. *Tatraiva saṁpralīyante*, and all of those activities which took place beforehand in the mind of the *sādhaka*, those activities all are dissolved along with the mind of the *sādhaka* in that supreme state of God consciousness. *Tena te śivadharmiṇah*, then all of these activities become divine. They are proved that they have become divine. And the mind of the *sādhaka* has become divine; *śivadharmiṇaḥ*, they possess the aspect of Siva. They don't possess any more aspects of individuality.

Now, the sixth explanation of *śakti cakra*:

Audio 8 - 31:39

śakti cakreṇa dīkṣānugrahadhyeya-samāpattyādinā sāmarthya saṁpadā vibhavo yasayācāryasya-udayastasya prabhavaṁ / yat abhidhāsyati /

Śakti cakreṇa, *śakti cakra* means here, in this sixth explanation, *dīkṣa anugraha dhyeya samāpattyādinā*, to initiate disciples, *anugraha*, to bless disciples, to bestow . . .

ERNIE: Boons.

SWAMIJI: . . . boons to disciples, and *dhyeya samāpattyādinā*, and [to] bestow the *samāpatti*, the achievement of *dhyeya*, the achievement which is to be meditated upon, the achievement of that element which is to be meditated upon. What is that? That is God, that is your own nature, your real nature. Who is working on it? The master. The master blesses you with initiation, he blesses you by *dhyeya samāpatti*, by which you are established in the state of *samādhi*, and this is *sāmarthya saṁpadā*, this *saṁpadā*, this glory, comes from the nature of *ācāryādi*, *yasya ācāryasya* (*ācāryasya* means, the master), when the master has risen in you, risen in your mind, when the glory of the master has risen in your mind. What is that glory?

JOHN: God consciousness.

SWAMIJI: Yes, when God consciousness is existing. When God consciousness begins to shine in your mind, it means your master's grace is residing in your mind. And it is definitely . . . all *yogi*s have perceived [that] when you meditate wholeheartedly, one-pointedly on God consciousness, [then] whenever you dream, whenever you fall asleep, you will dream [that your] master is . . .

ERNIE: Is watching.

SWAMIJI: . . . is watching you.

ERNIE: Over you.

SWAMIJI: Over you, yes. You will feel that [your] master is like this. You will feel, you will dream [of him looking over you].

ERNIE: His presence.

SWAMIJI: His presence, his presence is always there. If you don't meditate, you won't find any sign of [your] master in your dreaming state. This is a fact.

JOACHIM: But I dreamed of you also before I started to meditate.

SWAMIJI: (laughter) Then you have got the master's grace.

JOACHIM: Even before I knew you.

ERNIE: This is the sixth explanation of *śakti cakra*.

SWAMIJI: Yes, this is *śakti cakra vibhava*.

Yat abhidhāsyati, he will explain this point in these *ślokas* in the *Spanda* [*Kārikā*]:

Audio 8 - 34:35

'ayamevodayastasya dhyeyasya . . . . /'[303]

This is the rise of that God consciousness in the mind of the *sādhaka*, and this is the *dīkṣā*, this is the initiation, real initiation, what the *sādhaka* gets. What is that?

'. śivasadbhāvadāyinī //'[304]

Which sentences the *sādhaka* to that point of God consciousness. This is the master's grace.

api ca

The seventh explanation of *śakti cakra vibhavaṁ*:

śaktayoḥ . . .

Śaktyaḥ, energies, what are energies?

303 *Spanda Kārikā* 2.6, page 50.
304 Ibid., 2.7, page 51.

śaktayaḥ brāhmyādi devyaḥ

Brāhmī, māheśvarī, kaumārī, vaiṣṇavī, all of these energies of the Lord are energies, *śaktis*.[305]

brahmādikāraṇamālā

All of these garlands of gods and goddesses.

tāsāṁsbandhīcakram

And the wheel of those is:

Audio 8 - 35:40

svabhāvaśūnyapaśupramātuḥ advayarūpordhva-bhūmyanārohaṇakṣamo bhedamayādharasaraṇisaṁcāra-caturaśca vyūhaḥ, . . .

Brahmādi kāraṇamālā, and its *cakra*, its *cakra* is just to carry you away from God consciousness. Those also work in this universe.

ERNIE: Which? What?

SWAMIJI: *Brahmī, ityādi*, all gods and goddesses, they work in this field of the world, as they [are] carrying you–I can't pronounce English–carrying you away from God consciousness.

ERNIE: Distract you.

SWAMIJI: Distract you from God consciousness (laughter). *Svabhāva śūnya* . . . but they distract you from God consciousness only. Which "you"? *Svabhāva śūnya*, he who has not maintained awareness. One who is aware, they cannot carry [him away]. They cannot carry that person who is aware, who is always aware, who is always . . .

JOHN: Steadfast.

---

305 *Brāhmī, Māheśvarī, Kaumārī, Vaiṣṇavī, Vārāhā, Indrāṇī, Cāmuṇḍā*, and *Mahālakṣmī*. "They rule out this section of the eight organs: the five organs of knowledge, mind, intellect, and ego." *Parātrīśikā Vivaraṇa* (LJA archive).

SWAMIJI: . . . watchful, watchful. When you are not watchful, [when] you don't remain watchful always (internally watching)–it is not [simply] watching the construction of this house, you must be watchful inside, what is going on within you–when you don't remain watchful, they will carry you from that state of God consciousness, and *bheda mayādharasaraṇi saṁcāra caturaśca*, and you will become clever in the outside activities of the world. You will become clever in going to pictures and going to . . . and having discussions, parties, and everything.

Audio 8 - 37:36

ERNIE: Cars and . . .

SWAMIJI: Cars and . . . and we have to go on Saturday to a movie.

ERNIE: (laughs)

JOHN: This means that you become more clever?

SWAMIJI: No, this is also *śakti cakra* on the other side. It is the opposite side of *śakti cakra*.

ERNIE: Objective side.

GANJOO: This is the very nature of these *śakti*s.

SWAMIJI: To make you . . . they push you away from God consciousness.

JOHN: So, is this *bhoga*[306]?

SWAMIJI: *Bhoga*, yes.

JOHN: If a *sādhaka* came and wanted to achieve this, he could achieve this state also which is . . .

SWAMIJI: Yes, they are pushed. Some *sādhaka*s who are not aware, who are not always watchful, they are pushed in the outside world for *bhoga*s, for enjoyment.

ERNIE: Yes, but isn't that also some awareness though? It's not internal awareness, but there is some awareness involved there?

SWAMIJI: What awareness? There is no [awareness], no.

ERNIE: Nothing.

306 Worldly enjoyment.

SWAMIJI:

Audio 8 - 38:24

[*tasya yo*] *vibhavaḥ* . . .

And glory of that is:

. . . *tathākāryakāritvaṁ tasya prabhavam* /

Tat-kāryakāritvaṁ, *bas*, [you are] always filled with torture, always filled with grief, always filled with [thoughts of] what to do, what to take, what to eat, what to make, how to prepare, what should I do with Ganesha and Mohammed Sultan[307], and all of those [concerns]–these.

JOACHIM: Electricity bills.

SWAMIJI: (laughter) Yes.

ERNIE: But isn't that impossible to escape from?

SWAMIJI: No, you will escape from this only when you are watchful. When you remain always watchful inside, you will escape from it. Although you remain in this, you remain handling Mohammed Sultan and all other household work, still you will be above that.

[*Yadvakṣyati*, it is said in the *Spanda Kārikā*]:

Audio 8 - 39:16

śabdarāśisamutthasya śaktivargasya bhogyatām /
kalāviluptavibhavo gataḥ sansa paśuḥ smṛtaḥ //*3.13*//

When *śabdarāśi samutthasya*[308], by those varieties of sounds (*śabda*), *sparśa*, *rūpa*, *rasa*, and *gandha*, you are pushed away from God consciousness–you can't find That.

'*bandhayitrī* . . . . //'[309]

---

307 John Hughes' cook and gardener, respectively.

308 As Swamiji explains in the *Spanda Kārikā* (3.13), "God consciousness has produced the biggest cycle of Its energies. That is *śabdarāśi*. *Śabdarāśi* is the cycle of sounds, the cycle of words, the cycle of sentences. It has got great power."

309 *Spanda Kārikā* 3.16. page 80.

And it entangles you (laughter) in the repeated cycle of births and deaths–*bandhayitrī*. When–there is yet hope, there is yet hope (laughter), there is yet hope–*svamārgasthā*, when you again become watchful, when you again hold the watchful state again, *jñātā siddhi upapādikā*[310], it will give you again push to that God consciousness.

ERNIE: So, actually, they could . . .

SWAMIJI: So, no worry. No worry. If you are down, if you are pushed down, no worry, you can rise also.

ERNIE: You could use those activities to strengthen that awareness.

SWAMIJI: Yes, yes, yes.

The eighth explanation [of *śakti cakra*]:

Audio 8 - 40:25

tasyaiva śakticakrasya yo vibhavaḥ
svasvabhāvapadāpekṣayā adharādharabhūtyāgena
ūrdhvodhvārohaṇakṣamatā, tasyāpi prabhavaṁ prāgvat /

Tasyaiva śakti cakrasya, and that *śakti cakra*, that is the same *śakti cakra*, the glory of *śakti cakra*, when *svasvabhāva-padāpekṣayā*, when you are elevated, when you remain always watchful [with] what you are doing inside, how does your mind work inside, [when] you remain watchful to that, this mind won't move from that one-pointedness. [Your mind] will become just like a dead element. It will be under your command. It will remain under your command only when you are watchful to that [mind].

Do you understand?

ERNIE: And "watchful" is? What does "watchful" mean?

SWAMIJI: What [your mind] is doing–just watching. But, this mind is going, this mind is going. When you remain watching [it], it won't go, it won't go at all! *Bas*, it will stay [at a] standstill, *bas*. [Your mind] only will watch [for] your unwatchful state. At the point of [your] unwatchful state, it will begin to move. Whenever you watch [it], at the time, at the span of that time [of your] watchful state, it won't move.

---

310 *Spanda Kārikā*, 3.16.

ERNIE: So you watch your thoughts?

SWAMIJI: Watch your thoughts, the movement of thoughts.

ERNIE: As they go through.

SWAMIJI: They won't move, they won't move. At that time [of being watchful] they won't move at all.

ERNIE: Then?

SWAMIJI: Then, when they won't move, you become unminded and you get entry in God consciousness. Finished. You become *mukta, jīvan mukta*.[311] That is *vibhavaḥ*.[312]

Svasvabhāvapadāpekṣayā adharādhara bhūtyāgena, so, this movement, the movement in the worthless cycle of universe, is to be stopped.

Audio 8 - 42:34

Adharādhara bhūmi, this *adhara bhūmi*, . . .
What is *adhara*?

GANJOO: Lower.

SWAMIJI: Lower, the lower cycle of . . . the worldly cycle.

. . . when you leave that, *ūrdhvordhva ārohaṇakṣamata*, you get the capacity of how to rise. You get the capacity of how to rise by this, by remaining in the watchful state of your mind.

Always be watchful. When you remain watchful, leave your comfort, leave everything. Remain watchful. Only sleep when you are forced to sleep. Don't sleep by your own will. [You say], "No, we must take rest". *Bas*, you take a *razoi*[313] and *bas*, stretch your legs and that is all. No, this is not the way how *yogi*s do. *Yogi*s only sit for . . . and they watch their nature of mind. And, at the emergency point of sleeping, they go to sleep. They don't sleep till then.

Do you understand what I mean?

You should not sleep at leisure. You have to do so [many] things in this world, you see. What can we do? You have to work.

ERNIE: When you said, "leave those lower worlds", it is by watching your mind.

---

311 Liberated while embodied.

312 The glory (*vibhavaḥ*) of *śakti cakra*.

313 A blanket.

SWAMIJI: Watching, *bas*, yes.

ERNIE: That is how you leave those worlds?

SWAMIJI: Yes.

ERNIE: And then you come to . . . ?

SWAMIJI: Then you rise, then you rise!

ERNIE: I see.

SWAMIJI: Then you get the capacity, more and more. The more capacity [that] is there, [that] much more will [you] rise, much more will again appear, much more will again appear day-by-day, second-by-second.

Tasyāpi prabhavaṁ, and He is the creator of that. God is doing that way also. God is working that way also.

yadatraiva vadiṣyati

He will explain this in this very *Spanda* [*Kārikā*]:

Audio 8 - 44:37

'. . . . . *svamārgasthā jñātā siddhyupapādikā* //'[314]

When you step on the real pathway, the real pathway of the watchful state, *jñātā*, and you remain always elevated, *siddhi upapādikā*, these *śakti cakra*s, the wheel of energies of Lord Śiva, give you push to that God consciousness, instantaneously.

Audio 8 - 45:03 / Audio 9 - 00:00

[*kiṁ ca śakticakraṁ*] *khecarī gocarī dikcarī bhūcaryādiḥ*

The ninth explanation of *śakti cakra*:

Śakti cakra is the wheel of energies of Lord Śiva, and that you must understand that *śakti cakra* is *khecarī*, *gocarī*, *dikcarī*, and *bhūcarī*.[315] *Khecarī* is that [energy which] handles

---

314 *Spanda Kārikā* 3.16, page 80.

315 "They are produced by God for governing all of these organs so that the activity of these organs should be experienced properly. For instance, you see an *aloo bhukara* (plum) fruit and it gives you a taste in [your mouth]. But from the eyes, how has it reached in your

in the vacuum, voidness. *Gocarī* are those energies who handle this *gocarī*.

JOACHIM: Objects.

SWAMIJI: No. *Gocarī* means, the organs of action and the organs of senses. And *dikcarī* are [the energies] who act in the atmosphere of your own world. You know, you have got your own world, he has his own world, I have my own world. That is the environment in which we are placed. That is *dikcarī*. Those who are by your side, kith and kin, and boys and girls, you know, daughters, sisters, servants, motorcars, houses, [and all of those things] belonging to you.

JOACHIM: This is objective world, also?

SWAMIJI: Not the objective world.

JOACHIM: No?

SWAMIJI: No. *Bhūcarī* means, the outside objective world everywhere. So these energies . . .

JOHN: What is *dikcarī* then? Things that belong to you or your own . . . ?

SWAMIJI: *Dikcarī* is your own environment/circle.

DEVOTEE: Your immediate world.

SWAMIJI: Yes.

JOHN: So you are talking about the subjective immediate world? The things you make yours . . . ?

SWAMIJI: No. Objective worlds are two-fold. One is the objective world of your own[316] and another is the universal objective world (that is *bhūcarī*).

Audio 9 - 01:51

bāhyantaratābhedabhinno nānāyoginīgaṇaḥ, . . .

And these are *yoginīgaṇaḥ*, these are the masses of *yoginīs*, the energies of Lord Śiva, who handle all of these fourfold states of the universe. The first is [the energy] which is

---

[mouth] and you want to eat it? This conducting union is done by these *śaktis*." Swami Lakshmanjoo, trans., *Special Verses on Practice* (LJA archive).

316 *Dikcarī*.

residing in the vacuum,[317] vacuum means in forgetfulness. That is also another world which belongs to you. *Gocarī* is the world which is residing in your cognitive world–the organs of action and knowledge.[318] And *dikcarī* is your own environment, e.g., Viresh, Shanna[319], and all of those things, and your house, etc. And *bhūcarī* is the outside world with which you have no concern. *Bāhyantaratā-bhedabhinno nānāyoginī gaṇaḥ*, and it is handled by the various masses of *yoginī*s.

JOHN: Ladies, lady . . .

SWAMIJI: Energies, energies.

Audio 9 - 02:56

tadupalakṣito vīravrātaśca

It is not only *yoginī*s. There [are] male energies also.

JOACHIM: *Vīra*s.

SWAMIJI: *Vīra*s.[320]

JOHN: There are both male and female energies?

SWAMIJI: Yes.

JOHN: What is the difference between a male and a female energy? Most energies are always considered to be female, is that right?

SWAMIJI: Yes.

JOHN: Most energies are female.

SWAMIJI: Not most. Half!

DEVOTEES: (laughter)

SWAMIJI: Half are female and half are male.

DEVOTEE: But I thought they were offshoots of Lord Śiva, who is also considered to be male and . . .

SWAMIJI: But Lord Śiva is not residing on His own throne always.

---

317 *Khecarī*.

318 "*Gocarī* is the cycle of energies that reside in the organs of cognition. *Dikcarī* means those energies which reside in the organs of action." *Parātrīśikā Vivaraṇa* (LJA archive).

319 The son and daughter of John and Denise Hughes.

320 Lit., heroes.

JOHN: He is also . . .

SWAMIJI: . . . with Pārvatī. He is also . . . He pervades all of these energies.

JOHN: So, in pervading, He is the *vīra*s?

SWAMIJI: *Vīra*s and *yoginī*s also.

JOHN: Both?

SWAMIJI: *Vīra* is Śiva, that of Śiva, and *yoginī* is that of Śakti.

And the glory of those energies, what is the glory? *Tat śakticakra vibhavaḥ* (*vibhavaḥ* means "glory").

tasya yo vibhavaḥ

What is *vibhava*, glory?

Audio 9 - 04:00

atītānāgatajñānāṇimādiprāptisvaviṣayābhogasamaya-pūrṇaprathāvāptyādyanantakṣudrākṣudrādisiddhilābham [*aiśvaryaṁ*] . . .

All limited and unlimited attainment of powers, *yogic* powers, and [they are] concerned with *atīta-anāgata-jñānam*, that knowledge which has been established in the past and that knowledge which is [yet] to come (that is *anāgata*). *Atīta* is that [knowledge of] the past . . .

JOHN: Past knowledge.

SWAMIJI: . . . past knowledge and [*anāgata* is] future knowledge. Present knowledge is vividly open to all–the present things–but the *yogic* powers make you understand the past and the future also. And *aṇimā*, etc., these eight great *yogic* powers also [are attained]. This is the glory of these *śakti cakra*s, these masses of energies of Lord Śiva.

And it is the attainment of the powers [of] *kṣudrā* and *akṣudra*. *Kṣudra* is power which is a worthless power, e.g., black magic, it is a worthless power. And [*akṣudra* is] the power to insert the attainment of God consciousness in you. That is a worthwhile power.

JOHN: Those are the same powers?

SWAMIJI: These powers are handled by these energies. This is the glory of these energies.

JOHN: That they bring you down and they also . . .

SWAMIJI: And *prabhavaṁ*:

Audio 9 - 05:57

prāti pūrayati yaḥ, sa śakti cakra vibhavaḥ
[sa ca asau bhavo bhavati, tena tena rūpeṇa iti kṛtvā, taṁ], . . .

And that [Being] who fills these powers in human beings, that is *prabhava. Prabhava*, the creator of those powers is Lord Śiva.

JOHN: So these very same powers push you down and also lift you up.

SWAMIJI: Yes.

yadvakṣyati vibhūtispande

This will be explained in the *Spanda śāstra* in the section of *vibhūtiḥ. Vibhūtiḥ* is [pertaining] to powers, *yogic* powers.

Yathecchābhyarthito, the first power he attains in wakefulness.

yathecchābhyarthito dhātā jāgrato'rthān hṛdi sthitān /
somasūryo . . . . //[321]

Just he has to breathe in and out [and] think this must be done[322], breathe in and out in God consciousness, and it is done. That is the power achieved in wakefulness.

Audio 9 - 06:54

. . . . *kutaḥ sā syādahetukā* //[323]

And then, when he has got these powers, where is the place for torture and a sad universe to exist then? This is explained in the *Spanda* [*Kārikā*].

321 *Spanda Kārikā* 3.1, page 52.
322 Whatever the *yogi* wants to accomplish.
323 *Spanda Kārikā* 3.8, page 65.

ityantena ślokāṣṭakena /

These [previous] eight *ślokas*[324] explained this thing there in the *Spanda* [*Kārikā*].

[Now], the tenth explanation of *śakti cakra vibhavaḥ*. The ninth is over.

śrīvāmeśvaryādhiṣṭhitāni khecarī-gocarī-dikcarī-bhūcarī-cakrāṇi āntarāṇi,

This is internal, the internal wheel of energies, which is handled by Vāmeśvarī.[325] Vāmeśvarī is the chief energy of all of these four energies–*khecarī*, *gocarī*, *dikcarī*, and *bhūcarī*. *Khecarī* is that of the vacuum, *gocarī* is that of the organs, *dikcarī* is that of your own personal world, *bhūcarī* is the universal world. Vāmeśvarī is the chief energy who handles all of these fourfold worlds. And these are internal *cakra*s, internal energies.

bāhyāni ca vyākhyāyante /
External energies will be explained now.

Audio 9 - 08:14

yatra vā manti viśvaṁ bhedābhedamayaṁ bhedasāraṁ ca, gṛṇanti ucchairgiranti ca bhedasāraṁ, bhedābhedamayaṁ ca abhedasāram āpādayanti iti saṁsāravāmācārāḥ vāmāḥ śaktāyaḥ, . . .

Vāmā is the left-handed energies. You know the left-handed energies? If you walk on the path of straightforwardness, this is the right-handed energy, this is handled by the right-handed energy. The left-handed energy, it does not allow you to walk on [the path of] straightforwardness–just opposite to that. [If] you tell the truth always [and] don't tell lies, this is

324 Ibid., chapter 3, verses 1 to 8, pages 52 to 65.

325 "She is nominated as Vāmeśvarī because She is *vāmā*, She walks in a crooked way, in an order-less way, so She is nominated as Vāmeśvarī. It means that She goes in the objective world and *vamati*, and, at the same time, She is residing in the subjective world. So it is *vāmācāra*." *Tantrāloka* 4.177 (LJA audio archive).

the straight-forward path. [That which] makes you tell lies, this is the *vāmā* energy, this is handled by the *vāmā* energy. This is not . . . everything, whatever is existing in this world, is handled by these energies. You are not to be blamed for that. If you commit theft, you are not to be blamed. It is [these] energies who are to be blamed, but only you have to know that, "The energies are doing this, I am not doing this." This ego involves you in this . . .

ERNIE: Guilt.

SWAMIJI: . . . in this guilt. When there is ego, you are involved. When there is not ego and you think that, "The energies are doing [these actions], I have done nothing; I have committed this sin but this is committed by the energies, not me", then you won't be involved. So you must be above this, you must be above the sphere of being involved.

Audio 9 - 10:03

ERNIE: But isn't that an easy excuse to not be . . .

SWAMIJI: No, you have to find out within your own nature. It is not an excuse. It is not just [pretend]. You should not pretend that, "I have not done it." You have to see, you have to . . .

ERNIE: Understand.

SWAMIJI: . . . understand that you are not actually doing it, [that] it is the energies who are doing it. *Vāmā* energies is, *vāma* means, that who takes out all the substance which resides inside, inside your consciousness. *Vāmanti*, that who (Swamiji demonstrates vomiting). What is that?

DEVOTEES: Vomits.

SWAMIJI: Vomits, yes. Vomits *viśvaṁ*–what?–this whole universe. *Bhedāhedamayaṁ saṁsāram bhedasāram ca, bheda-abhedamayaṁ bhedasāram ca. Bhedābheda*[326] and *bheda* is vomited in the outside cycle.

JOHN: What is vomited?

SWAMIJI: Kept out, placed out.

JOHN: So, you mean *bhedābheda* and *bheda*?

326 That which is mono-dualistic (*bhedābheda*) and dualistic (*bheda*).

SWAMIJI: *Bhedābheda* and *bheda*, from *abheda*[327], . . .

JOHN: From *abheda*.

SWAMIJI: . . . from the store of *abheda*. *Abheda* is the storage of all of these two.

JOHN: Monism is the storage.

SWAMIJI: Monism is the storage [of] mono-dualistic and of dualistic, . . .

JOHN: Is vomited out.

SWAMIJI: . . . the dualistic world. That is *saṁsāra vāmācāra*. That is *saṁsāra vāmācara*; *saṁsāra*, this universal existence, is *vāmācāra*, it is . . .

JOHN: Vomited.

SWAMIJI: . . . just the vomiting of God consciousness outside. This [universe] is the vomiting of that supreme monistic state. And *abhedasāramāpādayanti*, and sometimes you just return to your own abode of God consciousness, the monistic state of thought. That too is handled by these energies. Sometimes outside, sometimes inside. When you are placed outside, you are involved by two energies, twofold energies. What are those? *Bhedābheda* and [*bheda*].

These are *vāmācāra*s. This is handled by *vāmā* energies, so they are Vāmeśvarī. Vāmeśvarī is the chief cycle of energies that governs and rules these other four energies (*khecarī*, *gocarī*, *dikcarī*, and *bhūcarī*).

tāsām īśvarī [*svāminī*]

Vameśvarī. And She is the *īśvarī*; *svāminī* is the . . .
What is "*svāminī*"? Marstress?

DENISE: Mistress.

SWAMIJI: Mistress, mistress (*svāminī*).

ekaiva bhagavatī

And that is the supreme energy of Lord Śiva.

327 That which is non-dual (*abheda*).

tadadhiṣṭhitatvāt vāmācakramapi vāmeśvarī cakram abhidhiyate [*iti*] /

So, as Lord Śiva's energy holds and gives Her the position of that energy, so that energy too is nominated as *vāmā śakti*. *Vāmā śakti* is not only Pārvatī, the immediate energy of Lord Śiva. Vāmeśvarī is also that energy.

Now, Vāmeśvarī handles this *khecarī*, *gocarī*, *dikcarī*, and *bhūcarī*, and they are now explained. And *khecarī–khecarī* handles in both ways (in the internal cycle and in the external cycle). *Gocarī* is also in the internal cycle and in the external cycle. *Dikcarī* is internal and external. *Bhūcarī* is internal and external. What do they do? He explains that.

This is the internal cycle:

khe bodhagagane caranti iti khecaryaḥ [*pramātṛbhūmi sthitā*]

Khecarī is the cycle of those energies, void energies (*khecarī*), who make one reside in *bodha gagane*, the ether of God consciousness. The *yogi* resides in the ether of, in the cycle of, the ether of God consciousness. That is handled by the *khecarī cakra*s for those who are to be elevated. For those who are to be elevated, for those, *khecarī* functions this way. Which way? They let him reside in the cycle, in the void-cycle, of God consciousness. So, he enjoys the blissful state of God consciousness in that way.

JOHN: This is the void state.

SWAMIJI: Void-blissful state.

JOHN: So, "it's a void" means, without *svātantrya*? Is that that state? Is this *māhāmāyā*?

SWAMIJI: No, no.

JOHN: What is the void state of God consciousness?

SWAMIJI: The void state is the void of duality. Void of duality.

JOACHIM: *Khecarī* is the subject, isn't it? Somehow the subject . . .

SWAMIJI: Subjective consciousness.

JOACHIM: Subjective consciousness completely out of objectiveness.

SWAMIJI: Yes, out of . . . there is no [objectivity]. So it is void of an object–an objective void.

JOHN: So, it is not *pramiti* either.

SWAMIJI: Huh?

JOHN: *Pramiti bhāva*.

SWAMIJI: Right, right, you are right. It is *pramiti bhāva*.[328]

JOHN: But I thought *pramiti bhāva* included objectivity. But that's universal objectivity, isn't it? Without . . .

SWAMIJI: It is not without [objectivity], it is with, it is with . . . it is the void of duality, not the void of the monistic state of thought.

So,

Audio 9 - 16:06

paraśaktipātapavitritānāṁ

Those who are purified by the supreme *śaktipāta* (grace) of Lord Śiva, they become, they enjoy, this state of *khecarī*, this internal state of *khecarī*.

cidānandaprasara-udvamanasārā

So, they get, they possess, the "vomit" of *cidānanda*.[329]

DEVOTEE: Isn't there a more acceptable word?

DEVOTEE: (laughter)

SWAMIJI: She vomits the nectar of *cidānanda*, *cit* and *ānanda*. What?

DEVOTEE: Normally, what one vomits is not the best, but when one is talking about *ānanda*, then it is more of a gushing, a rushing of . . .

SWAMIJI: No, it is internal . . . this is not . . . it is "*vaman*". *Vaman* is just to . . .

---

328 See Appendix 6 for an explanation of *pramiti bhāva*.

329 The bliss (*ānanda*) of consciousness (*cit*).

JOHN: Vomit.

SWAMIJI: . . . just to take it out. It is not that [which] we vomit, the substance we take from outside–that is filthy. The substance which we take from outside and vomit that, that is filthy. But this is the substance which is already existing inside, inside God consciousness, and . . .

ERNIE: The purest.

SWAMIJI: . . . it is the purest. It is just the vomiting of nectar. It is just the vomiting of this . .

JOHN: Bee pollen.

SWAMIJI: Bee what?

ERNIE: Honey.

SWAMIJI: Bee honey.

JOHN: They do that also, don't they? They take it in and do something and vomit it out?

SWAMIJI: So, the taste changes in that. Yes! This is why taste changes after sometime. After a pretty long time, the taste changes of that honey if you keep it in a bottle.

ERNIE: They lose that.

SWAMIJI: It is because it was derived from flowers, outside flowers. But that God consciousness [is] already existing inside, so it is always pure.

Audio 9 - 18:07

akālakali tatvātabhedasarvakartṛtvasarvajñatvapūrṇatva-
vyāpakatvasvarūponmīlanaparamārthāḥ /

And [the *khecarī* energies] expose, they give the exposition of, *sarvakartṛtva*, the power of all-doing, the power of all-knowledge[330], the power of fullness[331], the power of pervasion[332], [and *nityatva*, eternality],[333] and this kind of power they achieve from that *khecarī*–those *yogi*s. And, on the other hand, these *khecarī* work on us also, on those who are unfortunate,

330 *Sarvajñatva.*
331 *Pūrṇatva.*
332 *Vyāpakatva.*
333 These are the principal attributes of Lord Śiva.

who have [been caught] by mis[fortune], who have become . . .

ERNIE: Trapped.

SWAMIJI: . . . involved in a misfortunate state. That is,

> *māyāmohitānām anānandapradāḥ śūnyapramātṛ bhūmīcāriṇyaḥ* [not rectied in full]

Māyāmohitānām, those who are *mohita* (*mohita*[334] is kept away from God consciousness by *māyā*), these *khecarīs* work on them also. Which way? *Anānandapradāḥ*, they don't bestow *ānanda* to them. *Śūnyapramātṛ bhūmīcāriṇyaḥ*, they sentence them in *śūnya pramātṛ bhāva, deha pramātṛ bhāva, prāṇa pramātṛ bhāva*, all of these [states of the limited individual]. In wakefulness, in dreaming, and in the dreamless state, they are thrust in those three states. And there is never hope for them to achieve the state of *turya* and *turyātītā*.[335]

Audio 9 - 19:42

> *kālakalā śuddha vidyārāganiyatimayatayā bandhayitryaḥ* /

Kāla kalā śuddha–"*śuddha*" must be omitted, "*śuddha*" must be cut–*kāla-kalā-vidyā-rāga-niyati mayatayā bandhayitryaḥ*. So, they are entangled in *kāla*, in *kalā*, in *vidyā*, in *rāga*, and in *niyati*.[336] *Kāla*: they are entangled in *kāla* because

---

334 Lit., the stupefied, bewildered, infatuated, deluded.

335 See Appendix 5 for an explanation of *turya*. "The difference between *turya* and *turyātītā* is, in *turya* you find in *samādhi* that this whole universe is existing there in seed form, germ. The strength, the energy, of universal existence is existing there, but here he has [yet] to come out [into activity]. In *turyātītā*, he comes out in action and feels universal consciousness. This is the difference between *turya* and *turyātītā*. So, *turyātītā* is just like *jagadānanda* and *turya* is *cidānanda*." *Tantrāloka* 10.288 (LJA audio archives). See also *Kashmir Shaivism–The Secret Supreme*, 11.72-84.

336 Along with *māyā*, these are the *ṣaṭ kañcukas*, the sixfold coverings. "*Kalā*, *vidyā*, *rāga*, *kāla*, and *niyati*, these five elements are just offshoots of *māyā*. See Appendix 14 for an explanation of *kañcukas*.

they understand, he understands, "I am thirty years old. I am not forty years old. I'll be forty years old after ten years". *Kalā*: "I know only the electronic state of action. I know how to handle with electronic activity. I don't know . . ."

ERNIE: Milking a cow.

SWAMIJI: . . . milking a cow", all of these. That is *kalā*. *Vidyā*: "I know only the *Parātriṁśikā*, I don't know the *Tantrāloka*".[337] *Rāga*: "I have got attachment for Denise. I have no attachment for Marion". This is *rāga*, this is attachment. Attachment and detachment both work. *Niyati*: "I live in such and such house. I don't live everywhere." So, they are involved by this and they are entangled in the state of the world, the worldly state. And this is done by which energies? *Khecarī* energies.

Now, the action of *gocarī* energies will be explained.

gauḥ vāk . . .

Gauḥ is just sound, speech.

Audio 9 - 21:25

. . . tadupalakṣitāsu saṁjalpabhūmīṣu buddhyahaṁkāra-manobhūmiṣu caranti

So, by that speech, you must understand that *buddhi*, *ahaṁkāra*, and *manas*[338], he resides in these three states of mind by the handling of the *gocharī* energies.

iti gocaryaḥ

And they work [to uplift] those who are touched by the grace of Lord, *śaktipāta*. How?

Audio 9 - 21:57

śaktipātavatāṁ śuddhādhyavasāyābhimānasaṁkalpa-prarohiṇyaḥ, . . .

Those who are touched by *śaktipāta*, the grace of Lord Śiva,

---

337 *Parātrīśikā Vivaraṇa* and the *Tantrāloka* are both written by Abhinavagupta.

338 Intellect, ego, and mind, respectively.

and their intellect (*buddhi*) becomes divine, their *ahaṁkāra* (ego) becomes divine, and their thought (*manas*) becomes divine.

What is that divinity?

That is *śuddhādhyavasāya*, whatever they get in their intellectual world[339], that is pure, everything is pure (*śuddha adhyavasāya*). And *abhimāna*, by ego, *śuddha abhimāna*[340], they think that they are one with God. They never think [in] that shrunken state. They are never shrunken.

ERNIE: Do they just think it or they really are?

SWAMIJI: They really are. They become by the touch of these *gocharī śakti*s, but [only] those who are blessed by Lord Śiva's *śaktipāta*. And *saṅkalpa*, *śuddha saṅkalpa*, whatever they think, they think divine, divinely. They don't think just like beasts, as we think.

ERNIE: (laughter)

SWAMIJI:

pareṣāṁ tu viparyāsinyaḥ /

Those who are not blessed by the touch of *śaktipāta*, for those, these *gocarī* energies *viparyāsinyaḥ*, they take [them] on the other side. That is, the intellect is impure (impure intellect), impure ego, and impure thought always resides in them, those who are not touched by *śaktipāta*. This is the handling of the energies of *gocarī śakti*.

Now, *dikcarī śakti*.

Dikcarī śakti–what are *dikcarī śakti*s first?

Audio 9 - 23:54

dikṣu ca daśasu bāhyendriyabhūmiṣu caranti iti dikcaryaḥ

Those energies which are residing on your ten sides.[341] What is behind you? Behind you is the bedroom. What is on the right side? The bathroom. The left side? The kitchen. The

---

339 *Adhyavasāya*: a subtle type of understanding or judgement based on direct perception.

340 Lit., "pure", i.e., divine.

341 The *dikcari* energies govern the ten directions (*dik*), i.e., north-south-east-west; the four directions in-between, above and below.

front side? The yard, garden. The upper-side? The balcony. Down below?

ERNIE: The ground.

SWAMIJI: The ground and the earth and the floor.

ERNIE: Then the four corners?

SWAMIJI: The four corners also. So, these are *dikcarīs*. And in these *dikcarīs*, these *dikcarīs* handle those who are blessed by *śaktipāta* [in] this way:

anugṛhitānāṁ advayaprathanasārāḥ

Whatever you find, e.g., the bathroom, the bathroom is also divine. In here, divine. Everything is divine. Everything is divinely fixed for you if you are blessed by *śaktipāta*.

pareṣāṁ tu dvayapratītipātinyaḥ /

Pareṣāṁ, those who are not blessed by *śaktipāta*, [the *dikcarī śakti*s] handle [them] in *dvaya pratītiḥ*, in the dualistic way, not in the way of divinity.

Now, *bhūcarī*:

Audio 9 - 25:23

bhūḥ rūpādipañcakātmakaṁ meyapadaṁ

Bhūḥ is *śabda*, *sparśa*, *rūpa*, *rasa*, and *gandha*, from outside, which comes from the outside world.

tatra caranti

Those energies who are residing there, . . .

tadābhogamayya āśyānībhāvena tanmayatām āpannāḥ bhūcaryaḥ [*prabuddhānām*]

. . . those are *bhūcarīs*[342] because this is the coagulation of

342 External existents or objects.

the internal world in the outside state.[343] And *prabuddhānām*, [those] who are touched by *śaktipāta*, . . .

citprakāśaśarīratayā sphurantyaḥ

. . . for those, if he perceives some plant in his garden or [in the] outside world, outside in town, he feels that *cit prakāśa śarīrata*, this is also the expansion of God consciousness there. Everywhere there is the expansion of [God consciousness]. [If he sees] one who is dying, [he feels that] this is the expansion of God consciousness.

DENISE: There is harmony everywhere.

SWAMIJI: Yes.

itareṣāṁ sarvato vyavacchedakatāṁ darśayantyaḥ /

And those who are not touched by, those who are not blessed by, *śaktipāta*, for them, *sarvato vyavacchedakatāṁ darśayantyaḥ*, they feel separatedness everywhere.

Audio 9 - 26:41

ityevaṁ vāmeśvarīśaktyā prasāritāni āntarāṇi aparaparāparaparaparaprathāhetutvāt aghora-ghora ghorataranāma-niruktāni catvāri khecarī-gocarī-bhūcarī-dikcarī-cakrāṇi tathāvidha viravrātasahitāni tāni /

Prasāritāni āntarāṇi, the internal wheels, the four internal wheels (*khecarī*, *gocarī*, *dikcarī*, and *bhūcarī*), which has come out from the Vāmeśvarī energy, and this is the root of the *aparā* energy, *parāparā* energy, and *parā* energy. *Aparā* energy is that of the dualistic state, *parāparā* energy, that is the dualistic and monistic state, and *parā* energy is that of . . .

JOHN: Monistic state

SWAMIJI: . . . the monistic state. And [these energies are] *aghora*, *ghora*, and *ghoratarā*. *Aghora* is the supreme state of energies–*aghora*. *Aghora* is *parā*, *ghora* is *parāparā*, and *ghoratarā* is *aparā śakti* (*aparā* energy), and they work,

343 See footnotes 196 and 197, p131, for a discussion of ”coagulation”.

khecarī-gocarī-dikcarī-bhūcarī cakrāṇi, they work in *khecarī*, *gocarī*, *dukcarī*, *bhūcarī*, in these four *cakras*, *tathā-vidha-vīravrāta-sahitāni tāni*, and they are, they work, along with their husbands, along with their Śivas. They work on those both classes of the world. One class is that class who have got the touch of *śaktipāta* and another class is who have not received the grace of *śaktipāta*.

For instance, you are touched by *śaktipāta*, and you are not touched by *śaktipāta*–for instance. You are also touched by *śaktipāta*, don't worry.

DEVOTEE: (laughter)

SWAMIJI: Because you have come to me.

That is, it is said in the *pūrva śāstra*[344], in the *Mālinīvijaya* [*Tantra*][345]:

Audio 9 - 29:00

viṣayeṣveva saṁlīnānadhodhaḥ pātayantyaṇūn /
rūdrāṇūnyāḥ samāliṅgya ghortaryo'parāḥ smṛtāḥ //[346]

First He[347] explains the functioning, handling, of *aparā* energies. *Aparā* energies [are the] inferior energies of the Lord. The inferior energies of the Lord are called *ghoratarya*, *ghoratarī* energies. And the medium energies[348] are called *ghorā* energies. The supreme energies[349] are called *aghorā* energies. *Aghorā*, *ghorā*, and *ghoratarī*.

Ghoratarī [are the] very frightful energies.

What they do? How they act?

Viṣayeṣveva saṁlinānadho'dhaḥ pātayantyaṇūn. Viṣayeṣveva saṁlīnān aṇūn, those people who are attached to *śabda*,

344 Lit., the ancient scripture. *Pūrva śāstra* is another name for the *Mālinīvijaya Tantra*.

345 "The *Mālinīvijaya tantra* is the chief *tantra* for Kashmir Shaivism." *Tantrāloka* 13.198 (LJA archive). Abhinavagupta's *Tantrāloka* is based on the teachings of the *Mālinīvijaya tantra*.

346 *Mālinīvijaya Tantra*, 3.31.

347 The *Mālinīvijaya Tantra* is a discourse between Lord Śiva and Parvātī.

348 *Parāparā*.

349 *Parā*.

sparśa, *rūpa*, *rasa*, and *gandha* in the outside cycle of the world, those who are attached to these . . .

JOHN: Five senses and . . .

SWAMIJI: . . . sensual pleasures, those who are, those who have sunk . . .
"Sunk"?

ERNIE: Yes.

SWAMIJI: . . . in that world of . . .

ERNIE: Sensuality.

SWAMIJI: . . . sensual pleasures, happiness (that is *viṣayeṣeva saṁlīnān*), for those, these *aparā* energies (*ghoratarī* energies), act in this way that *pātayantyan*, *adho'dhaḥ pātayantya*, they kick them . . .

ERNIE: Sink them further.

SWAMIJI: . . . sink them further on, further on. They are sunk more and more.

JOHN: Push them down, push them down.

SWAMIJI: They push them down. And, at the same time, *rūdrāṇūnyāḥ samāliṅgya* (*rūdrāṇu* are those who are elevated souls), they embrace [elevated souls]. They embrace them, they don't kick them from their state. They embrace them at the same time and kick those who are attached to . . .

ERNIE: Their senses.

SWAMIJI: . . . senses, sensual pleasures. This functioning is done by the *ghoratarī śakti*s, which are *aparā* energies.

Audio 9 - 31:22

> *miśrakarmaphalāśaktiṁ pūrvajjanayanti yāḥ* /
> *muktimārganirodhinyāstāḥ syurghorāḥ parāparāḥ* //[350]
> [not recited in full]

Now, these are *parāparā* energies (*ghorā* energies); *parāparā* energies, and another name for these energies is *ghorā śakti*. *Ghorā* energies do *miśra-karma-phalā-śaktim*, they keep you attached to *miśra-karma*, sometimes [you have] worldly pleasures, sometimes, "Oh no, [I'll] meditate. Medi-

350 *Mālinīvijaya tantra*, 3.32.

tate, meditate for some time, it will give you peace." So, he or she begins to meditate. After a while, she wants to go to a movie or some . . .

ERNIE: He wants to go to . . .

JOHN: Anything.

SWAMIJI: Anything.

ERNIE: Read magazines.

JOHN: Do anything, work in his garden or . . .

SWAMIJI: That is *miśra-karma*. *Miśra-karma* is mixed activity. Mixed activity: sometimes God consciousness, sometimes towards God consciousness, sometimes toward worldly pleasures. This attachment is created by those energies. Which energies? *Parāparā* energies. And those *parāparā* energies are called *ghora* energies. *Mukti mārga nirodhinyaḥ*, but they don't allow that person, or that boy, or that girl, to go inside God consciousness, to dive deep inside the state of God consciousness–they don't allow.

DENISE: They just tease him.

SWAMIJI: They keep them pending on. Those are *ghorā* and those are called *parāparā* energies.

Now, *pūrvavat jantu-*. . . now this third cycle of energies is called *parā* energies, and those are *aghorā* energies.

Audio 9 - 33:02

pūrvavajjantujātasya śivadhāmaphalapradā /
parāḥ prakathitāstajjñairaghorāḥ śivaśaktyaḥ //[351]
[not recited]

Pūrvavajjantujātasya śivadhāma, to any who are . . . for instance, you are attached to worldly objects, worldly pleasures, you are attached to worldly [things]. If *aghorā* energies work on you, then you will just lose interest in the outside world at once! You won't know how it happened. He won't know how it happened because it was handled by *aghorā* energies. *Śivadhāma-phalapradā*, and you are just . . .

DENISE: Dragged.

351 *Mālinīvijaya tantra*, 3.33.

SWAMIJI: . . . dragged, dragged to God consciousness without your consent.

DENISE: Whether you like it or not.

SWAMIJI: If you don't like or if you like, you are dragged there. *Parā*, those are supreme energies, and these are called, these are nominated by those elevated beings [as] *aghorā*. And these are the immediate energies of Lord Śiva.

Audio 9 - 34:04

bāhyāni punaretadvāmeśvaryadhiṣṭhitānyeva khecarī-bhūcarī-gocarī-dikcarī-cakrāṇi /

In the outside circle is this Vāmeśvarī, Vāmeśvarī who handles this way in *khecarī*, *gocarī*, *bhūcarī*, and *dikcarī*.

What is *khecarī*?

tatra ākāśe carantyo aśarīrāḥ khecaryaḥ,

This is the [literal] meaning of *khecarī*. Those energies who reside in the ether, *aśarīrāḥ*, without bodies, those are *khecarī* energies.

yadīcchāmātrādhiṣṭhitamithunaprayogajaḥ prabuddha-śuddhavidyodayo yoginī-garbhodbhūto bhavati /

Yad icchāmatra adhiṣṭhitaḥ, and those *khecarī*, by the will of the *khecarī śaktis* . . . for instance, if you are attached to your [husband]–at some stage, when you are attached to your husband–and you are engaged in the sex act, if *khecarī*, if there is the touch of *khecarī* energies at that moment, . . .

You know? Do you understand?

. . . if there is the touch of the *khecarī* energies at that moment of worldly activities–for instance, this sex act–what is done by that? What is the outcome of that? That is, *icchāmātrādhiṣṭhita-mithuna-saṁprayogajaḥ*; *mithunasaṁ-prayogajaḥ*, when you are, when you get . . .

What is it called, that climax?

ERNIE: Uh, huh.

SWAMIJI: . . . when you get that climax state, *prabuddha* *śuddhavidyodayaḥ*, at that moment you both feel divinity, both feel an elevated state–sometimes. Sometimes they feel an elevated state at that moment. And *yoginī-garbha-udbhūto bhavati*, that [child which] comes out from that womb, he becomes a "*yoginī bhūḥ*"[352]. *Yoginī bhūḥ* is the state of *yoginī*s, and that boy or that girl becomes divine afterwards.

yathoktam śrītantrāloke

It is said in the *Tantrāloka*:

Audio 9 - 36:31

anyāśca gurutatpatnayaḥ śrimatkālīkuloditāḥ /
anantadehāḥ krīḍantyastaistairdehairaśaṁkitaiḥ //
prabodhitatadicchāke tajjaṁ kaulaṁ prakāśate /[353]

Those chief masters ("masters" are those energy holders and "*tat patnayaḥ*" are those energies, *khecarī* energies), *khecarī* energies and the masters of *kecharī* energies, *śrimat kālīkuloditāḥ*, those are explained in the *Kālīkula śāstra*. *Anantadehāḥ*, and they possess numberless bodies–those . . .

ERNIE: Energies and masters.

SWAMIJI: . . . energies and masters. And they work, they work in this world, in the activity of the world. Sometimes, whatever you do, if they touch you, you will become divine; at that moment you will become divine in that action. Whatever action you do, it becomes divine, if they indulge in your action. If they don't indulge, then it is just like ordinary activity.

DENISE: What makes them indulge? Why should they indulge?

SWAMIJI: Just . . .

DENISE: They just do.

SWAMIJI: . . . [they] just do, because it is the outcome of *śaktipāta*.

---

352 Produced of a *yoginī*, a *yogic* child.

353 *Tantrāloka*, 29.43-44a. Swamiji did not translate this last line: "*Prabodhita tad icchāke tajjaṁ kaulaṁ prakāśate*, because the inherent desire in that couple is enlightenment, the knowledge of Kaula shines in that offspring." [*Editors's note*]

There was one western lady who used to come to me and [she told me that] at the moment she would have, she would do sex, with her husband, the rise of *kuṇḍalinī* would take place in her body. Yes, it is true.

And *gocarī*[354]:

Audio 9 - 38:25

gocaryastu gośabdavācyapaśuhṛdayasārāharaṇaratāḥ tenaiva krameṇaiva svātmanaḥ, paśūnāṁ ca tattatsiddhi-sādhanapravaṇā ekajanmanaḥ prabhṛti saptajanmāntam-api paśumāharantyaḥ /

Gocarī energies: *Gocarī* energies work on those who are slaughtered in a sacrifice.

ERNIE: Like Kurbāni.

SWAMIJI: Kurbāni, yes.[355]

DEVOTEE: Huh?

SWAMIJI: Like Kurbāni, when you . . .

ERNIE: Eid.[356]

SWAMIJI: This Eid, that. . . . *Gocarī* energy, it [works for] some. All sheep do not get that state of *gocarī*, but some which are blessed by Lord Śiva. So, the *śaktipāta* of Lord Śiva does not work in human beings only. It works everywhere!

DENISE: All beings.

SWAMIJI: All beings, because He is the same to every being. He is so divine and so kind to all . . . but only to a few.

DEVOTEES: (laughter)

DENISE: Not all.

SWAMIJI: But in all of sections [of beings]. Not only in . . .

---

354 "*Gocarī* is the cycle of energies that reside in the organs of cognition." *Parātrīśikā Vivaraṇa* (LJA archive).

355 Also spelled Qurbāni, an annual Islamic festival (Eid) in which a prized animal is sacrificed to commemorate Abraham's willingness to sacrifice his own son for God.

356 Eid al-Adha, another name for Kurbāni.

JOHN: Kashmiri Brahmins.

SWAMIJI: . . . [not] only pure Kashmiri Brahmins with a long *tīlak*[357] up to [their] forehead, here . . . but those also.

DEVOTEES: (laughter)

Audio 9 - 39:53

SWAMIJI: (laughter) You should not keep them out of the scene.

Gocaryastu gośabda vācya paśu hṛdayasāra-āharaṇaratāḥ. [The *gocarī* energies] extract the heart[358] of *paśu*, the heart of this sheep, *tenaiva krameṇaiva svātmanaḥ, paśunāṁ ca tattatsiddhi-sādhana pravaṇā ekajanmanaḥ prabhṛti sapta-janmāntamapi*, right from one life up to the seventh life. It is already explained in the *Tantrāloka*.

JOACHIM: In book seventeen of the *Tantrāloka*.

SWAMIJI: Yes, yes. When in [his] first life he was slaughtered and [then] he became in the next [life] again another sheep and he was slaughtered [again]–this is the second *janma*[359]. So, . . .

ERNIE: Third, fourth, fifth, sixth, seventh.

SWAMIJI: Third, fourth, fifth, [sixth], and seventh.

ERNIE: And then?

SWAMIJI: And *sapta-janma-paśu*[360] is very dear to those *gocarī śaktis*. So, *sapta-janma-paśu*, when he is slaughtered at the time of the seventh time, he becomes *jīvan mukta*. He is dragged there!

DEVOTEE: So, it is not necessary to take human . . .

SWAMIJI: Blood?

DEVOTEE: No, to be born as a human being to achieve *jīvan mukti*?

SWAMIJI: No, no. His grace works everywhere, not only in

---

357 A mark on the forehead (made with coloured earths, sandalwood, or unguents, either as an ornament or a sectarial distinction).
358 The "heart" means, consciousness, not the physical heart.
359 Life.
360 A being (*paśu*) who has been slaughtered in a sacrifice in seven of its lifetimes (*sapta janma*).

sheep, in plants also, in plants also, in birds, in everybody.

ERNIE: So, if you . . .

DENISE: In rocks?

SWAMIJI: In rocks also.

Dikcaryastu . . . *dikcarī*[361] [will be explained] now:

Audio 9 - 41:26

dikcaryastu bhrāntacakravat sarvatra carantyaḥ parāparasiddhipravaṇāḥ /

Dikcarī cakra is *bhrānta cakravat sarvatra carantyaḥ parāparasiddhipravaṇāḥ*, sometimes you get a son and he becomes debauched, sometimes you get a son who becomes divine. You don't know how it happened. It happened because of *dikcarī*, the handling of *dikcarī*. *Dikcarī* handles in both ways. If there is the touch of *śaktipāta*, he becomes divine. If there is the touch of not-*śaktipāta*, the absence of *śaktipāta*, then he becomes a rascal, he begins to commit thefts and everything; whatever is a nasty thing, he does that in this world.

Audio 9 - 42:20

bhūcaryastu svasvabhāvatayaiva kuṁkuma-nārikelādivat tattatpītadibhūmijātāḥ pūrṇatvāpūrṇatvādinānābhedit-tad-devatāṁśaka-udbhūtāḥ /

Bhūcarī[362]: *bhūcarī* energies work *svasvabhāvataiva*, this is the nature, the nature of *bhūcarī* energies [is like] that *kuṁkuma nārikelādivat*. *Kuṁkum* is saffron. What is that?

JOACHIM: Saffron, saffron.

SWAMIJI: You call it "saffron" in English?

JOACHIM: Yes, saffron.

SWAMIJI: Saffron. And *nārikela* is that coconut. A coconut is white, *kuṁkuṁ* is . . .

DENISE: Orange.

---

361 "*Dikcarī* means, those energies which reside in the organs of action." *Parātrīśikā Vivaraṇa* (LJA archive).

362 "*Bhūcarī* are the energies which reside in the outside world." Ibid.

SWAMIJI: . . . orange-red. *Tattat pītādi bhūmijātaḥ*, *kuṁkuṁ* and *nārikela*, by taking the consideration, the example, of these two things, *bhūmijātaḥ pūrṇatvāpūrṇatvādinānā bhedita tat devatā aṁśaka udbhūtāḥ*, [*nārikela* is] *pūrṇatu* and [*kuṁkuṁ* is] *apūrṇatā*.[363] *Apūrṇatā* is found if it is divine. *Kuṁkuṁ* is divine [and] *nārikela rasa*[364] is divine. But in *nārikela rasa*, you will find fullness. In *kuṁkuṁ*, you won't find fullness–fullness is not there. Completion is not found in saffron. Completion is found in *nārikela*.

JOHN: Why is that? Because it is white?

Audio 9 - 43:59

SWAMIJI: No. White is the chief . . .

ERNIE: Aspect.

SWAMIJI: . . . chief aspect of fullness. And *kuṁkuṁ*, the *pita*[365] . . .

ERNIE: Red.

SWAMIJI:. . . red, . . .

JOHN: Is partial.

SWAMIJI:. . . it is partial, it is created. The pure *raṅga*, the pure color, which is in its fullness, it is white. From white is the production of all colors. And this whiteness is attributed to the sun. You know?

JOACHIM: Like the spectrum, the spectrum light from sunlight. If . . .

SWAMIJI: Yes.

JOHN: You get all of those colors.

SWAMIJI: You get . . . this is the production of all of those colors. All colors are produced from that fullness.[366]

JOACHIM: From the white mixture of all the colors through light.

---

363 Fullness and non-fullness, respectively.

364 Coconut juice.

365 *Kumkum* is a yellowish-red color.

366 Just as "all of those colors [of a peacock] are residing in that white liquid inside [a peacock] egg." *Parātrīśikā Vivaraṇa* (LJA archive).

SWAMIJI: Yes. This is handled by *bhūcarī śakti*s. Now, there is the eleventh explanation [of *śakti cakra*].

DEVOTEE: A human being has no control over these energies?

SWAMIJI: No, you get that controlling power when there is the touch of the grace of God consciousness, otherwise not.

ERNIE: But still, in your tradition . . .

Audio 9 - 45:19

[Lecture on one-pointedness and understanding sexuality.]

SWAMIJI: But from my viewpoint, I will tell you some secret. Should I tell you?

DENISE: Yes.

SWAMIJI: There is one secret. If this one-pointedness is developed [before the] 40th year, [then] it is developed, it is really developed. If you begin [to develop] it after the 30th year, or after the 40th year, it does not develop in that way. It develops very mildly. You don't get that [development]. So, this is the golden opportunity for you to meditate. You are young. For me, there is no time now.

DEVOTEE: What about people like me who can't pass that (laughter)?

SWAMIJI: What?

DEVOTEE: (laughs)

SWAMIJI: No, this is the golden . . . the sex age is the golden opportunity for meditation–the sex age. As long as you have got the curiosity for sex, you are living, you are living! You are dead afterwards. When curiosity of sex fades . . .

JOHN: Then all of your drive . . . you are saying that when the curiosity for sex fades, your drive also fades. Your, that . . .

ERNIE: Energy.

SWAMIJI: Yes, yes, that fades. There is no hope then. There is no hope. If you meditate at the time when you are running in the twenties, or even the thirties, if you meditate for one hour wholeheartedly, you will get some . . .

ERNIE: Progress.

SWAMIJI: . . . some progress. If you meditate after 50 years [of age], if you meditate–this is a secret–if you meditate after 50 years, you will meditate [but] nothing will happen after. [Even] if you meditate for 24 hours, nothing will happen. Because the one-pointed, the strength of one-pointedness, fades.

ERNIE: But isn't it possible that you could be 50 years old and still interested in sex?

JOHN: Like Hans.

SWAMIJI: Hans?

ERNIE: Or Donald Gates?

DEVOTEE: (laughs)

JOHN: No, but Hans was . . . in Japanese Zen Buddhism and a lot of Japanese feel . . .

Audio 9 - 47:37

SWAMIJI: No, that does not, that won't work. That is . . .

ERNIE: That's the same thing!

SWAMIJI: No, that kind of sex is . . .

ERNIE: Frustration?

SWAMIJI: . . . sexless-sex. Truly speaking, that is sexless-sex. [At that age, there is] not that much curiosity, [so] you won't get that much pleasure.

JOHN: But isn't it true that some people lose their sex . . .

SWAMIJI: It is just [like] the sex of eunuchs.

ERNIE: (laughter)

SWAMIJI: It is like the sex of eunuchs (Swamiji demonstrates), *bas*!

DEVOTEES: (laughter)

SWAMIJI: They taste it, [but] it is not that. There must be energy. The sex age is the . . . and we pass the sex age and make it worthless by doing these things.

ERNIE: But don't you . . .

SWAMIJI: You must get it diverted towards God consciousness, meditation, this . . .

ERNIE: Urge.

SWAMIJI: . . . this urge. This urge for [sex], the curiosity for sex, must be diverted towards the curiosity for God consciousness, and then you will know how divine you'll become, in days, not in months.

ERNIE: With *śaktipāta*.

SWAMIJI: *Śaktipāta* is there as long as I am at your disposal.

ERNIE: But don't you have in your tradition, aren't there rituals and *pūjā*s and things that you do for . . .

SWAMIJI: [For] duffers, yes.

ERNIE: No, but isn't it also in the *Tantrāloka*?

SWAMIJI: Yes.

ERNIE: That whole text was for . . .

JOACHIM: There are duffer-parts also in the *Tantrāloka*.

SWAMIJI: [There are] duffer-parts but . . .

ERNIE: For these energies to support the individual.

SWAMIJI: But topmost duffers do not get [anything] in this [advanced] age. They have to enter in the next life and they'll get. Topmost duffers, you know? (Swamiji demonstrates)

DEVOTEES: (laughter)

JOACHIM: There are ninety-nine percent duffers.

Audio 6 - 49:37

JOHN: Is it true that some people have . . . ?

SWAMIJI: And this sex act will make you a duffer, day-by-day, truly speaking, by God.

ERNIE: What is it?

SWAMIJI: This sex act. Too much of the sex act will make you a duffer (laughter), will make you enter in the field of duffers (laughter).

ERNIE: This is the *ghorā*? What is . . . *aghora*, *ghora*, and . . .

SWAMIJI: No, it is *ghoratarī*.

ERNIE: *Ghoratarī*.

SWAMIJI: So, take good opportunity of your age, this youth, please. I request it.

JOHN: Does everybody lose their sex age at the same time or some have longer and some have less or . . . ?

JOACHIM: Are you afraid?

JOHN: As a matter of fact, I am.

DEVOTEES: (laughter)

JOHN: I'm forty years old!

SWAMIJI: Have you lost?

JOHN: No, I haven't lost.

SWAMIJI: *Bas*, then . . .

JOHN: No, but then you said that somebody like Hans, say, in other cultures, people have strong sex urges when they are 65 or 70 years old, because they are taught that that is the right thing to have. But in . . .

SWAMIJI: No, there must be *vīrya* (*vīrya* means, this semen).[367] Semen must be, as Abhinavagupta has explained in the *Pratyabhijñā Vimarśinī*, . . .

Audio 9 - 50:52

paripūrṇam mahāvīryameva puṣṭisṛṣṭikāri /

Paripūrṇam mahāvīryameva. *Paripūrṇam* is "full", *mahāvīryameva*, supreme *vīrya* (semen), produces *puṣṭi* (strength)

367 "In the end of old age, that *vīrya* is fruitless, and in the early period of youth, that *vīrya* is fruitless. And this fruitful strength is produced by first-class music, first-class perceiving of beautiful ladies, beautiful flowers, beautiful roses–they create *vīrya* inside the body–and beautiful fragrances, various scents, will create that *ānanda śakti*. Concentration also requires *vīrya*. Without *vīrya*, you can't remain successful in concentrating also. Meditation also becomes weak if *vīrya* is not there, if *vīrya* is weak in you. If you have no *vīrya*, [it means that] you have exhausted it in other ways of life. That *vīrya* is the purest element in the body. It is not impure in any way as Vedānta holds. Vedānta holds that it is exactly an impure substance in the body. But it is not that way. It is the purest element in the body, that *vīrya* [which] is there. If the *vīrya* is there, everything is there." *Tantrāloka* 3.228-229 (LJA archive).

and *sṛṣṭi* (and the creative power). It will never fail if you have got *mahāvīrya*, great semen, strong semen. It won't fail. It will give you, it will produce . . .

ERNIE: That affect of enlight[enment], or . . .

SWAMIJI: Enlightenment? No.

DENISE: Offspring.

SWAMIJI: Offspring, offshoot. Offshoot it will produce. And it won't produce only this. It will give you strength, you will become fat, you will become energetic, if you have got that *vīrya* in you.

nāpi kṣiṇa, nāpi apūrṇa, . . .

Nāpi kṣiṇa–these are the words of Abhinavagupta–*nāpi apūrṇa, nāpi kṣiṇa*, this [*vīrya*] must be *pūrṇa*, it must be full. It must not be *kṣiṇa*, exhausted. It must not be *apūrṇa* (not come in fullness). *Śaiśava vārdhakeva*–how?–in *śaiśava*, in youth from 12 to 20 years, from the 12th year to the 20th year, the *vīrya* of that boy is *apūrṇa.*

JOHN: Not full.

SWAMIJI: No (affirmative). That won't work, that *vīrya* won't work.

Audio 9 - 52:34

And *vārdhakayoreva*, after the 50th [year], after 50 years, that *vīrya*, if he has got *vīrya*, that also won't work. That won't give you strength. It will make you weak and weak day-by-day. The strengthening *vīrya* is [present] only in the sex age and that you should preserve for meditation. If you meditate, then you can have sex, as much as you can. But meditate, take good opportunity of this occasion. This is a golden opportunity for you.

When I was in my old/previous ashram[368], I used to meditate on chairs. I used to sit on chairs and meditate. I used to sit on the ground of my orchard and meditate. At the same time, I would go inside *samādhi*, in the daytime also, in the night time, every[time], anytime. So, this works. This is a

368 Swamiji lived in his old ashram from 1933 to 1962, from the age of 26 to 55.

golden opportunity for everybody. This sex age, it must not be misused.

JOHN: So, "misused" means having sex too much, or what, or what? Or not doing . . . ? How do you define "misused"? You said, "don't misuse".

SWAMIJI: Not to be . . . play sex, don't be played by sex. That is misuse.

DENISE: Play sex, don't be played by play.

SWAMIJI: Yes. Be the player, [do] not be played. I don't mean that you should [abstain from] sex.

ERNIE: Although that's not a bad . . .

SWAMIJI: Are you people angry with me? You are angry with me by this?

ELLEN: Yes.

SWAMIJI: You are angry?

ELLEN: Angry? No, I thought [you said] "agree". I'm not angry.

DEVOTEES: (laughter)

JOHN: So, is Ernie's point right? [To Ernie]: What was your point? What did you say? You should stop or you shouldn't do it?

ERNIE: No, no, you said that you shouldn't totally withdraw, but I say . . .

SWAMIJI: No, you should not [abstain] if you have got a partner.

ERNIE: If you have that desire, but it doesn't hurt for you to abstain, to . . .

DENISE: Completely?

SWAMIJI: Too much, too much, too much, too much is . .

ELLEN: No, he means, totally abstain.

SWAMIJI: No.

ERNIE: It's not a bad thing to abstain for six months, three months, a year, just to have that strength built up inside and . . .

SWAMIJI: Yes, yes.

ERNIE: . . . to use that is not a bad thing. In fact, it is a good thing.

SWAMIJI: Yes, a good thing. [Just] don't be given to this sex. I mean that. Do you understand what I mean?

ERNIE: Yes, we are out of control.

DEVOTEE: Do not be a slave to it.

ERNIE: We have no control.

DEVOTEE: Not to be a slave to it.

SWAMIJI: Yes. And, by God, I bet . . .

ERNIE: How much?

SWAMIJI: I think one *paisa*[369].

. . . if you have sex after three months, four months, it will give you more pleasure, and that is the end of my story.

DEVOTEES: (laughter)

Audio 9 - 55:51 / Audio 10 - 00:00

[*api ca śakticakrasya*]

SWAMIJI: This is *śakti cakra vibhava prabhavam*. What is *śakti cakra*, the wheel of energies? What do you understand from this word "wheel of energies" in the eleventh way?

āgamsaṁpradāyaprasiddhanānādevātā-paramārthasya rāgadveṣakrodhavikalpādipratyayagrāmasya,

This perception, the perception of attachment, the perception of detachment, the perception of *krodha* (losing temper), *vikalpa* (thoughts, various thoughts), all of these classes of perceptions means *śakti cakra*, the wheel of energy. This is also handled by, this is also the wheel of energies of, Lord Śiva–this *śakti cakra*. This has got power; when there is attachment, it has power. It can do any mischief. If there is *dveṣa* (detachment[370]), it can do . . . you can kill each other.

JOHN: Who can? What can?

SWAMIJI: *Dveṣa*, when there is hatred.

369 One hundredth part of a rupee.

370 Lit., hatred, dislike, repugnance, enmity to.

JOHN: Oh, yes. The person who has attachment can kill any other . . .

SWAMIJI: Yes. Attachment or detachment. When [you have] detachment, then you can kill. When [you have] attachment, at that moment also, you can kill others who stand in opposition. That is *śakti cakra*.

Tathā, in addition, . . .

Audio 10 - 01:36

dehāśṛtatataddevatāparamārthanānādhātvadigaṇasya, yo vibhavaḥ tattadupaniṣatsiddhaḥ prabhāvaviśeṣaḥ, . . .

. . . *dehāśṛtat-tad-devatā-paramārtha-nānādhātvādigaṇasya*, that which is residing in *deha*, in your body, i.e., the classification, the multitude, of gods (the multitude of gods, that is, the *indriyas*, the organs[371]), *devatā parmārtha nānā dhātu*, . . .

Nānā dhātu means, . . .

JOACHIM: Different elements.

SWAMIJI: Different elements, that mass of those different elements of the organs.

. . . the glory of that, the glory of both–the glory of that *rāga-dveṣa* (attachment-detachment), losing temper, etc., and all of those organs, the multitude of organs (this is *śakti cakra*)–and the glory of *śakti cakra* is *tat-tat-upaṇiṣat-siddhaḥ prabhāva viśeṣa*, the strength, the force that it produces. When you perceive some enemy, when you see an enemy, you get upset–at once you get upset. You can't control your temper. You lose your temper altogether. That happens. It has got such strength. That is *devatāgaṇa* (*devatāgaṇa* means, the organs, the classes of organs). That is *vibhavaḥ*, that is the glory of this [*śakti cakra*]–the force.

---

371 "That ego, keep that ego on one side. But take care, take care of your senses. Those are gods. *Deva indriyāni vṛttāya*, your own organs are *devas*, gods. You have to serve those gods, and in return, they will make you achieve that God consciousness." Swami Lakshmanjoo, trans., *Bhagavad Gītā* audio (LJA archive).

Audio 10 - 03:32

māyāmūḍhān prati bandhahetutvaṁ [*ca*], *tasya ubhayasyāpi prabhavam* /

And this is for those who are elevated. This force, for elevated souls, pushes them up in the cycle of God consciousness. And those who are not elevated, they are digested by these and they get stuck, they get stuck in the downward field of bondage. And this way, the *prabhavaḥ*, the creator of these two-fold powers, is Lord Śiva. The creator of these two-fold powers deriving from what? From *raga-dveṣa*, etc., . . .

JOHN: And the organs, the mass of organs.

SWAMIJI: . . . and the organs.

tadetat upadekṣyati

This will be explained in this *Spanda* [*Kārikā*] in these *ślokas*:

guṇādispandaniṣyandāḥ sāmānyaspandasaṁśrayāt /[372]

When *guṇādi spanda* [*niṣyandāḥ*], the force of all of these organs (*guṇā*s means here "organs"; this *spanda niṣyandāḥ* is the movement of all of these organs), when these movements of all of the organs are stuck in *sāmānya spanda*, not *viśeṣa spanda*, . . .[373]

There are two movements, two-fold movements of these organs. One is *sāmānya spanda*, undifferentiated movement. When you remain in the cycle of the undifferentiated state, there, you become elevated. When you are merged in the

372 *Spanda Kārikā* 1.19, page 30.

373 "That elevated soul takes hold of that *sāmānya spanda*, not *viśeṣa spanda*. In the activity of *viśeṣa spanda*, he takes hold of *sāmānya spanda*. So he is fine, he does not go down, he is not trodden down from the kingdom of God consciousness. His kingdom of God consciousness is still prevailing there, in *viśeṣa spanda* also. That is what is called *karma yoga*, *yoga* in action." *Spanda Kārikā* 1.19.

differentiated state[374] of these organs and senses, you get stuck and you are tossed downwards and get bondage.

"Guṇādi spanda niṣyandāḥ sāmānya spanda . . . ", this *sūtra* is for an elevated soul, because they hold, they take hold, of *sāmānya spanda* at that moment. When there is wrath, losing temper, they find out the root[375] of that losing temper. They can do any mischief afterwards when they lose their temper, but those who are elevated souls, they catch hold of *sāmānya spanda* at that moment. What is the *sāmānya spanda*, wherefrom this has risen, they catch that point. As soon as they catch that point, they get entry in God consciousness.

JOHN: That is the same *spanda* that exists in sex, and eating, and all of those things.

SWAMIJI: Everything. And . . .

Audio 10 - 06:27

. . . . . saṁsāravartmani //[376]

. . . is for those who are not elevated; *sāṁsāra vartmani*, this next section of *spanda*.[377]

JOHN: Twentieth verse.

SWAMIJI: For those, they are tossed, they are kicked, on the path of *saṁsāra*, on the path of the cycle of repeated births and deaths. *Saṁsāra* means, the cycle of repeated births and deaths [upon which they] have gone.

ityantam[378] */ tathā*
seyaṁ kriyātmikā śaktiḥ śivasya . . . . /[379]

---

374 Viz., *viśeṣa spanda*.
375 *Prathama ābhāsa,* the first movement.
376 The path (*vartmani*) of *saṁsāra*. *Spanda Kārikā* 1.20, page 33.
377 *Viśeṣa spanda*, "where you find differentiatedness of everything." *Parātrīśikā Vivaraṇa* (LJA archive).
378 *Ityantam*: the following *śloka* from the *Spanda Kārikā* explains the same point.
379 *'svacittottha-vikalpāndhā niraye nipatanti te.' Spanda Kārikā* 3.16 page 80.

This energy of action of Siva kicks down Siva on the path of ignorance only when Śiva does not understand what is happening to Him. As soon as He understands what is happening to Him[self], then He is elevated, then He is no more kicked.

Do you understand?

As soon as you get this kind confirmation that, "I am going to be kicked out", you won't be kicked out.

DENISE: Really?

SWAMIJI: Yes, really, yes. It is nature. As soon as you don't remain aware at that moment when you are kicked out–you don't remain aware–you are kicked out. When you are aware, you won't be kicked out. This is what he says.

JOHN: In fact, it will sentence you to God consciousness, that energy.

SWAMIJI: Yes.

JOHN: It becomes force.

SWAMIJI:

[*ityādi*] / *anyatrāpi āgameṣūktam*

In other *śāstra*s also, this point is touched.

Audio 10 - 08:03

kulasāramajānanto hyadvaye nipatanti ye /[380]

Those *sādaka*s, those aspirants, who, not knowing the essence of the Kula *śāstra*, not knowing the essence of the Trika *śāstra*, *hyadvaye nipatanti*, they are moved down from *advaya*, they are moved down from the monistic state of God consciousness. *Hyadvaye nipatanti* means, they . . .

JOACHIM: They fall into a double heart or something.

SWAMIJI: Yes. *Svacittotha vikalpāndhā*, they have become blind (*andha* means "blind"), they have become blind by their own ways and thinkings of the mind (*svacitta vikalpāndhā*). *Niraye nipatanti*, they just are sentenced to hells, various hells, in continuation.

380 Unstated source.

Next:

yena yena nibadhyante jantavo raudrakarmaṇā /
sopāyena tu tenaiva mucyante bhavabandhanāt //[381]

By those actions, those very actions, those actions which toss one down in the field of repeated births and deaths, *yena yena nibadhyante*, they are entangled, entangled in the trap of *saṁsāra* (worldly torture). Taking hold of those very actions, those who are elevated, they are pushed up in God consciousness.

So, this is the way, this is the way on which you are treading, the way on which you are treading and fall down. This is the way . . . there is a trick, just to hold a trick and you will rise on the same [path], by the same treading. The treading is the same. The pathway is one and the traveling is also one. Only, there is a trick just to divert it in . . .

GANJOO: To the right or the left.

SWAMIJI: Not "right". To divert your attention. When you divert your attention towards that point that, "There is nothing, this is all divine", you will become divine. When you divert your attention [towards the thought that], "No, this is not divine, I am sinking and sinking day by day", you sink. Finished.

Audio 10 - 10:51

evaṁprāyaṁ ca vyākhyānaṁ nānāgamasaṁvāditam asti

This kind of explanation you will find in various *Tantra*s (*nānāgamasaṁvāditam*, various other *Tantra*s also). So there is no worry to find out the proofs for this.

grantha-gauravabhayāt tu na likhītam,

I won't put those references also here because it will make this book very big.

Who says that?

JOHN: Kṣhemarāja.

---

381 Jayaratha also quotes this verse in his commentary on *Tantrāloka*, 5.27. The source of this verse is unknown.

SWAMIJI: Kṣhemarāja.

svayameva paraśaktipātapavitritaiḥ anusartuṁ śakyaṁ /

Those who are blessed by the grace of Lord Śiva, they can find out those *Tantra*s and read that there. I won't put those references here.

ERNIE: But it is referred to so many times.

SWAMIJI: Yes.

anyeṣāṁtu saṁvādaśatairapi pradarśyamāṇaṁ idaṁ vastutattvaṁ nidāghātapataśilāpatitajalabinduvat na kṣanamapi tiṣṭhati iti alam /

Those who are blessed by the grace of Lord Śiva can understand it by my explanation also. They have not to worry to go and to see the other references in the *Tantra*s for satisfaction, for confirmation. But those who are not blessed by the grace of Lord Śiva, they cannot understand, they cannot understand by my explanation also. What to speak of going and searching for other references? My saying, my explanation, becomes for them just like–what?–*nidāghātapa* (*nidāgha* means, [creating] too much heat).[382]
When there is . . . how much heat is extreme heat?

JOHN: Depends. For a human being, anything over . . .

SWAMIJI: No, no, no, I mean in the atmosphere, in the summer months.

ERNIE: 45, 50.

SWAMIJI: No. Say, 175, 175 degrees.

GANJOO: In the deserts of Africa.

SWAMIJI: In the deserts of Africa. And there is a rock, see, in that midday sunshine, there is a rock, and on . . .

Audio 10 - 13:17

. . . on this [rock, a drop of water is sprinkled] to make it cool. What will happen to that drop of water?

---

382 *Nidāgha*, of the summer; *ātapa*, by the glaring sun.

DENISE: *Sssssssh.*

SWAMIJI: *Ssssssssh*, and [the water] will vanish altogether. It won't remain, it won't exist at all. You will find there is no water at all, it is gone. Just as it falls on it, it vanishes.

ERNIE: Disappears.

SWAMIJI: It disappears at once. Like this, it will disappear. The confirmation, for those who are not elevated, who are not blessed by the grace of Lord Śiva, my explanation to them will act like this. There will be no affect in their thought.

ERNIE: Understanding.

SWAMIJI: In their understanding. *Na kṣaṇamapi tiṣṭhati*, not even for one moment will it exist in their brain–my explanation. *Iti alam*, let us close this chapter.

Anyacca, now the twelfth explanation of *śakti cakra*. *Anyacca* means, now the twelfth explanation of what is *śakti cakra*, the wheel of energies.

śakticakrasya svantrādvayanijamahāprakāśānupraveśa-kāri-svamarīcinicayasya,

Śakti cakra means, your own multitude of energies, one's own multitude of energies.

Which multitude?

Svatantra-ādvaya-nija-mahā-prakāśa-anupraveśakāri, that multitude of energies that diverts you towards God consciousness. There are some energies, waves, tides of energies, working in human beings at least one or two times in twenty-four hours. And when they increase and increase by meditation–if you meditate wholeheartedly, go on meditating, meditating, those energies will get established in your mind–so, those energies will work more in the daytime also, in midnight also, in the dreaming state also. Those are also *śakti cakra*. Those are also the energies of Lord Śiva. Those energies also work.

Audio 10 - 15:40

svāmodajṛmbhātmanā vibhavena

And the glory of the *śakti cakra* is, you get the fragrance of

God consciousness by those (*svāmoda jṛmbhātmanā*). *Sva-āmoda* is fragrance (*āmoda* means "fragrance"), the fragrance of your own Self (*sva-āmoda*). And the expansion of that (*jṛmbhātmanā* means "expansion of your own fragrance") will be established, and that is the glory of those energies.

prakāśitahṛdaya-saṅtoṣa-kāriṇyalpādīptiḥ,

Just one ray of that will work, one ray of that fragrance.

mitayogījanaprayatna sādhyāpi

Mita yogījana, those *yogis* who are not established in *yoga*, who are inferior, who remain in the inferior state of *yoga* (those are called *mita yogis*), *prayatna sādhyāpi*, but those *yogis* can attain this glory of *śakti cakra*. This kind of glory of *śakti cakra* will be attained by those inferior *yogis* also by what? By *prayatna*, by effort of meditation (*prayatna sādhyāpi*). But . . .

Audio 10 - 17:08

ayatanena svabhāvāvaṣṭambhamātrasiddhabindunādādi-prakāśamayī kṣobhakatvena utthitā yasya jñānijanasya,

. . . but those who are elevated (*jñānijana* means, the one who is elevated), for an elevated *sādhaka* it is *svabhāva*, it becomes nature for them to get absorbed in that state of God consciousness by these energies.

So this is a two-way cycle of energies. One way is with effort; with effort you can achieve that if you are an inferior *yogi*. If you are not an inferior *yogi*, if you are a *jñāni* (elevated[383]), then there is no worry to [use] effort. It will come automatically.

---

383 Swamiji explains the difference between *jñānis* and *yogis*: "*Jñānis* who are filled with knowledge, filled with God consciousness, they are not afraid of this universe–*jñānis*. *Yogis* are afraid of this universe. *Yogis* are afraid of objectivity with this apprehension [that] they may fall in the pit of that objective consciousness. [*Jñānis*] are Shaivites always. They find divinity in each and every action of the world. There is no apprehension of falling down." *Tantrāloka* 10.244-246 (LJA archive).

tam, svabhāvāvaṣṭambhamātra, alpā diptiḥ mitayogī janaprayatna sādhyāpi ayatnena svabhāvāvaṣṭambha-mātrasiddhabindu nādādi prakāśamayī [repeated]

Bindu and *nāda* is *prakāśa* and *vimarśa.*[384] And *kṣobha-katvena*, it agitates your inferior mind, your polluted mind; it agitates and crushes it and pushes you up in the state, in the supreme cycle, of God consciousness.

taṁ vayati anuttarādvaya saṁvittantu saṁtānitaṁ saṁpādayati /

And this way, *anuttara-advaya saṁvittantu saṁtānitaṁ saṁpādayati*, it diverts you, directs you, towards that supreme state of *advaya. Advaya* means, where there is no . . .

GANJOO: Duality

SWAMIJI: . . . duality.

Yatprathayiṣyati, this he will clarify in the *Spanda* [*Kārikā*]; this point also he will clarify in this [verse]:

Audio 10 - 19:00

ato bindurato nādo rūpamasmādato rasaḥ /
pravartante'cireṇaiva kṣobhakatvena dehinaḥ //*SpK 3.10*//

At the very moment of establishing your mind towards meditation, what happens? You find, you perceive, some *bindu* (*bindu* is effulgent light, *prakāśa*) between your two eyebrows–you perceive that. You perceive *nāda*, sound, divine sound; divine sound comes in your understanding while doing this meditation. *Rūpaṁ*, a divine formation of a lady. If you are lady, then you will find a divine formation of a gentleman. If you are a gentleman, you will find, you will perceive, a divine formation of a lady. [These perceptions are] just to divert your attention from that point, to take you away from God consciousness.

DENISE: Distractions.

ERNIE: The sound and the form and . . .

SWAMIJI: Yes.

384 See Appendix 12 for explanation of *prakāśa* and *vimarśa*.

GANJOO: *Bindu* and *nāda* also have that.

SWAMIJI: *Nāda* also. *Nāda* is sound, *rūpaṁ* is formation (beautiful formation). Divine formation, divine sound, everything divine, but that divine sound also will distract you from that state of God consciousness, one-pointed God consciousness. *Pravartante* . . .

JOHN: Is this the state . . .

SWAMIJI: This is the state that . . .

JOHN: Is this *prāṇāyāma*? This, in meditation, you said that you go first in *turya*[385], you enter that point, then you have those, that whirling here, and then you feel that you are losing your self . . .

SWAMIJI: No, no, no, that is . . .

JOHN: . . . then after that you hear divine sounds.

SWAMIJI: No, it is before that, it is before that.

JOHN: You hear divine sounds.

SWAMIJI: Divine sounds, divine formation.

JOHN: From the *tanmātrā*[386] level.

SWAMIJI: Yes.

JOHN: Divine sound, divine *rūpa*, divine . . .

SWAMIJI: No, that is the final state. You must have it, you must crave for that, you must long for that, desire for that.

JOHN: That final state.

SWAMIJI: That. That. That.

JOHN: You mean this twirling?

SWAMIJI: Yes, yes. Who will experience it? Only blessed souls will experience it.

JOHN: So, this comes before that?

SWAMIJI: [These divine perceptions] come before that to distract you from that state, to keep you away from that state.

JOHN: But this is also in *samādhi*. This is a lower state of *samādhi*.

---

385 See appendix 5 for an explanation of *turya*.

386 *Śabda*, *sparśa*, *rūpa*, *rasa*, and *gandha*.

SWAMIJI: Yes, in *samādhi*, but in *samādhi*, it will take you, carry you, away from *samādhi*.

GANJOO: Distractions.

SWAMIJI: Yes.

JOHN: But this is after *turya* takes place, *turya* has started.

SWAMIJI: Huh?

JOHN: This entering that gap, *turya* has started.

SWAMIJI: Yes, yes, yes, this is the beginning in *turya*.

Ato bindurato nāda kṣobhakatvena dehinaḥ, it just agitates you and diverts your attention of God consciousness, from God consciousness.

Audio 10 - 21:37

evaṁvidho yaḥ taṁ śakticakravibhavaprabhavaṁ
vyākhyāta rūpaṁ śaṁkaraṁ svasvabhāvaṁ stumaḥ iti /
[not recited in full]

And this is handled also by Lord Śiva. This kind of handling also is done by whom?

ERNIE: Lord Śiva.

SWAMIJI: Lord Śiva, that I, we, talked about that 'Bloody Fellow'.

Śakti cakra vibhava prabhavaṁ, *vyākhyāta rūpaṁ*, we have already explained Him, that Lord Śiva, *śaṁkaraṁ svasvabhāvaṁ*, is your own nature. *Stumaḥ*, we bow to Him, we prostrate before Him.

evamanena śloka-bhāgena

So, we have explained this *śloka bhāga*, only one portion of the *śloka*, that is, "*yasyonmeṣanimeṣa*". This is the commentary on "*yasyonmeṣanimeṣa*", the first *śloka* of the *Spanda* [*Kārikā*].

JOHN: The first *śloka*.

SWAMIJI: That is *śloka bhāgena*.

vartamānarthopakṣepagarbheṇa

In this first *śloka*, we have kept, we have treasured, all other . . .

JOHN: *Śloka*s of . . .

SWAMIJI: . . . all other points of *śloka*s, which are coming in the . . .

ERNIE: Following.

SWAMIJI: . . . in the following, up to the end of this *Spanda śāstra*. *Vartamāna artha upakṣepagarbheṇa*, it is *upakṣepa garbheṇa*, it is kept in the heart of this first *śloka*.

visvottīrṇo . . .

So, what have we understood from this, from this first *śloka*?

Audio 10 - 23:03

viśvottīrṇo viśvamayaśca uttama akula-trikādi-āmnāya-upadeśadiśā svasvabhāva eva śaṁkaraḥ iti upapāditam,

Viśvottīrṇā, He is above this, above the level of the universe. *Viśvamayaśca*, He is one with the universe. He is one with the universe . . .

Who?

Lord Śiva.

. . . He is one with the universe and above the level of the universe, both (*viśvottīrṇā* and *viśvamaya*[387]). *Uttama*, and He is supreme. *Akula*, without . . . He is *akula* (*akula* means, *anuttara*, the most supreme state[388]). *Trikādi āmnāya upadeśadiśā*, and this is calculated, this is taught, in the *Tantra*s which are nominated as *Trika Tantra*s, Bhairava *Tantra*s–monistic *Tantras* (that is *trikādyi āmnāya upadeśa-diśā*). By that, we come to this point that *svasvabhāva eva śaṁkaraḥ*, this Śaṁkara, Lord Śiva is your own Self. You have not to go to search [for] It. Wherever you are already existing, that is the state of Lord Śiva. *Bas*, remain there. This is what he says.

---

387 Transcendent and immanent, respectively.

388 On another occasion, Swamiji defined *akula* as "undifferentiated totality". *Śiva Sūtras–The Supreme Awakening* (LJA archives).

Audio 10 - 24:26

na tu vedāntavādivat'viśvaṁ yat na tadeva brahma'ityevaṁ prāyam,

This statement of the Vedānta theory is absolutely incorrect. What statement of Vedānta? That where this state of worldliness ends, there you find the state of God consciousness.

DENISE: It's wrong.

SWAMIJI: It is wrong.

JOHN: Say that one more time, sir.

SWAMIJI: What?

JOHN: That statement.

SWAMIJI: No, when this is discarded, this state of . . .

ERNIE: Renounced.

SWAMIJI: . . . the state of . . .

ERNIE: The world.

SWAMIJI: . . . of the world is neglected, then you find the shining of God consciousness.

JOHN: Like "*neti-neti*"?[389]

SWAMIJI: "*Neti-neti*", yes.

GANJOO: Negative.

SWAMIJI: This is not the real thing, this is not . . . what is the Real [thing]? Wherever you are, you are There! Don't worry.

DEVOTEES: (laughter)

Audio 10 - 25:23

'nābhāvo bhāvyātāmeti . . . . /'[390]

Abhāva, the negation cannot exist. When you negate this state of God consciousness from the world, [then the world] is already negated, it is nowhere existing then. How could the

389 Lit., "not this, not that", the *via negativa* of Vedāntic philosophy.
390 *Spanda Kārikā* 1.12, page 19.

world exist? How could the world appear from God consciousness if it was to be negated? It has come out from That body. Which body?

ERNIE: God consciousness.

SWAMIJI: The body of God consciousness. This [universe] is the outcome of That body. This is the reflection of His own body, [so] why should you neglect it? Go on enjoying this world and you are There.

DENISE: *Zuruhr*[391]?

SWAMIJI: But not always.

DENISE: Not always.

DEVOTEES: (laughter)

SWAMIJI: Once a month (laughter). Don't be given to these pleasures.

Nābhavo bhāvyatāmeti, it is not *abhāva*. *Abhāva* is not, this is not . . .

JOHN: The negation of being or the negation of existence.

SWAMIJI: . . . negation is not the point. Affirmation is the point. As long as you negate, you are nowhere. As you . . .

JOACHIM: And a dualist. Negation is dualism.

SWAMIJI: Yes, negation is dualism. Negation is dualism between the world and Śiva. Affirmation is, the world is Śiva and Śiva is the world. There is nothing [but Śiva].

śaktayo'sya jagatkṛtsanaṁ śaktimāṁstu maheśvaraḥ /[392]

This whole universe is His multitude of energies, and the holder of this multitude of energies is He Himself–I mean, Lord Śiva . . . or you.

ityādinā

And we have also explained in the *Spanda* [*Kārikā*]:

---

391 Kashmiri for "surely".

392 This quote from the *Sarvamaṅgalā śāstra* does not appear in the text of *Spanda*. See: *Śiva Sutras* 3.8, and *Tantrāloka* 5.40.

Audio 10 - 27:20

na tvevaṁ smaryamāṇatvaṁ tattattvaṁ pratipadyate //[393]

This reality of *spanda* cannot be perceived in the cycle of memory. It cannot be perceived in the cycle of memory.[394]

Once Vivekānanda asked Rāmakṛṣṇa, "Have you seen God?"

He said, "Yes, I have seen Him."

"How have you seen Him?" he asked. Who?

DEVOTEES: Vivekānanda.

SWAMIJI: Vivekānanda.

[Rāmakṛṣṇa] said, "Just as I [see you]."

"Do you talk to God?"

He said, "Yes, just as I talk to you, I talk to God."

Like that. So, he meant that, Rāmakṛṣna meant that. He was really, inside, he was a Śaivite. But he had no theory in hand of Shaivism, but he was a Śaivite–Rāmakṛṣṇa Paramahaṁsa.

JOACHIM: Does that mean that he was a real Śaivite if he had no theory at hand or he is only . . . ?

SWAMIJI: No, he was a Śaivite.

JOACHIM: He was a real Śaivite.

SWAMIJI: A real Śaivite, internally a Śaivite.

JOACHIM: So, everybody of any religion . . .

SWAMIJI: But he thought he had only the substance of Vedānta, so he would . . .

ERNIE: Draw from that.

SWAMIJI: . . . he would draw from that, that this is the point.

JOACHIM: Is it possible to say that he was a real Śaivite?

SWAMIJI: Because it can be drawn from anything.

---

393 *Spanda Kārikā* 1.13, page 19.

394 This is refuting the Vedantic idea (as stated in *Spanda Kārikā* 1.13) that the state of the Absolute is a void (*śunya*), which can only be remembered afterwards when one come out of *samādhi*. According to Shaivism, this kind of *samādhi* is just like deep sleep.

JOACHIM: Yeah, I know that.

SWAMIJI: This Shaivism can be drawn from anything, anything rubbish also.

DENISE: Jesus Christ.

SWAMIJI: Yes.

JOACHIM: But he is a dualist–Jesus Christ. How can it be monist Shaivism then? It is so dualistic.

SWAMIJI: Who?

JOACHIM: Jesus Christ. Christianity is a very harsh dualism.

SWAMIJI: No, then you have not understood this.

JOACHIM: But the orthodoxy is really based on dualism.

SWAMIJI: Who? Which author?

ERNIE: The church, the religion.

JOACHIM: The church and for the mystics . . .

SWAMIJI: Who, who, who?

ERNIE: The people.

SWAMIJI: The people don't think . . .

DENISE: They didn't understand.

SWAMIJI: They didn't understand Christ, the theory of Christ.

JOACHIM: But the church, for example, forbade the mystics.

SWAMIJI: Then keep him on the shelf.

DENISE: Keep him on the shelf (laughter).

SWAMIJI: Then keep him on the shelf for the time being (laughter) and go on with Shaivism then if it is so, because I have not gone through that theory properly.

GANJOO: Christianity says, "thou art that".

JOACHIM: No, I don't believe that it is a monism.

SWAMIJI:

Audio 10 - 29:37

nāpi siddānta dṛṣṭivat viśvottīrṇam eva paraṁ tattvaṁ ityevaṁrūpaṁ,

This also cannot be admitted. This also cannot be admitted, this theory that the state of God consciousness is above the universe. First, we have explained that point. Which point?

JOHN: The world is not the non-existence of . . .

SWAMIJI: When the negation of the world takes place, then the state of God consciousness shines.

ERNIE: This is the first point and this is wrong.

SWAMIJI: This is wrong. The second point is, He is above this; He has created this universe and He remains above this, above the universe. This point is also wrong.

Then?

DENISE: He is above the universe and He is in the universe.

SWAMIJI: No, being and becoming, being and becoming. This is the theory of *Pratyabhijñā darśana.*[395] Being and becoming. He has become the universe. He has become the universe, He has not created the universe. There is a vast difference between "creating" and "becoming".

DENISE: This is His body.

SWAMIJI: This is His body![396]

---

395 The school (*darśana*) of Recognition (*Pratyabhijñā*). "The word *pratyabhijñā* means "to spontaneously once again recognize and realize your Self." Here you have only to realize, you do not have to practice. There are no *upāyas* (means) in the *Pratyabhijñā* system. You must simply recognize who you are. Wherever you are, whether you are at the level of Supreme Being, at the level of *yoga*, or at that level which is disgusting, you can recognize your own nature then and there without moving anywhere or doing anything." *Kashmir Shaivism–The Secret Supreme*, 19.130.

396 "This whole universe rises from that *sāmānya spanda. Sāmānya spanda* is where there is no differentiateness, and that is Śiva. *Svaśaktyā*, from His *svātantrya śakti*, [the universe] is created. It is created from *sāmānya spanda*, and then, *tatraiva*, in that *sāmānya spanda*, [the universe] appears in *bhairava-viśeṣa-spandātmani*, in *viśeṣa spanda* of Bhairava–that is *śakti pradhānāt*, the predominance of Śakti. Śakti is *viśeṣa spanda*, where you find differentiatedness of each and every object. So it is created like that, this whole universe." *Parātrīśikā Vivaraṇa* (LJA archive). See Appendix 15 for

So, *viśvottīrṇa*[397] is also not applicable; *viśvottīrṇa*, that He is above this universe. "He is universal (*viśvamaya*)", this also is not correct. "He is above the universe", this is also not correct. Because . . .

Audio 10 - 31:12

tasyopalabdhiḥ satataṁ tripadāvyabhicāriṇī /[398]

Viśvottīrṇa, "He is above the universe", it is incorrect how? It is said in the *Spanda* [*Kārikā* that] you find/realize the state of God consciousness in wakefulness, in dreaming, and the dreamless state also. How can It be above this?

Do you understand what I mean? You don't understand.

ERNIE: What does waking, dreaming, and deep sleep have to do with His involvement in this universe?

SWAMIJI: No, if He would have been existing only in the state of *turya* and *turyātītā*, then He would not have been perceived in the state of wakefulness, in the state of dreaming, and the dreamless state. As long as He is perceived in the dreamless state, the dreaming state, and wakefulness, it means He is everywhere!

JOACHIM: And not isolated only in *turya* as marked by the Vedānta.

SWAMIJI: Yes. That is what he says here.

Audio 10 - 32:10

nāpi aprakaṭita akula svarūpa kula prakriyā śāstravat, viśvamayameva pūrṇaṁ rūpaṁ [*ityevaṁ svabhāvam*] /

This also cannot be admitted that, "He is universal (*viśvamaya*)". He is not universal also. How can He be universal? If He is universal, [then] beyond the universal state (*viśvottīrṇa*) is not existing–then beyond the universal state is not existing. There are one hundred and eighteen worlds, which our *yogi*s have perceived in the state of *samādhi*–one hundred and

---

an explanation of 'Creation in Kashmir Shaivism'.

397 *Viśvottīrṇa* (transcendental, i.e., above the universe), *viśvamaya* (immanent, i.e. universal).

398 *Spanda Kārikā* 1.17, page 26.

eighteen worlds–but there are more worlds which they have not perceived. It is not only one hundred and eighteen worlds that have been created in this universe. There are numberless one hundred and eighteen worlds, numberless twenty million worlds. And above that is also existing God consciousness. So, it is vast. You cannot understand His tricks, ways. Whose?

DENISE: Lord Śiva's.

SWAMIJI: It is why I call Him always "a Bloody Fool".

DEVOTEES: (laughter)

SWAMIJI: Because He has kept so much treasure, so much treasure under His possession, and given us only just a blow.

DEVOTEES: (laughter)

SWAMIJI: This is unjust. Is it not unjust?

ERNIE: We must deserve this.

SWAMIJI: We are deserving, yes, because we have it.

Audio 10 - 33:47

yadā kṣobhaḥ pralīyeta tadā syātparamaṁ padam //[399]

This won't fit then if It is just introverted. The state of God consciousness would be only . . .

JOHN: Introverted.

SWAMIJI: . . . introverted, yes.

JOHN: Without having . . .

SWAMIJI: Without having adjustment in the world. If It is aloof from the world, then this part of the *śloka* won't fit.

JOHN: If it is only transcendental meditation and not . . .

SWAMIJI: Yes.

---

399 "*Yadā kṣobhaḥ*, and this is agitation; these [organs] are agitated by this, by being [in] the extroverted position. The position must be diverted inside. *Yadā kṣobhaḥ pralīyet*, when that position will be diverted inside and this agitation will be vanished, *tadā syāt paramaṁ padam*, then the supreme state of God consciousness will be there, in the organs also. The organs will be divine. . . . *Tadā syāt paramaṁ padam*, then that supreme state is shining already there." *Spanda Kārikā* 1.9, page 13.

iti samastaśātrārthaṁ vākaikavākyatayā paryālocya [sarvāsu daśasu]

This way, the essence of all *śāstra*s–he has come to this point after going through the essence of all *śāstra*s; he has come to this point, we have come to this point–that *sarvadā* (always), *sarvāsu daśasu*, in all activities, in all states of your life, . . .

Audio 10 - 34:43

dṛḍaśaṁkarātmakasvasvabhāvapratipattyā [avasthātavyam],

. . . you must attain the perception of *śaṁkara svabhāva*, the nature of Śiva, and you should remain there, you should establish your mind there.

natu atra manāgapi avajñā [*atra*] *vidheyā* /

You should not neglect this point.

akhyātinirharaṇāyaiva tu sarvadā yatna āstheyaḥ

So, for removing away, putting aside, the ignorance, you have always to [apply] yourself with absolute effort.

na tu sā daśāsti yatra śivatā na sphurati,
iti upadiṣṭaṁ bhavati / [not recited]

Na tu sā daśāsti, in other words, there is no such state of life where *śivatā* does not exist, where the state of Śiva is not present. This is what we understand through this book.

yadādiṣṭaṁ parameṣṭhinā śrīsvacchandādiśāṣtreṣu

Lord Śiva has also explained this in the *Svacchanda Śāstra* and other *śāstra*s also.

Audio 10 - 36:06

yatra yatra nilīyeta manas tatraiva bhāvayet /
calitvā yāsyati kutra sarvaṁ śivamayaṁ yataḥ //[400]
[not recited in full]

Wherever your mind flows, fix your awareness of God consciousness there. Don't try to put your mind away from that point. Wherever this mind . . .

JOHN: Is carried to.

SWAMIJI: Goes.

JOHN: Goes.

SWAMIJI: Yes.

JOHN: So don't spend your energy trying to move your mind . . .

SWAMIJI: No (affirmative).

JOHN: . . . to some other point, just be . . .

SWAMIJI: Just think that *there* also is the existence of God. *Calitvā yāsyati kutra*, if it goes, moves here and there, this mind, where will it move? It will move in the cycle of God consciousness, so you are [always] There.[401]

ihāpi vakṣyati

In this also, he will explain in this *Spanda* [*Kārikā*]:
'. *na sāvasthā na yā śivaḥ* /'[402]

That state is not existing where Śiva is not present.

The Śiva *sūtra* also says this. Not this Śiva *Sūtra* which we have read.[403] This is some other Śiva *sūtra*:

400 The verse as it appears in the *Svacchanda tantra* reads: *yatra yatra mano yāti jñeyaṁ tatraiva cintayet* | *calitvā yāsyate kutra sarvaṁ śivamayaṁ yataḥ* ||4.313||

401 See also *Vijñāna Bhairava, Dhāraṇā* 90.

402 *Spanda Kārikā* 2.4, page 47.

403 The *Śiva Sūtra Vimarśini* of Vasugupta. This text has been published as the *Shiva Sutras–The Supreme Awakening* (Lakshmanjoo Academy Book Series, 2015).

'sakṛdvibhāto'yamātmā pūrṇo'sya . . .'

This nature of your Self is always perceived, is always present, in fullness.

'. . . na kvāpi aprakāśa saṁbhavaḥ /'[404]

There is no question of Its absence anywhere, in any state of life.

There is another reference:

Audio 10 - 37:33

'cidghanamātmapūrṇaṁ viśvam'[405]

This whole universe is filled with God consciousness.

JOHN: Why do they always use "*cidghanam*"? *Ghanam* means "mass of consciousness" or . . .

SWAMIJI: No, *ghanam* is just like in a rock of salt, this salty taste is *ghana*, filled.

JOHN: Compacted in there.

SWAMIJI: It is all salt, nothing else.

JOHN: So *ghana* doesn't really mean "a mass" like that. It's not like a "mass of consciousness".

SWAMIJI: No, *ghana* is just . . .

ERNIE: Concentrated.

SWAMIJI: . . . concentrated.

JOHN: Concentrated pure consciousness.

SWAMIJI: Yes.

vyākhyātamidaṁ samastaśāstrāthasūtraṇaparamārtham-atiprasannagambhīramādisūtraṁ, [karotu sarvasya śivam] //

---

404 This verse is quoted by Abhinavagupta in his *Īśvara Pratyabhijñā Vivṛtti Vimarśini*. It is from the *Sārasvatasaṅgraha Sūtra* which is no longer available.

405 Unstated source.

So this way, we have explained this first *sūtra* of the *Spanda* [*Kārikā*], which is *samastaśāstrārtham*, where all of the points of *śāstra*s, all *śāstra*s, are existing in this first *sūtra* of the *Spanda* [*Kārikā*]. It is *prasanna*, it is quite clear [and] *gambhīram*, it is deep. So, we have explained this deep and . . .

ERNIE: Clear.

SWAMIJI: . . . clear *sūtra*, clear *śloka*, the first *śloka*, and this will make everybody peaceful in the state of Śiva–this explanation of mine.

Kṣhemarāja's concluding verses

Now these three *śloka*s of Kṣhemarāja:

Audio 10 - 39:02

śāstrābderarthamātraṁ parimitamatayaḥ ke'pi saṁprāpya tuṣṭāḥ

There are some *yogi*s, some *sādhaka*s, in this world found, but they have got *parimitamataya*, very inferior knowledge, they possess very inferior knowledge. There are some people like that, some *sādhaka*s, some aspirants, like that [who] *śāstrabdher arthamātram*, they just go through *śāstra*, through this *Trika śāstra*, and derive from that the [literal] meaning of that and are satisfied with that. They don't go deep in the . . .

ERNIE: The real meaning.

JOHN: What the real . . . what it is pointing to.

SWAMIJI: . . . in the depth of that *śāstra*. They just understand the word meaning and they are satisfied. They say, "We have . . ."

ERNIE: Understood.

SWAMIJI: ". . . we have understood." There are such people.

ERNIE: (laughter)

SWAMIJI:

kecit naivāpnuvanti pravitata-yatanāḥ pāramasyāpare tu /

There are some classes of aspirants who *pravitatayatanāḥ*, they are bent upon, they strive to find out, the reality of God, the reality of *śāstra*, what is behind that, what is existing, what truth is existing behind . . .

ERNIE: The word.

SWAMIJI: . . . behind the word. They are trying, they are striving to find out that truth, but they don't come to that end. They don't understand that in the real sense.

JOHN: Even though they want to.

SWAMIJI: There are some people like that.

Audio 10 - 40:49

poplūyante'rdhabhāge tṛṇavadatha
pare majjanonmajjanābhiḥ
khidyante'nye tu netuṁ nikhilam-
idamathāpyarthiṣūdvāntamīśaḥ //1//

There are some people, some aspirants, they dive deep in the *śāstra*s, they want to find out that [knowledge], but they flow on the surface, they partly flow on the surface of that great ocean of the knowledge of *śāstra*s. They float on the surface of that . . .

JOHN: Ocean of knowledge.

SWAMIJI: . . . ocean of knowledge, and sometime *majjana-unmajjanābhiḥ*, they dive deep in that sometimes. At some stages, they dive deep in its truth, but then they come out again and float [on the surface] again. So, they get some touch of that God consciousness when diving deep, and they come out again and float on the surface of that ocean.

ERNIE: Is that also the "words understanding" . . . ?

SWAMIJI: Yes, they just are going to understand and then come out again.

ERNIE: *Acha.*

SWAMIJI: [They understand] halfway and then float on the surface again. *Khidyante'nye tu netuṁ nikhilamidam athāpy-arthiṣūdvāntamiśāḥ*, and some are *iśāḥ* (masters); some masters, they strive wholeheartedly (*khidyante* means, they strive wholeheartedly) to dive deep in the essence of all *śāstra*s and they vomit the essence of *śāstra*s [to] people. There are some people like that also. So, you should prefer those.

ERNIE: (laughter)

SWAMIJI:

Audio 10 - 42:51

smṛtipathajuṣi yasminpāśabandhaprabandhā
jhaṭiti vighaṭitāntargranthayo viślathante /
sphurati ca citicandrānandaniḥṣyandidhārā-
mṛtarasapariṣekastaṁ śivaṁ saṁśrayāmaḥ //2//

I bow, I prostrate, at the feet of Lord Śiva. I prostrate at the feet of Lord Śiva whose *smṛtipathajuṣi*, when you remember Him, when you remember Him in your mind, in your thought, at that moment, what happens to that [person] who remembers His name–whose name? Lord Śiva's name–*pāśa-bandha-prabandhā jhaṭiti vighaṭita antara granthayo viślath-ante*, all bondage and all obstacles on the spiritual path, all obstructions and all knots, . . .

"Knots" you know?

ERNIE: *Saṁsāra.*

SWAMIJI: . . . they get loosened, they are . . .

ERNIE: Dissolved.

SWAMIJI: . . . dissolved, they get dissolved, and instantaneously (*jhaṭiti*).

ERNIE: Just by the thought.

SWAMIJI: By thinking, by whose thinking, by whose thought. *Sphurati*–and they are removed at once, instantaneously, and then, what happens next to them?–*sphurati ca citi candra ananda niḥṣyandi dhārā*, and that stream of *ānanda*, the supreme bliss of consciousness, the stream of supreme consciousness, flows in their mind with great force. *Amṛta rasa pariṣekaḥ*, and they dive deep in that *rasa* of nectar. In that water of nectar, they dive deep and get purified instantaneously by whose memory, by whose remembrance.

ERNIE: Śiva.

SWAMIJI: I bow to that Lord Śiva.

Audio 10 - 45:13

sarvatra pratibodhaviddhamahaso vidyābdhiśītadyuter-
helālokanakarmamocitanatānantārthisārthādguroḥ /
śrutvā samyagidaṁ prabhorabhinavātsmṛtvā ca
kiṁcinmayā

My master was Abhinavagupta. *Prabhor abhinavāt*, from the lips, from the divine lips of [my] master, I have heard the essence of this *spanda*, the essence of this . . .

JOHN: He has learned this from Abhinavagupta or Abhinavagupta's master?

SWAMIJI: No, Abhinavagupta. Abhinavagupta was his immediate master.

JOHN: He says here, "The lips of my master".

SWAMIJI: *Idaṁ samyak prabhor-abhinavāt śrutvā*, this theory of *spanda* I have learnt and I have understood from the lips of my master who was, whose name was, Abhinavagupta.

JOHN: The glorious Abhinavagupta.

SWAMIJI: And *smṛtvā ca kiṁcit mayā*, and I have thought over it afterwards, myself also, what I heard from his divine lips. Whose [lips]?

JOHN: Abhinavagupta's. Kṣhemarāja's thinking.

SWAMIJI: Who was Abhinavagupta? *Sarvatra pratibodha-viddhamahaso*, all-round he was pierced with the knowledge of God consciousness–he himself. Who?

DEVOTEES: Abhinavagupta.

SWAMIJI: Abhinavapupta. All-round, from all sides, he was pierced, he was penetrated, with the knowledge of God consciousness.

ERNIE: Saturated.

SWAMIJI: Yes.

Audio 10 - 46:51

Sarvatra pratibodhaviddhamahasaḥ. And *vidyābdhiśītad-yuter*, and he was *vidyābdhi-śītadyuteḥ* (*vidyābdhiḥ* means "ocean of knowledge"), for the ocean of knowledge, he was *śītadyuteḥ* (the moon).

GANJOO: He was . . . ?

SWAMIJI: The moon (*śītadyutiḥ*). *Śītadyutiḥ* [means], who has got cold rays, the holder of cold rays. Who is the holder of cold rays?

DENISE: The moon.

SWAMIJI: Yes.

GANJOO: This [moon] attracts the sea to itself.

SWAMIJI: Because when the moon rises, the tides get agitated at once without a storm, without wind.

ERNIE: Without effort.

SWAMIJI: Without effort. So, he was *śītadyutiḥ* for . . .

JOHN: Knowledge, the ocean of knowledge.

SWAMIJI: . . . for the ocean of knowledge.

GANJOO: Knowledge would go to him rather than he would go to the knowledge.

SWAMIJI: *Helālokanakarmamocitanatānantārthisārthā-guroḥ*, and he was that master who would adjust friendliness with those who were *anantasārthisārthāt*; *anantasārthi*, who were treading [according to] his directions, who were treading on the path, on the spiritual path . . .

JOHN: Under his direction.

SWAMIJI: . . . under his directions. He was very friendly to them.

DENISE: Abhinavagupta.

SWAMIJI: Abhinavagupta. And being very friendly to them, he would remove all of the dirt of ignorance from their minds playfully.

GANJOO: *Helā.*

ERNIE: Friendly.

SWAMIJI: No. *Helā* [means] "playfully", without any effort. It was no problem for him to remove that dirt from their minds. It was just a play for him.

Audio 10 - 49:06

kṣemeṇārthijanārthitena
vivṛtaṁ śrīspandasūtraṁ manāk //3// [not recited]

And from that Abhinavagupta's lips, I have heard the essence of this *Spanda* [*Kārikā*] and I have thought over it myself for some time. *Kṣemeṇa*, I am Kṣhemarāja, *ārthi-janārthitena*, and I was forced, I was compelled, by my devotees, by my immediate devotees, to do the exposition of this *Spanda* [*Kārikā*], so I have completed the exposition of this [first] *Spanda sūtra*.

GANJOO: *Manāk*.

SWAMIJI: *Manāk* means, . . .

GANJOO: A little.

SWAMIJI: . . . just a little. *Bas*!

iti spanda sandoha samāptā

This is your lesson. This is finished.

| | Here ends the Spanda Sandoha | |

Audio 10 - 49:54

[Additional Questions]

SWAMIJI: What would you like me to explain now after you leave?

DEVOTEE: What is the meaning of "*spanda*"? [inaudible]

SWAMIJI: Established stable movement.

ERNIE: And "*sandoha*" means?

SWAMIJI: *Sandoha* means "the exposition".

ERNIE: Of that movement.

SWAMIJI: Yes, *sandoha* means, just milking the cow; you derive milk from the udders of the cow. This is *sandoha*, *sandohana*, *dvyayam*.

GANJOO: *Dohana*.

ERNIE: So, "milking" the understanding of *spanda*. Is that the idea?

SWAMIJI: Yes.

ERNIE: So, that *śakti cakra* is just explaining that movement in that . . .

SWAMIJI: God consciousness.

ERNIE: . . . of those energies

SWAMIJI: Yes.

ERNIE: I see.

GANJOO: This is the first kick of the vibratory world.

ERNIE: And this *Spanda* [*Kārikā*] was before Abhinavagupta?

SWAMIJI: Of course.

JOHN: No, he means the teaching, the *spanda śāstra*s.

SWAMIJI: No, it was lying in the body of Tantras, hiddenly.

ERNIE: Which? Which?

SWAMIJI: The *spanda*. The theory of *spanda* was hidden in the body of the Tantras.

ERNIE: And how was it extracted?

SWAMIJI: And it was extracted by Vasugupta.

ERNIE: I see.

GANJOO: The *Kārikā*s are from Vasugupta.

ERNIE: So, all *spanda*s came after him?

SWAMIJI: No, he reproduced it, reinstalled it separately.

ERNIE: Under his investigation.

Audio 10 - 51:35

SWAMIJI: Yes. Because, afterwards, there were reproducers of Shaivism in four sections from the Tantras. They got this exposition from the Tantras. So, it was reproduced; it was not the first production, it was not a new production.

JOHN: "Four sections" means?

SWAMIJI: The Spanda section . . .

JOHN: Oh, and then the Krama section.

SWAMIJI: . . . Krama section, Pratyabhijñā *śāstra*, and Kula system.

JOHN: Kula *śāstra*.

ERNIE: But all of those come from the Tantras.

SWAMIJI: Tantras, yes. And those masters have . . .

ERNIE: Seen those.

SWAMIJI: . . . have exposed that [*spanda* principle]. . .

ERNIE: I see.

SWAMIJI: . . . from Tantras.

ERNIE: After Vasugupta.

SWAMIJI: No. Vasugupta did it first. Vasugupta's [*Spanda Kārikā*] is the exposition of the *spanda* theory.

ERNIE: The theory.

SWAMIJI: The theory of *spanda*.

ERNIE: But this *Spanda Sandoha* . . .

SWAMIJI: It is exposition of that theory.

ERNIE: Of the *spanda* theory.

DEVOTEE: The main *śloka* is from Vasugupta.

ERNIE: But the text came from Tantra.

SWAMIJI: No, the text is of Vasugupta.

ERNIE: I see.

SWAMIJI: He composed these *śloka*s of the Spanda [*Kārikā*].

JOHN: *Śiva Sūtra*s.

SWAMIJI: *Śiva Sūtra*s, yes. *Śiva Sūtra*s and *Spanda* [*Kārikā*].

JOHN: And the *Spanda Kārikā*s.

GANJOO: *Spanda Kārikā*s, yes.

JOHN: So, in our Shaivism, we hold that nothing's new?

SWAMIJI: No (affirmative). Erakanātha[406] [provided] the exposition of this Krama system.

JOHN: In ancient times.

Audio 10 - 53:10

SWAMIJI: And Somānanda was the reproducer of the Pratyabhijñā system, the theory of recognition.

ERNIE: But, it was all there all the time.

SWAMIJI: Yes, yes. It was lying, it was lying secretly in Tantras.

ERNIE: And they just extracted it . . .

SWAMIJI: Yes, extracted it.

ERNIE: . . . and presented.

JOHN: Somānanda then . . . who were the other two from Krama and Kula school?

SWAMIJI: No, Krama I told you. Krama is . . .

JOHN: Vasagupta?

SWAMIJI: No, Erakanātha. Erakanātha is the reproducer of the Krama system.

JOHN: And Somanātha is the Pratybhijña system.

JOHN: Somānanda.

---

406 In *Tantrāloka* chapter 4, Swamiji says it was Avatārakanātha, and not Erakanātha who was the founder of Krama System. Avatārakanātha was another name for Śivānandanātha.

SWAMIJI: Somānanda. Somānanda is reproducer of the Pratybhijña system.

ERNIE: Vasagupta is?

SWAMIJI: No. Vasagupta is of Spanda.

ERNIE: Spanda.

GANJOO: Kula is?

SWAMIJI: Maccandanātha. Maccandanātha is the reproducer of . . .

ERNIE: This knowledge.

SWAMIJI: . . . of the Kula system.

JOHN: So, these are the four . . .

SWAMIJI: Four sections of Shaivism, Trika.

ERNIE: All based on Tantra . . .

SWAMIJI: Tantras.

ERNIE: . . . which is *āgama*s.

SWAMIJI: Yes, *āgama*s. It is just an offshoot from the lips of Lord Śiva with five mouths [i.e., Svacchandanātha][407].

ERNIE: There are other *āgama*s that are not Kashmiri *āgama*s?

SWAMIJI: There are many other *āgama*s, yes. They are not recognized here.

ERNIE: They are not recognized. So, what does the word *āgama* mean?

SWAMIJI: *Āgama* means, that [which] has come out from above.

GANJOO: *Ā-gama*, origin.

SWAMIJI: From the original source, that is Śiva.

Audio 10 - 54:43

JOHN: Why do they use the word "*tantra*" then more. They like "*tantra*"? *Tantra* means "expansion"?

SWAMIJI: Expansion [is the meaning of] *tantra*; *tanu*

---

407 See *Secret Supreme, Birth of The Tantras,* 13.87; and also Self Realization in Kashmir Shaivism, 4.71-72, 91.

vistāre, expansion.[408]

And Abhinavagupta is the reproducer of all the four sections in the *Tantrāloka*. He has put all the four sections in the *Tantrāloka*. I mean, Pratyabhijñā, in this *Parātriṁśikā* also.

GANJOO: All the four systems.

SWAMIJI: Abhinavagupta was a tiger . . .

GANJOO: Giant.

SWAMIJI: . . . on this path of this Trika. I think Abhinavagupta was more important than Śiva!

ERNIE: (laughter)

SWAMIJI: Yes.

Audio 10 - 55:29

| | END | |

408 "Expanded *śāstras* are *tantras* and not-expanded *śāstras* are *āgamas*. *Āgamas* [are residing] in His own supreme Self. They are already existing in Lord Śiva, in the shape of an *āgama*, but in the shape of illuminating way, these very *āgamas* are called *tantras*." *Kashmir Shaivism–The Secret Supreme* (LJA, Los Angeles, 2000).

Appendix

1. The Spanda System

"The fourth system which comprises the Trika philosophy is called the Spanda system. The word *spanda* means "movement". The Spanda school recognizes that nothing can exist without movement. Where there is movement, there is life, and where there is no movement, that is lifelessness. They realize that there is movement in wakefulness, dreaming, deep sleep, and *turya*. Though some thinkers argue that there is no movement in deep sleep, the philosophers of the Spanda system realize that nothing can exist without movement.

The teachings of the Spanda system, which is an important practical system, are found embodied in the *Vijñāna Bhairava Tantra*, the *Svacchanda Tantra*, and in the sixth chapter of the *Tantrāloka*."

Kashmir Shaivism–The Secret Supreme, 19.134.

"This universe, which is a world of consciousness, is filled with and is one with the supreme state of God consciousness. God consciousness is *spanda*, a unique reality of supreme movement filled with nectar and an outpouring of the supreme bliss of independence."

Shiva Sutra–The Supreme Awakening, 1.9.

"*Spanda* is nominated as *sphurattā* (vigor, life, life-giver, power of existence), *ūrmiḥ* (tide), *balam* (strength), *udyoga* (force), *hṛdayam* (heart), *sāram* (essence), and *mālinī* (supreme energy). These are nominations which are attributed to this *spanda* in the *śāstra*s."

Spanda Sandoha of Kṣhemarāja (LJA archive).

"The element of *spanda* is that being of God consciousness in which this whole universe exists and from which this whole universe comes out. And [God consciousness] is not only the resting place of the universe, this is the *prasara sthana* also, the flowing energy. This universe comes out from That. It *has* to exist in God consciousness and it is coming out from God consciousness *in* God consciousness, because there is no other space for the universe to exist."

Parātrīśikā Vivaraṇa (LJA archive).

2. *Svātantrya*

"All these five energies of God consciousness are produced by His *svātantrya śakti* of freedom, His free power. That is called *svātantrya śakti. Svātantrya śakti* produces these five energies of Lord Śiva. And *cit śakti* is actually based on His nature, *ānanda śakti* is based on His *śakti* (on His Pārvatī), *īcchā śakti* is based in *Sādaśiva*, and *jñāna śakti* (the energy of knowledge) is based on *Īśvara*, and the energy of *kriyā* is based on *Śuddhāvidya*. All these five pure states of Lord Śiva are one with Lord Śiva. *Cit śakti* indicates Lord Śiva's actual position, *ānanda śakti* indicates Lord Śiva's position of *śakti*, and *icchā śakti* indicates Lord Śiva's position of *Sādaśiva*, and *jñāna śakti* indicates His position of *Īśvara*, and *Śuddhāvidya* is [His] fifth position [viz., *kriyā śakti*]. All these five positions are filled with God consciousness. Below that is the scale of *māyā*, illusion. That will go from *māya* to earth."

Swami Lakshmanjoo, *Special Verses on Practice* (LJA archive).

"The definition of *svātantrya* is "freedom in action and freedom in knowledge"; when you know with your freedom, when you act with your freedom. When you know and you don't succeed in that knowledge, there is not *svātantrya*. When there is not *svātantrya*, it is not really knowledge. When there is not *svātantrya*, it is not really action. The action of individuals is just like that. Individuals know, they know something–you can't say that they don't know anything–they know something, but that knowledge has not *svātantrya*. And they act also, they do something, but that doing also has not *svātantrya*. So, without *svātantrya*, doing and knowing has no value. When there is *svātantrya*, it is fully valued.

That essence of *svātantrya* is *anavacchinna* (beyond limitation), all-round beyond limitation. There is no such limit found in that state. *Vicchinna camatkāra maya viśrāntyā*, and this limited state of being is also found there. [Lord Śiva] is unlimited, but the limited cycle of God consciousness is also found there. So it is both limited and unlimited. That being who is limited only, he is not true. That being who is unlimited only, he is not true. Why? Because he is limited. The being who is unlimited is not true because he is unlimited only [and] not limited. That fullness of God consciousness is found [in one] who is limited and, at the same time, unlimited also. That is the fullness of God consciousness. The fullness of God consciousness is where nothing is excluded. Whatever is excluded, it is also one with that. That is the fullness of God consciousness."

Parātrīśikā Vivaraṇa (LJA archive).

"Lord Śiva creates this external universe for the sake of realizing His own nature. That is why this external universe is called "Śakti", because it is the means to realize one's own nature. Therefore, in order to recognize His nature, He must first become ignorant of His nature. Only then can He recognize it.

Why should He want to recognize His nature in the first place? It is because of His freedom, His *svātantrya* (independence). This is the play of the universe. This universe was created solely for the fun and joy of this realization. It happens that when His fullness overflows, He wants to [become] incomplete. He wants to appear as being incomplete just so He can achieve completion. This is the play of His *svātantrya*: to depart from His own nature in order to enjoy it again. It is this *svātantrya* that has created this whole universe. This is the play of Śiva's *svātantrya*.

This kind of action cannot be accomplished by any power in this universe other than Lord Śiva. Only Lord Śiva can do this. Only Lord Śiva, by His own *svātantrya*, can totally ignore and mask His own nature. This is His *svātantrya*, His glory, His intelligence. Intelligence does not mean that in this super-drama called creation you will only play the part of a lady or a man. With this kind of intelligence, you will also play the part of rocks, of trees, of all things. This kind of intelligence is found only in the state of Lord Śiva and nowhere else."

Self Realization in Kashmir Shaivism–Fifteen Verses of Wisdom, chapter 1, Verses 5, 6 and 7, pp23-26.

"*Svātantrya śakti* and *māyā* are one. *Svātantrya śakti* is that state of energy which can produce the power of going down and coming up again. And *māyā* is not like that. *Māyā* will give you the strength of coming down and then no ability of going up. Then you cannot go up again. This is the state of *māyā*. And all these three *mala*s (impurities) reside in *māyā śākti*, not *svātantrya śakti*, although *svātantrya śakti* and *māyā śakti* are one. *Māyā śakti* is that energy, universal energy, which is owned by the individual being, the individual soul. The same energy, when it is owned by the universal Being, is called *svātantrya śakti*.

Svātantrya śakti is pure universal energy. Impure universal energy is *māyā*. It is only the formation that changes through a difference of vision. When you experience *svātantrya śakti* in a crooked way, it becomes *māyā śakti* for you. And when you realize that same *māyā śakti* in Reality, then that *māyā śakti* becomes *svātantrya śakti* for you. Therefore, *svātantrya śakti* and *māyā śakti* are actually only one and the three impurities (*mala*s), which are to be explained here, reside in *māyā śakti*, not in *svātantrya śakti*."

Kashmir Shaivism–The Secret Supreme, 7.47.

"In Vedānta, [*māyā* is] unreal. In Shaivism, *māyā* is transformed at the time of knowledge. At the time of real knowledge, *māyā* is transformed in His *śakti*, in His glory. *Māyā* becomes the glory of Paramaśiva then. When *puruṣa* realizes the reality of his nature, *māyā* becomes glory for him–*śakti*, his energy, great energy, [i.e., *svātantrya śakti*]."
Kashmir Shaivism–The Secret Supreme (LJA audio archive).

3. *Samādhi*

The state of *samādhi* is the last limb (*aṅga*) of the eight limbs of *yoga*. The eight limbs are *yama*, *niyama*, *āsana*, *prāṇayama*, *pratyāhāra*, *dhāraṇā*, *dhyāna*, and *samādhi*. In classical *yoga* texts, the state of *samādhi* is recognized to be the hightest state, but Kashmir Shaivism treats that kind of *samādhi* as a purely internal state. [*Editor's note*]

"So, if you want to perceive Him, perceive the state of Lord Śiva, as it ought to be in its real sense, enjoy this universe. You will find the exact state of Lord Śiva in the universe. You won't find the real state of Lord Śiva in *samādhi*. In *samādhi*, you will find Its not-vivid formation. The vivid formation will be found only in the universal state."
Shiva Sutras–The Supreme Awakening, 2.7.

"When this kind of existence is experienced by such a *yogi* in the very active life of the universe, in *kriyā śakti*–not only in the state of knowledge (*jñāna śakti*), not in your internal state of consciousness of Self (*icchā śakti*), but also in the active life; in the active life also he feels and experiences the state of universal consciousness of Śiva–this is called real *samādhi* for him."
Shiva Sutras–The Supreme Awakening, 3.6

yāmavasthāṁ samālambya yadayaṁ mama vakṣyati /
tadavaśyaṁ kariṣye'hamiti saṁkalpya tiṣṭhati //SpK 23//

"*Yāmavasthāṁ samā lambya*, when a *yogi* takes hold, catches hold, of that *avastha*, [establishment in] that state of *turya*, the beginning of *turya*–when a *yogi* takes hold of that state, which is felt at the beginning of *turya*–when he is likely to go in *samādhi* (he has not yet gone in *samādhi*), before going [into] that, he takes an oath in his own self according to the directions of his master [who said], "*Yadayaṁ mama vakṣyate*, you go ahead according to that which you are taught from within. You have not to listen to my directions afterwards."

When you are about to enter in *samādhi*, then you have to do according to the directions which come [from] above in *samādhi*. You have to go ahead according to the directions of *samādhi*, not according to the directions of *śāstras* or according to the directions of the master. The master's job is over there when [the disciple] is going inside. So, [the disciple takes this oath] that, "*Tad avasyaṁ kariṣye'ham*, that I will definitely do what informs me [from] within at that time of going in; *tadavasyaṁ kariṣye'ham*, I will do that definitely." *Iti saṁkalpya tiṣṭhate*, so he has to remain there with this oath that, "Whatever is felt within me, whatever order is felt within me, from myself, that I have to obey." It is the direction he gets from his master. Up to that point, he has to tread according to the directions of the master. Afterwards, the master's job is over." *Special Verses on Practice*, 44 (LJA archives).

4. The Seven Perceivers

"The first state is called *sakala*. The *sakala* state is that state where perception takes place in the objective world and not in the subjective world. In other words, I would call this state the state of *prameya*, the state of the object of perception. It is realized by its *pramātṛ*, the observer who resides in this state, in the field of objectivity and its world.

The second state is called *pralayākala*. This is the state of negation, where the whole world is negated. And the one who resides in this world of negation is called *pralayākala pramātṛ*, the observer of the *pralayākala* state. And this *pramātṛ*, this perceiver, does not experience the state of this voidness because it is actually the state of unawareness. This state would be observed at the time of *mūrcchā*, when one becomes comatose, which is like unnatural and heavy sleep, like deep sleep devoid of dreams. And the observer, *pralayākala pramātṛ*, resides in that void of unawareness. These two states [*sakala* and *pralayākala*] function in the state of individuality, not in the state of your real nature. These are states of worldly people, not spiritual aspirants.

The third state is called *vijñānākala pramātṛ*. This state is experienced by those who are on the path of *yoga*. Here, the *yogi* experiences awareness at times (but this awareness is not active awareness), and at other times, his awareness is active but he is not aware of that active awareness. This *vijñānākala pramātṛ*, therefore, takes place in two ways: sometimes it is full of action (*svātantrya*) without awareness, and sometimes it is full of awareness without action.

The fourth state of the observer is called *śuddhavidyā* and its observer is called *mantra pramātṛ*. In this state, the observer is always aware with *svātantrya*.

The next state is called *īśvara* and its observer is called *mantreśvara pramātṛ*. The word "*mantreśvara*" means "the one who has sovereignty on *mantra* (*ahaṁ*–I)." This state is like that of *mantra pramātṛ*, full of consciousness, full of bliss, full of will, full of knowledge, and full of action, however, this is a more stable state. The aspirant finds more stability here. The *mantra* for this state is "*idaṁ-ahaṁ*". The meaning of this *mantra* is that the aspirant feels that this whole universe is not false. On the contrary, he feels that this whole universe is the expansion of his own nature. In the state of *mantra pramātṛ*, he felt that the universe was false, that he was the truth of this reality. Now he unites the state of the universe with the state of his own consciousness. This is actually the unification of *jīva*, the individual, with Śiva, the universal.

The next state is the state of *sadāśiva*. The observer of this state is called *mantra maheśvara*. In this state, the observer finds himself to be absolutely one with the universal transcendental Being. He experiences this state to be more valid, more solid, and deserving of confidence. Once he enters into this state, there is no question at all of falling from it. This is the established state of his Self, his own Real nature. The *mantra* of this state is "*ahaṁ-idaṁ*". The meaning of this *mantra* is, "I am this universe." Here, he finds his Self in the universe, while in the previous state of *mantreśvara*, he found the universe in his Self. This is the difference.

The seventh and last state is the state of Śiva and the observer of this state is no other than Śiva Himself. In the other six, the state is one thing and the observer is something else. In this final state, the state is Śiva and the observer is also Śiva. There is nothing outside Śiva. The *mantra* in this state is "*ahaṁ*", universal-I. This-ness is gone, melted in His I-ness. This state is completely filled with consciousness, bliss, will, knowledge, and action."

Kashmir Shaivism–The Secret Supreme, 8.51-54.

5. *Turya* and *Turyātītā*

"When, by the grace of a master, this subjective body enters into subjective consciousness with full awareness, and maintaining unbroken awareness becomes fully illumined in its own Self, this is called the fourth state, *turya*.

From the Trika Shaivite point of view, predominance is given to the three energies of Śiva: *parā śakti* (the supreme energy), *parāparā śakti* (medium energy), and *aparā śakti* (inferior energy). The kingdom of *aparā śakti*, the lowest energy, is found in wakefulness and dreaming. The kingdom of *parāparā śakti*, the medium energy, is established in the state of sound sleep. And lastly, the kingdom of *parā śakti*, the supreme energy, is found in the state of *turya*.

The state of *turya* is said to be the penetration of all energies simultaneously, not in succession. All of the energies are residing there but are not in manifestation. They are all together without distinction. *Turya* is called "*savyāpārā*" because all of the energies get their power to function in that state. At the same time, this state is known as "*anāmayā*" because it remains unagitated by all of these energies.

Three names are attributed to this state; by worldly people, by *yogin*s, and by illuminated humans (*jñānī*s). Worldly people call it "*turya*", which means "the fourth." They use this name because they have no descriptive name for this state. They are unaware of this state and, not having experienced it, simply call it "the fourth state". *Yogin*s have attributed the name "*rūpātītā*" to this condition because this state has surpassed the touch of one's self and is the establishment of one's Self. The touch of one's self was found in sound sleep, however, the establishment of one's Self takes place in *turya*. For illuminated humans, *jñānī*s, the entire universal existence is found in this state of *turya*, collectively, as undifferentiated, in the state of totality. There is no succession here. *Jñānī*s, therefore, call this state "*pracaya*", the undifferentiated totality of universal existence.

Turyātīta is that state which is the absolute fullness of Self. It is filled with all-consciousness and bliss. It is really the last and the supreme state of the Self. You not only find this state of *turyātīta* in *samādhi*, you also find it in each and every activity of the world. In this state, there is no possibility for the practice of *yoga*. If you can practice *yoga*, then you are not in *turyātīta*. In practicing *yoga*, there is the intention of going somewhere. Here, there is nowhere to go, nothing to achieve. As concentration does not exist here, the existence of the helping hand of *yoga* is not possible.

There are only two names actually attributed to this state of *turyātīta*, one given by worldly people and one by *jñānī*s. Worldly people, because they know nothing about the state, call it "*turyātītā*", which means "that state which is beyond the fourth". *Jñānī*s, on the other hand, also have a name for it. They call it "*mahāpracaya*", which means "the unlimited and unexplainable supreme totality". *Yogin*s do not actually attribute any name to this state because they have no knowledge of it. It is completely outside of their experience. *Yogin*s have though, through the use of their imagination and guesswork, imagined one name which might be appropriate for this state: "*satatoditam*", which means "that state which has no pause, no break". It is a breakless and unitary state. In *samādhi*, It is there. When *samādhi* is absent, It is there. In the worldly state, It is there. In the dreaming state, It is there. And in the state of deep sleep, It is there. In each and every state of the individual subjective body, It is there."

Kashmir Shaivism–The Secret Supreme, 11.72-84.

"*Pūrṇatūnmukhyī daśā*, [*turya*] is situated towards the fullness of God consciousness, it is not the fullness of God consciousness. It is situated *towards* the fullness of God consciousness." *Tantrāloka* 10.271-278 (LJA archive).

"The difference between *turya* and *turyātīta* is, in *turya*, you find in *samādhi* that this whole universe is existing there in a seed form, a germ. The strength, the energy, of universal existence is existing there, but here he has [yet] to come out [into activity]. In *turyātīta*, he comes out in action and feels universal consciousness. This is the difference between *turya* and *turyātīta*."

Tantrāloka 10.288 (LJA archive).

6. *Pramiti, pramātṛ, pramāṇa, prameya bhāva*

"*Pramiti bhāva* is the supreme subjective state, *pramātṛ bhava* is the pure subjective state, *pramāṇa bhava* is the cognitive state, and *prameya bhāva* is the objective state. There is a difference between *pramātṛ bhāva* and *pramiti bhāva*. *Pramātṛi bhāva* is that state of consciousness where objective perception is attached. When that state of *pramātṛ bhāva* is attached with objective perception, that is the pure state of *pramātṛ bhāva*. When it moves to the state where there is no objective perception, there is no touch of objective perception, it is beyond objective perception, that is *pramiti bhāva*."
Tantrāloka 4.124, commentary (LJA archive).

"[*Pramiti bhāva* is an] object-less subjective state. It is residing in only pure subjective consciousness. It has nothing to do with the object. When there is the objective state also attached to the subjective state, that is not *pramiti bhāva*, that is *pramātṛ bhāva*. And when that objective state is connected with the cognitive state, that is *pramāṇa bhāva*. When that objective state is completely a pure objective state, that is *prameya bhāva*. And *pramiti bhāva* is complete subjective consciousness without the slightest touch and trace of this object. In the long run, everything resides in *pramiti bhāva*; *pramiti bhāva* is the life of all the three. This is pure consciousness, and that *pramiti bhāva* is absolutely one with *svātantrya śakti*, it is one with Lord Śiva."
Tantrāloka 11.72-73a, (LJA archive).

"In fact, this *pramiti bhāva* is the real source of understanding anything. Whatever you see, it must touch the state of *pramiti bhāva*, otherwise you won't understand it. For instance, you see [an object]. You'll only know [that object] when this sensation of [that object already] resides in *pramiti bhāva*, in that super state of subjective consciousness. And the super state of subjective consciousness is not differentiated. From that undifferentiated point of *pramiti bhāva*, the differentiated flow of *pramātṛ bhāva* and *pramāṇa bhāva* flow out." *Tantrāloka* 11.62 (LJA archive).

"It is *nirvikalpa*, it is a thoughtless state. And in that thoughtless state, [all knowledge] must reside, otherwise it is not known. It will be unknown for . . . eternity."
Tantrāloka, 11.68-69 (LJA archive).

"For instance, when you are [giving a lecture while] reading your book, your consciousness is *with* an object. When you are giving a lecture without a book, without any support, your consciousness is *without* an object, it flows out. This is the state of *pramiti bhāva*."
Tantrāloka 6.180 (LJA archive).

7. *Malas*

The three impurities are gross (*sthūla*), subtle (*sūkṣma*), and subtlest (*para*). The gross impurity is called *kārmamala*. It is connected with actions. It is that impurity which inserts impressions such as those which are expressed in the statements, "I am happy", "I am not well", "I have pain", "I am a great man", "I am really lucky", etc., in the consciousness of the individual being.

The next impurity is called *māyīyamala*. This impurity creates differentiation in one's own consciousness. It is the impurity of ignorance (*avidyā*), the subtle impurity. The thoughts, "This house is mine", "That house is not mine", "This man is my friend", "That man is my enemy", "She is my wife", "She is not my wife", are all created by *māyīyamala*. *Māyīyamala* creates duality.

The third impurity is called *āṇavamala*. It is the subtlest impurity.* *Āṇavamala* is the particular internal impurity of the individual. Although he reaches the nearest state of the consciousness of Śiva, he has no ability to catch hold of that state. That inability is the creation of *āṇavamala*. For example, if you are conscious of your own nature and then that consciousness fades away, and fades away quickly, this fading is caused by *āṇavamala*.

Āṇavamala is *apūrṇatā*, non-fullness. It is the feeling of being incomplete. Due to this impurity, you feel incomplete in every way. Though you feel incomplete, knowing that there is some lack in you, yet you do not know what this lack really is.

You want to hold everything, and yet no matter what you hold, you do not fill your sense of lacking, your gap. You cannot fill this lacking unless the master points it out to you and then carries you to that point.

Of these three impurities, *āṇavamala* and *māyīyamala* are not in action, they are only in perception, in experience. It is *kārmamala* which is in action."

Kashmir Shaivism–The Secret Supreme, 7.47-49.

*"*Āṇavamala* is the root of the other two impurities. Which are those other two impurities? *Māyīyamala* and *kārmamala*."

Parātrīśikā Vivaraṇa (LJA archive).

"This whole universal existence, which is admitted by other thinkers that it is ignorance, that it is *māyā* (illusion), that is pain, it is torture–they explain it like that–but we Shaivites don't explain like that. We Shaivites explain that this [universe] is the expansion of your own nature. *Mala* is nothing; *mala* is only your free will of expanding your own nature.

So we have come to this conclusion that *mala* is not a real impurity [i.e., substance]. It is your own choice; it is the choice of Lord Śiva. The existence of impurity is just the choice of Lord Śiva, it is not some thing. It is *svarūpa svātantrya māṭraṁ*, it is just your will, just your independent glory.

If you realize that it is *svarūpa svātantrya māṭraṁ*, [that] it is your own play, then what will an impure thing do? An impure thing will only infuse purity in you if you realize that the impurity is not existing at all, it is just your own play, just your own independent expansion.

[So], *mala* is neither formless nor with form. It is just ignorance. It doesn't allow knowledge to function, knowledge is stopped. *Mala* is the absence of knowledge. *Mala* is not something substantial. So, this absence of knowledge takes place only by ignorance, otherwise there is no *mala*. In the real sense, *mala* does not exist, impurity does not exist."

Tantrāloka 9.79-83, (LJA archive).

8. Seven States of *Ānanda* (*turya*)

The following paraphrase is from *Kashmir Shaivism–The Secret Supreme*, 16.107:

The practical theory of the seven states of *turya*, also known as the seven states of *ānanda* (bliss), was taught to the great Śaivite philosopher, Abhinavagupta, by his master, Śaṁbhunātha.

The first state of *turya* is called *nijānanda*, which means "the bliss of your own Self." When you concentrate in continuity with great reverence, with love, affection, and devotion, then your breath becomes very fine and subtle. Automatically, you breathe very slowly. At that moment, you experience giddiness. It is a kind of intoxicating mood. And when the giddiness becomes firm and stable, this is the second state of *turya* known as *nirānanda*, which means "devoid of limited bliss." Here the aspirant falls asleep at once and enters that gap or junction which is known to be the start of *turya*. At that moment the aspirant hears hideous sound and sees furious forms. For example, he may experience that the whole house has collapsed upon him, or he may experience that there is a fire burning outside and this fire will burn everything including himself. He may actually think that he is going to die, but these thoughts are wrong thoughts and he must ignore them. When the aspirant desires to move from individuality to universality, all of these experiences occur because individuality has to be shaken off.

If you continue with tolerance, breathing, and internally reciting your *mantra* according to the instructions of your master, then these terrible sounds and forms vanish and a pulling and a pushing in your breathing passage begins to occur and you feel as if you are choking, that you cannot breathe. At that point you must insert more love and affection for your practice, and then after some time, this choking sensation will pass.

This state of hideous sounds and forms, followed by the sensation that you are choking and that your breathing is about to stop, is called *parānanda*, which means "the *ānanda* (bliss) of breathing." Here, your breathing becomes full of bliss and joy even though you are experiencing terrible forms and sounds. If you maintain your practice continuously with intense devotion, your breath stops at the center of what we call *lambikā sthāna*, which in English is known as the "soft palate." This *lambikā sthāna* is found on the right side near the pit of the throat. Here the aspirant experiences that his breath is neither moving out nor coming in. He feels that his breath is moving round and round, that it is rotating at one point. This state is called *brahmānanda*, which means, "that bliss which is all-pervading."

Here, as his breathing has stopped, the *yogi* must put his mind on his *mantra* and only his *mantra* with great devotion to Lord Śiva. If he continues this practice with great devotion, then a myriad of changes take place on his face and the apprehension of death arises in the mind of this *yogi*. He feels now that he is really dying. He is not afraid but he is apprehensive. This is the kind of death which takes place when individuality dies and universality is born. It is not a physical death, it is a mental death. The only thing the *yogi* must do here is to shed tears of devotion and pray for the experience of universal-I. After a few moments, when the whirling state of breath becomes very fast, moving ever more quickly, you must stop your breath at once. You must not be afraid. At this point, it is in your hands to stop it or to let it go.

When you stop your breathing, then what happens next is, the gate of the central vein (*madhyanāḍī*) opens at once and your breath is "sipped" down and you actually hear the sound of sipping. Here, your breath reaches down to that place called *mūlādhāra*, which is near the rectum. This state of *turya* is called *mahānanda* which means, "the great bliss."

After *mahānanda*, no effort is required by the aspirant. From this point on, everything is automatic. There is however one thing that the aspirant should observe and be cautious about, and that is that he should not think that "everything is now automatic." The more he thinks that everything will be automatic, the more surely he will remain at the state of *mahānanda*. This is why masters never tell what will take place after *mahānanda*.

From the Śaiva point of view, from *mahānanda* onwards, you must adopt *bhramavega* which means "the unknowing force." Here you have to put your force of devotion, without knowing what is to happen next. You cannot use your *mantra* because when your breath is gone, your mind is also gone, as the mind has become transformed into the formation of consciousness (*cit*). Here, breathing takes the form of force (*vega*). It is this *vega* which pierces and penetrates *mūlādhāra cakra* so that you pass through it.

When the penetration of *mūlādhāra cakra* is complete, then this force rises and becomes full of bliss, full of ecstasy, and full of consciousness. It is divine. You feel what you are actually. This is the rising of *cit kuṇḍalinī*, which rises from the *mūlādhāra cakra* to that place at the top of the skull known as *brahmarandhra*. It occupies the whole channel and is just like the blooming of a flower. This state, which is the sixth state of *turya*, is called *cidānanda*, which means, "the bliss of consciousness."

This force then presses the passage of the skull (*brahmarandhra*), piercing the skull to move from the body out into the universe. This takes place automatically, it is not to be "done." And when this *brahmarandhra* is pierced, then at once you begin to breathe out. You breathe out once for only a second, exhaling from the nostrils. After exhaling, everything is over and you are again in *cidānanda* and you again experience and feel the joy of rising, which was already present. This lasts only for a moment and then you breathe out again. When you breathe out, your eyes are open and for a moment you feel that you are outside. You experience the objective world, but in a peculiar way. Then once again, your breathing is finished and your eyes are closed and you feel that you are inside. Then again your eyes are open for a moment, then they close for a moment, and then they again open for a moment. This is the state of *krama mudrā*, where transcendental I-consciousness is beginning to be experienced as one with the experience of the objective world.

The establishment of *krama mudrā* is called *jagadānanda*, which means "universal bliss." This is the seventh and last state of *turya*. In this state, the experience of Universal Transcendental Being is never lost and the whole of the universe is experienced as one with your own Transcendental

I-Consciousness.

All of the states of *turya* from *nijānanda* to *cidānanda* comprise the various phases of *nimīlanā samādhi*. *Nimīlanā samādhi* is internal subjective *samādhi*. In your moving through these six states of *turya*, this *samādhi* becomes ever more firm. With the occurrence of *krama mudrā*, *nimīlanā samādhi* is transformed into *unmīlanā samādhi*, which then becomes predominant. This is that state of extraverted *samādhi*, where you experience the state of *samādhi* at the same time you are experiencing the objective world. And when *unmīlanā samādhi* becomes fixed and permanent, this is the state of *jagadānanda*.

In terms of the process of the seven states of the perceiver, the *sakala pramātṛ*, or the waking state, is the first state of *turya*, which is the state of *nijānanda*. *Vijñānākala* is the state of *nirānanda*. *Śuddhavidyā* is the state of *parānanda*. *Īśvara* is the state of *brahmānanda*. *Sadāśiva* is the state of *mahānanda*. *Śiva* is the state of *cidānanda*. And *Paramaśiva* is the state of *jagadānanda*.

In respect of the above experiences, Swamiji once wrote the following poem.

> There is a point twixt sleep and waking
> Where thou shalt be alert without shaking.
> Enter into the new world where forms so hideous pass;
> They are passing—endure, do not be taken by the dross.
> Then the pulls and the pushes about the throttle,
> All those shalt thou tolerate.
> Close all ingress and egress,
> Yawnings there may be;
> Shed tears—crave—implore, but thou will not prostrate.
> A thrill passes—and that goes down to the bottom;
> It riseth, may it bloom forth, that is Bliss.
> Blessed Being, Blessed Being,
> O greetings be to Thee.

For the full explanation of the seven states of *ānanda* (*turya*), see *Kashmir Shaivism–The Secret Supreme*, 16.107.

In the fifth *āhnika* of *Tantrāloka* (5.43-45), Abhinavagupta explains God consciousness and the states of *turya* in relation to the five subtle *prāṇas*: *prāṇana*, *apānana*, *samānana*, *udānana*, and *vyānana*. Swamiji translates:

"*Nijānanda* is no state. It is the beginning point of putting awareness on subjective consciousness, *pramātṛ bhāva*. The first state is *nirānanda*, when you go inside, inside, inside, inside. But this is not the point to be maintained. You have to rise from that [*nirānanda*]. And the rising point is from *parānanda*.

When this *prāṇana* takes place, that is the state of *spanda*. When awareness resides in *śūnyatā* (voidness), then the rise of *prāṇana* takes place and then he enters in another world. And that is the world of *apānana vṛtti*.[409]

> Just close your eyes tightly, just close your eyes tightly–tightly, squeeze it–and you will hear that sound from inside. Don't you hear? In sexual intercourse also that sound is there. That is the sound of *apānana* that gives you joy, happiness and entire bliss.

Apānana vṛtti is the supreme *ānanda* (bliss). That is the next state of *yoga* called *parānanda*, the absolute state of happiness. There, you feel that you have drowned in the sound of that bliss. In this state of *apāna vṛtti* you feel that breathing in and out is gathered in one point. Not only breath. All differentiated perceptions of the organic field and objective field are also gathered and balled in one point. It is why he sees that this whole universe has fallen down and is shattered to pieces; this whole world, all mountains have fallen down on him, in that *apānana vṛtti*. And it takes place on the right side here just below *tālu* (the soft palate). And when you establish your awareness in *apāna vṛtti*, then those fearful forms, fearful apparitions, and fearful impressions that take place in your awareness, they subside.

---

409 *Vṛtti* means, the established state. *Prāṇana vṛitti* is that kind of state of breath which is not moving, breath without movement.
For instance, *prāṇana vṛtti* means, the established state of *prāṇa*, and *apānana vṛtti* means, the established state of *apāna*, etc.

Now, when you find that everything is completely balled inside peacefully, and there is no breathing in and out, and all the objective and cognitive world is balled inside in one pointedness without fear, then what happens next?

That *yogi* is absolutely filled with the state of joy, with the state of bliss, and that is the state of *samānana vṛtti* which is the state of *brahmānanda*.

Then that fourth state of *udānana vṛtti* takes place, where the *yogi* finds that this ball is melted in that sound of bliss. *Shssssssssssssssssssssssssssssssssss*, this very long sound is produced there and this ball is melted inside. Finished. There is no breath; this breathing process is finished. This is the state of *mahānanda*. And that sound that is not only the *shssssssssssssssssss* sound, sexual joy appears there with that sound. When you are fully established there, and have settled your awareness fully there, then, in that supreme *tejas*, the supreme light, he gets dissolved, he gets melted. He melts for good.

In the process of rising through these states, *prāṇa vṛtti* travels to *prāṇana vṛtti*, *apāna vṛtti* travels to *apānana vṛtti*, *samāna vṛtti* travels to *samānana vṛtti*, *udāna vṛtti* travels to *udānana vṛtti*, and *vyāna vṛtti* has to travel to *vyānana vṛtti*.

And when *vyāna vṛtti* travels to *vyānana vṛtti*, this is the fifth state of *ānanda* called *cidānanda*. This is the state of *mahāvyāpti*, the great pervasion, where you pervade this whole universe. But, you don't pervade this whole universe only. You pervade the negation of this whole universe also. When the state of *cidānanda* takes place, nothing is excluded, nothing remains outside. *Cidānanda* includes everything in Its being.

Now the sixth state of *ānanda* is called *jagadānanda*. This is that universal state which shines in the whole cosmos and which is strengthened and nourished by that supreme nectar of God consciousness, which is filled with knowledge which is beyond knowledge. Here there is no entry, there is no acceptance of remaining in *samādhi* or remaining in awareness and so on. That is the state of *jagadānanda*.

Abhinavagupta concludes by saying, "This state of *jagadānanda* was explained to me by my great master, Śambhunātha."

The fifth *āhnika* of the *Tantrāloka* also discusses God consciousness and the states of *turya* in relation to the five activities of Lord Śiva: creation (*sṛṣṭi*), protection (*stithi*), destruction (*samhāra*), concealing (*tirodhāna*), and revealing (*anugraha*, grace).

The creation [act] of God consciousness is in the state of *nirānanda*, the protecting [act of] God consciousness is in the state of *parānanda*, the destroying [act of] God consciousness (it is not destroying God consciousness, it is destroying differentiated God consciousness) is *brahmānanda*, the concealing [act] of God consciousness is *mahānanda*, and the revealing [act of] God consciousness is *cidānanda*. And *jagadānanda* is *anākhyā*[410], where God consciousness is not felt [because] It becomes your nature.

9. *Upāyas* (the "means" or "ways")

"The difference between *āṇavopāya*, *śāktopāya*, and *śāmbhavopāya* is this: In *āṇavopāya*, the strength of your awareness is such that you have to take the support of everything as an aid to maintain and strengthen your awareness. In *śāktopāya*, your awareness is strengthened to the extent that only one point is needed as a support for your concentration and that point is the center. In *śāmbhavopya*, the strength of your awareness is such that no support is needed. You are already residing in the meant (*upeya*). There is nowhere to go, just reside at your own point. The rest is automatic.

It is important to realize that though there are different *upāyas*, all lead you to the state of one transcendental consciousness. The difference in these *upāyas* is that *āṇavopāya* will carry you in a long way, *śāktopāya* in a shorter way, and *śāmbhavopāya* in the shortest way. Although the ways are different, the point to be achieved is one."

Kashmir Shaivism–The Secret Supreme, 5.39-40.

---

410 The literal meaning of *anākhyā* is "unspeakable". Here, *anākhyā* is being used in the sense of "the absolute void which is known in the state of the unknown. It is unknown and at the same time it is known." *Tantrāloka* 11.86 (LJA archives).

10. Yoga Vasiṣṭha

"Vasiṣṭha *ṛṣi* was explaining the state of God Consciousness to Rāma, his disciple. At one place he has explained to him: *Hastaṁ hastena saṁpīḍya*, just squeeze your hands, *dantair-dantāṁśca pīḍayan*, just squeeze your teeth, *aṅgāny-aṅgairsamākramya*, and squeeze all your organs. *Jayedādau svakaṁ manaḥ*, conquer your mind first, this is the only thing you have to do in this world, in this life. You have to conquer your mind. Don't [allow] your mind going astray here and there. So this is the most essential thing one has to do: just to conquer your mind. Don't let it go astray here and there. Because [the mind] goes astray without any purpose. There is no purpose. For instance, [the mind] thinks, "This is a tape recorder". This is untimely thinking. "This is a tape recorder", what will come out of it? [You are] only becoming astray. "This is a chair", what to me? Why this thought came at all? It is no use to think these things. You should think only [of that] which you need. For instance, you have to prepare your meals. [Just] think that. Don't think that, "This is a [microphone]", "This is a table", "This is a tablecloth"–it is not needed. So you should not [let] your mind go astray like this. This is what Vasiṣṭha explained to Rāma in that *śloka*.

Swami Lakshmanjoo, *Bhagavad Gītā–In the Light of Kashmir Shaivism*, ed, John Hughes, Lakshmanjoo Academy Book Series, (Los Angeles, 2015).

11. The thirty-six elements (*tattvas*)

Śuddha tattvas – Pure Elements

Śiva = I-ness (Being)
Śakti = I-ness (Energy of Being)
Sadāśiva = I-ness in This-ness
Īśvara = This-ness in I-ness
Śuddhavidyā = I-ness in I-ness / This-ness in This-ness

Ṣaṭ kañcukas – Six Coverings

(Mahāmāyā = gap of illusion)*

Māya = illusion of individuality
Kalā = limitation of creativity/activity
Vidyā = limitation of knowledge
Rāga = limitation of attachment
Kāla = limitation of time
Niyati = limitation of place
Puruṣa = ego connected with subjectivity
Prakṛti = nature
(Guṇa tattva = manifest guṇas)*

Antaḥkaraṇas – Three Internal Organs

Buddhiḥ = intellect
Ahaṁkāra = ego connected with objectivity
Manas = mind

Pañca jñānendriyas – Five Organs of Cognition

Śrotra = ear, organ of hearing
Tvak = skin, organ of touching
Cakṣu = eye, organ of seeing
Rasanā = tongue, organ of tasting
Ghrāṇa = nose, organ of smelling

Pañca karmendriyas – Five Organs of Action

Vāk = speech
Pāṇi = hand
Pāda = foot
Pāyu = excretion
Upastha = procreative

Pañca tanmātras – Five Subtle Elements

Śabda = sound
Sparśa = touch
Rūpa = form
Rasa = taste
Gandha = smell

Pañca mahābhūtas - Five Great Elements

Ākāśa = ether
Vāyu = air
Tejas = fire
Jala = water
Pṛthvī = earth

Though Kashmir Shaivism recognises 36 *tattvas* (elements), Abhinavagupta adds an additional two states:

1) * *Mahāmāyā*: Swamiji says, "It is the gap and power of delusion. Delusion, where you won't know that you are deluded. You will conclude that you are established on truth, but that is not truth, that is not the real thing." This is the abode of the *vijñānākalas*.
2) * *Guṇa tattva*: The state where the three *guṇas* first manifest. Swamiji says, "In *prakṛti*, you can't see the three *guṇas* [because] this is the seed state of the three *guṇas*. It is why in Shaivism we have put another element, and that is the element of *guṇa tattva*."

For a complete explanation of the thirty-six *tattvas*, see *Kashmir Shaivism–The Secret Supreme*, chapter 1.

12. *Prakāśa* and *Vimarśa*

"In the world of Shaivite philosophy, Lord Śiva is seen as being filled with light. But more than this, Lord Śiva is the embodiment of light and this light is different than the light of the sun, of the moon, or of fire. It is light (*prakāśa*) with Consciousness (*vimarśa*), and this light with Consciousness is the nature of that Supreme Consciousness, Lord Śiva.

What is Consciousness? The light of Consciousness is not only pure Consciousness, It is filled with the understanding that, "I am the creator, I am the protector, and I am the destroyer of everything". Just to know that, "I am the creator, I am the protector, and I am the destroyer", is Consciousness. If Consciousness was not attached to the light of Consciousness, we would have to admit that the light of the sun or the light of the moon or the light of a fire is also Lord Siva. But this is not the case.

The light of Consciousness (*vimarśa*) is given various names. It is called *cit-caitanya*, which means, the strength of consciousness; *parā vāk,* the supreme word; *svātantrya*, perfect independence; *aiśvarya*, the predominant glory of supreme Śiva; *kartṛtva*, the power of acting; *sphurattā*, the power of existing; *sāra*, the complete essence of everything; *hṛdaya*, the universal heart; and *spanda*, universal movement. All these are names in the *Tantra*s, which are attributed to this Consciousness.

This I-Consciousness, which is the reality of Lord Śiva, is a natural (*akṛtrima*), not a contrived, I. It is not an adjusted I-Consciousness. Limited human beings have an adjusted I-Consciousness. Lord Śiva has a natural or pure I-Consciousness. There is a difference between an adjusted consciousness and a natural Consciousness. An adjusted or artificial consciousness exists when this I-Consciousness is attributed to your body, to your mind, to your intellect, and to your ego. Natural consciousness is that consciousness that is attributed to the reality of the Self, which is all-Consciousness.

This universe, which is created in His Consciousness, is dependent on that Consciousness. It is always dependent on that Consciousness. It cannot move outside of that Consciousness. It exists only when it is residing in His Consciousness. This is the way the creation of His universe takes place."

Self Realization in Kashmir Shaivism, 3.56-57.

"There are two positions of Śiva. One is *prakāśa* and another is *vimarśa.* When He feels this blissful state as His own nature, that is *prakāśa.* When He feels, "That blissful state is My glory", that is *vimarśa.* When He feels that, "This blissful state is My being", that is Śiva. When He believes that, "This is My glory", that is *śakti.* The cycle of glory is residing in *śakti*, and the cycle of *prakāśa* is residing in Śiva. Both are in one. That is indicated by *visarga* in Śiva, i.e., [the vowel] '*aḥ*' or ':'. So, *vimarśa śakti* is supreme *parā parameśvarī* attributed to *svātantrya śakti.* It is the intensity of independence of the *svātantrya* of Bhairava."

Parātrīśikā Vivaraṇa (LJA archives).

13. *Nirvikalpa*

"In reality, everything, whatever exists, it is in *nirvikalpa* state [where] you can't define anything. You can define only in the *vikalpa* state, in the cycle of *vikalpa*, e.g., when you say, "This is a specks cover". But it is not a specks cover in the real sense, in the state of God consciousness. It is just *nirvikalpa*–you can't say what it is, but it is! *Saṁketādi smaraṇam*, when you understand, "This is mine", "O, this was in my house and this is mine", this memory takes place in the *vikalpa* state, not the *nirvikalpa* state. And that *vikalpa* state cannot exist without *anubhavam*, the *nirvikalpa* state.

Nirvikalpa is the cause of all *vikalpa*s; the undifferentiated state is the cause of all *vikalpa*s. It is not something foreign [to *vikalpa*s]. It is their life, It is the life of all *vikalpa*s."

Parātrīśikā Vivaraṇa (LJA archives).

As long as the kingdom of God consciousness is there, there is no place for the kingdom of the mind. The junk of thoughts don't come in God consciousness. They have no right to come, they have no room to come.

DENISE: But a person who's in God consciousness and in the world, don't they have to think a thought before they perform an action?

SWAMIJI: No, that thought is not thought. That thought is . . . a fountain of bliss. You can't imagine unless you realize it, experience it.

JOHN: So we can't say that a man in God consciousness thinks. But he's in the world doing and acting and so many things.

SWAMIJI: But he is rolling in God consciousness. There is no worry about him. He can do everything, each and every act that an ordinary person, an ignorant person, does, but for him, all is divine, all is lying in his nature (*svarūpa*).

JOHN: So thought is by its nature limited. The definition of thought is something that is limited.

SWAMIJI: Limited, yes.

JOHN: And since a man in God consciousness doesn't have a limited anything, then he doesn't have thoughts.

SWAMIJI: Unlimited thought is not thought, it is

nirvikalpa. It is the state of your own nature where there is no limitation.

Special Verses on Practice, 65 (LJA archive).

14. *Kañcukas* (lit., coverings)

"Directly, universal consciousness can never travel to individual consciousness unless universal consciousness is absolutely disconnected. *Māyā* is the disconnecting element from God consciousness. *Kalā* (limited action) is the connecting element to that dead being in some limited thing. So he does something by *kalā*. When he does something, then individuality shines. Otherwise, direct from God consciousness, individual consciousness would never come in existence."

Tantrāloka 9.175-6 (LJA archive).

"*Kalā*, *vidyā*, *rāga*, *kāla*, and *niyati* are the limiting connecting rods [between the individual and God]."

Ibid., 9.257.

"[The five pure states of Lord Śiva] take the formation of *ṣaṭ kañcuka* in the individual. Because, whatever is manifested in the universe, it is not manifested [as] other than Śiva. The same thing has come out in manifestation; the same thing what existed in Paramaśiva, that same thing is manifested outside also."

Ibid., 6.41.

"*Kalā*, *vidyā*, *rāga*, *kāla*, and *niyati*, these five elements are just offsprings of, offshoots of, *māyā*. *Kalā* means, "the capacity of doing something", *vidyā* means "the capacity of knowing something", *rāga* means "the capacity of some attachment (not universal attachment)", *niyati* means "the capacity of the limitation of space", *Kāla* means "the limitation of time".

Ibid., 9.41.

"These [*kañcukas*] are pertaining to the individual being. It is why [the grammarian] Pāṇini has also accepted these, the representatives of these [*kañcukas* as the letters] *ya*, *ra*, *la*, *va*;

these letters as *antaḥstha*. And all these [subtle] energies are found, not outside the individual being, but inside the individual being, inside the thought of the individual being, inside the perception of the individual being. So they are named, nominated, by the grammarian [Pāṇini], as "*antaḥ-stha*". *Antaḥstha* means, that which is residing inside of the individual being. We say that it is not *antaḥstha*, it is *dhāraṇā* [lit., the bearing or support] because it gives *life* to the individual being. The individual being is created, the individual being is glorified, by these five elements ("five" means, the five coverings); the glory of his own place, not the glory of Śiva; glorified with his own . . . that limited sphere."

Swami Lakshmanjoo, *Shiva Sutra Vimarśinī* (LJA archive).

"In [the Śaiva] *tantras*, they are nominated as "*dhāraṇā*". These five elements (*kalā*, *vidyā*, *rāga*, *kāla*, *niyati*, with *māyā*) are called "*dhāraṇā*" because they give life to the individual being; the individual being lives in these five elements. Without these five elements, there was no life to the individual being, there was only the sphere of Lord Śiva. If these five elements would not be there, there was no question of the individual being to exist. The individual being lives only on the basis of these five elements. So they are nominated as *dhāraṇā*. *Dhāraṇā* means, that which gives you life to exist."

Swami Lakshmanjoo, *Śiva Sūtra Vimarśinī* (LJA) archive.

For a further explanation of the *kañcukas*, see *Kashmir Shaivism–The Secret Supreme*, 1.7.

15. Creation in Kashmir Shaivism

"He has created this universe in His own Self as the reflection of His sweet will. The creation of this universe is the outcome of this reflection. In Shaivism, the sweet will of God is known as *icchā śakti*, the energy of the will. It is through His will that the reflection of the universe takes place in His own nature. This reflection, however, is not like that reflection which takes place in an ordinary mirror where the mirror is the reflector and that which is reflected in the mirror is external to it. The reflection of the universe, which takes place in Lord Śiva's own nature, is like the reflection which takes place in a cup-shaped mirror. Here, Lord Siva takes the form of a cup-[shaped mirror] and puts another cup [shaped mirror] in front of His nature. And in that second cup-[shaped mirror], which is inseparable from Him, the reflection of the universe takes place."

Kashmir Shaivism–The Secret Supreme, 3.15.

"The universe, therefore, is reflected in the mirror of consciousness, not in the organs nor in the five gross elements. These are merely *tattva*s and cannot reflect anything. The real reflector is consciousness. In consciousness, however, you see only the reflected thing and not the object that is reflected. That which is reflected (*bimba*) is, in fact, *svātantryā*. This whole universe is the reflection of *svātantrya* in God consciousness. There is no additional class of similar objects existing outside of this world that He reflects in His nature. The outside element, that which is reflected, is only *svātantrya*. The infinite variety which is created is only the expansion of *svātantrya*."

Ibid., 4.29-30.

"In fact, there is one God and no one else. You have to accept that there is only one God, not individuals, nothing–only one God. This [universe] is the kingdom of God in the body of God. This is only the kingdom of God. And that God is *svatantrya* (independent), *cidrūpa* (filled with consciousness), *svabhāvata prakāśa ātmā* (by nature He is all-light). He has become many by the playful act of His concealing way, *svātma*, concealing His own nature, whenever He likes to conceal His own nature. And that is a blissful act–that too is a blissful act. And when He conceals His nature, He becomes many. When He reveals His nature, He becomes one. *Svayaṁ*, by His own nature, by His own divine will, *kalpita ākāra vikalpātmaka*, [He] creates an artificial way of thoughts, many thoughts, e.g., 'This is a stove', 'This is specks', 'This is good, this is bad', 'This is a brick', 'This is Denise', 'This is a book', or all of these things, *vikalpātmaka*, by His own playful act of *vikalpa*s, thoughts, many thoughts. Otherwise, in God you will see only one thought. That thought is *ahaṁ*, universal-I. That thought is the real nature of God. And by that real nature of God, [He] creates various thoughts, variety of thoughts, by His own free will. *Karmabhiḥ*, and He creates variety of actions. Otherwise, there is only one act: creation, protection, destruction, concealing and revealing. This is only one act–the fivefold act. The fivefold act is His own nature, but He wants to conceal It. For instance, anybody who is overjoyed, he wants to jump, he wants to kill himself, he wants to slaughter himself because of the reaction of being overjoyed. In the same way, God is overjoyed by that blissful state of His own nature. And by that, the reaction is that He wants to conceal His nature of that blissful joy, then He becomes many. This is the reality of God."

Tantrāloka 13.104 (LJA archive).

"All of the thirty-six elements, from Śiva to earth, are created by that natural I-Consciousness. And not only are they created by that Consciousness, they also shine in that Consciousness. His creation is not outside of His nature, it exists in His own Self. He has created this whole universe in the cycle of His Consciousness. So, everything that exists resides in that Consciousness.

This must be your understanding. The creative energy which is attributed to Lord Śiva is not that energy of Lord Śiva that creates the universe outside of His Consciousness as we create outside of our consciousness. His creation is not insentient (*jaḍa*) as our creations are.

This universe, which is created in His Consciousness, is dependent on that Consciousness. It is always dependent on that Consciousness. It cannot move outside of that Consciousness. It exists only when it is residing in His Consciousness. This is the way the creation of His universe takes place."

Self Realization in Kashmir Shaivism, Kṣhemarāja's *Parāprāveśikā*–Entrance Into the Supreme Reality, 3.57.

Bibliography

Published text of Lakshmanjoo Academy Book Series:

Bhagavad Gita, in the Light of Kashmir Shaivism (with original video), Swami Lakshmanjoo, ed. John Hughes (Lakshmanjoo Academy Book Series, Los Angeles, 2015), xxi, 683.

Essence of the Supreme Reality, Abhinavagupta's Paramārthasāra, with the commentary of Yogarāja, translation and commentary by Swami Lakshmanjoo with original video recording, (Lakshmanjoo Academy Book Series, Los Angeles, 2015).

Festival of Devotion and Praise, Shivastotravali, Hymns to Shiva by Utpaladeva, Swami Lakshmanjoo, ed. John Hughes, (Lakshmanjoo Academy Book Series, Los Angeles, 2015).

Kashmir Shaivism, The Secret Supreme, Swami Lakshmanjoo, ed. John Hughes (Lakshmanjoo Academy Book Series, Los Angeles, 2015).

Self Realization in Kashmir Shaivism, The Oral Teachings of Swami Lakshmanjoo, ed. John Hughes (State University of New York Press, Albany, 1995).

Shiva Sutras, The Supreme Awakening, Swami Lakshmanjoo, ed. John Hughes (Lakshmanjoo Academy Book Series, Los Angeles, 2015).

Vijñāna Bhairava, The Manual for Self Realization, Swami Lakshmanjoo, ed. John Hughes (Lakshmanjoo Academy Book Series, Los Angeles, 2015).

Unpublished texts from the Lakshmanjoo Academy (LJA) archives:

Bhagavad Gitartha Samgraha of Abhinavagupta, translation and commentary by Swami Lakshmanjoo (original audio recording, LJA archives, Los Angeles, 1978).

Janmamaraṇavicāragranthaḥ, Janma Maraṇa Vicāra of Bhaṭṭa Vāmadeva, Swami Lakshmanjoo (original audio recording, LJA archives, Los Angeles, 1980).

Kashmir Shaivism, The Secret Supreme, Swami Lakshmanjoo (original audio recording, LJA archives, Los Angeles, 1972).

Parātriśikā Laghuvṛtti with the commentary of Abhinavagupta, translation and commentary by Swami Lakshmanjoo (original audio recording, LJA archives, Los Angeles, 1982).

Parātriśikā Vivaraṇa with the commentary of Abhinavagupta, translation and commentary by Swami Lakshmanjoo (original audio recording, LJA archives, Los Angeles, 1982-85).

Stava Cintāmaṇi of Bhaṭṭanārāyaṇa, translation and commentary by Swami Lakshmanjoo (original audio recording, LJA archives, Los Angeles, 1980-81).

The Tantrāloka of Abhinavagupta, Chapters 1 to 18, translation and commentary by Swami Lakshmanjoo (original audio recording, LJA archives, Los Angeles, 1972-1981).

Vātūlanātha Sūtras of Anantaśaktipāda, translation and commentary by Swami Lakshmanjoo (original audio recordings, LJA archives, Los Angeles, 1979).

Additional sources - Books

Iśvarapratyabhijñā Kārikā (*Siddhitrayī*) by Utpaladeva, with commentary (*vivṛti*) by Utpaladeva, Edited by Pandit Madhusudan Kaul Shastri, *KSTS*, Vol. XXXIV, Srinagar, Kashmir, 1921.

Iśvarapratyabhijñā Vivṛti Vimarśinī of Abhinavagupta, Edited by Pandit Madhusudan Kaul Shastri, *KSTS*, Vol. LX, Srinagar, Kashmir, 1938.

Kaṭha Upaniṣad, Sacred Books of The East, Translated by Various Oriential Scholars, Edited by Max Müller, Vol XI, p1, Clarendon Press, Orford, 1884.

Mahābhāṣya of Patañjali, a commentary on selected rules of Sanskrit grammar, from Pāṇini's *Aṣṭādhyāyi*.

Mālinīvijayottara Tantram, Edited with Preface abd English Introduction by Pandit Madhusudan Kaul Shastri, *KSTS*, Vol. XXXVII, Srinagar, Kashmir, 1922.

Pratyabhijñāhṛdayam, *The Secret of Self-Recognition*, Sanskrit Text with English Translation, Notes and Introduction by Jaideva Singh (Motilal Banarsidass, Delhi, 1963-2011).

Rājamārtaṇḍavṛtti – Bhojavṛtti, King Bhojadeva's commentary on Patañjali's *Yoga Sūtras*.

Śivastotrāvalī of Utpaladevācaryā With the Sanskrit commentary of Kṣhemarāja, edited with Hindi commentary by Rājānaka Lakṣmaṇa (Swami Lakshmanjoo) (Chowkhamba Sanskrit Series 15. Varanasi, 1964).

Spanda Kārikās – The Divine Creative Pulsation. Jaideva Singh, (Delhi: Motilal Banarsidass, 1980).

Śvetāśvatara Upaniṣad, Sacred Books of The East, Translated by Various Oriential Scholars, Edited by Max Müller, Vol XI, p231, Clarendon Press, Orford, 1884.

The Śivadṛṣṭi of Sri Somānandanātha, with the *vṛtti* by Utpaladeva, Edited with Preface, Introduction and English Translation by Pandit Madhusudan Kaul Shastri, *KSTS*, Vol. LIV, Srinagar, Kashmir, 1934.

The Spanda Karikas of Vasugupa, with the *Nirnaya* by Ksemaraja. Edited with Preface, Introduction and English Translation by Pandit Madhusudan Kaul Shastri, Superintendant of The Research Department of The Kashmir State, Kashmir Series of Texts and Studies, Vol. XLII, Srinagar, Kashmir, 1917.

The Spanda Sandoha of Kṣhemarāja. Edited with notes by Mahamohapadhaya Pandit Mukunda Rama Shastri, Officer in Charge Research Department Jammu and

Kashmir State, Srinagar, *KSTS*, Vol. XVI, Srinagar, Kashmir, 1925.

Yoga and the Luminous: Patañjali's Spiritual Path to Freedom Christopher Key Chapple, State University of New York Press (October 30, 2008).

INDEX

ābhāsa 110–111, 116, 158, 160, 164, 173
abhāsavāda 112
abhāva 20–21, 168, 170, 249
abheda 102, 118, 156, 211
abhedāṁśa 167
abhimāna 217
abhiyoga 21
ability 281
absence 282
absent 279
absolute 10, 158, 255, 278, 287
achieve 34, 42, 49, 53, 86, 112–113, 200, 214–215, 226, 243, 273, 279
action 15, 25, 30–35, 37, 46, 160, 205–206, 216, 224, 239, 272–273, 277, 279, 281–282, 294–295
activity 30–31, 33, 49, 58, 74, 119, 122, 161–162, 167–168, 216, 222, 224, 279, 291
adhara 203
adhvans 156
advaita 153
agādha 85
āgama 184, 268
aghora 219, 231
agitated 13, 263
agni 182
ahaṁ 5, 45, 128–131, 133, 192–193, 277, 297
ahaṁkāra 216–217
aiśvarya 174, 293
akrama 135
akula 247, 253
alertness 90, 178
amṛta 51
anākhyā 101
anāmayā 278
ānanda 89, 92, 179–180, 213, 215, 261, 272, 283, 286–288
āṇavamala 56, 281–282
āṇavopāya 70, 289
aṇḍa 181
anger 36, 38–43, 122, 124
antaḥkaraṇa 9
antaḥstha 296
antar 25, 90, 191
anubhava 185
anugraha 95, 159, 161, 167–168, 173–174, 197, 289
anuttara 174, 244, 247
apāna 287–288
apānana 287–288
aparā 66, 219–221, 278
appear 273

aprabuddha 27
aprakāśa 160, 257
apūrṇa 233
argue 271
āsana 275
aspirant 277, 283–284
aśuddhi 13
ātma 119, 126
attachment 5–6, 52, 62–63, 186, 216, 222, 235–236, 291, 295
automatic 289
avidyā 281
avikalpa 96–97
aware 276–278, 289
awareness 13, 34, 41–42, 45, 55–56, 58–59, 62, 70, 174, 190, 194–195, 199–200, 202, 256, 276–278, 287–289
ayatnena 244
bala 45–46
balam 271
bandha 261
Being 6, 9–10, 64, 106, 112, 135–136, 143, 208,252, 272, 274, 277, 285–286, 290
bhāga 246
bhagavatī 211
bhairava 271, 293
bhava 280
bhāva 7, 16, 25, 29, 31, 36, 39, 48, 51, 80, 96, 98–99, 105, 120, 144, 172–173, 213, 215, 280–281, 287
bheda 117–118, 155–156, 200, 210–211
bhokta 52
bhūcarī 204–206, 209, 211–212, 218–220, 223, 227, 229
bhūmi 119, 161, 203
bhuvana 182
bīja 173
bimba 297
bindu 244
birth 82
bliss 89, 95, 175, 261, 271, 277–278, 283–285, 287–288, 293–294
bodha 212
body 1–2, 8, 46, 53–54, 57, 61–65, 81, 83, 127, 150, 179–180, 192, 225, 236, 249, 252, 265, 278–279, 285, 293, 297
brahma 285
brahmānanda 284, 286, 288–289
brahmāṇḍa 41
brahmarandhra 285
break 279
breath 18–19, 34–36, 41, 62, 283–285, 287–288
breathe 18, 53–54, 56, 62, 208, 283, 285
breathing 18–19, 35, 40, 54, 62, 283–285, 287–288
breathless 19
breaths 41, 56, 62, 72
bubhukṣitaḥ 62
buddhi 81, 216–217
caitanya 94–95, 293
cakra 2, 41, 92–94, 177–178, 188–193, 195–200, 202, 204, 208–209, 227, 229, 235–236, 242–243, 246, 265, 285

cakreśvaraḥ 83
camatkāra 273
candra 261
catch 281
cause 2, 13, 69, 118, 294
center 27, 32, 34, 39, 72, 130, 157, 284, 289
central 41, 130, 164, 284
cetanā 14
ceti 14
channel 285
chapter 271, 274
choice 282
choking 283
church 251
cidānanda 213, 285–286, 288–289
cidānandaghanaḥ 179
cidātma 131
cidghanam 257
cidrūpa 130, 297
cinema 13, 17
cinmayaḥ 28
circle 205, 223
cit 118, 174, 213, 219, 272, 285, 293
citi 261
cittasya 149–150, 195
climax 223
cognition 46
cognitive 28–29, 206, 280, 288
comatose 276
commentary 87, 149, 151, 280
commit 210, 227
complete 63, 89, 280, 285, 292–293
completely 39, 147, 159, 213, 277, 279–280, 288
composed 77, 267
con 15, 20, 136, 179, 245, 289, 293
conceal 33, 103–104, 115, 161, 297–298
concealing 33, 106, 166, 289, 297–298
concentrate 75, 283
concentration 279, 289
conclusion 282
condition 278
connected 280
conscious 12, 22, 27, 33, 71–72, 74, 101, 111–112, 115, 130, 133, 146, 148, 155, 172–173, 179, 184, 195, 199, 230–231, 237, 240, 242, 248–249, 271–272, 277–278, 281, 289, 292–295, 297
consciousness 3, 6, 10–23, 25–27, 29, 31–34, 40–42, 45–53, 56, 58–60, 62, 64–72, 74–80, 82, 86, 88, 90, 99–103, 105, 109–116, 118, 120–127, 130–134, 136–138, 140, 145–148, 155, 158–161, 164, 171–180, 185, 187, 189–204, 207–208, 210–215, 219, 222–223, 229, 238–239, 243–246, 248–249, 252–254, 256–257, 260–262, 265, 271–273, 275, 277–281, 285, 287–289, 293–295, 297–298

cover 294
create 274, 281, 293
creation 58, 87, 93, 117, 130, 134, 136–137, 140–141, 144, 154–156, 158–161, 163–165, 171–172, 178, 181–182, 189–191, 274, 281, 289, 293, 296, 29
creator 94, 160, 181, 184–186, 190, 204, 208, 237, 292
curiosity 91, 165–168, 229–231
cycle 2–5, 8–9, 13–18, 21, 24, 26–27, 33, 46–48, 60, 62, 64, 69, 73–77, 80, 82–83, 85, 88, 90, 95, 97, 101–102, 113, 117–120, 125–126, 128–131, 137, 180–182, 184, 188–192, 202–203, 210–212, 221–222, 237–238, 243–244, 250, 256, 273, 293–294, 298
darśana 149–150, 153, 252
daśā 118, 126–128, 279
death 75, 284
deha 96, 175, 215, 236
delusion 292
demon 35
dependent 293
deśa 162–163
desire 11, 15, 48, 52–54, 62, 122, 234, 245
desires 283
destroy 45–46, 77, 79, 96, 117, 120, 136, 147–148, 150, 154, 160, 164–165, 171, 178, 184, 189, 191, 292
destruction 76, 87, 93–94, 102–103, 106–107, 117, 130, 134, 138, 140–141, 144, 154, 158–161, 164–166, 170–172, 178, 181–182, 189–191, 289, 29
detachment 216, 235–236
deva 175
devī 137
devotion 10–11, 43, 189, 283–285
dhāraṇā 275, 296
dharma 14–15
dhātu 236
dhyāna 275
die 283
difference 29, 38, 60, 98, 111, 139, 143, 206, 252, 274, 277, 279–280, 289, 293
differentiated 94, 117–118, 123, 134, 155–156, 167, 172–173, 238, 280, 287, 289
dikcarī 204–206, 209, 211–212, 217–220, 223, 227
dīkṣa 197
diptiḥ 195, 244
diśā 247
disciple 134, 276, 290
dissolved 288
divine 4, 13, 17–18, 29, 68–69, 72–75, 84, 190, 192, 196, 217–218, 224–225, 227–228, 231, 240, 244–245, 262, 285, 294, 297
doubt 50, 85, 183
drama 5, 49, 138, 148, 274

dream 26, 48, 55, 58–60, 185, 195, 197–198, 215, 271, 276, 278–279
drop 138, 167, 241
dualism 249, 251
duality 142, 212–213, 244, 281
duffer 231
duḥkha 6
dvanda 149
dveṣa 235–237
ear 8, 46, 80, 291
earth 117, 218, 272, 292, 298
ecstasy 285
effort 9, 11, 24, 34, 43, 65, 67 –69, 78, 88, 116, 189, 243, 255, 263, 284
ego 9, 81, 96–98, 191, 210, 217, 291, 293
egress 286
element 4, 32, 48, 69, 139, 179, 182, 197, 202, 272, 292, 295, 297
embodiment 116, 130, 175, 292
emptiness 175
enemy 281
energies 2, 75, 77, 79–80, 83, 94, 109, 174, 177, 184–185, 188, 192, 198–199, 204–212, 214, 216–227, 229, 231, 235, 242–243, 249, 265, 272, 278, 296
energy 19, 28–29, 80, 107–110, 115–117, 124, 131, 138–139, 184–185, 204–206, 209–212, 219, 224–225, 230, 235, 239, 256, 271–272, 274, 278–279, 296, 298
enjoy 82, 213, 273, 275
enters 283, 287
entry 288
erotic 39
essence 7, 109, 116, 176, 178, 239, 255, 260, 262–263, 271, 273, 293
establish 255, 287
established 288
establishment 278, 285
eternal 105–107
eternity 281
ether 212, 223, 292
eunuchs 230
everything 280, 283–285, 288–288
existence 3, 72, 138–139, 180, 185, 194, 211, 249, 252, 256, 271, 275, 278–279, 282, 295
experience 23, 42, 89, 98, 100–101, 123, 128, 185, 245, 274, 276, 279, 282–286, 294
external 273
extreme 36, 40, 241
eye 18, 291
eyes 285, 287
face 284
fear 37–39, 74, 80, 82, 122, 124, 288
feel 281
female 206
field 276
fire 283, 292

fivefold 155, 159, 161–162, 164, 166, 168, 171, 174, 178, 298
flower 285
focus 11, 13, 74, 82
force 9, 13–14, 25, 38, 41, 54, 60, 116, 236–237, 239, 261, 271, 285–285
forgetfulness 206
form 10, 12, 17, 25, 68, 80–81, 120–123, 141–144, 146, 148–149, 151–154, 163, 191, 244, 279, 282, 285, 291, 297
formation 274, 285
formless 282
forms 10, 68–69, 283, 286–287
free 138, 272, 282, 29
freedom 137, 272–273
friend 281
fullness 130, 138, 151, 158, 171–172, 228, 233, 257, 273, 278–279, 281
fully 288
fun 273
function 11–12, 14, 19, 25, 36, 46, 50, 276, 278, 282
furious 283
gandha 11, 17, 30, 81, 188, 193, 201, 218, 221
gap 27, 35, 52, 68, 123–124, 129–130, 246, 282–283, 290, 292
garbha 224
germ 279
ghee 70
ghora 219, 222, 231
ghoratarī 220–221, 231
giddiness 283
girl 63, 222, 224
giver 271
glory 2, 57, 88, 174, 178, 186, 188, 190, 195, 197, 201–202, 207–208, 236, 242–243, 273–274, 282, 293, 296
gocarī 204–205, 209, 211–212, 216–217, 219–220, 223, 225–226
God consciousness 3, 6, 10–23, 25–27, 29, 31–34, 40–42, 45–53, 56, 60, 62, 64–72, 74–80, 82, 86, 88, 90, 101–103, 105, 109–115, 118, 120–127, 130–131, 134, 137–138, 148, 155, 158–161, 171, 173–180, 185, 189–204, 207–208, 211–212, 214–215, 219, 222–223, 229, 238–239, 243–246, 248–249, 252–254, 256–257, 260, 262, 265, 271–273, 279, 287–289, 294–295, 297
govern 59
grace 9, 12, 27, 42–43, 94–95, 159, 197–198, 213, 216, 220, 226, 229, 241–242, 278, 289
grāhaka 11, 168–172
grammar 149–152
great 9–11, 56, 62, 68, 75, 77, 79, 85, 88, 91, 100, 150, 183, 189, 207, 233, 260–261, 274, 281, 283–284, 288
guṇa 292
guṇādi 32, 237

guṇādispanda 30
guru 90, 92, 135
hand 117, 146, 214, 250, 279, 284, 291
happiness 221, 287
head 37, 108
hear 8, 46, 245, 284, 287
heart 87, 116, 175, 226, 239, 247, 271, 293
heavy 276
hell 24, 158–159
herbs 149
hero 24, 89–90, 175
hetu 105
hideous 283, 286
house 24, 131–133, 185, 200, 206, 216, 281, 283, 294
hṛdaya 178, 293
hṛdayaṁ 271, 293
hṛdi 52–53, 87, 208
human 6, 128, 208, 225–226, 229, 241–242, 293
icchā 28, 32, 272, 275, 296
idaṁ 2–3, 128–130, 161, 241, 277
ignorance 25, 124, 175, 239, 255, 263, 281–282
ignore 283
illumined 278
illusion 32, 96, 119, 124, 272, 282, 290–291
imagination 72–73, 279
immanent 144
impression 159, 167, 173, 281
impressions 287
impure 13, 44, 47, 156, 217, 282
impurity 13, 150, 274, 281–282
incomplete 273, 281
independence 10, 271, 273, 293
individual 11–12, 14, 18, 26, 47, 49, 64–65, 80, 82, 85, 147, 161–164, 168, 215, 231, 274, 276–277, 279, 281, 295–296
individuality 283–284
indriya 189, 193
inferior 278
ingress 286
initiate 197
insentient 298
instantaneously 261
instruction 130
instrument 11–12
intellect 9, 14, 33, 81, 151, 174–175, 191, 217, 291, 293
intelligence 273–274
intensity 293
intercourse 287
internal 9, 36, 67, 82, 90–91, 101, 130, 145–148, 191, 193, 196, 200, 209, 212–213, 219, 275, 281, 286
internally 283
intoxicating 283
introverted 14–15, 25, 90, 189–190, 254
īśvara 128–131, 133, 277
īśvarī 211
jaḍa 298

jagadānanda 285–286, 288–289
jagat 49, 74, 106, 141, 144
jāgrat 2, 4–5, 27, 29, 34
jala 182
janma 226
jīva 187, 277
jīvan 50, 203, 226
jñāna 28–28, 31–32
jñānendriyas 291
jñāni 243
jñātā 80, 202, 204
journey 17, 169, 196
joy 36, 39–41, 273, 28 , 285, 287–288, 298
kalā 215–216, 295–296
kāla 163, 215, 295–296
kālāgnirūdra 182
kañcuka 295
kāraṇa 2, 106
karaṇeśvarī 189–192
karma 31–32, 221–222, 281–282
kārmamala 56, 281–282
kartṛtā 160–161
Kashmir 37, 147, 271, 274–275, 277, 279, 282–283, 286, 289–290, 292–293, 296–298
kaumārī 199
khecarī 192, 204, 209, 211–214, 219–220, 223–224
kingdom 278
know 280
knower 98–99
knowing 285
knowledge 15, 25, 28–30, 32, 86, 99, 168, 206–207, 259–260, 262–263, 268, 272, 274–275, 277, 279, 281–282, 288, 291
known 30, 49, 98–99, 101–102, 111–112, 122, 185, 278, 281, 283–285, 296
krama 135, 285–286
krama mudrā 285–286
kriyā 28, 30, 32, 272, 275
krodha 235
Kṣhemarāja 14, 74, 87, 91–92, 112, 240–241, 259, 263, 271
kṣobha 244
kula 90, 253
kuṇḍalinī 225, 285
lady 274
lambikā 284
lelihānā 137
life 5, 9, 11, 13–14, 18, 25, 30, 34, 47, 49, 64, 80, 99, 119–123, 187, 189, 226, 231, 255, 257, 271, 275, 280, 290, 294, 296
light 67–68, 92, 95, 109, 116, 185, 190, 195–196, 228, 244, 288, 292–293, 297
limited 283
logic 105
lolībhūtā 158
love 63, 283
madhyanāḍī 284
mahābhūtas 292
mahāmudrā 89
mahānanda 284, 286, 288–289
mahāvīrya 233

mahāvyāpti 288
maheśvara 92, 184, 277
Maheśvara 277
māheśvarī 199
mala 56, 282
malā 274, 282
mālinī 116, 271
man 42, 59, 63, 106, 115, 274, 277, 281, 294
manas 217, 256
manifest 80, 291–292
manifestation 278
mantra 44–45, 47, 192–195, 277, 283–285
mantreśvara 277
master 2, 6, 21–22, 27, 43, 57, 85, 90–92, 135, 158, 197–198, 262–263, 275–276, 278, 282–283, 288
masters 284
māyā 89, 96, 112, 119, 124, 161, 215, 272, 274, 282, 295–296
māyīya 56
māyīyamala 56–57, 281–282
means 1, 4, 6, 16–17, 21, 30, 34, 38, 40, 44, 47, 50–53, 55, 58, 70, 73, 75, 77, 83–85, 88, 90, 92–95, 101–106, 115, 118, 126, 138, 141–143, 144–145, 147–149, 151–153, 157, 159–160, 163, 170–171, 175, 179–180, 183, 187, 189, 194–197, 200, 205–207, 210, 212, 232, 234–239, 241–244, 247, 253, 257, 260, 262–266, 268, 271, 273, 277–279, 283–285, 289, 293, 295–296
meditation 9, 50, 53, 55–56, 58, 62, 65, 70, 78, 80, 84, 150, 192, 229–230, 233, 243–245, 254
memory 49, 164, 173, 250, 261, 294
mental 284
mind 9, 14, 19, 40, 43, 49, 51, 58, 66–67, 70–72, 78, 81, 84, 86, 111, 133, 145, 150, 162, 166, 173, 191, 195–198, 202–203, 216, 239, 242, 244, 255–256, 261, 284–285, 290–291, 293–294
mine 281, 294
mirror 3, 296–297
mithuna 223
moha 175
moment 14, 18, 21, 37, 40–42, 78, 127–128, 136–137, 162, 170–172, 223–225, 236, 238–239, 242, 244, 261, 283, 285
moments 284
monistic 105, 153, 211, 213, 219, 239, 247
mood 283
moon 262–263, 292
mountains 287
move 283, 285
movement 4, 7, 11, 30–31, 66, 106, 116, 118, 203, 237, 265, 271, 293
moves 280
mūḍha 7

mudrā 91, 192–193, 285–286
mukta 203, 226
mūlādhāra 284–285
mūrcchā 276
nābhiḥ 87
nāda 68, 244–246
name 278–279, 293
nātha 283, 288
nature 289
nectar 288
negation 248–249, 252, 276, 288
neti 248
nijānanda 283, 286
nimeṣa 2, 93, 103–112, 114–120, 122, 128–130, 134, 140–144, 146–148, 152–159, 179–180, 183, 187, 189
nimīlanā 286
nirañjanāḥ 44, 46, 194
nirodha 4
nirvāṇa 51
nirvikalpa 97, 169, 281, 294–295
niṣyandāḥ 30, 237–238
nitya 74
niyama 275
niyati 215, 295–296
nostrils 285
nothing 280, 288
object 7, 16, 28–28, 40, 60, 75, 98–99, 101, 119–121, 126–128, 131, 136, 145, 147–148, 153–154, 163–166, 169–173, 213, 276, 280–281, 297
objective 7, 10, 16, 28–29, 48, 73, 99, 101, 136, 186, 190–191, 193, 205, 213, 276, 280, 285–288
observe 284
observer 276–277
oṁ 79, 194–195
once 283–286
oneness 110, 115, 125–126, 130, 143, 173
onwards 284
open 285
order 273
organ 9, 12–13, 30, 291
organic 12–14, 287
outside 277, 279, 283, 285, 288, 293
pāda 20, 30
pain 6–7, 13, 281–282
palate 284, 287
pāṇi 30
parā 116, 121–122, 158, 219, 221–222, 227, 278, 281,
paramānanda 175
parāmarśa 116, 133
paramārtha 110–111, 160, 236
parameśvara 120, 180, 183
parameśvarī 293
parānanda 283, 286–287, 289
parāparā 219, 221–222, 278
Parātrīśikā 272–273, 282, 293–294
parimita 96
pāśa 261
paśu 76, 80, 175, 226

path 41–42, 76, 80, 196, 209 –210, 238–240, 261, 263, 269, 276
pathway 17, 76, 196, 204, 240
pāyu 30
peacefully 288
penetrate 278
penetrates 285
perceiver 101, 169–173, 276, 286
perception 6–7, 12, 16, 21, 25, 122–123, 128, 145, 167–169, 171, 184, 187, 235, 255, 276, 280, 282, 296
perceptions 287
pervading 284
pervasion 64–65, 135, 288
philosophy 271, 292
physical 284
piercing 285
play 49, 69, 73, 87, 177, 234, 263, 273–274, 282
pleasure 6–7, 13, 17, 230, 235
point 280, 283–284, 286–287
pointedness 288
power 9–12, 45, 52–55, 57–62, 69–70, 75, 80, 109, 189, 192, 194–195, 207–208, 214, 229, 233, 235, 271–274, 278, 292–293
prabuddha 26–28, 42, 223
practical 283
practice 27, 57, 73–74, 279, 283–284
prādhānya 141, 143–144
prakāśa 92, 94–95, 116, 124, 130, 135, 160, 163, 184–185, 219, 242, 244, 292–293, 297
prakāśaḥ 292–293
prakṛti 59–60, 181, 292
pralaya 144, 148
pralayākala 276
pramāṇa 280
pramātṛ 96, 161, 215, 276–277, 280, 286–287
prameya 29, 276, 280
pramiti 98–99, 213, 280–281
prāṇa 19, 175, 215, 288
prāṇana 287–288
prāṇāyāma 245
prasara 157, 272
prathama 169
pratyāhāra 275
prayatna 24, 243
predominance 278
present 285
process 286, 288
produced 288
protection 289
protector 292
pṛthvī 117, 144, 181–182
pṛthvyaṇḍa 181
pūjās 231
pure 44–45, 47, 116, 133, 135, 150, 156, 173, 192, 214, 217, 226, 228, 257, 272, 274, 280, 292–293, 295
purity 282
pūrṇa 89, 233
pūrṇāhanta 126
pūrṇānanda 89
puruṣa 12, 187, 274

pūrva 119, 183, 220
puryaṣṭaka 82, 175
puṣṭi 232
question 277
rāga 6, 215–216, 236, 295–296
randhra 285
rasa 8, 11, 17, 30, 76, 81, 188, 193, 201, 218, 221, 228, 261
real 280
reality 7, 11, 20–22, 27, 34, 47–48, 51, 53, 60, 69, 73, 92, 95, 106, 109–114, 122, 135, 154, 157–158, 176–178, 250, 259, 271, 274, 277, 293–294, 298
realization 17–18, 49, 273
rebirths 17
reciting 45, 283
recognition 53, 267
rectum 284
reflection 3, 249, 296–297
religion 250–251
remember 42, 147, 261
reside 274, 281, 289
resides 280, 287
residing 280
respect 286
rest 289
revealing 106, 161, 174, 289, 298
right 284, 287
rise 287
rises 285
rising 285, 287–288
root 145, 219, 282
round 31, 63, 159–160, 174, 262, 273, 284
rūpa 8, 11, 17, 30, 68, 76, 81, 188, 193, 201, 218, 221, 245
rūpātītā 278
śabda 8, 11, 17, 76, 81, 188, 193, 201, 218, 220
Sadāśiva 277
sadāśiva 87, 117, 128–131, 133, 144, 277
sādhaka 10, 50, 58, 136, 195–196, 198, 200, 243
sādhana 192, 226
sādhus 162
sakala 276, 286
sakalā 276
śakti 2, 19, 28–28, 32, 75, 80, 88–89, 92–94, 107, 109, 116, 122–123, 131, 139, 151–152, 188, 190, 192–193, 195–198, 200, 202, 204, 207–209, 212, 217, 219, 221, 229, 235–236, 242–243, 265, 272, 274–275, 278, 280, 293, 296
śaktiḥ 273–274, 278, 293
śaktimān 161
śaktopāya 289
śāktopāya 68–70, 289
samādhi 21–23, 29, 31, 49, 53–54, 56, 62–63, 96, 174, 192, 197, 233, 245–246, 253, 275–276, 278–279, 286, 288
samāna 288
sāmānya 30–31, 35–39, 45–46, 48, 64, 66–67, 237–238
samāveśa 180
śāmbhavopāya 289

Saṁdoha 271
saṁhāra 87, 117, 159, 161, 170
saṁkalpa 40
śaṁkara 94, 109, 111, 255
saṁsāra 33, 82, 136, 211, 238, 240
saṁskāra 173
saṁvedana 47
saṁvit 134
saṁyojana 186
Sandoha 87, 146, 264–266, 271
saṅkalpa 217
śāntarūpā 44, 46
saṅtoṣa 243
sāra 293
sāram 116, 271
śarīra 2
sarva 10, 25, 101, 122, 186
sarvabhāva 47, 187
sarvajña 45–46
sarvakartṛtva 214
śāstra 30, 109, 132, 155, 175–176, 184, 186, 188, 190, 196, 208, 224, 239, 247, 255, 259, 266, 271
satatoditam 279
sauḥ 192
second 276
secret 73, 135, 229–230, 271, 274, 277, 279, 282, 289
seed 279
self 1, 8, 12, 14, 71, 73, 183, 185, 239, 245, 274–275, 277–278, 293
semen 232–233
sensation 8, 46, 280, 283
sense 22, 30, 57, 260, 275, 282, 294
sex 8–9, 13, 17, 223, 225, 229–235, 238
sexual 30, 122, 287–288
Shaivaite 278, 292
Shaivism 21, 23, 33, 106–110, 112, 115, 151, 153, 250–251, 266–268, 271, 274–275, 277, 279, 282–283, 286, 289–290, 292–293, 296–298
Shaivite 21–22, 63, 278, 292
Shiva 271, 275, 296
siddha 28, 185
siddhi 192, 202, 204
simultaneous 104, 135
simultaneously 278
śiva 47, 51, 87, 133, 151–152
śivaśaktī 142, 153
sleep 21–22, 27, 29, 96–97, 123, 180, 203, 253, 271, 276, 278–279, 286
smaraṇam 294
smell 8, 17, 46, 81, 196, 291
soma 53
sound 17, 68, 81, 96, 216, 244–245, 278, 283–284, 287–288, 291
sounds 283–28
source 280
sovereignty 277
space 272
spanda 4–11, 17–18, 30–32, 34–39, 44–46, 48, 52, 64, 66–67, 87–88, 91, 94, 99, 101–102, 114, 116–117, 119, 147,

154–155, 166, 169–170, 178, 189–190, 194, 237–238, 250, 262, 264–266, 271–272, 274, 278, 280–281, 282, 287, 289–290, 292–296, -PAGE-
sparśa 8, 11, 17, 30, 76, 81, 188, 193, 201, 218, 221
specks 294
speech 30, 150, 216, 291
sphurati 255, 261
sphurattā 116, 271, 293
spiritual 80, 168, 170–173, 261, 263, 276
squeeze 83, 287, 290
sṛṣṭi 87, 161, 190, 233, 289
sthana 272
sthāna 284
sthiti 9, 136, 157–158, 161, 164, 172–173, 188
sthūla 2, 281
straightforwardness 209
strength 41–42, 45–46, 55, 62, 64, 69–70, 78–79, 116, 230, 232–234, 236, 271, 274, 279, 289, 293
stumaḥ 2, 92–95, 101–102, 246
subjective 7, 16, 39, 48, 99–101, 136, 205, 276, 278–280, 286–287
subtle 283, 287
succession 115, 135, 190, 278
śuddhavidyā 277
sūkṣma 2, 121, 281
Sun 292
śūnya 20–21, 199, 215
śūnyatā 287
support 289
suprabuddha 26–29
supreme 13–14, 36, 41, 45, 47, 51, 74, 76, 85, 88–90, 92, 94–95, 101–102, 107, 112, 116, 122, 124–126, 130, 136, 138–140, 158, 174–175, 190, 192, 196, 211, 213, 219–220, 223, 232, 244, 247, 261, 271, 274, 277–280, 282, 287–289, 292–293
suṣumnā 41
suṣupti 4–5, 22, 27, 29, 41
Sūtra 271
svabhāva 16, 111, 120, 243, 255
svapna 5, 27, 29, 55, 57–59, 184
svaprakāśa 174
svarūpa 92, 102–104, 109, 114, 155, 158, 179, 193, 253, 282, 294
svarūpaṁ 282
svātantrya 7, 20, 57, 88–89, 107, 118–119, 131, 139, 212, 272–274, 277, 280, 282, 293, 297
sweet 65, 131, 296
system 271
tādātmya 47
tālu 287
Tantrāloka 271, 279, 282
tantras 293
taste 12–13, 17–18, 23, 46, 68–69, 81, 167, 190, 193, 214, 230, 257, 291

tattva 4, 10, 34, 111–112, 139, 181–182, 291–292
technique 90–91
teeth 83, 290
tejas 288
temper 235–236, 238
third 276, 281
thought 19–20, 36, 38, 40, 42–43, 50, 53–54, 66–70, 73, 78–79, 84, 103, 105, 107, 110–111, 114, 129–130, 153, 206, 211, 213, 217, 234, 240, 242, 250, 261–263, 281, 290, 294, 296–297
thoughts 283
throat 284
tide 271
time 283, 286
tirodhāna 123, 160–161, 166, 173, 289
tolerate 103–104, 112, 286
top 285
torture 6, 75, 95, 201, 208, 240, 282
touch 8, 11–12, 17, 33, 46, 81, 142, 188, 217, 220, 223–224, 227, 229, 260, 278, 280, 291
transcendent 277, 289
transcendental 285
tree 274
trick 184, 189, 240
Trika 116, 239, 247, 259, 268–269, 271, 278
truth 34, 50, 209, 259–260, 277, 292
turya 26–27, 34, 68, 96–97, 177, 215, 246, 253, 271, 275, 278–279, 283–287, 289
turyātīta 278–279
turyātītā 278–279
tuṭi 127
tuṭipāta 127
udāna 288
udānana 287–288
udaya 144, 178
udyoga 116, 271
unaware 42, 278
unawareness 276
unconscious 41–42
understand 280
understanding 280, 292
undifferentiated 118, 120, 140, 155–156, 237, 278, 280, 294
unification 277
universal 19, 31, 45, 47, 49, 59, 64, 138, 144–145, 147, 153–154, 161–163, 205, 209, 211, 213, 253, 274–275, 277–279, 282, 284–285, 288, 293, 295, 297
universality 284
universe 285, 287–288
unknown 281
unlimited 82, 207, 273, 279
unmeṣa 2, -PAGE-, 65–68, 93, 102–112, 114–119, 122–123, 128–130, 134, 140–144, 146–148, 152–159, 179–180, 183, 187, 189
unmīlanā 286
upastha 30

upāya 289
ūrmiḥ 271
USF 271–272, 293–294
vācā 149–150
vacuum 205–206, 209
vācya 226
vaiṣṇavī 199
vāk 30, 216, 293
vaktra 90
vāmā 210–212
vaman 213
vāmeśvarī 212
varga 2–3, 75, 189
vartmani 238
vedana 187
vedha 100
vega 285
veil 124–125
vein 41, 284
verse 274
vibhava 2, 75, 92–94, 188, 196, 198, 207, 235, 246
vibhūtispande 208
vibrating 116–117
vicitra 190
vidha 154, 161, 174, 192, 220
vidyā 215, 295–296
vighna 77
vigor 77, 271
vigraha 175
vikalapa 294
vikalpa 66, 96–97, 235, 294
vilaya 165–168, 173
vimarśa 92, 122, 140, 244, 292–293
vimūḍha 189
vinā 79
vīra 89, 175, 182
vīrabhairava 175
vīrya 232–233
visarga 293
visargaḥ 293
viṣaya 188
viśeṣa 30–31, 35, 236–237
vision 274
viśva 253
viśvamaya 253
viśvottīrṇa 253
Vivaraṇa 272, 293–294
vivekaḥ 148
void 20–21, 212–213, 276
voidness 21, 205, 276, 287
vomited 210–211
vṛtti 287–288
vyāna 288
vyānana 287–288
vyutthāna 180
wakefulness 4–5, 26–29, 34, 52–56, 58–60, 96, 101, 123, 125, 162, 176–177, 208, 215, 253, 271, 278
waking 28, 181–182, 253, 286
watch 34, 51, 66, 202–203
watchful 200–204
way 277, 289
wheel 2, 94, 136, 174, 177–178, 185, 188, 199, 204, 209, 235, 242
white 145, 227–228
wife 281
wonder 16, 41, 169
wonderstruck 16–17, 136

word 17, 85, 90, 94, 107, 141–142, 151–153, 213, 235, 259–260, 268, 271, 276–277, 293
world 285–288
worldly 48, 80, 121, 168, 203, 216, 221–223, 240, 276, 278–279
yama 275
yoga 31–32, 149–150, 192, 243, 275–276, 279, 287
yogi 284, 288
yogī 284, 288
yoginī 207, 223–224
yukti 184

Teachings of Swami Lakshmanjoo published by The Lakshmanjoo Academy

Bhagavad Gita, In the Light of Kashmir Shaivism

Festival of Devotion & Praise, Hymns to Shiva
Shivastotravali by Utpaladeva

Vijñāna Bhairava, The Manual for Self Realization

Shiva Sutras, The Supreme Awakening

Kashmir Shaivism, The Secret Supreme

Self Realization in Kashmir Shaivism,
The Oral Teachings of Swami Lakshmanjoo

The Mystery of Vibrationless-Vibration
in Kashmir Shaivism,
Vasugupta's Spanda Kārikā & Kṣemarāja's Spanda Sandoha

Lakshmanjoo
ACADEMY

The teachings of Swami Lakshmanjoo are a response to the urgent need of our time: the transformation of consciousness and the evolution of a more enlightened humanity.

The Universal Shaiva Fellowship and its educational branch, The Lakshmanjoo Academy, a fully accredited non-profit organization, was established under Swamiji's direct inspiration, for the purpose of realizing Swamiji's vision of making Kashmir Shaivism available to the whole world. It was Swamiji's wish that his teachings be made available without the restriction of caste, creed or color. The Universal Shaiva Fellowship and the Lakshmanjoo Academy have preserved Swamiji's original teachings and are progressively making these teachings available in book, audio and video formats.

This knowledge is extremely valuable and uplifting for all of humankind. It offers humanity a clear and certain vision in a time of uncertainty. It shows us the way home and gives us the means for its attainment.

For information on Kashmir Shaivism or to support the work of The Universal Shaiva Fellowship and the Lakshmanjoo Academy email us at info@LakshmanjooAcademy.org or visit the Lakshmanjoo Academy website.

www.LakshmanjooAcademy.org
www.IshwarAshramTrust.com

Instructions to download audio files

1. Open the link below to download the free audio
   https://www.universalshaivafellowship.org/Spanda

   You will be **directed** to "**The Mystery of Vibrationless-Vibration in Kashmir Shaivism, Vasugupta's Spanda Kārikā & Kṣemarāja's Spanda Sandoha - Audio**".

2. Select "**Add to basket** " which will send you to the next page.

3. Copy "**Spanda**" into the "**Add Gift Certificate or Coupon"** box

4. Click "**Checkout**" and fill in your details to process the free downloads.

   If you have any difficulties please contact us at:
   www.LakshmanjooAcademy.org/contact

www.ingramcontent.com/pod-product-compliance
Lightning Source LLC
Chambersburg PA
CBHW050527300426
44113CB00012B/1986
9780996636575